Great Documents in
American Indian History

GREAT DOCUMENTS IN AMERICAN INDIAN HISTORY

EDITED BY WAYNE MOQUIN
WITH CHARLES VAN DOREN

Afterword by Robert Powless

DA CAPO PRESS • NEW YORK

Library of Congress Cataloging in Publication Data

Great documents in American Indian history / edited by Wayne Moquin with
    Charles Van Doren; new foreword by Dee Brown; afterword by Robert
    Powless.—1st Da Capo Press ed.
        p.   cm.
    Originally published: New York: Praeger, 1973.
    Includes bibliographical references and index.
    ISBN 0-306-80659-2
    1. Indians of North America. 2. Indians of North America—History—Sources.
I. Moquin, Wayne. II. Van Doren, Charles Lincoln, 1926–
E77.2.G74   1995
970.004′97—dc20   95-20373
                                                                                            CIP

First Da Capo Press edition 1995

This Da Capo Press paperback edition of *Great Documents in
American Indian History* is an unabridged republication of the
edition originally published in New York in 1973, with the
addition of a new foreword by Dee Brown. It is reprinted
by arrangement with Praeger Publishers, an imprint of
Greenwood Publishing Group, Inc.

Published by Da Capo Press, Inc.
A Subsidiary of Plenum Publishing Corporation
233 Spring Street, New York, N.Y. 10013

Manufactured in the United States of America

CONTENTS

Foreword	*Dee Brown*	xi
Introduction		xv
Acknowledgments		xix

PART ONE: THE INDIAN WAY ... 1
Epigraphs ... 3
The Beginning of Newness: A Zuñi Creation Legend ... 7
Origin of the Arikara ... 10
Journey to the West in Search of Tribal Origins
Moncachtape (Yazoo) ... 16
Constitution of the Iroquois Federation
Degandawida (Mohawk) ... 20
A Visit to the "Master of Life": A Delaware Legend
Pontiac (Ottawa) ... 27
Speech in Response to Missionary Efforts, 1805
Red Jacket (Seneca) ... 31
A System of Religion *Tenkswataya, or the Prophet (Shawnee)* ... 34
An Indian Cosmogony *Chief Smohalla (Wanapum)* ... 36
Courtship and Marriage *James Larpenteur Long and*
Red Feather (Assiniboine) ... 38
Indian Family Life *Luther Standing Bear (Sioux)* ... 41
A Winnebago Father's Instructions to His Son ... 46
A Pawnee Mother's Advice to Her Son, Lone Chief ... 52
Life in the Woods: Boyhood Memories of Autumnal Tribal
Activities (c. 1870-72) *Charles Eastman, or Ohiyesa*
(Santee Sioux) ... 54
The Years of a Warrior *Wooden Leg (Cheyenne)* ... 60
Buffalo—Staff of Life for the Indians
James Larpenteur Long (Assiniboine) ... 62
Stealing Horses from the Arapahoe
Chief Plenty-Coups (Crow) ... 66
An Indian Deer Hunt
James Paytiano, or Flaming Arrow (Ácoma Pueblo) ... 70
The Sun Dance *Chief Dick Washakie (Shoshone)* ... 74

Human Sacrifice   *Eagle Chief (Pawnee)*   77
"Our People Are Ebbing Away Like a Rapidly Receding Tide":
A Speech to Governor Isaac Stevens of the Washington Terri-
tory, 1885   *Chief Seattle (Puget Sound Tribes)*   80
An Account of Wovoka, the Paiute Messiah
                                         Porcupine (Cheyenne)   84
A Defense of the Ghost Dance Religion
                                         Masse Hadjo (Sioux)   90
Autobiography   *Poor Wolf (Gros Ventre)*   92
Funeral Oration   96
The End of the World: A Pawnee Myth
                                  Young Bull (Pitahaunat Pawnee)   97

PART TWO: CAPTIVE NATIONS   101
Epigraphs   104
Remarks to Captain John Smith (c. 1609)
                            Powhatan (Powhatan Confederacy)   111
Reasons for the Pueblo Revolt of 1680 in New Mexico: Testi-
mony Given to Spanish Authorities on December 19, 1681
                                 Pedro Naranjo (Queres Pueblo)   112
Speeches to the Governors of New York and Virginia, in a
Council Assembled at Albany in August, 1684
                            Onondaga, Cayuga, and Seneca Chiefs   116
Speech in Behalf of the Six Nations to Pennsylvania Officials,
July 7, 1742   *Canassateego (Seneca)*   119
Address to an Englishman on British-French Relations with the
Indians, 1761   *Minavavana (Chippewa)*   122
Speech to the French on Reasons for Making War on the
English, May 25, 1763   *Pontiac (Delaware)*   124
Speech at the End of Lord Dunmore's War   *Logan (Mingo)*   126
Speech to the British at a Council in Detroit, November, 1781
                                 Captain Pipe (Delaware)   127
Letter to President Washington, 1790
                       Big Tree, Cornplanter, and Half-Town (Seneca)   129
Relations with the United States and Britain
                                 Blue Jacket (Shawnee)   131
Speech to Governor William Henry Harrison at Vincennes,
August 12, 1810   *Tecumseh (Shawnee)*   133
Refusal of a Land-Purchase Offer, in a Speech Made at Buffalo
Creek, New York, in May, 1811   *Red Jacket (Seneca)*   135
Letter to William Eustis, Secretary of War, December 19, 1811
                                 Farmers-Brother (Seneca)   137
Speech on the Futility of Fighting the Americans in the War
of 1812   *Between-the-Logs (Wyandot)*   139
Speech to American Commissioners in Response to the Allega-
tion That Indians Had Broken Treaty Obligations, July, 1815
                                 Black Thunder (Fox)   141
Letter to the Governor of Pennsylvania, February, 1822
                                 Cornplanter (Seneca)   143

Why the Indians Will Not Give Up Their Land, 1827
            Känakûk (Kickapoo)   146
Response to a Message from President Andrew Jackson Concerning Indian Removal, 1830   Speckled Snake (Cherokee)   149
Farewell Letter to the American People, 1832
            George W. Harkins (Choctaw)   151
Farewell Speech at Prairie du Chien, Wisconsin, at the End of the Black Hawk War, August, 1835
            Black Hawk (Sac-Potawatomi)   154
Surrender of a Seminole Band, 1841   Coacooche (Seminole)   156
A Portion of a Speech to a Meeting of the New York Historical Society, May, 1847   Peter Wilson (Cayuga)   159
Speech to Canadian Officials on Land-Purchase Policy, Given at a Council at the Sault Ste. Marie, August 9, 1848
            Peau de Chat (Ojibway)   160
An Interview with Governor Alexander Ramsey of Minnesota, December, 1852   Red Iron (Sisseton Sioux)   163
Fourth of July Address at Reidsville, New York, 1854
            John Quinney (Mahican)   166
Speech to Council of War on the Eve of the Sioux Uprising in Minnesota, August 18, 1862   Little Crow (Santee Sioux)   171
The Great Sioux Uprising of 1862   Big Eagle (Santee Sioux)   173
Letter to General Ulysses S. Grant, January 24, 1864
            Ely S. Parker, or Donehogawa (Seneca)   186
An Eyewitness Report of the Sand Creek Massacre, November 28, 1864   George Bent (Cheyenne)   191
How the Indians Are Victimized by Government Agents and Soldiers   Palaneapope (Yankton Sioux)   195
The Condition of the Winnebago Indians in Nebraska, October 3, 1865   Little Hill (Winnebago)   204
Speech at the Medicine Lodge Indian Council, Addressed to the Indian Commissioner Nathaniel G. Taylor, October 20, 1867   Ten Bears (Comanche)   208
Speech at Cooper Union, New York, July 16, 1870
            Red Cloud (Oglala Sioux)   211
Remarks Made to General Gordon Granger During a Conference on the Matter of Going to a Reservation, 1871
            Cochise (Apache)   214
Events Leading Up to the Modoc War, 1873
            Captain Jack (Modoc)   216
Testimony About the White Man's Promises and Intentions, August 11, 1873   Blackfoot (Crow)   222
The Battle of the Little Bighorn, Narrated by an Indian Who Fought in It, June 25, 1876
            Two Moons (Cheyenne)   226
The Black Hills Is Our Country: Testimony to a Federal Commission, September, 1876   Black Coal (Arapahoe)   230
Indian Conditions for Treaty Renewal, October 11, 1876
            John Grass (Blackfoot Sioux)   232

A Protest to Governor John W. Hoyt of the Wyoming Territory,
 1878   *Washakie (Shoshone)*   235
The Fate of the Nez Percés Tribe, 1879
                                   Chief Joseph (Nez Percés)   237
A Message for the President of the United States, 1881
                             Sitting Bull (Hunkpapa Sioux)   252
The Killing of Big Snake, a Ponca Chief, October 31, 1879
                                        Hairy Bear (Ponca)   254
"The American Nation Is Too Powerful for Us to Fight"
                                    Manuelito (Navajo)   256
Reasons for Leaving the Reservation
                          Geronimo (Chiracahua Apache)   259
Keeping Treaties   *Sitting Bull (Hunkpapa Sioux)*   262
Reasons for the Trouble Between the Indians and the Govern-
 ment During the Ghost Dance Excitement of 1890
                                Red Cloud (Oglala Sioux)   263
The Massacre at Wounded Knee, on December 29, 1890
          *Turning Hawk, Captain Sword, Spotted Horse, and
                               American Horse (Sioux)*   267

PART THREE: HEADING TOWARD THE MAINSTREAM   273
Epigraphs   275
The Reservation School (c. 1900)   *Don C. Talayesva (Hopi)*   278
How Allotment Impoverishes the Indians: Testimony Before a
 Senate Committee Investigating Conditions in the Indian
 Territory, November, 1906   *D. W. C. Duncan (Cherokee)*   286
The Reservation System   *Thomas L. Sloan (Omaha)*   290
Testimony During a 1915 Trial for Violating a Washington State
 Code on Salmon Fishing
                      Chiefs Meninock and Wallahee (Yakima)   297
"Let My People Go": An Address Delivered at the Conference
 of the Society of American Indians in Lawrence, Kansas,
 September 30, 1915   *Carlos Montezuma (Apache)*   301
What the Indian Means to America (1933)
                             Luther Standing Bear (Sioux)   306
Indian Self-Determination (1934)
                         Ralph Fredenberg (Menominee)   309
The Indian in Wartime (1944)   *Ella Deloria (Sioux)*   314
"Shall We Repeat Indian History in Alaska?": Speech to the
 Annual Meeting of the Indian Rights Association, January 23,
 1947   *Ruth Muskrat Bronson (Cherokee)*   319
Problems of off-Reservation Employment (1948)
                                  Jim Becenti (Navajo)   326
An Appeal for Justice (1948)   *Indians of the St. Regis
                  Reservation, Hogansburg, New York*   328
"Whither the American Indian?": A Symposium, 1954
          *Daisy Albert (Hopi), Clarence Wesley (Apache), and
                               N. B. Johnson (Cherokee)*   330

The Importance of Keeping the Land (1955)
Dan Monongye (Hopi) 334
The Voice of the American Indian 337
The Indian Tests the Mainstream
D'Arcy McNickle (Flathead) 347
Testimony Against Proposed Congressional Legislation, 1966
Earl Old Person (Blackfoot) 351
The War on Poverty (1967) *Clyde Warrior (Ponca)* 355
A Symposium on Indian Education, June, 1968
*Allen Quetone (Kiowa), Alex Saluskin (Yakima), Joshua
Wetsit (Assiniboine), and Ben Black Elk (Oglala Sioux)* 360
Fishing Rights for the Indians of Washington State (1968)
Sidney Mills (Yakima-Cherokee) 366
The Native Alaskans' Land Rights (1969)
John Borbridge (Tlingit) 371
Planning Grant Proposal to Develop an All-Indian University
and Cultural Complex on Indian Land, Alcatraz
Indians of All Tribes 374
Consolidating Indian Efforts (1970)
Vine Deloria, Jr. (Standing Rock Sioux) 380
Appeal to Congress for the Return of Blue Lake, 1970
Taos, New Mexico, Pueblo Delegation 385

Afterword *Robert Powless (Oneida)* 389
Glossary of Tribes 403
Recommended Reading 409
Index 411

Sections of illustrations follow pages 14 4 *and* **288.**

FOREWORD

We all are fascinated by our origins, and so it is proper that this comprehensive volume begin with representative creation myths. What is most striking about these legends are the similarities that occur among myths of varied tribes and the resemblances to the tales of diverse peoples all around the earth. A supreme being is usually the central figure, translated into such English names as Sky-Father, Earth-Mother, All-Father, Old Man, Master of Breath. Accompanying are basic sustainers of the life force—corn and buffalo, the sun and clouds, light and water. Animals are usually principal characters in origin myths and naturally the species involved are those indigenous to the geographical areas of specific tribes. For example, badgers, gophers, and long-nosed mice appear in the northern Great Plains legend of the Arikari. In North America the coyote is almost universal.

Within the Zuni myth, which has endured orally through past centuries, are significant passages. The legend tells us that after the Sun-Father impregnated the Great Waters, in the heat of his light the waters grew green, scum rose upon them, and from this came terrestrial life. As Vine Deloria, Jr., the Sioux educator and author, has been telling us, the western world's scholars and scientists have neglected our American Indian heritage as a source for knowledge of the past, present, and future.

These documents of the tribal past, collected in the pages that follow, have, of course, been translated into English—a necessity for preservation in print. Some passages are so lyrical or so philosophical that literary scholars and others have questioned the authenticity. One such is the 1854 speech of Seattle, the Suquamish leader of Puget Sound, which responded to Governor Stevens of Washington Territory after the governor told how much land he was going to take from Seattle's people. Disparagement of the speech reached a high point during the 1970s, the reason being that *two* different Seattle speeches were in circulation. The second version, written for television and filled with anachronisms and modern phrasing, was an unfortunate example of TV's distortion of American Indian history. The Seattle speech in this collection is the authentic version, but it also has been questioned because of its poetic images. Some non-Indians have difficulty believing that an untutored primitive could use such phrases as "waves of a wind-ruffled sea." Perhaps the translator, Henry Smith, who knew the tribal language well, did add a bit of English alliteration to his rendition, but the thoughts are those of Seattle.

A generation after Seattle, similar controversies arose over the speeches of Chief Joseph of the Nez Percés. (The Suquamish and the Nez Percés were Washington Territory neighbors.) Included in this volume is Joseph's famous address before a large assembly of Congressmen, government officials, and other national leaders in Washington, D.C. It is not as well-known as the oft-published surrender speech, but it contains some of the most poignant passages in English in his appeal for freedom for his people, who at the time were literally prisoners in Indian Territory. During the score or so years of Joseph's public life, his words were translated into English by three quite different interpreters: Perrin Whitman, a nephew of Marcus Whitman, the American pioneer and missionary; James Reuben, an English-speaking Nez Percés; and Arthur Chapman, who was married to a member of the Umatilla tribe. The English passages written by Joseph's disparate translators all bear the stamp of his phraseology, his simple and direct presentation, his rhythmic figures of speech and images drawn from the natural world, and his irony. He did not want the white man's churches because they would teach the Nez Percés to quarrel about God. "We never quarrel about God," he said. "We do not want to learn that."

Throughout the years of the American Indians' early confrontations with other cultures, the world saw the creation of new philosophies and much romantic poetry. As the documents within this book attest, some contributions to this universal culture came from the tribes of North America.

And what documented words do we have from other great Indians—those names that appear so frequently now in our popular literature? Sitting Bull is here with a message for the President of the United States. His speech proves the notion that a person's words set down in print will often tell the reader as much about that person as will a meeting in the flesh. Sitting Bull dictated his words concisely, coming directly to the point in telling the President why he had led his people into Canada, why he had brought them back, and what they now needed. From the beginning of Sitting Bull's contact with intruders from the east, he repeated again and again that he wanted only to be let alone, that he had never attacked the intruders, but had defended himself when attacked. Surviving documents show that Sitting Bull was a complex man, a warrior in his youth, a spiritual leader in his maturity. He listened to the messages of meadowlarks and composed songs as succinct as his message to the President: "A warrior / I have been / Now / It is all over / A hard time / I have."

In a stirring narrative Two Moons describes Sitting Bull's great camp on the Little Bighorn, Crazy Horse's bravery, and how they triumphed against Custer. Unlike other leaders, Crazy Horse attended no treaty meetings, therefore few words of his were ever recorded. His speeches survive in the remembrances of his comrades.

From the far southwest, Geronimo tells General Crook several good reasons why he and his Chiracahua Apaches had to leave their reservation. A victim of the print media of his time, Geronimo found it difficult, as he said, "to do right." Only the Earth-Mother would listen to him. "In the papers all over the world they say I am a bad man."

Red Cloud of the Oglala Sioux addresses a large audience at Cooper Union in New York City and receives a standing ovation. At the Medicine Lodge Council, Ten Bears, the Comanche poet, sings of "where the wind blows free" on his native High Plains.

Eastern tribesmen from an earlier time contribute fluently to this documentary record. The voice of Red Jacket, the Seneca leader, is heard twice. His was the largest tribe of the League of the Iroquois, a people much admired by Benjamin Franklin who borrowed some ideas from them for the new nation he helped to create. Here in 1805 Red Jacket, like Chief Joseph later in the century, tells a group of missionaries that his people do not need any of the several religions offered by the whites, who quarrel about their God. The Senecas, he says, rely on the Great Spirit. "We are determined not to sell our lands," he says. "They are fruitful, and produce corn in abundance for the support of our women and children, and grass and herbs for our cattle."

Pontiac was one of the first Indian leaders to organize a confederation of tribes to resist the unceasing encroachment of whites moving westward. Herein is a speech in which he declares himself to be a Frenchman, seeking the aid of the French in driving back his British enemies. In this collection Pontiac also tells a traditional Indian tale about a Delaware who travels to Paradise to seek advice from the Master of Life. The denouement is quite unexpected.

In the early part of the nineteenth century, a generation after Pontiac's efforts, Tecumseh of the Shawnees did succeed in forming a large confederation of tribes east of the Mississippi valley. Known widely as Shooting Star, he traveled thousands of miles, visiting dozens of tribes in his endeavor to unite them. In order to deal with his adversaries, he learned to speak, read, and write English. Tecumseh's remarks to Governor William Henry Harrison, which are included here, sum up his motivations and goals. He advocated common ownership of land by all tribes and organized a united armed force to defend it. His principal aim was to create an Indian nation strong enough to confront the United States government as an equal.

In addition to the documents that were left by these representative, renowned leaders, hundreds of lesser known native peoples also speak their thoughts here. Their affirmations and dissents, their simple accounts of rights and wrongs, are as eloquent as those of more prominent Indians. In past years words endured only if printed in ink on paper. Poor communications, accidents, and pure chance often obscured the words of persons who should have become much better known. In this anthology the best of these are made available for discerning readers who can form their own judgments.

It has become fashionable for the popular media to condemn all white Europeans and their descendants as arch-villains in their relations with American Indians. The historical record may sometimes give that impression, yet there were many non-Indians who defended native tribes. In this book their voices (along with those of a few arch-villains) can be found in the sections titled "Epigraphs." Among them are Thomas Jefferson, Walt Whitman, Benjamin Franklin, Francis Parkman, Ralph Waldo Emerson, John Collier, and Edward Wynkoop. The last name is significant because Wynkoop is an example from a small company of military men who risked their careers, and sometimes their lives, to defend the people they were supposed to fight as enemies. Had Major Wynkoop not been transferred out of Colorado against his will, he probably could have prevented the horrible slaughter at Sand Creek. After the event he hastily returned to Colorado to demand exposure and punishment of the perpetrators.

The numerous documents in this book are all "parts of one stupendous whole." Here is a vast assemblage of words that reveal who the first Americans were. Speaking from their hearts, they disclose their world far better than any historian could. They tell of wrongs done, of splendid deeds, of evil and redemption. Their words are messengers from the past, bringing intelligences necessary for our full understanding of the American experience.

DEE BROWN
Little Rock, Arkansas
May 1995

Dee Brown, a distinguished scholar in American Indian, Civil War, and frontier history, is the author of Bury My Heart at Wounded Knee, Dee Brown's Folktales of the American Indian, Showdown at Little Big Horn, Grierson's Raid, Morgan's Raiders, Hear That Lonesome Whistle Blow, The Gentle Tamers: Women of the Old Wild West, Wondrous Times on the Frontier, When the Century Was Young, *and, most recently,* The American West.

INTRODUCTION

To study one particular ethnic group in American society can be a precarious undertaking because the course of no people has ever proceeded without a variety of outside influences and apart from the over-all context of events at any given time. To focus on too small an area may result in distortion if we see only what we are studying at the moment and do not take into consideration other facts and trends. This is especially true in the case of what might be called a persecuted minority.

There have been a number of such minorities in our national life. The Germans, Irish, Italians, Chinese, Japanese, blacks, and Mexican Americans all have had (and in some cases still have) experience of the under side of our history. But a close look at American Indian history calls forth a particular sense of outrage; for it can be asserted without qualification that no other ethnic group has been so consistently treated with such malevolence over so long a period of time—indeed, right up to the present moment. The outrage is almost unavoidable because in this case, as in several others, the Anglo-American majority is found to be without excuse in the face of its own claims concerning justice, and in the light of its own "Christian" heritage. If one is searching for evidence of moral bankruptcy and the failure of American ideals, the study of Indian-white dealings is the place to find it.

Indian history is not all of American history, however, nor is it a paradigm of the whole. What has happened to the Indians since 1492 has constituted only one portion of a marvelously variegated and multifaceted national development. And from the time of President Washington, at least, the number of Anglo-Americans in contact or concerned with the Indians at any given moment has been a small fraction of the national population. Unfortunately, that fraction rarely had much to recommend it in the way of humanitarianism. Most citizens and immigrants paid only scant attention to the fate of the aboriginal peoples. The United States was engaged in many activities besides that of dealing with some four hundred tribes along a steadily advancing frontier. To say this may, from a contemporary Indian point of view, verge on typical American chauvinism. Not to say it, however, puts us in the position of interpreting all the ambivalence and variety of our national history much too narrowly. It is like suggesting that everything that has happened here since the founding of the English colonies can be expressed in terms of the average Hollywood western.

What is most needed is that we learn something from our history so we can make correctives that are long overdue. The problem, and the rationale of a volume such as this, is that we have tended to repeat our mistakes and to perpetuate attitudes that are wrong in every way. Only haltingly, and almost grudgingly, have we come even to recognize the most horrendous situations. The experiences of recent years have prompted us to see that, when any segment of the population is forced to exist under conditions closely resembling a police state, the rest of society has no sure guarantee of its rights. From this fact it is easy to proceed to another: To improve the quality of life for large numbers of people who only want the same opportunities so many take for granted is much less costly and difficult than an equivocal policy of systematic deprivation for short-term gains.

The condition of the American Indians in the United States is therefore a measure of national failure amidst many successes, and therefore a continuing impetus to the attainment of our own pretensions. But Indians are not just symbols; they are also people—an inherently diverse group with a culture, heritage, humor, self-consciousness, and outlook that will not be dissipated by evanescent notions of a melting pot. They will rightfully insist on maintaining their own identity as a contribution to vital cultural pluralism.

This book is not, strictly speaking, a documentary history of all Indians. Such a work, if it could be accomplished at all, is beyond the competence of any one scholar. What we have tried to present is a survey of Indian life and history in the words of Indians of many tribes from all areas of the country. In doing this, we admit that the differences between the tribes may be lost to view in favor of highlighting the similarities. We are not trying to perpetuate the myth that all Indians are the same, for there were, after all, more than four hundred tribes existing under many different natural conditions and with several language groupings. But the portrayal here is of the native Americans vis-à-vis the white man's world. And for all the striking differences between tribes, there are also striking similarities. Most tribes had cosmologies, creation legends, myths of origin, religious-nature rituals, a fairly democratic infrastructure, patterns of family life, education, hunting, war, agriculture, and funeral customs. To select instances of these life-styles from many tribes allows us to present a mosaic of Indian-ness that would not be possible by concentrating on one tribe or language family.

Probably the severest limitation imposed on us as editors is in the matter of available documents. The Indians were not a record-keeping people in the modern sense, despite the excellence and accuracy of their oral traditions. There are no masses of letters, diaries, speeches, newspaper articles, pamphlets, books, or tracts hidden away in tribal archives awaiting the efforts of translators. In pre-twentieth-century material, we have to rely almost entirely on the transcriptions by white redactors of what Indians said. What has come to us, therefore, is almost as much the product of who wrote it down as it is of the actual author. The speeches and articles reprinted here were meant mostly for white audiences, and, insofar as they were so directed, they may say something other than what an Indian would have said to his own people. Then, too, the circumstances of a particular speech are often obscure, and the speaker himself may be largely unknown to history except for his known encounter with white listeners. To aid readers who may puzzle over the many tribal ascriptions, the glossary at the end provides pertinent information on the more important tribes.

In this book, American Indians of many tribes speak for themselves. Part One is a general, somewhat ahistorical, and admittedly incomplete depiction of life within the tribal communities. Part Two covers the long, tortuous series of confrontations between red and white men that included broken treaties, land cession and theft, banishment to reservations, a lost way of life, wars, and occasional massacres. Part Three affords a glimpse of some of the issues with which the twentieth-century Indian has had to deal.

The reader will note that each section opens with a series of short quotations, or epigraphs, by Anglo-Americans and other non-Indians. The attitudes expressed in these statements range from the sympathetic to the condescending and downright hostile. They are placed here to give a brief suggestion of the societal milieu with which the Indians had to deal from the seventeenth century onward.

Grateful acknowledgment is made to the following for selections obtained for this book: the libraries of the University of Minnesota; the libraries of the University of Illinois, both at Champaign and Chicago; the Chicago Public Library; and Malcom Rosholt, of Rosholt, Wisconsin.

The editors are particularly grateful to our consultant, Robert Powless, for the concluding chapter he has written for this book. A member of the Oneida tribe in Wisconsin, he is currently Director of the American Indian Studies program at the University of Minnesota, Duluth Branch.

ACKNOWLEDGMENTS

The editors wish to express their gratitude for permission to reprint material from the following sources:

Association on American Indian Affairs, Inc., for portions of "Jim Becenti speaks for the Navajo" and "An Appeal for Justice" taken from *The American Indian*, Vol. IV, No. 3 (1948), © 1948 by Association on American Indian Affairs, Inc. (Note: *The American Indian* is out of print.)

Curtis Brown Ltd. and William Morrow and Company, Inc., for portions of *Wilderness Messiah: The Story of Hiawatha and the Iroquois* by Thomas R. Henry, © 1955 by Thomas R. Henry.

The Arthur H. Clark Company for portions of *Washakie: Account of Indian Resistance* by Grace Raymond Hebard, © 1930 by The Arthur H. Clark Company.

The John Day Company Inc. for portions of *American: The Life Story of a Great Indian* by Frank B. Linderman, © 1930.

Dodd, Mead & Company for portions of *Flaming Arrow's People* by James Paytiamo, © 1959.

Friendship Press for portions from *Speaking of Indians* by Ella Deloria. Copyright Friendship Press, New York, 1944. Used by permission.

The Indian Rights Association, Inc., for portions of "Shall We Repeat Indian History in Alaska?" An address by Ruth Muskrat Bronson taken from *Indian Truth*, January–April, 1947, © 1947.

Mrs. May Jones for portions of *Land of the Spotted Eagle* by Chief Standing Bear, © 1933, published by Houghton Mifflin Company.

The Minnesota Historical Society for portions of "Taoyateduta Is Not a Coward" taken from *Minnesota History*, Vol. 28, No. 3 (September, 1962), © 1962.

The Myrin Institute, Inc., for portions of *Can the Red Man Help the White Man?* A Denver Conference with the Indian Elders, edited by Sylvester M. Morey, © 1970 by the Myrin Institute, Inc.

The Nation for portions of "The Indian Tests the Mainstream" by

D'Arcy McNickle from the September 26, 1966, issue of *The Nation*.

The New York Times Company for portions of "This Country Was a Lot Better Off When the Indians Were Running It" by Vine Deloria, Jr., taken from *The New York Times Magazine*, March 8, 1970, © 1970.

Pan American Union for portions of "Nash and Crow Tribe Delegates on U.S. Indians Today" taken from *Americas*, Vol. 14, No. 9 (September, 1962), © 1962.

Rotarian Magazine for passages from *The Rotarian Magazine* of August, 1954.

Straight Arrow Books for portions from *Of Utmost Good Faith*, edited by Vine Deloria, Jr., © 1971 by Vine Deloria, Jr.

University of Nebraska Press for portions from *Wooden Leg: A Warrior Who Fought Custer*, interpreted by Thomas B. Marquis, © 1931.

University of New Mexico Press for portions from *Revolt of the Pueblo Indians of New Mexico and Otemin's Attempted Reconquest 1680–1682*, translated by Charmion Clair Shelby, Ph.D., with Introduction and Annotations by Charles Wilson Hackett, Ph.D., © 1942 by The University of New Mexico Press.

University of Oklahoma Press for portions from *The Fighting Cheyennes* by George Bird Grinnell, © assigned 1955 to the University of Oklahoma Press; and for portions from *The Assiniboines*, edited by Michael Stephen Kennedy, New Edition, © 1961 by the University of Oklahoma Press.

Yale University Press for portions from *Sun Chief: The Autobiography of a Hopi Indian*, edited by Leo W. Simmons, © 1942.

Part One

THE INDIAN WAY

The spiritual chasm that separates white Americans from the Indians has been so great that it has become nearly impossible to bridge the gap. Anglo-American society represents man conquering nature and erecting a technological superstructure over it. It is a society, moreover, that is thoroughly individualized, compartmentalized, personalized, and in which the components are grasped and dealt with far more readily than the whole. It is a society and a culture in which it is possible to select the aspects with which to deal, be they work, leisure, politics, economics, entertainment, sports, religion, and so forth. Identity is sought as much in what one does and through the groups one joins as it is in discovering whom one is to begin with.

It was not so with the American Indian. Aboriginal society comprised what theologian Paul Tillich called a "theonomous culture." Such a society was integral; all the components fit together to form a whole. Today the term "ecology" is often used to describe such an interplay of related factors and parts. It is an apt word here, for the Indians viewed themselves not as subduers of nature but as part of the natural world, to destroy which meant to attack the basis of life itself. Tribal life was first of all an accommodation to the world around it, and this was expressed in a mythic-religious way that gave a rationale to existence and unified everything. There was no sense of individuality without community, yet among the Indians there was a highly developed awareness of both. Neither the "quest for meaning" nor a search for identity was an issue for the Indian. Nor were there politics, agriculture, hunting, home-building, art, morality, or religion as separate categories in society.

1

Everything "fit" into the over-all scheme of things. Everyone had a place in nature, therefore in life, therefore in society.

The preceding description, of course, does no more than define the prevailing ethos in the most general of terms. It is not meant to suggest that tribal life was everywhere the same in North America or that the Indians lived in an idyllic paradise. They were a stone age people who struggled to survive under harsh conditions. And their ways varied markedly from one section of the country to another. Communities as widely separated as the Iroquois federation in the Northeast, the Seminoles of Florida, the Apaches, Comanches, and Dakotas of the Plains, the Pueblos of the arid Southwest, the coastal tribes of California, the Yakima of Puget Sound, and the Tlingit and Haida of Alaska all developed distinctive life-styles.

The selections in this section depict in a fragmentary way something of how the first Americans lived within their tribal environments. Many selections have dates; some do not. Chronology is not particularly important here, because the material is arranged to cover the sweep of Indian thought and activity, beginning with legends of origin, continuing with matters of family life, education, and tribal practices, and culminating in selections about funeral traditions, death, and the afterlife. It is perhaps obvious, but still to be emphasized, that much of what the Indian spokesmen say was conditioned by numerous contacts with white society, just as most of the readings were originally directed to white audiences, for the Indians had little need to explain themselves to each other.

EPIGRAPHS

As soon as they see that they are safe and have laid aside all fear, they are very simple and honest and exceedingly liberal with all they have; none of them refusing anything he may possess when he is asked for it, but, on the contrary, inviting us to ask them. They exhibit great love toward all others in preference to themselves. . . . They practise no kind of idolatry, but have a firm belief that all strength and power, and indeed all good things, are in heaven, and that I had descended from thence with these ships and sailors, and under this impression was I received after they had thrown aside their fears. Nor are they slow or stupid, but of very clear understanding.
—CHRISTOPHER COLUMBUS. Letter to Rafael Sanchez. March 14, 1493

As to the natives of this country, I find them entirely savage and wild, strangers to all decency, yea, uncivil and stupid as garden stakes, proficient in all wickedness and ungodliness, devilish men who serve nobody but the devil, that is, the spirit which in their language they call Menetto [Manitou], under which title they comprehend everything that is subtle and crafty and beyond human skill and power. They have so much witchcraft, divination, sorcery, and wicked arts that they can hardly be held in by any bands or locks. They are as thievish and treacherous as they are tall, and in cruelty they are altogether inhuman, more than barbarous, far exceeding the Africans.
—JONAS MICHAELIUS. Letter to Adrian Smoutius. August 11, 1628

They go naked, both men and women; they have well-shaped bodies, and in colour nearly red; they bore holes in their cheeks, lips, noses and ears, and stuff these holes with blue stones, crystals, marble and alabaster, very fine and beautiful. This custom is followed alone by the men. They have no personal property, but all things are in common. They all live together without a king and without a government, and every one is his own master. They take for wives whom they first meet, and in all this they have no rule. They also war with each other, and without art or rule. And they eat one another, and those they slay are eaten, for human flesh is a common food. In the houses salted human flesh is hung up to dry. They live to be a hundred and fifty years old, and are seldom sick.

—Description of a wood engraving illustrating
the South American Indians. 1505

Thus mankind is one, and all men are alike in that which concerns their creation and all natural things, and no one is born enlightened. From this it follows that all of us must be guided and aided at first by those who were born before us. And the savage peoples of the earth may be compared to uncultivated soil that readily brings forth weeds and useless thorns, but has within itself such natural virtue that by labour and cultivation it may be made to yield sound and beneficial fruits.

—Bartolomé de las Casas. *Apologetica Historia.* 1550

The people bothe men and women are naked, neither suffer they any heare to growe on their bodies, no not on their browes, the head excepte. . . . There is no law or order observed of wedlocke, for it is lawful to have so many women as they affect, and to put them away with out any daunger. They be filthy at meate, and in all secrete acts of nature, comparable to brute beastes.

—William Cunningham. *The Cosmographical Glasse.* 1559

I am safe in affirming that the proofs of genius given by the Indians of North America place them on a level with whites in the same uncultivated state. The North of Europe furnishes subjects enough for comparison with them, and for a proof of their equality, I have seen some thousands myself, and conversed much with them, and have found in them a masculine, sound understanding.

Thomas Jefferson. 1785

I have had frequent opportunities to observe moral dispositions in the men we call savages, that would do much honour to the most civilized European.

—Pierre Marie François de Pages.
Travels Round the World in the Years 1767–1771

From what I have seen of these people I feel authorised to say, that there is nothing very strange or unaccountable in their character; but that it is a simple one, and easy to be learned and understood, if the right means be taken to familiarise ourselves with it. Although it has its dark spots; yet there is much

in it to be applauded, and much to recommend it to the admiration of the enlightened world. And I trust that the reader, who looks through these volumes with care, will be disposed to join me in the conclusion: that the North American Indian in his native state is an honest, hospitable, faithful, brave, warlike, cruel, revengeful, relentless,—yet honourable, contemplative and religious being.
—GEORGE CATLIN. *The North American Indians.* 1841

Some races of men seem molded in wax, soft and melting, at once plastic and feeble. Some races, like some metals, combine the greatest flexibility with the greatest strength. But the Indian is hewn out of rock. You cannot change the form without destruction of the substance. Such, at least, has too often proved the case. Races of inferior energy have possessed a power of expansion and assimilation to which he is a stranger; and it is this fixed and rigid quality which has proved his ruin. He will not learn the arts of civilization, and he and his forest must perish together. The stern, unchanging features of his mind excite our admiration, from their very immutability; and we look with deep interest on the fate of this irreclaimable son of the wilderness, the child who will not be weaned from the breast of his rugged mother. And our interest increases when we discern in the unhappy wanderer, mingled among his vices, the germs of heroic virtues —a hand bountiful to bestow, as it is rapacious to receive, and, even in extreme famine, imparting its last morsel to a fellow-sufferer; a heart which, strong in friendship as in hate, thinks it not too much to lay down life for its chosen comrade; a soul true to its own idea of honor, and burning with an unquenchable thirst for greatness and renown.
—FRANCIS PARKMAN. *The Conspiracy of Pontiac.* 1851

The customs and institutions of the red man, like the laws of the Medes and Persians, have no change. They are true to nature as it appears to them. Their minds seem stereotyped by nature in its wildness. The charms of purity and refinement in social life, when chastened into living form by the aid of art and science may excite an emotion of pleasure, but have no response in their nature of enduring sentiment.
—Oshkosh (Wisconsin) *Democrat.* June 25, 1852

As to our aboriginal or Indian population—the Aztec in the South, and many a tribe in the North and West—I know it seems to be agreed that they must gradually dwindle as time rolls on, and in a few generations more leave only a reminiscence, a blank. But I am not at all clear about that. As America, from its many far-back sources and current supplies, develops, adapts, entwines, faithfully identifies its own—are we to see it cheerfully accepting and using all the contributions of foreign lands from the whole

outside globe—and then rejecting the only ones distinctively its own—the autochthonic ones?
—WALT WHITMAN. Letter to the city officials at
Santa Fe, New Mexico. 1883

To the Indians the buffalo was the staff of life. It was their food, clothing, dwellings, tools. The needs of a savage people are not many, perhaps, but whatever the Indians of the Plains had, that the buffalo gave them. It is not strange, then, that this animal was reverenced by most Plains tribes, nor that it entered largely into their sacred ceremonies, and was in a sense worshiped by them. The Pawnees say "Through the corn and the buffalo we worship the Father." The Blackfeet ask, "What one of all the animals is most sacred?" and the reply given is "The buffalo."
—GEORGE BIRD GRINNELL. *Scribner's Magazine.* September, 1892

What, in our human world, is this power to live? It is the ancient, lost reverence and passion for human personality, joined with the ancient, lost reverence and passion for the earth and its web of life.

This indivisible reverence and passion is what the American Indians almost universally had; and representative groups of them have it still.
—JOHN COLLIER. *Indians of the Americas.* 1947

THE BEGINNING OF NEWNESS: A ZUÑI CREATION LEGEND

Before the beginning of the new-making, Awonawilona (the Maker and Container of All, the All-father Father), solely had being. There was nothing else whatsoever throughout the great space of the ages save everywhere black darkness in it, and everywhere void desolation.

In the beginning of the new-made, Awonawilona conceived within himself and thought outward in space, whereby mists of increase, steams potent of growth, were evolved and uplifted. Thus, by means of his innate knowledge, the All-container made himself in person and form of the Sun whom we hold to be our father and who thus came to exist and appear. With his appearance came the brightening of the spaces with light and with the brightening of the spaces the great mist-clouds were thickened together and fell, whereby was evolved water in water; yea, and the world-holding sea.

With his substance of flesh outdrawn from the surface of his person, the Sun-father formed the seed-stuff of twain worlds, impregnating therewith the great waters, and lo! in the heat of his light these waters of the sea grew green and scums rose upon them, waxing wide and weighty until, behold! they became Awitelin Tsita, the "Four-fold Containing Mother-earth," and Apoyan Tä'chu, the "All-covering Father-sky."

From the lying together of these twain upon the great world-waters, so vitalizing, terrestrial life was conceived; whence began

From *Thirteenth Annual Report of the Bureau of American Ethnology*, p. 379.

7

all beings of earth, men and the creatures, in the Fourfold womb
of the World.

Thereupon the Earth-mother repulsed the Sky-father, growing
big and sinking deep into the embrace of the waters below,
thus separating from the Sky-father in the embrace of the waters
above. As a woman forebodes evil for her first-born ere born,
even so did the Earth-mother forebode, long withholding from
birth her myriad progeny and meantime seeking counsel with
the Sky-father. "How," said they to one another, "shall our children
when brought forth, know one place from another, even by the
white light of the Sun-father?"

Now like all the surpassing beings the Earth-mother and the
Sky-father were changeable, even as smoke in the wind; trans-
mutable at thought, manifesting themselves in any form at will,
like as dancers may be mask-making.

Thus, as a man and woman, spake they, one to the other.
"Behold!" said the Earth-mother as a great terraced bowl
appeared at hand and within it water, "this is as upon me the
homes of my tiny children shall be. On the rim of each world-
country they wander in, terraced mountains shall stand, making
in one region many, whereby country shall be known from
country, and within each, place from place. Behold, again!" said
she as she spat on the water and rapidly smote and stirred it
with her fingers. Foam formed, gathering about the terraced
rim, mounting higher and higher. "Yea," said she, "and from
my bosom they shall draw nourishment, for in such as this shall
they find the substance of life whence we were ourselves sustained, for see!" Then with her warm breath she blew across the
terraces; white flecks of the foam broke away, and, floating over
above the water, were shattered by the cold breath of the Sky-
father attending, and forthwith shed downward abundantly fine
mist and spray! "Even so, shall white clouds float up from the
great waters at the borders of the world, and clustering about
the mountain terraces of the horizons be borne aloft and abroad
by the breaths of the surpassing of soul-beings, and of the children,
and shall hardened and broken be by thy cold, shedding downward, in rain-spray, the water of life, even into the hollow places
of my lap! For therein chiefly shall nestle our children mankind
and creature-kind, for warmth in thy coldness."

Lo! even the trees on high mountains near the clouds and
the Sky-father crouch low toward the Earth-mother for warmth
and protection! Warm is the Earth-mother, cold the Sky-father,
even as woman is the warm, man the cold being!

"Even so!" said the Sky-father; "Yet not alone shalt *thou* helpful
be unto our children, for behold!" and he spread his hand abroad
with the palm downward and into all the wrinkles and crevices
thereof he set the semblance of shining yellow corn-grains; in the
dark of the early world-dawn they gleamed like sparks of fire,
and moved as his hand was moved over the bowl, shining up

from and also moving in the depths of the water therein. "See!" said he, pointing to the seven grains clasped by his thumb and four fingers, "by such shall our children be guided; for behold, when the Sun-father is not nigh, and thy terraces are as the dark itself (being all hidden therein), then shall our children be guided by lights—like to these lights of all the six regions turning round the midmost one—as in and around the midmost place, where these our children shall abide, lie all the other regions of space! Yea! and even as these grains gleam up from the water, so shall seed-grains like to them, yet numberless, spring up from thy bosom when touched by my waters, to nourish our children." Thus and in other ways many devised they for their offspring.

ORIGIN OF THE ARIKARA

A long time ago, people lived in the ground. Mother-Corn engaged the animals to help her to get these people out of the ground. The animals came, and said, "Mother-Corn, we will help." There was a Badger, a Gopher, the long-nosed Mouse, and a Mole.

The Badger was the first to stand up, and he said, "Mother-Corn, I will be the first to dig." So the Badger went to work digging through the earth. The Badger gave out. He came back, and said, "Mother-Corn, I am tired." The next animal went and dug, became tired, and came back. The Mole then went to work, but the long-nosed Mouse was the last to go. He dug through the earth with his nose. Then the Mole asked to see the light, and it went through and was blinded. The Mole went back, and said, "Mother-Corn, I will stay under ground always."

The next animal to try was a Gopher. He went up, and tried to go out of the hole. It was late in the evening, so that this animal received only a black streak across his eyes. The Badger then went to work and dug the hole larger, and went out, and it was morning, for the sun was up. The sun burned the fore legs of the Badger, also around his face, but he was not blinded. The long-nosed Mouse stood up, and said, "Mother-Corn, in trying to open the doorway of the earth for the people, my nose was squeezed, and made pointed. My snout has been made small, and I shall keep this shape always, so that the people will know that I was the one that opened the doorway of the earth for the people."

The Mole stood up, and said, "Mother-Corn, I am blinded. I

From George A. Dorsey, ed., *Traditions of the Arikara* (Washington, D.C., 1904).

can not go with you, and your people will have to allow me to remain here, that I may always stay under the ground." Mother-Corn gave her consent, and that is why the Mole is in the ground. If it comes out, it will come out in the night, and if the sun comes up on it, it has to sit still all day, until the night comes, then it will travel again.

The people now came out from the ground and stood outside. They saw other pathways, where other people had gone out from the ground, by the help of the Buffalo.

Now the people started upon a journey. This journey was stopped; for the leaders said, "Here is an obstacle, a deep crevice. What shall we do, Mother-Corn?" Mother-Corn said, "Help! Hurry!" And she called upon the gods. The gods sent a Kingfisher, who said, "Mother-Corn, I will be the one to make a way for you and your people." The Kingfisher flew and shot through the side of the bank, and the bank fell. The Kingfisher flew around to where the company of people were, and shot through the other bank, and this bank also fell, so that the two banks, meeting, formed a pathway. Some of the people who saw these banks torn up, turned to Mother-Corn, and said, "Mother-Corn, we want to stay here in the banks, as Worms." So Mother-Corn allowed some of the people to remain in the banks as Worms. The people started, and when they got across this crevice they started on their journey.

Again they met another obstacle—thick timber—and Mother-Corn called on the gods, and said, "Hurry! Help!" So the gods sent the wonderful Owl to the people. This wonderful Owl flew and lighted by Mother-Corn, and said, "Mother, I will be the one to make a pathway." The Owl flew through the timber, and there was a pathway. The people went through the timber, and some of them liked the timber, and they turned to Mother-Corn, and said, "Mother, we want to stay with the wonderful Owl." So some of the people turned into animals and birds, and they stayed in the timber.

Again the people started to journey, and they came to another difficulty. This time they came to a lake, whose banks were mountains, but they managed to get down to the lake. Then the people said, "Mother-Corn what shall we do, for the lake is in the way?" Mother-Corn called upon the gods, and said, "Hurry! Help!" The gods sent a Loon. The Loon came down and stood by the people, and said, "Mother-Corn, I will help to make a pathway for your people." The Loon flew down to the lake, and flew through the waters, and the waters opened, leaving the bottom of the lake dry so that the people could cross; some drank from the lake, turned into fish, and remained behind. When they had crossed the lake, some of the people said, "Mother-Corn, we want to stay with the wonderful bird, the Loon." Mother-Corn gave her consent. Some of them turned into Loons, and they stayed behind. The obstacles were overcome.

It was now time for Mother-Corn to smoke to the gods. The smoke was ready. Animals and birds were sent out to find offerings.

When the pipe was made the animals and the birds went out to find the offering. The Prairie-chicken found a wild-cat and killed it. The Prairie-chicken brought the wild-cat to the people and laid it down outside of the camp. The Prairie-chicken then went to Mother-Corn, and said, "Mother, I have killed for the offering." Mother-Corn, said, "What kind of an animal is it that you have killed?" The Prairie-chicken said, "It is an animal that is speckled." Mother-Corn said, "You have done right. The animal that is speckled represents the heavens, and the white spots represent the stars. So you will bring it and we will make an offering." The Prairie-chicken went and brought the animal.

When it came time to offer the smoke the people found that they had not the pipe with which to form the smoke. There were three Stars in the heavens, and they saw the pipe was lacking. They said, "Mother-Corn, we will get you the pipe." So the three Stars went and found a stone, and brought it to Mother-Corn. They said, "We are the three Stars that come up in the East. We know the pipe smoked to us." They were Red-Star, Yellow-Star, and the Big-Black-Meteoric-Star. So Mother-Corn had the stone made into a pipe.

When the pipe was made and filled with native tobacco Mother-Corn called the Prairie-chicken, and said, "You must carry this pipe to the God in the Southeast." So the Prairie-chicken took the pipe and flew to the Southeast. It was gone for some time, and when the Prairie-chicken came back it said, "The God in the Southeast received the pipe and smoked." Mother-Corn again filled the pipe with native tobacco and called on the Prairie-chicken again, gave it the pipe, and told it to go to the God in the Southwest with it. The Prairie-chicken flew away again and was gone for some time. When it came back it said to Mother-Corn, "The God in the Southwest has received the pipe and smoked." Then Mother-Corn took the pipe again and filled it with native tobacco, called the Prairie-chicken, and said, "Take this pipe to the God in the Northwest." The Prairie-chicken took the pipe and flew away again to the Northwest. When it came back it told Mother-Corn that the God in the Northwest had received the pipe and smoked. Again Mother-Corn filled the pipe, gave it to the Prairie-chicken, and it flew away to the God in the Northeast. The Prairie-chicken came back, and said, "Mother-Corn, the God in the Northeast has received the pipe and smoked." Then the pipe was filled again and the Prairie-chicken was called to carry it to Nesaru, which it did. The Prairie-chicken flew up into the heavens, and said, "Nesaru has received the pipe and smoked. Other animal gods also smoked with Nesaru." Then Prairie-chicken said, "Mother-Corn, these journeys were very hard. The wind was blowing hard, sand-stones were thick, the little stones struck upon my feathers and made white spots upon them. Flying through these hard winds gave me power to fly through storms. The stones hit upon my feathers and made white spots upon them. I wish to remain as I am now." Mother-Corn said, "It is well. You shall be as you are always." (This is why the Prairie-chicken has white spots upon its feathers.) "As you have carried the pipes yourself to the gods, so it shall be to all people who shall make a sacrifice to the gods that they themselves must go through the smoke ceremony, that the gods may receive the smoke offering from the person himself who makes the offering."

In the smoking Nesaru let the gods know that he had given his consent to Mother-Corn to have people upon the earth; and that the gods were also to give their power to the people and protect them. So it was the place of the gods to help Mother-Corn whenever she called upon them for help.

After they had smoked to the gods there came a Dog running into the camp and telling Mother-Corn that one of the gods, the Whirlwind, who stands a little to the southwest, had been slighted in the smoke ceremony and the Whirlwind was angry. Then the Dog said to Mother-Corn, "That God, the Whirlwind, is coming. Be quick and do something for the people, for the gods in the heavens promised you aid when the people should be in trouble." Mother-Corn stood up and spoke, saying, "Nesaru and the gods, I want help, for the Whirlwind is coming to destroy my people!" A woman stepped in front, and said, "I will be the one to save the people." She stood up and was turned into a Cedar-Tree. Then there was a noise in the heavens and a Rock fell by the Cedar-Tree. A voice spoke from the heavens, and said, "I am the Big-Black-Meteoric-Star. I shall assist the Cedar-Tree to save the people." The people then ran up to the Cedar-Tree and around the rock. The Whirlwind came, and some of the people ran away, some going north, some west, some south and some east, and when the Whirlwind struck these people it changed their language. The people who stood upon the Cedar-Tree and the Rock remained as the Arikara. When the Whirlwind struck Mother-Corn she vomited red water, and after the water there came out a red ear of corn. Again she vomited and threw up yellow water, which was followed by a yellow ear of corn. Again she vomited, and there came up black water and a black ear of corn. Now she vomited and there came up white water and a white ear of corn. The Whirlwind passed the people and it turned back and came to Mother-Corn. It said to her: "You slighted me in your smoke. I became angry. I have left behind me diseases, so that the people will become sick and die. You wanted your people to live forever, but I have left sickness behind, so that it will fall upon the people who are proud and dress fine; but always remember when you offer smoke to the gods to give me smoke towards the last, so that I shall not visit the people very often." The Whirlwind went on. The Cedar-Tree spoke, and said: "Mother-Corn, the Whirlwind twisted my body until, you see, it is bent in many places.

Let me remain this way. Let the people know me as the 'Wonderful Grandmother.' They shall place me in front of their medicine-lodge and they shall have a ceremony that I shall give them when they place me in front of their lodge." Then the Big-Black-Meteoric-Star said: "Mother-Corn, I wish to be known as the 'Wonderful Grandfather.' I shall sit by the Wonderful Grandmother, in front of the medicine-lodge, so that the people will always remember that it was I who saved them from the Whirlwind." Then the Dog spoke, and said: "Mother-Corn, I brought the news. I followed up the people from where they came out from the ground. I am always to remain with the people, so that I may guard their camps and villages, and when enemies are approaching their camps or villages I shall let them know by my barking. My spirit is up to all the gods. My flesh is good to eat, and the grease of my body is curative for sores. Let the people in all their ceremonies kill me and offer my flesh to the different gods in the heavens. Let the medicine-men use my fat for their sores." Mother-Corn was satisfied.

Mother-Corn then stood up and said: "My people, this corn is for you. They are seeds. You shall plant them, so that in time you can offer this corn to the gods also. This will be done to remind them that I was once Corn up in the heavens and was sent down to take you from the ground. These people who have scattered out shall be your enemies. The people who have gone to the Southwest you shall call 'Sahe' (Strike-Enemy); the people who have gone to the Northeast you shall call 'Pichia' (People-of-Cold-Country); the people who have gone to the East you shall call 'Wooden-Faces' (Iroquois), for they shall wear wooden faces in their ceremonies. The people who have gone to the South you shall call 'Witchcraft-People,' for they shall understand how to practice witchcraft. They will understand the mysteries of the Owl, Woodpecker, Turkey and the Snakes." (These were the Wichita.) Other people also were named at this time.

Mother-Corn stayed with the people until she had taught them the bundle ceremonies. When she had completed telling them concerning these ceremonies, she told them that she was now to go back to the place where they had come from and that they should sing the bundle songs that she had taught them. She also told them to bring all of the children's little moccasins, and to tie them together and place them upon her back; that it was time now for her to go. She then told them they must take her to the river and throw her in. The people did not understand this, as they kept up the singing in the night. When daylight came they looked behind where Mother-Corn was sitting, and there they found that she had turned into an ear of corn. The buffalo robe that she had about her was tied to the corn. It was told the people through the village, and the people came with their children's moccasins and placed them with Mother-Corn. Then the priests took Mother-Corn and the robe to the river, and threw her into it.

For many years she did not return, but one fall, when they were having their bundle ceremonies, a mysterious-looking woman entered the lodge where the bundle ceremony was being given and they finally recognized her as Mother-Corn. She taught them some more bundle ceremony songs and before daylight disappeared, and was never seen again.

JOURNEY TO THE WEST IN SEARCH OF TRIBAL ORIGINS
Moncachtape (Yazoo)

[This travel account was given to the French historian Le Page Du Pratz, who conducted extensive research among the Indians of the Lower Mississippi region for his *History of Louisiana* (1758). Du Pratz was particularly interested in demonstrating the Asian origin of America's Indians.]

I had lost my wife, and all the children whom I had by her, when I undertook my journey towards the sun-rising. I set out from my village contrary to the inclination of all my relations, and went first to the Chicasaws, our friends and neighbors. I continued among them several days, to inform myself whether they knew whence we all came, or, at least, whence they themselves came; they, who were our elders; since from them came the language of the country. As they could not inform me, I proceeded on my journey. I reached the country of the Chaouanous, and afterwards went up the Wabash, or Ohio, near to its source, which is in the country of the Iroquois, or Five Nations. I left them, however, towards the north; and, during the winter, which, in that country, is very severe and very long, I lived in a village of the Abenaquis, where I contracted an acquaintance with a man somewhat older than myself, who promised to conduct me, the following spring,

From Samuel G. Drake, *Biography and History of the Indians of North America*, 11th ed. (Boston, 1841), Chapter 5.

to the great water. Accordingly, when the snows were melted, and the weather was settled, we proceeded eastward, and, after several days' journey, I at length saw the great water, which filled me with such joy and admiration, that I could not speak. Night drawing on, we took up our lodging on a high bank above the water, which was sorely vexed by the wind, and made so great a noise that I could not sleep. Next day, the ebbing and flowing of the water filled me with great apprehension; but my companion quieted my fears, by assuring me that the water observed certain bounds, both in advancing and retiring. Having satisfied our curiosity in viewing the great water, we returned to the village of the Abenaquis, where I continued the following winter; and, after the snows were melted, my companion and I went and viewed the great fall of the River St. Lawrence, at Niagara, which was distant from the village several days' journey. The view of this great fall, at first, made my hair stand on end, and my heart almost leap out of its place; but afterwards, before I left it, I had the courage to walk under it. Next day, we took the shortest road to the Ohio, and my companion and I, cutting down a tree on the banks of the river, we formed it into a pettiaugre, which served to conduct me down the Ohio and the Mississippi, after which, with much difficulty, I went up our small river, and at length arrived safe among my relations, who were rejoiced to see me in good health.—This journey, instead of satisfying, only served to excite my curiosity. Our old men, for several years, had told me that the ancient speech informed them that the red men of the north came originally much higher and much farther than the source of the River Missouri; and, as I had longed to see, with my own eyes, the land from whence our first fathers came, I took my precautions for my journey westwards. Having provided a small quantity of corn, I proceeded up along the eastern bank of the River Mississippi, till I came to the Ohio. I went up along the bank of this last river, about the fourth part of a day's journey, that I might be able to cross it without being carried into the Mississippi. There I formed a cajeux, or raft of canes, by the assistance of which I passed over the river; and next day meeting with a herd of buffaloes in the meadows, I killed a fat one, and took from it the fillets, the bunch, and the tongue. Soon after, I arrived among the Tamaroas, a village of the nation of the Illinois, where I rested several days, and then proceeded northwards to the mouth of the Missouri, which, after it enters the great river, runs for a considerable time without intermixing its muddy waters with the clear stream of the other. Having crossed the Mississippi, I went up the Missouri, along its northern bank, and, after several days' journey, I arrived at the nation of the Missouris, where I staid a long time to learn the language that is spoken beyond them. In going along the Missouri, I passed through meadows a whole day's journey in length, which were quite covered with buffaloes.

When the cold was past, and the snows were melted, I continued my journey up along the Missouri, till I came to the nation of the west, or the Canzas. Afterwards, in consequence of directions from them, I proceeded in the same course near 30 days, and at length I met with some of the nation of the Otters, who were hunting in that neighborhood, and were surprised to see me alone. I continued with the hunters two or three days, and then accompanied one of them and his wife, who was near her time of lying in, to their village, which lay far off betwixt the north and west. We continued our journey along the Missouri for nine days, and then we marched directly northwards for five days more, when we came to the fine river, which runs westward in a direction contrary to that of the Missouri. We proceeded down this river a whole day, and then arrived at the village of the Otters, who received me with as much kindness as if I had been of their own nation. A few days after, I joined a party of the Otters, who were going to carry a calumet of peace to a nation beyond them, and we embarked in a pettiaugre, and went down the river for 18 days, landing now and then to supply ourselves with provisions. When I arrived at the nation who were at peace with the Otters, I staid with them till the cold was passed, that I might learn their language, which was common to most of the nations that lived beyond them.

The cold was hardly gone, when I again embarked on the fine river, and in my course I met with several nations, with whom I generally staid but one night, till I arrived at the nation that is but one day's journey from the great water on the west. This nation live in the woods about the distance of a league from the river, from their apprehension of bearded men, who come upon their coasts in floating villages, and carry off their children to make slaves of them. These men were described to be white, with long black beards that came down to their breast; they were thick and short, had large heads, which were covered with cloth; they were always dressed, even in the greatest heats; their clothes fell down to the middle of their legs, which, with their feet, were covered with red or yellow stuff. Their arms made a great fire and a great noise; and when they saw themselves outnumbered by red men, they retired on board their large pettiaugre, their number sometimes amounting to thirty, but never more.

Those strangers came from the sun-setting, in search of a yellow stinking wood, which dyes a fine yellow color; but the people of this nation, that they might not be tempted to visit them, had destroyed all those kind of trees. Two other nations in their neighborhood, however, having no other wood, could not destroy the trees, and were still visited by the strangers; and being greatly incommoded by them, had invited their allies to assist them in making an attack upon them, the next time they should return. The following summer I accordingly joined in this expedition, and, after travelling five long days' journey, we came to the place where the bearded men usually landed, where we waited seventeen days for their arrival. The red men, by my advice, placed themselves in ambuscade to surprise the strangers, and accordingly when they landed to cut the wood, we were so successful as to kill eleven of them, the rest immediately escaping on board two large pettiaugres, and flying westward upon the great water.

Upon examining those whom we had killed, we found them much smaller than ourselves, and very white; they had a large head, and in the middle of the crown the hair was very long; their head was wrapt in a great many folds of stuff, and their clothes seemed to be made neither of wool nor silk; they were very soft, and of different colors. Two only, of the eleven who were slain, had fire-arms, with powder and ball. I tried their pieces, and found that they were much heavier than yours, and did not kill at so great a distance.

After this expedition, I thought of nothing but proceeding on my journey, and, with that design, I let the red men return home, and joined myself to those who inhabited more westward on the coast, with whom I travelled along the shore of the great water, which bends directly betwixt the north and the sun-setting. When I arrived at the villages of my fellow-travellers, where I found the days very long, and the nights very short, I was advised by the old men to give over all thoughts of continuing my journey. They told me that the land extended still a long way in a direction between the north and sun-setting, after which it ran directly west, and at length was cut by the great water from north to south. One of them added, that, when he was young, he knew a very old man who had seen that distant land before it was eat away by the great water, and that when the great water was low, many rocks still appeared in those parts. Finding it, therefore, impracticable to proceed much further, on account of the severity of the climate, and the want of game, I returned by the same route by which I had set out; and, reducing my whole travels westward to days' journey, I compute that they would have employed me 36 moons; but, on account of my frequent delays, it was five years before I returned to my relations among the Yazoos.

CONSTITUTION OF THE IROQUOIS FEDERATION

Degandawida (Mohawk)

[Although the Iroquois federation was founded about 1500, the constitution was not put into writing until after 1850. This version was inscribed by Seth Newhouse, a Seneca, in 1880.]

Constitution of the Five Nations Indian Confederacy.

This is wisdom and justice of the part of the Great Spirit to create and raise chiefs, give and establish unchangable laws, rules and customs between the Five Nation Indians, viz the Mohawks, Oneidas, Onondagas, Cayugas and Senecas and the other nations of Indians here in North America. The object of these laws is to establish peace between the numeras nations of Indians, hostility will be done away with, for the preservation and protection of life, property and liberty.

Laws, rules and customs as follows:

1. And the number of chiefs in this confederation of the five Nation Indians are fifty in number, no more and no less. They are the ones to arrange, to legislate and to look after the affairs of their people.*

---

* These fifty include the long dead Degandawida and Hiawatha, who are supposed to be present in spirit. Their places have never been filled by living men.

From Thomas R. Henry, *Wilderness Messiah: The Story of Hiawatha and the Iroquois* (New York, 1955), Appendix 2.

2. And the Mohawks, an Indian Nation, forms a part of the body of this Five Nation Indians confederation, and their representatives in this confederation is nine chiefs.

3. And the Oneidas, an Indian Nation, forms a party of the body of this Five Nation Indians confederation, and their representatives in this confederation is nine chiefs.

4. And the Onondagas, an Indian Nation, form a part of the body of this Five Nation Indians confederation, and their representatives in this confederation is fourteen chiefs.

5. And the Cayugas, an Indian Nation, forms a part of the body of this Five Nation Indians confederation, and their representatives in this confederation is ten chiefs.

6. And the Senecas, an Indian Nation, forms a part of the body of this Five Nation Indians confederation, and their representatives in this confederation is eight chiefs.

7. And when the Five Nation Indians confederation chiefs assemble to hold a council, the council shall be duly opened and closed by the Onondaga chiefs, the Firekeepers. They will offer thanks to the Great Spirit that dwells in heaven above: the source and ruler of our lives, and it is him that sends daily blessings upon us, our daily wants and daily health, and they will then declare the council open for the transaction of business, and give decisions of all that is done in the council.

8. And there are three totems or castes of the Mohawk Nation viz. the Tortoise, the Wolf and the Bear; each has 3 head chiefs, 9 in all. The chiefs of the Tortoise and Wolf castes are the council by themselves, and the chiefs of the Bear castes are to listen and watch the progress of the council or discussion of the two castes; and if they see any error they are to correct them, and explain, where they are wrong; and when they decide with the sanction of the Bear castes then their speaker will refer the matter to the other side of the council fire, to the second combination chiefs, viz The Oneidas and Cayugas.

9. And the council of the five Nations shall not be opened until all of the three castes of the Mohawk chiefs are present; and if they are not all present it shall be legal for them to transact the business of the council if all the three totems have one or more representatives present, and if not it shall not be legal except in small matters; for all the three castes of the Mohawk chiefs must be present to be called a full council.

10. And the business of the council of the Five Nation Indians is transacted by two combination of chiefs; viz first the Mohawks and Senecas, and second the Oneidas and Cayugas.

11. And when a case or proposition is introduced in the council of the five nations, the Mohawk chiefs with the Senecas shall first consider the matter, and whatever the decision may be; then the speaker will refer the matter to the other side of the council fire; to the second combination chiefs, the Oneidas and Cayugas, for their consideration, and if they all agree unanimously then the

speaker of the council shall refer the matter to the Fire keepers; and it is then their duty to sanction it; and their speaker will then pronounce the case as passed in council.

12. And if a dissention arises between the two combination chiefs in council, and they agree to refer the matter to the Fire keepers to decide, then the Fire keepers shall decide which of the two or more propositions is most advantageous to their people, and their decission is final.

13. And when any case or proposition has passed unanimously between the two combination chiefs, and the case or proposition is then referred to the Fire keepers for their sanction: and if the Fire keepers see that the case or proposition is such that it will be injurious and not to the advantage of their people, then they will refer the case or proposition back to the Mohawk chiefs, and point out where it would be injurious to the people and then they will reconsider the case. When it is right the case is then referred again to the Fire keepers and then they will pass it.

14. And when there is a case, proposition, or any subject before the council of the Five Nation Indians, no chief or chiefs has any right to stand up to speak without permission from the council, and if he has anything to say by way of explanation, he can do so in a low tone to the combined chiefs whereof he is a member.

15. And when anything is under the consideration of the council, they must agree unanimously if possible before it is referred to the other side of the council fire, to the second combination chiefs; otherwise it would be illegal so to do by one or more chiefs, unless sanction[ed] by the rest of the combined chiefs of which he or they is a member.

16. The speaker of the council of the Five Nations council shall be appointed from time to time when it is necessary, by the first combined chiefs Viz the Mohawks and Senecas during the day or days when the council is in session.

17. And the duty of the speaker of the council as aforesaid is to order the Fire keepers to open and close the council, and to address the council when necessary and to refer cases propositions etc. to the second combined chiefs and to the Fire keepers, and to proclaim a sanctioned cases, or anything when passed by the council.

18. A speaker of the Fire keepers shall be chosen from time to time, as occasion shall require; by the Onondaga chiefs themselves.

19. The speaker of the Second Combined Chiefs appointment, shall be on the same condition as the speaker of the Fire keepers.

20. Each of the Principal chiefs has one war chief and a runner, and should war break out then the office of the principal chief ceases during the war; then the war chiefs will take their places and council for the Five Nations till the end of the war; then the office will cease and the principal chiefs shall resume their places and their duties as before.

21. And if the Principal chief desires to have anything to do

with the war, this he can do by giving up the emblem which he received by his relatives when he was first made chief.

22. And the duty of the messenger or runner is to carry tidings from place to place by Order of the Five Nation Indians confederation session, or by his superior chiefs.

23. And if the Principal chief does fail in his judgement in the Five Nation Indians confederation council of course the duty of his war chief is to assist him, and he is bound to listen.

24. And the duty of the Head Principal Chief of the Onondagas, Ododarho, is to keep the Five Nation Indians confederation council fire clean all around, that no dust or dirt is to be seen. There is a long wing of a bird, and a stick is placed by his side, and he will take the long wing and sweep or dust the dirt away from the council fire, and if he sees any creeping creature crawling towards the Five Nation Indians council fire he will take the stick and pitch the crawling creature away from the fire, and his cousin chiefs of the Onondagas will act with him at all times, and the crawling creature signifies any case or proposition or subject brought before the Five Nation Indians council which would be ruinous and injurious to their people, and they are to reject anything which on the nature would be ruinous and injurious and not to the advantage of their people, and they are to consider first by themselves during the council, and then call the attention of the council to the fact, case or proposition, and the council are not to receive it after it had been rejected by the council.

25. And the Fire Keepers of the Five Nation Indians confederation council the Onondaga principal chiefs are combined together by themselves expressly to open and close the Five Nation Indians confederation council and to sanction, and decide any case, proposition, subject, point or points, when it is referred to them and all the chiefs must be present during the session, an agre unanimously, for one or two or more chiefs to sanction, and to give decision is illegal if the rest of their cousin chiefs are present and the council shall not be organized if the Onondaga chief of chiefs are not present to open and close the council, but he or they shall not sanction, or give decision on any case, proposition, subject, point or points till all the rest of their cousin chiefs shall be present.

26. The duty of the two head Seneca chiefs, Viz, Ke non keri dawi and De yo nin ho hakarawen, who are stationed at the door of the Five Nations Indians confederation session, is to watch and if they see any crawling creature entering in the session they will disallow to enter in the session; Crawling creature signifies any case of proposition which brought before the session would be ruinous, or injourious to the people; and also if they see stranger near the door they will bring the stranger in their session and ask what is their message have they with them.

27. And if any one of the Five Nation Indians confederation chiefs should die, and there being no member in the caste fit for

the office to succeed him; then the chiefs of the Five Nation Indians shall take the emblem of chieftainship and put it in another family of the same caste as the deceased chief; until such time as they shall have a member qualified for the office, then the emblem of chieftainship shall be restored to the said family; on the female side.

28. And if the principal chief or chiefs of the Five Nation Indians confederation, disregards the constitution of the Five Nation Indians, then his female relatives will come to him and warn him or they to come back, and walk according to this constitution; if he or they disregards the warning after the first and second warnings, then she will refer the matter to the war chief, and the war chief will now say to him, so you did not listen to her warnings, now it is just where the bright noonday sun stands, an its before that sun's brightness I now discharge you as a chief an I now disposses you of the office of chieftainship. I now give her the chieftainship for she is the proprietor, and as I have now discharged you as a chief, so you are no longer a chief you will now go where you want it to go, an you will now go alone, an the rest of the people will not go with you for we know not of what kind of a spirit has got in you, and as the Great Spirit could not handle sin therefore he could not come to take you out of the prespice in the place of destruction, and you will never be restored again to the place you did occupy once. Then the war chief will notify the Five Nation Indians confederation of his dismissal and they will sanction it.

29. Kariwhiyho, the good message is the love of the Great Spirit, the Supreme Being, now this Kariwhiyho is the surrounding guard of the Five Nation Indians confederation principal chiefs, an this Kariwhiyho it loves all alike the members of the Five Nation Indians confederation, and other nations of Indians that are attached to it by an through customary way of treaties, an if the Five Nation Indians confederation principal chiefs were to submit to laws and regulations made by other people, or course he or they the chief or chiefs are now gone through outside the boundary of the Kariwhiyhos surrounding guard, but their chieftainship fell of from their heads, an it remains inside the Five Nation Indians confederation, and he or they are now gone outside of the Kariwhiyho's surrounding guard alone without his or their chieftainship, the emblem of his or their chieftainship, their authority an honour.

30. And there is Five arrows bound together. This is the symbol of Union, Power, Honour, and Dominion of the Five Nation Indians confederation, an if one of the Five arrows was to be taken out then the remainder is easily broken asunder. This signifies if one of the Five Nations were to emagrate to a distant country of course they now withdrawn from the confederation therefore the Power of the Five Nation Indians confederation decreased.

31. Adodarho, the head chief of the Ononadagas or fire keepers, it is them are entrusted the care of the Five Nation Indians confederation council fire, and if there is any business to be transacted, they will send a messenger to the head chief of the Fire Keepers Adodarho; and state the nature of the business to him. Then Adodarho will call his cousin chiefs together and hold a council by themselves and consider the matter, and if they find that the matter is worth the consideration of the council of the Five Nations, then Adodarho will send a messenger and notify the rest of the chiefs of the five nations to assemble at their council house, or wherever their residence where the council fire is keept, and its smoke assends up perpetually to the sky, this it signifies that other Indian Nations are allies to the Five Nation Indians confederation, and as an imperial council fire, and when the chiefs assemble together and the council fire opened according to their rules, then the Fire Keepers will announce to the council the nature business for which they came together to consider.

32. And when the Five Nation Indian chief dies, the council will be adjourned ten days if it is in session, and if it is not in session it will not be summoned before the ten days expire; and if the three Brothers, Viz; Mohawks, Ononadagas and Senecas, should lose one by death of their number, then the four brothers Ya dat he wah, Oneidas and Cayugas, shall come to the residence of the deceased chief on the tenth day and comfort and cheer up their spirits again and if it is to Ya dat ha wah that loses one of their number then the three Brothers will perform the ceremony according to their customs by passing a certain number of strings of wampum, and diring the ceremony is in progress, a successor must be pointed out to them; then the female relatives of the deceased chief shall select one out of kindreds fit for the office of a chief, and if they are not ready, then they will postpone it till another time, and when they are ready; all the chiefs will assemble together to perform a long ceremony of what is called Oka yon donts hera to install the new chief or chiefs.

33. Yoh he do da oe, this is the title of a chief, and it is a peculiar way of how he becomes chief when a warrior assists the chiefs in their councils and otherwise, and he is found to be a wise councilor in war and peace, and of sober habits trustworthy and honest, then the chiefs will place him among the rest of the chiefs; as a chief and proclaim in their council, that such a one has become what is called Wa ka dine dot he se he now becomes a chief. And also if a warrior do exploits that will tend to the advantage and interest of his people, he also will become Yo ne do da oe amongst them as well, so his class of chiefs are not of the same order as the principle chiefs; for when he departs this life no one is to take his place or succeed him, and if he does wrong in their councils he could not be put out of the council, but he will not be

allowed any more to speak in their council, and if he resign his office no one is able to prevent him.

34. And if the Five Nation Indian confederation chief die, then his comarades will send a messenger to notify the rest of the confederate chiefs to attend his funeral.

35. And when the Five Nation Indians confederation chief get sick, and as he is now approaching unto death, then his female relatives, or his comarade chiefs will come and disposses him the emblem of his chieftainship.

36. And you can create an install a new chief or chiefs when you will hear my words again, and the way that you will hear my words again is when you will read the wampams, for its the wampams that talls all my Laws, Rules, Customs, which I gave you the Five Nation Indians, on this occasion you can create and install a new chief in the first combined chiefs, the second and the third as well.

37. And when one is made chief his skin are said to be seven Ni yo roe ka ra ke (each of the seven is six inches) in thickness and they were made so when they were made a chief or chiefs; this symbolizes, that when they are in council and engaged in their duties they will not willingly offend, and they are not easily to be offended, and they are not to take offence in any thing that might be said in council against them; but to go one calmly, and of a good conscience to deliberate whatever is before them to council.

38. The title of the Five Nation Indians confederation principal chiefs are Lords, and this title was from the beginning when the confederation first established.

39. And if any of the chiefs resign his office as a chief, he shall tell his Brother chiefs, and if he selects one to take his place and be a chief instead, and his Brother chiefs accepts his resignation, and one to fill his place, but he will not be made a chief, untill sanctioned by his female relatives.

40. The Great Spirit the Supreme Being has chosen to Mohawk Nation as head in this confederation, for it is with them that the confederation originated. Therefore if the Mohawk chiefs disallow anything, or protest any case or proposition that is brought before the council it shall not be lawful for the council to pass it, for he hath chosen them to be the leader of this confederation government, and all the affairs of the Five Nation Indians, and others that are united with them are in their hands; and he hath given the Mohawk chiefs a calm and tender hearts towards their people, and if any difficulty arise amongst them the people the chiefs in council will settle it for them.

A VISIT TO
THE "MASTER OF LIFE":
A DELAWARE LEGEND
Pontiac (Ottawa)

An Indian of the Wolf [Delaware] nation, desirous to see the "Master of Life," as all Indians call the good God, resolved to undertake the journey to Paradise, which he knew to be his residence, without having communicated anything to his nation, or to his village. But the question arose as to the way leading there, in order to succeed in his project, and not knowing anyone who had been there and could show him the way, he began to juggle, in the hope of securing good luck, by dreaming, as it was the general rule amongst all Indians, even those who had freed themselves from most superstitions, to put great faith in their dreams, and try their best to dream them over, as this story will show farther on.

The Wolf [Delaware] Indian imagined in his dreams that it was only necessary for him to start, and that in his travel he would see the heavenly abode, which induced him, on the next day, early in the morning, to equip himself for traveling and hunting, not forgetting to take, besides his provisions and ammunition, a large kettle; and thus he set out on his journey to heaven.

The first seven days of his voyage were rather favorable for his design. He marched on without being discouraged, firmly convinced that he would arrive at his aim, and eight days had fairly passed without his having met with anything which would put ob-

From Pioneer Society of the State of Michigan, *Collections*, Vol. 8 (1907), pp. 268ff.

stacles to his desires. On the evening of the eighth day, at sundown, he stopped, as usual, at the border of a small prairie, which
seemed to him fit for camping, on the bank of a creek. While
preparing his sleeping place, he observed, on the other end of the
prairie where he camped, three rather wide paths starting from one
point, which seemed to him somewhat singular. Nevertheless, he
continued to work, preparing his resting place, so as to have shelter
against the weather, and built a fire. While doing his cooking, it
appeared to him that the more it darkened by the setting of the
sun, the brighter the three paths became, which surprised him to
the point of frightening him, and he hesitated some moments what
to do—whether to stay in his camp or to go away and camp further
off, but by thinking it over, he remembered his juggleries, or
rather his dream, and that he had only undertaken his journey in
order to see the Master of Life. This brought him back to his
senses, and believing one of these three roads to be the one which
he must take to reach the place he was seeking, he resolved to
remain where he was until the following day, when he would take
one of these three paths, without choosing. But his curiosity hardly
left him time to take rest. He abandoned his camp, started out on
the path which seemed to be the widest, and marched on for half
a day without seeing anything to stop him, but on resting awhile
to take breath, he suddenly saw a large fire, which came out of
the ground and drew his curiosity to it.

While going nearer to observe better what could only be fire,
the more he advanced the larger it seemed to grow, which frightened him to the point of returning in his steps to take another road
which was less wide than the first. When, having marched the same
length of time as on the other, he saw the same spectacle. This
awakened anew his fright, which had quieted by the change of the
road, and he was obliged to change once more and take the third
path, in which he marched a whole day without discovering anything. Suddenly something appeared in his view like a mountain
of marvelous whiteness, which astonished him greatly; nevertheless, he advanced resolutely enough to see what there was of this
mountain, at the foot of which he saw his road no longer, which
made him sorry, not knowing what to do to continue his way. In
this dilemma he looked all around him and saw on the top of this
mountain a woman whose beauty dazzled him and whose garments
made the whiteness of the snow appear dull, and who was seated.
This woman said to him in his own tongue: "Thou seemest astonished no longer to see the road which leads thee to where thou
woulds't go. I know that long thou hast desired to see and to speak
to the Master of Life and hast undertaken this journey only to see
him. The way to His abode leads over this mountain, and to scale
it thou must leave behind all that thou hast and undress entirely.
Leave all thy things and garments at the foot of the mountain, no
one will wrong thee and after bathing in the river which I shall
show thee, thou shalt ascend." The savage Wolf obeyed the voice

of this woman in every point, but there remained one difficulty to vanquish, that was, to know how to get to the top of the mountain which was plumb upright, without path and as smooth as glass. He questioned the woman upon the mode of ascending and was assured if he was truly anxious to see the Master of Life, he must make the ascent without other help than that of his left hand and left foot. This appeared impossible to the Wolf [Delaware], who, however, encouraged by this woman, commenced the task of ascending and succeeded by very hard work. When he arrived at the top he was very much astonished not to see any one. The woman had disappeared and he saw himself alone, without guide, to the right of three villages, which made him confused. He did not know them, but they appeared differently constructed from those of his people, handsomer and in better order. After dreaming some time as to what he should do, he advanced toward the one which seemed to him to look the handsomest, but after having proceeded a little more than half way along the top of the mountain, he bethought himself of being nude and was afraid to proceed farther; but he heard a voice which told him to go on, he need not fear; having bathed, as he did, he proceeded in confidence. Therefore, he did not hesitate to go up to a place, which seemed to him to be the village gate and stopped there, waiting for it to open that he might enter. While he examined the beautiful outside appearance of the village, the gate opened and he saw coming to him a beautiful man, clothed wholly in white, who took him by the hand and said that he would satisfy him and let him speak to the Master of Life. The Wolf [Delaware] allowed himself to be led and both arrived in a place whose beauty had no equal, and which the savage could not sufficiently admire, where he saw the Master of Life, who took him by the hand and gave him a hat trimmed all around in gold, to sit down upon. The Wolf hesitated to do so from fear of spoiling the hat, but was ordered to do so and obeyed without reply.

The savage being seated, the good God said to him: "I am the Master of Life, whom thou desirest to know and to whom thou wouldst speak. Listen well to what I am going to say to thee and all thy red brethren. I am he who made heaven and earth, the trees, lakes, rivers, all men, and all that thou seest, and all that thou hast seen on earth. Because [I have done this and because] I love you, you must do what I say and [leave undone] what I hate. I do not like that you drink until you lose your reason, as you do; or that you fight with each other; or that you take two wives, or run after the wives of others; you do not well; I hate that. You must have but one wife, and keep her until death. When you are going to war, you juggle, join the medicine dance, and believe that I am speaking. You are mistaken, it is to Manitou to whom you speak; he is a bad spirit who whispers to you nothing but evil, and to whom you listen because you do not know me well. This land, where you live, I have made for you and not for others. How comes it that you suffer the whites on your lands? Can you not do without them? I know that those whom you call the children of your Great Father supply your wants, but if you were not bad, as you are, you would well do without them. You might live wholly as you did before you knew them. Before those whom you call your brothers came on your lands, did you not live by bow and arrow? You had no need of gun nor powder, nor the rest of their things, and nevertheless you caught animals to live and clothe yourselves with their skins, but when I saw that you inclined to the evil, I called back the animals into the depths of the woods, so that you had need of your brothers to have your wants supplied and cover you. You have only to become good and do what I want, and I shall send back to you the animals to live on. I do not forbid you, for all that, to suffer amongst you the children of your father. I love them, they know me and pray to me, and I give them their necessities and all that they bring to you, but as regards those who have come to trouble your country, drive them out, make war on them. I love them not, they know me not, they are my enemies and the enemies of your brothers. Send them back to the country which I made for them. There let them remain.

SPEECH IN RESPONSE TO MISSIONARY EFFORTS, 1805
Red Jacket (Seneca)

Friend and Brother! It was the will of the Great Spirit that we should meet together this day. He orders all things, and he has given us a fine day for our council. He has taken his garment from before the sun, and caused it to shine with brightness upon us. Our eyes are opened that we see clearly. Our ears are unstopped that we have been able to hear distinctly the words you have spoken. For all these favors we thank the Great Spirit, and him only.

Brother!—This council fire was kindled by you. It was at your request that we came together at this time. We have listened with attention to what you have said. You requested us to speak our minds freely. This gives us great joy, for we now consider that we stand upright before you, and can speak what we think. All have heard your voice, and all speak to you as one man. Our minds are agreed.

Brother!—You say you want an answer to your talk before you leave this place. It is right you should have one, as you are a great distance from home, and we do not wish to detain you. But we will first look back a little, and tell you what our fathers have told us, and what we have heard from the white people.

Brother!—Listen to what we say. There was a time when our forefathers owned this great island. Their seats extended from the

From B. B. Thatcher, *Indian Biography* (New York, 1845), pp. 291-94.

rising to the setting sun. The Great Spirit had made it for the use of Indians. He had created the buffalo, the deer, and other animals for food. He made the bear and the beaver, and their skins served us for clothing. He had scattered them over the country, and taught us how to take them. He had caused the earth to produce corn for bread. All this he had done for his red children because he loved them. If we had any disputes about hunting-grounds, they were generally settled without the shedding of much blood. But an evil day came upon us. Your forefathers crossed the great waters, and landed on this island. Their numbers were small. They found friends and not enemies. They told us they had fled from their own country for fear of wicked men, and come here to enjoy their religion. They asked for a small seat. We took pity on them, granted their request, and they sat down amongst us. We gave them corn and meat. They gave us poison in return. The white people had now found our country. Tidings were carried back, and more came amongst us. Yet we did not fear them. We took them to be friends. They called us brothers. We believed them, and gave them a larger seat. At length their numbers had greatly increased. They wanted more land. They wanted our country. Our eyes were opened, and our minds became uneasy. Wars took place. Indians were hired to fight against Indians, and many of our people were destroyed. They also brought strong liquors among us. It was strong and powerful, and has slain thousands.

Brother!—Our seats were once large, and yours were very small. You have now become a great people, and we have scarcely a place left to spread our blankets. You have got our country, but are not satisfied. You want to force your religion upon us.

Brother!—Continue to listen. You say that you are sent to instruct us how to worship the Great Spirit agreeably to his mind; and if we do not take hold of the religion which you white people teach, we shall be unhappy hereafter. You say that you are right and we are lost. How do we know this to be true? We understand that your religion is written in a book. If it was intended for us as well as for you, why has not the Great Spirit given it to us; and not only to us, but why did he not give to our forefathers the knowledge of that book, with the means of understanding it rightly? We only know what you tell us about it. How shall we know when to believe, being so often deceived by the white people.

Brother!—You say there is but one way to worship and serve the Great Spirit. If there is but one religion, why do you white people differ so much about it? Why not all agree, as you can all read the book?

Brother!—We do not understand these things. We are told that your religion was given to your forefathers, and has been handed down from father to son. We also have a religion which was given to our forefathers, and has been handed down to us their children. We worship that way. It teaches us to be thankful for all the favors we receive, to love each other, and to be united. We never quarrel about religion.

Brother!—The Great Spirit has made us all. But he has made a great difference between his white and red children. He has given us a different complexion and different customs. To you he has given the arts; to these he has not opened our eyes. We know these things to be true. Since he has made so great a difference between us in other things, why may we not conclude that he has given us a different religion, according to our understanding? The Great Spirit does right. He knows what is best for his children. We are satisfied.

Brother!—We do not wish to destroy your religion, or take it from you. We only want to enjoy our own.

Brother!—You say you have not come to get our land or our money, but to enlighten our minds. I will now tell you that I have been at your meetings and saw you collecting money from the meeting. I cannot tell what this money was intended for, but suppose it was for your minister; and if we should conform to your way of thinking, perhaps you may want some from us.

Brother!—We are told that you have been preaching to white people in this place. These people are our neighbors. We are acquainted with them. We will wait a little while, and see what effect your preaching has upon them. If we find it does them good and makes them honest and less disposed to cheat Indians, we will then consider again what you have said.

Brother!—You have now heard our answer to your talk, and this is all we have to say at present. As we are going to part, we will come and take you by the hand, and hope the Great Spirit will protect you on your journey, and return you safe to your friends.

A SYSTEM OF RELIGION
Tenkswataya, or the Prophet (Shawnee)

[The Prophet was
the brother of Tecumseh, with whom he worked from 1808 to 1812
to forge a federation of tribes east of the Mississippi in order to
halt further white encroachments on Indian lands. They asserted
that all tribes possessed the land as a common heritage, and no
tribe could sell any portion of it to whites. This address was delivered to the governor of Indiana in August, 1808.]

Father:—It is three years since I first began with that system of
religion which I now practice. The white people and some of the
Indians were against me; but I had no other intention but to introduce among the Indians, those good principles of religion which the
white people profess. I was spoken badly of by the white people,
who reproached me with misleading the Indians; but I defy them
to say that I did anything amiss.

Father, I was told that you intended to hang me. When I heard
this, I intended to remember it, and tell my father, when I went
to see him, and relate to him the truth.

I heard, when I settled on the Wabash, that my father, the governor, had declared that all the land between Vincennes and fort
Wayne, was the property of the Seventeen Fires. I also heard that
you wanted to know, my father, whether I was God or man; and
that you said if I was the former, I should not steal horses. I
heard this from Mr. Wells, but I believed it originated with himself.

The Great Spirit told me to tell the Indians that he had made

From Benjamin Drake, *Life of Tecumseh, and of His Brother, the Prophet* (Cincinnati,
1841), pp. 107-9.

them, and made the world—that he had placed them on it to do good, and not evil.

I told all the red skins, that the way they were in was not good, and that they ought to abandon it.

That we ought to consider ourselves as one man; but we ought to live agreeably to our several customs, the red people after their mode, and the white people after theirs; particularly, that they should not drink whiskey; that it was not made for them, but the white people, who alone knew how to use it; and that it is the cause of all the mischief which the Indians suffer; and that they must always follow the directions of the Great Spirit, and we must listen to him, as it was he that made us: determine to listen to nothing that is bad: do not take up the tomahawk, should it be offered by the British, or by the long knives: do not meddle with any thing that does not belong to you, but mind your own business, and cultivate the ground, that your women and your children may have enough to live on.

I now inform you, that it is our intention to live in peace with our father and his people forever.

My father, I have informed you what we mean to do, and I call the Great Spirit to witness the truth of my declaration. The religion which I have established for the last three years, has been attended to by the different tribes of Indians in this part of the world. Those Indians were once different people; they are now but one: they are all determined to practice what I have communicated to them, that has come immediately from the Great Spirit through me.

Brother, I speak to you as a warrior. You are one. But let us lay aside this character, and attend to the care of our children, that they may live in comfort and peace. We desire that you will join us for the preservation of both red and white people. Formerly, when we lived in ignorance, we were foolish; but now, since we listen to the voice of the Great Spirit, we are happy.

I have listened to what you have said to us. You have promised to assist us: I now request you, in behalf of all the red people, to use your exertions to prevent the sale of liquor to us. We are all well pleased to hear you say that you will endeavor to promote our happiness. We give you every assurance that we will follow the dictates of the Great Spirit.

We are all well pleased with the attention that you have showed us; also with the good intentions of our father, the President. If you give us a few articles, such as needles, flints, hoes, powder, &c., we will take the animals that afford us meat, with powder and ball.

AN INDIAN COSMOGONY

Chief Smohalla (Wanapum)

[The message of this Indian "Preacher" to his people urged them to return to the traditional ways of the past and to abandon the customs of white men, the disrupters of nature. The law of which he speaks is the order of nature, which their god Saghalee Tyee did not want broken.]

Once the world was all water and God lived alone. He was lonesome, he had no place to put his foot, so he scratched the sand up from the bottom and made the land, and he made the rocks, and he made trees, and he made a man; and the man had wings and could go anywhere. The man was lonesome, and God made a woman. They ate fish from the water, and God made the deer and other animals, and he sent the man to hunt and told the woman to cook the meat and to dress the skins. Many more men and women grew up, and they lived on the banks of the great river whose waters were full of salmon. The mountains contained much game and there were buffalo on the plains. There were so many people that the stronger ones sometimes oppressed the weak and drove them from the best fisheries, which they claimed as their own. They fought and nearly all were killed, and their bones are to be seen in the hills yet. God was very angry at this and he took away their wings and commanded that the lands and fisheries

From *Fourteenth Annual Report of the Bureau of American Ethnology* (1896), Part 2, pp. 720–21.

should be common to all who lived upon them; that they were never to be marked off or divided, but that the people should enjoy the fruits that God planted in the land, and the animals that lived upon it, and the fishes in the water. God said he was the father and the earth was the mother of mankind; that nature was the law; that the animals, and fish, and plants obeyed nature, and that man only was sinful. This is the old law.

I know all kinds of men. First there were my people (the Indians); God made them first. Then he made a Frenchman [referring to the Canadian voyagers of the Hudson Bay company], and then he made a priest [priests accompanied these expeditions of the Hudson Bay company]. A long time after that came Boston men [Americans are thus called in the Chinook jargon, because the first of our nation came into the Columbia river in 1796 in a ship from Boston], and then King George men [the English]. Later came black men, and last God made a Chinaman with a tail. He is of no account and has to work all the time like a woman. All these are new people. Only the Indians are of the old stock. After awhile, when God is ready, he will drive away all the people except those who have obeyed his laws.

Those who cut up the lands or sign papers for lands will be defrauded of their rights and will be punished by God's anger. Moses was bad. God did not love him. He sold his people's houses and the graves of their dead. It is a bad word that comes from Washington. It is not a good law that would take my people away from me to make them sin against the laws of God.

You ask me to plow the ground! Shall I take a knife and tear my mother's bosom? Then when I die she will not take me to her bosom to rest.

You ask me to dig for stone! Shall I dig under her skin for her bones? Then when I die I can not enter her body to be born again.

You ask me to cut grass and make hay and sell it, and be rich like white men! But how dare I cut off my mother's hair?

It is a bad law, and my people can not obey it. I want my people to stay with me here. All the dead men will come to life again. Their spirits will come to their bodies again. We must wait here in the homes of our fathers and be ready to meet them in the bosom of our mother.

COURTSHIP
AND MARRIAGE
James Larpenteur Long and
Red Feather (Assiniboine)

When a young couple decided to marry, the young man brought his wife to the lodge of his folks, or he went to live with her people. Then the marriage was announced at the next dance and the relatives gave away presents.

The couple lived with either parents for a year or so. If they lived at the lodge of the wife's parents, the son-in-law was expected to supply the meat and do the man's work. The wife did most of the tasks in and about the lodge, if they lived with his folks.

The parents and relatives of a marriageable youth sometimes made a choice for him. Red Feather told the following story:

My father never talked to me about marriage, but one time, while on a visit to my aunt in another band, she talked right to the point. She always seemed to do the talking for the family. She had a son and a daughter. The youth was my age, and we were always together.

She said, "You and your cousin (meaning her son) have been visiting back and forth between the two bands and caused us much worry. There is so much danger from war parties traveling about and an enemy could easily waylay and kill you both. You are now grown up and should settle down. We have selected a young woman who lives in this band to be your wife. She is strong

From Michael S. Kennedy, *The Assiniboines* (Norman, Okla., 1961), pp. 30–32.

and well-trained by her mother and no one has, so far, asked for her. We have already arranged everything so you will be married tomorrow."

I was not surprised, for I was resigned to the will of my family and my aunt was like my own mother. A man was paid a fee and sent with three horses and some goods to my future wife's folks.

It was the custom for the bridegroom to paint the face of his bride upon her arrival in the lodge of her future husband, but my cousin said, "I will relieve you of that task and paint her face myself. Just leave that part to me."

The man returned, accompanied by my future wife. She brought food with her, which she placed in front of my aunt. My aunt then seated her beside me and told my cousin to paint her face as he had volunteered to do. My cousin was not so willing to keep his word now that the time had come and said I should paint my own wife's face.

By that time I thought my heart was going to pound its way out through my breast. I could not move to do anything and my aunt kept repeating that the bride should not be kept waiting. So finally I got up enough courage to perform the rite, and I did not do it so well either. My hands shook so that I just daubed a little paint on each cheek and was finished. After that she accompanied the man back to her home.

The next day, her folks brought her and two horses, which were loaded with goods, to my aunt's lodge. The horses they gave to my uncle and aunt, and the goods were bedding and things for us.

My aunt gave a large feast, and the marriage was announced, and many things were given away by both parties.

It was customary for older men to bargain for a wife. They gave a fee to a go-between, and he made the offer to the girl's parents. If the offer was attractive to the parents, they entreated their daughter to consent to the marriage. The girl could not be compelled to accept, but the parents always worked on her affection for her relatives and usually, in the end, there was a marriage.

Some poor parents, or parents who had daughters but no male provider in the family, "gave away" their daughters to prominent men, even though the men already had one or more wives.

There were cases where a child was promised to a grown man, and while the girl was growing up, the prospective husband provided for her and her parents. There were times when a girl, on reaching maturity, refused to fulfill the promise made by her parents.

A man boldly took back his gifts if the girl he bought left his lodge and went back to her folks. Some of these troubles, now and then, had serious consequences and someone was injured or killed.

If a man's wife had more work than she could do in their lodge and had one or more unmarried younger sisters, the man could through another person, ask her relatives for one of them to be his wife. He need not bargain for her, as it was considered her duty to her sister to accept and help with the tasks. The parents did not expect anything in return but continued support. Several sisters could marry a man if he was a prominent person, a good provider, and entertained a great deal.

The parents of a boy and the parents of a girl, if the families were close friends, usually planned that the two would marry at maturity. In that case, if someone else wanted the girl, she was already promised. And the maidens knew, too, that the young man was as good as married. From childhood, the two were taught to observe the rules that governed a person's behavior and speech when in the presence of a father-in-law or a mother-in-law.

Marriages were dissolved merely by living apart. Sometimes, if the husband was a member of a society, he announced through another that, "He has thrown her away." That was a sign that any-one was free to court the woman. If the man took his wife back and they lived together as before, it was considered a disgrace. He was dropped from his society, and if he had an office or rank in the organization, it was taken from him and given to someone else.

INDIAN FAMILY LIFE
Luther Standing Bear (Sioux)

The home was the center of Lakota society—the place where good social members were formed and the place whence flowed the strength of the tribe. Here it was that offspring learned duty to parents, to lodge, to band, to tribe, and to self.

Woman's work, generally, was to cook for the family, keep the tipi in order, and sew the clothing of the household members. The good wife never allowed one of the family to run low in clothing. There were garments to be made, and moccasins, robes and blankets, and sometimes gloves, caps and scarfs. Buttonholes were never made, probably never thought of, but very pretty buttons were fashioned of rawhide and either painted or covered with porcupine quills. Sinew was split for thread, coarse strands for heavy work and medium fine or very fine strands for decorative work, then folded into little bundles and placed in a sewing kit. When the men came home from the hunt there were skins to be cleaned and tanned. New tipis were made and old ones, for the sake of frugality, made into clothing for children. From rawhide were made moccasin soles, bags and trunks for holding ceremonial garments, head-dresses, and other articles to be kept in neatness and order.

The good wife always kept plenty of food stored and cooked so that it could be served at any moment. The thought was to not only meet the food requirements of the family, but to be able to serve any one who came to the tipi, strangers or relatives, children who came in from other tipis, or any old people whom the children might bring in. If the husband brought home friends unexpectedly,

From Chief Standing Bear, *Land of the Spotted Eagle* (Boston, 1933), pp. 84–93.

he could be sure that his wife would receive them hospitably without any request from him.

Many of the courtesies of Indian social life included the preparation and serving of food, and among the Lakota it was a custom of good will just as it is with the white man. When a white friend wishes to extend a courtesy it is usually by asking one to dine. A feast in honor of my father was sometimes given in this way: Some of my mother's relations would invite her over to their tipi. At once the women would begin preparing food for a number of people. When all was ready, they would tell mother to ask father to come to the feast and bring with him some of his friends. Father would gladly accept the invitation and would bring with him, as a rule, some of the old men of the village and there would be singing, eating, story-telling, and a general good time. The meal which the relations offered to father was their good will expressed in their most generous way. All his relations wished him to remain on good terms with his people, so if father could ask a number of old men to share good food with him, his chances for remaining popular would be better. The feast tended to strengthen the ties between father and the headmen of his band and also between him and his wife's relations.

Visiting bands were often received with a feast of welcome. As soon as the visitors stopped and began putting up their tipis, our women and girls built fires and cooked great quantities of food. They then carried the food over and spread the feast for the visitors, waiting upon them with every attention. The visitors ate and enjoyed themselves, but were never allowed to help in clearing away the remains of the feast. This was done by the women after the visitors had departed.

Sometimes a lone stranger came to our village for a visit. He was usually taken from tipi to tipi for a round of feasting and gossip, for the visitor was sure to have news to tell and he was encouraged to tell of his travels and of the people of his band. When the round of visits began, the stranger was given a long stick, pointed at one end, which he carried with him from tipi to tipi, each family putting on his stick some dried meat until it was full and sometimes more. This meat was to supply the visitor with food on his return or continued journey.

The serving of a family meal was a quiet and orderly affair. Mother placed the food in front of her while we children all sat quietly about, neither commenting on the food nor asking for any favors. Father, if at home, sat in his accustomed place at the side of the tipi. He, too, remained perfectly quiet and respectful, accepting the food that mother offered to him without comment. The serving was done on wooden plates, the soup being passed in horn spoons of different sizes, some of them holding as much as a large bowl. The food was portioned to each one of us as mother saw fit, her judgment being unquestioned, for we never asked for more.

Before serving us, however, mother put a small portion of the food in the fire as a blessing for the meal.

Grandmother, next to mother, was the most important person in the home. Her place, in fact, could be filled by no one else. It has been told and written that old people among the Indians were sacrificed when they became useless. If this is the case with other tribes, I do not know of it, but I do know that it was never done among the Lakotas. Most old people were revered for their knowledge, and were never considered worthless members to be got rid of. Parental devotion was very strong and the old were objects of care and devotion to the last. They were never given cause to feel useless and unwanted, for there were duties performed only by the old and because it was a rigidly-kept custom for the young to treat their elders with respect. Grandmother filled a place that mother did not fill, and the older she got the more, it seemed, we children depended upon her for attention. I can never forget one of my grandmothers, mother's mother, and what wonderful care she took of me. As a story-teller, she was a delight not only to me but to other little folks of the village. Her sense of humor was keen and she laughed as readily as we.

Mother's and grandmother's tipis were quite close together and they saw a good deal of each other, working together and visiting back and forth. The men folks of the family were, for the most part, away from home during the day on hunting or scouting parties. But whenever father was at home and he chanced to walk out of the tipi, he covered his face with his blanket until he was sure that he would not see his mother-in-law. In this way he showed his respect for her, and had he not observed this courtesy she would have had every right to be affronted. She, too, avoided him, and if by chance they met, she hid her face. Had she allowed him to look upon her, it would have been an unforgivable breach of manners. In order to show her great respect for my father, grandmother often cooked some meat in her tipi, and calling my mother over would give her the meat saying, "Take this to my son-in-law." In this way she let him know that she thought highly of him.

The men, when at home, were shown a good deal of attention by the women. This was but natural, as it was the hunters, scouts and warriors who bore the greatest dangers, and consequently were the recipients of much care and consideration. Young warriors bearing for the first time the hardships of life were specially considered by the women. I remember one winter a party of young hunters returned home exhausted and near starvation, having seen no game. On reaching the village, they entered the first tipi they came to, which happened to be that of an old woman. Without a word, these young men began putting the meat, which was strung on a pole inside the tipi, on the fire to cook, and feeding themselves until it was gone. All the while the old woman ran about crying, not with anger or sorrow, but with joy for the return of the young men, and with gladness for the supply of meat that she was able to furnish. Had a white man witnessed this occurrence, it would probably have been interpreted in a manner far from correct.

Women and children were the objects of care among the Lakotas and as far as their environment permitted they lived sheltered lives. Life was softened by a great equality. All the tasks of women —cooking, caring for children, tanning and sewing—were considered dignified and worth while. No work was looked upon as menial, consequently there were no menial workers. Industry filled the life of every Lakota woman.

The first thing a dutiful husband did in the morning, after breakfasting, was to arrange his wife's hair and to paint her face. The brush was the tail of the porcupine attached to a decorated handle, and in place of a comb a hair parter was used—a slender pointed stick, also with a decorated handle. The husband parted his wife's hair, then carefully brushed and plaited it into two braids which were tied at the ends with strings of painted buckskin. These hair-strings were sometimes works of art, being wrapped with brightly colored porcupine quills and either tipped with ball tassels of porcupine quills or fluffs of eagle feathers. Bead hair-strings were later made, and they, too, are very pretty. When the hairdressing was finished, the part in the hair was sometimes marked with a stripe of red or yellow paint. Next, the husband applied red paint to his wife's face, sometimes just to the cheeks, sometimes covering the entire face. If the woman was to be exposed to the wind and sun all day, she usually had her face covered with a protective coat of paint mixed with grease. It was "style" for the Lakota woman to use much red paint, but the custom was very likely a necessary and comfortable one before it became a mere matter of style. Many Lakota women had skins quite fine in texture and in childhood were light in color. Such skins, of course, burned easily in the hot wind and sun, consequently children were often painted with the red paint and grease, both boys and girls, the mother performing this duty and not the father.

If the man of the family was to be home for several days, he busied himself in many ways, lightening the work of the woman. He cut down trees for the ponies and for wood, made and repaired her saddles, cut up meat conveniently for drying, and, when there was nothing else to be done, gladly amused the baby of the family. A man who unduly scolded his wife or who beat her or his children was not considered a good man. A man who would inflict punishment upon the women and children was considered a weakling and a coward. Whenever it was said about a man, "He ought not to have a wife," that was expressing strong disapproval of him.

As soon as the wife realized that she was to become a mother, she withdrew from the society of her husband, though at all times he had her in his care. But the husband immediately found duties that occupied his time—the hunt, the war-party, or ceremonies. With the knowledge that a child was about to be born the thought of the couple was for its welfare, and both father and mother were willing to sacrifice for the sake of the health of the child and mother. Not till a child was five or six years of age did the parents allow themselves another offspring. As a consequence Lakota families were not large, four or five children being the rule. But disabled mothers were a rarity and many a grandmother was as strong as her granddaughter. And with all the demands placed by parenthood, seldom was the relationship between husband and wife weakened. Children were influential beings with parents also. I remember my stepmother's uncle, Horse Looking, who fell a victim to the habit of drinking. It made of him a terrible man when under its influence, though in his right mind he was the kindest of men. When he was in a drunken frenzy, the only way to curb him was to get his youngest child and present it to him. He would at once forget his temper and begin to pet and fondle the child.

With the nearing event much preparation took place. Sisters, aunts, and other relatives made clothes of the finest and softest doeskin. A cradle was decorated and paints and powders prepared. But to grandmother fell the honor of officiating as supervisor and adviser on all matters pertaining to the occasion. She had, in fact, started her preparations and arrangements for the event of birth from the day of the wedding. During the waiting period grandmother had baked a red earth clay and pounded it to a fine powder to mix with the buffalo fat which she had rendered into a creamy paste. This mixture served as a cleanser and also as a protector to the tender skin of the child. Then grandmother had gathered the driest of buffalo chips and ground them between stones to a powder as fine and soft as talcum. This powder was a purifier, and soothing to an irritated skin.

Perhaps the hardest duty in the performance of parenthood was not so much to watch the conduct of their children as to be ever watchful of their own—a duty placed upon parents through the method used in instructing their young—example. Children, possessors of extreme vigor of health, with faculties sensitized by close contact with nature, made full use of eyes and ears; and Lakota parents and elders were under scrutiny for conduct and conversation. They were consequently bound to act in as kind and dignified a manner as possible.

A WINNEBAGO FATHER'S INSTRUCTIONS TO HIS SON

My son, when you grow up you should see to it that you are of some benefit to your fellowmen. There is only one way in which you can begin to be of any aid to them, and that is to fast. So, my son, see to it that you fast. Our grandfather, the fire, who stands at all times in the center of our dwelling, sends forth all kinds of blessings. Be sure that you make an attempt to obtain his blessings.

My son, do you remember to have our grandfathers, the war chiefs, bless you. See to it that they pity you. Some day when you go on the warpath their blessings will enable you to have specific foreknowledge of all that will happen to you on that occasion. This will likewise enable you to accomplish what you desire without the danger of anything interfering with your plans. Without the slightest trouble you will then be able to obtain the prizes of war. Without any trouble you will be able to obtain these and in addition glory and the war honors. If, in truth, you thirst yourself to death, our grandfathers who are in control of wars—to whom all the war powers that exist in this world belong— they will assuredly bless you.

My son, if you do not wear out your feet through ceaseless activity (in fasting), if you do not blacken your face for fasting, it will be all in vain that you inflict sufferings upon yourself. Blessings are not obtained through mere desire alone; they are

From Paul Radin, *The Winnebago Tribe*. In the *Thirty-seventh Annual Report of the Bureau of American Ethnology* (1923), Chapter 7.

not obtained without making the proper sacrifices or without putting yourself time and again in proper mental condition. Indeed, my son, they are not to be obtained without effort on your part. So see to it that, of all those spirits whom Earthmaker created, one at least has pity upon you and blesses you. Whatever such a spirit says to you that will unquestionably happen.

Now, my son, if you do not obtain a spirit to strengthen you, you will not amount to anything in the estimation of your fellow-men. They will show you little respect. Perhaps they will make fun of you.

Do not die in the village. It is not good to die there. Whenever a person is grown up that is what is told him. Nor is it good, my son, to let women journey ahead of you from amidst the village. It is not good thus to let women die before you. Therefore, in order to prevent this, our ancestors encouraged one another to fast. Some day you will travel in a difficult road; there will be some crisis in your life, and then when it is too late you will begin to reproach yourself for not having fasted at the proper time. So that you may not have occasion to blame yourself at such a time I counsel you to fast. If you do not obtain a blessing when the other women are dividing the war prizes brought home from the warpath by their brothers, your sisters will stand aside envying them. If, however, you are blessed by the spirits in control of war power, and if you then return victorious, how proud your sisters will be to receive the war honors and to wear them around their necks and participate with them in the victory dance! And in this way your sisters likewise will be strengthened by your war deeds. You will keep well, in health.

My son, it will indeed be good if you obtain war powers, but our ancestors say it is difficult. Especially difficult is it to be leader on the warpath. So they say. If you do not become an individual warranted to lead a war party, yet mistaking yourself for one although really an ordinary warrior, you "throw away a man," your act will be considered most disgraceful. A mourner might harm you in revenge for the fact that you have caused him to mourn, and burn you with embers. Your people will all be sad, both on account of your disgrace and on account of the pain inflicted upon you.

My son, not with the blessing of one of the spirits merely, nor with the blessing of twenty, for that matter, can you go on the warpath. You must have the blessing of all the spirits above the earth, and of all those on the earth, and of all those who are pierced through the earth; of all those under the earth; of all those who are under the water; of all those that are on the sides of the earth, i.e., all the four winds; of the Disease-giver; of the Sun; of the Daylight; of the Moon; of the Earth; and of all those who are in control of war powers—with the blessings of all these deities must you be provided before you can lead a successful war party.

My son, if you cast off dress men will be benefited by your deeds. You will be an aid to all your people. If your people honor you, it will be good. And they will like you even the more if you obtain a limb. They will indeed like you very much if you obtain a limb, or, even better, two or three. If you do thus, wherever people boil an animal with a head you will always be able to eat.

If on account of your bravery you are permitted to tell of your war exploits during the Four Nights' Wake for the benefit of the soul of the deceased, do not try to add to your glory by exaggerating any exploit, for by so doing you will cause the soul to stumble on its journey to the spirit land. If you do this and add an untruth to the account of your war exploit, you will die soon after. The war spirits always hear you. Tell a little less. The old men say it is wise.

My son, it is good to die in war. If you die in war, your soul will not be unconscious. You will have complete disposal of your soul and it will always be happy. If you should ever desire to return to this earth and live here again, you will be able to do so. A second life as a human being you may live, or, if you prefer, as an inhabitant of the air (a bird) you may live, or you may roam the earth as an animal. Thus it is to him who dies in battle.

My son, fast for an honorable place among your fellowmen. Fast, so that when you are married you may have plenty of food; that you may be happy and that you may not have to worry about your children. If in your fastings you have a vision of your future home, the members of your family will be lacking in nothing during their life. Fast for the food that you may need. If you fast a sufficiently large number of times, when in after life you have children and they cry for food you will be able to offer a piece of deer or moose meat without any difficulty. Your children will never be hungry.

My son, never abuse your wife. The women are sacred. If you abuse your wife and make her life miserable, you will die early. Our grandmother, the earth, is a woman, and in mistreating your wife you will be mistreating her. Most assuredly will you be abusing our grandmother if you act thus. And as it is she that is taking care of us you will really be killing yourself by such behavior.

My son, when you keep house, should anyone enter your house, no matter who it is, be sure to offer him whatever you have in the house. Any food that you withhold at such a time will most assuredly become a source of death to you. If you are stingy about giving food the people will kill you on this account. They will poison you. If you hear of a traveler who is visiting your people and you wish to see him, prepare your table for him and have him sent for. In this manner you will be acting correctly. It is always good to act correctly and do good, the old people used to say.

If you see an old, helpless person, help him with whatever you possess. Should you happen to possess a home and you take him there, he might suddenly say abusive things about you during the middle of the meal. You will be strengthened by such words. This same traveler may, on the contrary, give you something that he carries under his arms and which he treasures very highly. If it is an object without a stem, keep it to protect your house. If you thus keep it within your house, your home will never be molested by any bad spirits. Nothing will be able to enter your house unexpectedly. Thus you will live. Witches, instead of entering your house, will pass around it. If, in addition to possessing this medicine, you also fast, your people will be benefited by it greatly. Earthmaker made spirits up above and some he made to live on this earth; and again some he made to live under the water and some to live in the water; and all these he put in charge of something. Even the small animals that move about this earth the creator put in charge of some power. Thus he created them. Afterwards he created us human beings and as he had exhausted all the powers to be disposed of we were not in control of anything. Then he made a weed and placed it in our charge. And he said that no matter how powerful are the spirits that exist they would not be able to take this weed from us without giving something in return. He himself, Earthmaker, would not be able to demand it for nothing. So he spoke. This weed was the tobacco plant. Earthmaker said that if we would offer a pipeful of tobacco to him, whatever we should ask of him he would immediately grant. Not only he, but all the spirits created, longed to have some of this tobacco. It is for this reason that when we fast and cry piteously for some spirit to take pity on us, if we give them tobacco they will bless us with those powers that the creator gave them. So it will be. Earthmaker made it thus. . . .

If you ever get married, my son, do not make an idol of your wife. The more you worship her, the more will she want to be worshipped. Thus the old people said. They warned the young men against the example of those men who always hearken to what the women say, who are the slaves of women. Often they would speak in the following manner: "You have had many warnings, but it may happen that some day you will not pay any attention to them. Then, when they call upon you to take part in the Winter Feast you may perhaps refuse to go. When a war party is leaving you may listen to the voice of your wife and not join them. Thus you will be as one who has been brought up as a woman. Men of every description do what is demanded of them, you alone do not act as a man should. You never perform a man's deed. If you were to go to a Winter Feast, you would be handed a lean piece of meat. Why should you subject yourself to the danger of being made fun of? A real brave man, when he goes to a Winter Feast, will receive a deer's head, while you will only receive a lean piece of meat. That is all they will give you to eat. It will stick in your throat."

My son, if you keep on listening to your wife, after a while she will never let you go to any feast at all. All your relatives will scold you and your own sisters will think little of you. They will say to one another, "Let us not ever go over to see him. He is of no help to anyone." Finally, when you have become a real slave to your wife, she might tell you to hit your own relatives, and you would do it. For these reasons, my son, I warn you against the words of women. Steel yourself against them. For if you do not do so you will find yourself different from other men. It is not good to be enslaved by a woman.

My son, this also I will tell you. Women can never be watched. If you try to watch them you will merely show your jealousy and your female relatives will also be jealous. After a while you will become so jealous of your wife that she will leave you and run away. First, you worshipped her above everything else, then you became jealous and watched her all the time, and the result will be that she will run away from you. You yourself will be to blame for this. You thought too much of a woman and in worshipping her you humbled yourself, and as a consequence she has been taken away from you. You are making the woman suffer and making her feel unhappy. All the other women will know of this, and no one will want to marry you again. Everyone will consider you a very bad man.

My son, whenever people go on the warpath go along with them. It is good to die on the warpath. You may perhaps say so, because you are unhappy that your wife has left you. My son, not for such reasons, however, must you go on the warpath. You will be merely throwing away a human life. If you want to go on the warpath, do so because you feel that you are courageous enough, not because you are unhappy at the loss of your wife. If you go on the warpath you will enjoy yourself. Do not go, however, unless you have fasted, and unless you have fasted for that particular warpath. If you have not fasted and attempt nevertheless to go on the warpath, a bullet will surely seek you out and kill you. This is what will happen to you if you do not fast.

If you exert yourself in fasting you will assuredly perform some brave war exploit. You must tell your sisters and sister's children and your mother's sisters all about your exploit. Remember, also, that the keepers of the war-bundles can give you good advice in all that pertains to war. For their deeds they will be given a good dish of meat. This they will give you to eat.

Of such things did my ancestors speak, and I would wish you to do as they did. That is why I am telling you all these things. I myself never asked for any of this instruction, but my father did. All human beings ought to ask for it. Never let anybody be in a position to puzzle you in regard to what is right. Ask for this instruction, my son, for it is not an ordinary thing. In the olden times if a person loved his child very much, he would only give him instruction after he had begun fasting all day for the first time. When a young boy has just matured, those who have been preaching to him always ask him one question, namely, whether he had begun to fast. And this the young boy must always answer truthfully, for if he has begun his fast the instruction would stop. The old men do not preach to men, but only to boys.

A PAWNEE MOTHER'S ADVICE TO HER SON, LONE CHIEF

You must trust always in *Ti-ra'-wa*. He made us, and through him we live. When you grow up, you must be a man. Be brave, and face whatever danger may meet you. Do not forget, when you look back to your young days, that I have raised you, and always supported you. You had no father to do it. Your father was a chief, but you must not think of that. Because he was a chief, it does not follow that you will be one. It is not the man who stays in the lodge that becomes great; it is the man who works, who sweats, who is always tired from going on the warpath.

When you get to be a man, remember that it is his ambition that makes the man. If you go on the warpath, do not turn around when you have gone part way, but go on as far as you were going, and then come back. If I should live to see you become a man, I want you to become a great man. I want you to think about the hard times we have been through. Take pity on people who are poor, because we have been poor, and people have taken pity on us. If I live to see you a man, and to go off on the warpath, I would not cry if I were to hear that you had been killed in battle. That is what makes a man: to fight and to be brave. I should be sorry to see you die from sickness. If you are killed, I would rather have you die in the open air, so that the birds of the air will eat your flesh, and the wind will breathe on you and blow over your bones. It is better to be killed in the open air than

From George Bird Grinnell, *Pawnee Hero Stories and Folk-Tales* (New York, 1889), pp. 45–47.

to be smothered in the earth. Love your friend and never desert him. If you see him surrounded by the enemy, do not run away. Go to him, and if you cannot save him, be killed together, and let your bones lie side by side. Be killed on a hill; high up. Your grandfather said it is not manly to be killed in a hollow. It is not a man who is talking to you, advising you. Heed my words, even if I am a woman.

LIFE IN THE WOODS: BOYHOOD MEMORIES OF AUTUMNAL TRIBAL ACTIVITIES (c. 1870–72)

Charles Eastman, or Ohiyesa (Santee Sioux)

The month of September recalls to every Indian's mind the season of the fall hunt. I remember one such expedition which is typical of many. Our party appeared on the northwestern side of Turtle mountain; for we had been hunting buffaloes all summer, in the region of the Mouse river, between that mountain and the upper Missouri.

As our cone-shaped teepees rose in clusters along the outskirts of the heavy forest that clothes the sloping side of the mountain, the scene below was gratifying to a savage eye. The rolling yellow plains were checkered with herds of buffaloes. Along the banks of the streams that ran down from the mountains were also many elk, which usually appear at morning and evening, and disappear into the forest during the warmer part of the day. Deer, too, were plenty, and the brooks were alive with trout. Here and there the streams were dammed by the industrious beaver.

In the interior of the forest there were lakes with many islands, where moose, elk, deer and bears were abundant. The water-fowl were wont to gather here in great numbers, among them the

From Charles Eastman, *Indian Boyhood* (New York, 1902).

crane, the swan, the loon, and many of the smaller kinds. The forest also was filled with a great variety of birds. Here the partridge drummed his loudest, while the whippoorwill sang with spirit, and the hooting owl reigned in the night.

To me, as a boy, this wilderness was a paradise. It was a land of plenty. To be sure, we did not have any of the luxuries of civilization, but we had every convenience and opportunity and luxury of Nature. We had also the gift of enjoying our good fortune, whatever dangers might lurk about us; and the truth is that we lived in blessed ignorance of any life that was better than our own.

As soon as hunting in the woods began, the customs regulating it were established. The council teepee no longer existed. A hunting bonfire was kindled every morning at day-break, at which each brave must appear and report. The man who failed to do this before the party set out on the day's hunt was harassed by ridicule. As a rule, the hunters started before sunrise, and the brave who was announced throughout the camp as the first one to return with a deer on his back, was a man to be envied.

The legend-teller, old Smoky Day, was chosen herald of the camp, and it was he who made the announcements. After supper was ended, we heard his powerful voice resound among the teepees in the forest. He would then name a man to kindle the bonfire the next morning. His suit of fringed buckskin set off his splendid physique to advantage.

Scarcely had the men disappeared in the woods each morning than all the boys sallied forth, apparently engrossed in their games and sports, but in reality competing actively with one another in quickness of observation. As the day advanced, they all kept the sharpest possible lookout. Suddenly there would come the shrill "Woo-coo-hoo!" at the top of a boy's voice, announcing the bringing in of a deer. Immediately all the other boys took up the cry, each one bent on getting ahead of the rest. Now we all saw the brave Wacoota fairly bent over by his burden, a large deer which he carried on his shoulders. His fringed buckskin shirt was besprinkled with blood. He threw down the deer at the door of his wife's mother's home, according to custom, and then walked proudly to his own. At the door of his father's teepee he stood for a moment straight as a pine-tree, and then entered.

When a bear was brought in, a hundred or more of these urchins were wont to make the woods resound with their voices: "Wah! wah! wah! Wah! wah! wah! The brave White Rabbit brings a bear! Wah! wah! wah!"

All day these sing-song cheers were kept up, as the game was brought in. At last, toward the close of the afternoon, all the hunters had returned, and happiness and contentment reigned absolute, in a fashion which I have never observed among the white people, even in the best of circumstances. The men were lounging and smoking; the women actively engaged in the preparation of the evening meal, and the care of the meat. The choicest of the game was cooked and offered to the Great Mystery, with all the accompanying ceremonies. This we called the "medicine feast." Even the women, as they lowered the boiling pot, or the fragrant roast of venison ready to serve, would first whisper: "Great Mystery, do thou partake of this venison, and still be gracious!" This was the commonly said "grace."

Everything went smoothly with us, on this occasion, when we first entered the woods. Nothing was wanting to our old way of living. The killing of deer and elk and moose had to be stopped for a time, since meat was so abundant that we had no use for them any longer. Only the hunting for pelts, such as those of the bear, beaver, marten, and otter was continued. But whenever we lived in blessed abundance, our braves were wont to turn their thoughts to other occupations—especially the hot-blooded youths whose ambition it was to do something noteworthy.

At just such moments as this there are always a number of priests in readiness, whose vocation it is to see into the future, and each of whom consults his particular interpreter of the Great Mystery. (This ceremony is called by the white people "making medicine.") To the priests the youthful braves hint their impatience for the war-path. Soon comes the desired dream or prophecy or vision to favor their departure.

Our young men presently received their sign, and for a few days all was hurry and excitement. On the appointed morning we heard the songs of the warriors and the wailing of the women, by which they bade adieu to each other, and the eligible braves, headed by an experienced man—old Hotanka or Loud-Voiced Raven—set out for the Gros Ventre country.

Our older heads, to be sure, had expressed some disapproval of the undertaking, for the country in which we were roaming was not our own, and we were likely at any time to be taken to task by its rightful owners. The plain truth of the matter was that we were intruders. Hence the more thoughtful among us preferred to be at home, and to achieve what renown they could get by defending their homes and families. The young men, however, were so eager for action and excitement that they must needs go off in search of it.

From the early morning when these braves left us, led by the old war-priest, Loud-Voiced Raven, the anxious mothers, sisters and sweethearts counted the days. Old Smoky Day would occasionally get up early in the morning, and sing a "strong-heart" song for his absent grandson. I still seem to hear the hoarse, cracked voice of the ancient singer as it resounded among the woods. For a long time our roving community enjoyed unbroken peace, and we were spared any trouble or disturbance. Our hunters often brought in a deer or elk or bear for fresh meat. The beautiful lakes furnished us with fish and wild-fowl for variety. Their placid waters, as the autumn advanced, reflected the variegated colors of the changing foliage.

It is my recollection that we were at this time encamped in the vicinity of the "Turtle Mountain's Heart." It is to the highest cone-shaped peak that the Indians aptly give this appellation. Our camping-ground for two months was within a short distance of the peak, and the men made it a point to often send one of their number to the top. It was understood between them and the war party that we were to remain near this spot; and on their return trip the latter were to give the "smoke sign," which we would answer from the top of the hill.

One day, as we were camping on the shore of a large lake with several islands, signs of moose were discovered, and the men went off to them on rafts, carrying their flint-lock guns in anticipation of finding two or three of the animals. We little fellows, as usual, were playing down by the sandy shore, when we spied what seemed like the root of a great tree floating toward us. But on a closer scrutiny we discovered our error. It was the head of a huge moose, swimming for his life! Fortunately for him, none of the men had remained at home.

According to our habit, we little urchins disappeared in an instant, like young prairie chickens, in the long grass. I was not more than eight years old, yet I tested the strength of my bow-string and adjusted my sharpest and best arrow for immediate service. My heart leaped violently as the homely but imposing animal neared the shore. I was undecided for a moment whether I would not leave my hiding-place and give a war-whoop as soon as he touched the sand. Then I thought I would keep still and let him have my boy weapon; and the only regret that I had was that he would, in all probability, take it with him, and I should be minus one good arrow.

"Still," I thought, "I shall claim to be the smallest boy whose arrow was ever carried away by a moose." That was enough. I gathered myself into a bunch, all ready to spring. As the long-legged beast pulled himself dripping out of the water, and shook off the drops from his long hair, I sprang to my feet. I felt some of the water in my face! I gave him my sharpest arrow with all the force I could master, right among the floating ribs. Then I uttered my war-whoop.

The moose did not seem to mind the miniature weapon, but he was very much frightened by our shrill yelling. He took to his long legs, and in a minute was out of sight.

The leaves had now begun to fall, and the heavy frosts made the nights very cold. We were forced to realize that the short summer of that region had said adieu! Still we were gay and light-hearted, for we had plenty of provisions, and no misfortune had yet overtaken us in our wanderings over the country for nearly three months.

One day old Smoky Day returned from the daily hunt with an alarm. He had seen a sign—a "smoke sign." This had not appeared in the quarter that they were anxiously watching—it came from the east. After a long consultation among the men, it was concluded from the nature and duration of the smoke that it proceeded from an accidental fire. It was further surmised that the fire was not made by Sioux, since it was out of their country, but by a war-party of Ojibways, who were accustomed to use matches when lighting their pipes, and to throw them carelessly away. It was thought that a little time had been spent in an attempt to put it out.

The council decreed that a strict look-out should be established in behalf of our party. Every day a scout was appointed to reconnoitre in the direction of the smoke. It was agreed that no gun should be fired for twelve days. All our signals were freshly rehearsed among the men. The women and old men went so far as to dig little convenient holes around their lodges, for defense in case of a sudden attack. And yet an Ojibway scout would not have suspected, from the ordinary appearance of the camp, that the Sioux had become aware of their neighborhood! Scouts were stationed just outside of the village at night. They had been so trained as to rival an owl or a cat in their ability to see in the dark.

The twelve days passed by, however, without bringing any evidence of the nearness of the supposed Ojibway war-party, and the "lookout" established for purposes of protection was abandoned. Soon after this, one morning at dawn, we were aroused by the sound of the unwelcome war-whoop. Although only a child, I sprang up and was about to rush out, as I had been taught to do; but my good grandmother pulled me down, and gave me a sign to lay flat on the ground. I sharpened my ears and lay still.

All was quiet in camp, but at some little distance from us there was a lively encounter. I could distinctly hear the old herald, shouting and yelling in exasperation. "Whoo! whoo!" was the signal of distress, and I could almost hear the pulse of my own blood-vessels.

Closer and closer the struggle came, and still the women appeared to grow more and more calm. At last a tremendous charge by the Sioux put the enemy to flight; there was a burst of yelling; alas! my friend and teacher, old Smoky Day, was silent. He had been pierced to the heart by an arrow from the Ojibways.

Although successful, we had lost two of our men, Smoky Day and White Crane, and this incident, although hardly unexpected, darkened our peaceful sky. The camp was filled with songs of victory, mingled with the wailing of the relatives of the slain. The mothers of the youths who were absent on the war-path could no longer conceal their anxiety.

One frosty morning—for it was then near the end of October—

the weird song of a solitary brave was heard. In an instant the camp was thrown into indescribable confusion. The meaning of this was clear as day to everybody—all of our war-party were killed, save the one whose mournful song announced the fate of his companions. The lonely warrior was Bald Eagle.

The village was convulsed with grief; for in sorrow, as in joy, every Indian shares with all the others. The old women stood still, wherever they might be, and wailed dismally, at intervals chanting the praises of the departed warriors. The wives went a little way from their teepees and there audibly mourned; but the young maidens wandered further away from the camp, where no one could witness their grief. The old men joined in the crying and singing. To all appearances the most unmoved of all were the warriors, whose tears must be poured forth in the country of the enemy to embitter their vengeance. These sat silently within their lodges, and strove to conceal their feelings behind a stoical countenance; but they would probably have failed had not the soothing weed come to their relief.

The first sad shock over, then came the change of habiliments. In savage usage, the outward expression of mourning surpasses that of civilization. The Indian mourner gives up all his good clothing, and contents himself with scanty and miserable garments. Blankets are cut in two, and the hair is cropped short. Often a devoted mother would scarify her arms or legs; a sister or a young wife would cut off all her beautiful hair and disfigure herself by undergoing hardships. Fathers and brothers blackened their faces, and wore only the shabbiest garments. Such was the spectacle that our people presented when the bright autumn was gone and the cold shadow of winter and misfortune had fallen upon us. "We must suffer," said they—"the Great Mystery is offended."

THE YEARS
OF A WARRIOR
Wooden Leg (Cheyenne)

The warrior days of a Cheyenne man began at the age of about sixteen or seventeen, or sometimes a little earlier for such activities as were not very difficult or risky. They ended somewhere between thirty-five and forty, according to particular circumstances. The regular rule was, every man was classed as a warrior and expected to serve as such until he had a son old enough to take his place. Then the father retired from aggressive fighting and the son took up the weapons for that family. If a man came into early middle age without any son, he adopted one. If he had more than one son, he might allow the additional one or more to be adopted by another man who had none. By following this system, all of the offensive fighting was done by young men, mostly the unmarried young men. The fathers and the older men ordinarily stayed in the background, to help or to shield the women and children. Or, if it was practicable, the fathers and old men and women followed out the young warriors and stayed at a safe distance behind, there to sing cheering songs and to call out advice and encouragement. If a warrior's father or some other old person put himself unnecessarily forward in a battle he was likely to be criticised for his needless risk, and also the young warriors felt aggrieved at his taking from them whatever of honors might be gained in the combat. In general, the young men were supposed to be more valuable as fighters and less valuable as wise counselors, while the older men were estimated in the opposite way. It was considered as being not right for an important older man

From Thomas B. Marquis, ed., *Wooden Leg: A Warrior Who Fought Custer* (Lincoln, Neb., 1962), pp. 118–22.

to place himself as a target for the missiles of the enemy, if he could avoid such exposure. Even in a surprise attack upon us, it was expected the seniors should run away, if they could get away, while the more lively and supposedly more ambitious young men met the attack.

Our war chiefs—that is, the three leading chiefs and the twenty-seven little chiefs of our three warrior societies—were more useful as instructors in quiet assemblage than as directors of operation in times of battle. There were frequent gatherings of the warrior societies, each in its own gathering, where the chiefs exchanged ideas about methods of combat and about daily care of the personal self, and where the listening young warriors learned their lessons. If some aggressive war was contemplated, these chiefs agreed upon the plans. But when any battle actually began it was a case of every man for himself. There were then no ordered groupings, no systematic movements in concert, no compulsory goings and comings. Warriors of all societies mingled indiscriminately, every individual went where and when he chose, every one looked out for himself only, or each helped a friend if such help were needed and if the able one's personal inclination just then was toward friendly helpfulness. The warrior chiefs called out advice, perhaps a reminder of some rule of action theretofore discussed in the gatherings, or perhaps some special suggestion that exactly fitted the immediate situation, such as, "Yonder is one whose horse is down; go right in after him." Ordinarily the advice of the chiefs was heeded. But the obedience was a voluntary one. In battle, the chiefs had not authority to issue commands that must be obeyed.

Special war parties made up of members of some certain warrior society often went out seeking conflict with the enemy. The warrior societies competed with each other for effectiveness in this kind of activity, as well as in all other activities regarded as commendable. At times, the members of some certain warrior society would be selected by the tribal chiefs to do all of the tribal fighting in some case where the opposition was looked upon as being not great enough to make necessary the use of the entire tribal military forces. If this appointed segment of our fighters did well they were acclaimed. If they did not do well, especially if other warriors had to go to their assistance, the original combatants were discredited. Ordinarily, whatever warrior society was on duty as camp policemen had also the duty as special camp defenders. It was their business to be the first ones out to meet any attack upon the camp. Members of the other societies added their help if necessary, refrained from doing so if they were not needed. If the enemy onset was sufficient to render needful the resistance of all of the warriors in the camp, all of them were called by the heralds of the tribal chiefs. In cases of extreme danger, even the old men and some of the women might use whatever weapons they could seize and wield.

BUFFALO—
STAFF OF LIFE
FOR THE INDIANS
James Larpenteur Long (Assiniboine)

There is an old Assiniboine saying, "The buffalo gives food from his flesh and clothing from his hide. The marrow, sinew, bones, and the horns can be used by the people, so that a skilled woman can make many different kinds of food and the family does not eat the same thing each day. It is so also with the man, who can make many things from the buffalo for use in war, hunting, and pleasure. All these things the buffalo offers to the ones who heed the talks of the old men and the old women who know that the lives of the people and the growth of children depend on the buffalo." . . .

To the Assiniboines, the buffalo was more than an animal. It was the staff of life. No other animal gave so much to the people as that great shaggy creature. For that reason, the buffalo was studied more closely than any other animal.

Its name was given to children so they would be hardy and reach maturity quickly, organizations were named after it, and medicine men relied on the powers of the Spirit Buffalo to help them perform their rituals more successfully. A chief had the long forelock of a bull tied to the tip of a lodge pole and had it placed among the rest of the poles of his lodge as an emblem. The head was placed on the ground, outside, and close to the back of the lodge with offerings laid on top of it.

From Michael S. Kennedy, ed., *The Assiniboines* (Norman, Okla., 1961), pp. 63–69, 78–79.

To an unobservant person, all buffaloes in a herd looked alike. Only the usual kinds that made up the herd, such as the bulls, cows, heifers, young bulls, and the general run of the calves, were noticeable. But not so with the Assiniboines. To them there were many kinds and sizes of buffaloes in a herd and much to know about them.

Mating time was in Red Berries Moon (July). The bulls, grouped in small and large herds, roamed peacefully by themselves. But after they joined the cows, the bull buffaloes became mean and vicious both toward each other and toward any Indians who approached them.

Whenever two bulls fought each other, the main herd circled around them. Other bulls in the herd would be pawing dirt and bellowing deep down in their throats while the cows looked on. The battle was always to the death of one of the warriors. They fought forehead to forehead, pushing each other backwards. If one gave up and turned or tried to jump out of the way, he was gored in the flank. One swift move forward and a quick turn of the head made a long and deep gash in the flank. The intestines immediately came out, resulting in death. The victor never paid any attention to the victim after the fatal hook was made.

It is told that during a fight the bulls paid no attention to persons. Although the main herd fled at the approach of a mounted person, the pair fought on so that many times Assiniboine onlookers saw at close range the outcome of such encounters.

Oddly, old bulls mated with young cows, and young bulls with the matured cows. Early in the mating season, perhaps to avoid fighting, a bull with one or more cows would stay in deep coulees, quite a distance from large herds. That was a common sight, and when a group was seen, the following remark was usually made: "He [the bull] has stolen the women [the cows], so he is hiding out with them."

From late summer to early fall, all the buffaloes were together in small and large herds. Bull fights then were rare. With feed ripe and at its best at that time of the year, the buffaloes began to get fat. Long files of them leisurely went to water and back to feeding grounds. They traveled in single file, and the buffalo trails, belly deep in places that can be seen to this day, were thus made.

At that time, too, the animals were at ease. During the heat of the day they lay around a great deal, because the big hunting days, which always molested them, had not arrived. They were not disturbed by hunters except occasionally for a supply of fresh meat.

When a herd of buffalo crossed a large river such as the Missouri, they swam across in small groups, one group after another. Because of the extensive size of the herds, the leaders were, many times, already across and far on their way to new feeding grounds while the last groups were still moving up to the river. It often took several hours before the last group was across. It is told that when buffaloes were swimming they blew water through their nostrils. This made a peculiar noise that could be heard for a long distance down stream. . . .

The main hunting time for the Assiniboines was in Join Both Sides Moon (October), at which time in good years the buffaloes were very fat and the bulls were still in the herds. This hunting was devoted to obtaining all the meat needed for drying and storing away for winter. The chase for robes came later.

When the Frost Moon (November) appeared, the bulls left the herds and gathered in groups and remained away from the main herds until breeding time. In this moon the hides from four-year-old cows were taken. The hair was not prime, but the hides were at their best for new lodges.

Buffalo calves started to drop about the full of the Frog Moon (April) and up to the time when Idle Moon (May) appeared. As far as is known, no twins were ever seen, but it is told by a man named Crazy Bull that he saw a two-headed unborn calf while butchering a cow which was killed in the Sore-Eye Moon (March). In a chase, calves never ran close to their mothers. All of them fell to the rear, so even if there were twins, they were not noticed as such.

The hair on calves was of a yellowish color and remained that shade until they were almost a year old. Calves were called Little Yellow Buffaloes. Robes for children were made from these skins, which were tanned with the hair intact.

After a big hunt, in the early fall, a large number of motherless and deserted calves remained on the hunting ground. The cows deserted their calves as soon as the hunters gave chase and, usually, were in the lead of a running herd. The bulls ran just behind the cows while the yearlings and calves were in the rear. Some hunters claimed that the cows ran much faster than any other buffaloes in a herd, and that for this reason they were always in the lead. Yet, some said, the bulls ran just behind the cows to protect them, and at no time were they ever left behind. They always kept right at the heels of the cows.

If a chase was near an encampment and many calves remained afterwards, boys mounted on yearling ponies and using their small bows and arrows staged a miniature chase, much to the delight of the hunters who looked on. Very young calves left motherless or deserted after a chase were known to follow the hunters back to camp.

When the calves were one year old, their coats turned from the yellowish color to a dark shade. A calf was so fluffy that it usually looked big for its age. Instead of calling calves "yearlings," the Assiniboines called them "Little Black-haired Ones," or "Fluffed-hair Ones."

Two-year-old buffaloes were called "Two-Teeth," having two full teeth at that age. Just before they reached the second year, their horns stood out and commenced to curve. At that age the tips of the horns were blunt, so they were also called "Blunt-Horns."

After they passed the second year, their horns curved and a three-year-old was known as "Curved-Horns," because of the short, small, curved horns.

"Small-built Buffalo" was the name applied to the four-year-olds, which were also called "Four Teeth." Robes taken in the Middle (January) and Long Day (February) moons from those animals were considered the best of all. The hides were not too thick, but the hair was fluffed out, silky and thick.

When the robe hunters rode into a herd, they looked only for "Small-built Ones," both males and females, the ones with trim and neat bodies whose coats of hair looked much like fine fur.

At the age of six, cows were known as "Big Females," which meant matured. The bulls were called "Horns Not Cracked" because of their fine polished horns. They spent much time polishing their horns by rubbing them against low cut banks. Sometimes these bulls pawed down the upper sides of washouts and used that as polishers.

When hides were taken from the bulls, they were skinned only to the shoulders and cut off, leaving out the parts that covered the humps. In skinning a mature bull, the Assiniboines laid the animal in a prone position; then an incision was made along the back, starting a little above and between the tips of the shoulder blades and ending at the tail. When the skinning was completed, the hide was in two pieces.

Fat from matured animals, when rendered, was soft and yellowish in color. The tallow from young buffaloes was always hard and white.

When buffaloes got very old, they became thin. The horns, especially on the bulls, were cracked, and there were deep grooves around the butts on account of the brittle condition of the horns. Old bulls congregated in groups. They remained away from the main herds and usually died of old age or other natural causes because no one wanted their meat or robes.

STEALING HORSES
FROM THE ARAPAHOE
Chief Plenty-Coups (Crow)

On Cloud Peak
we met the other parties and soon picked up the enemy's trails,
one coming in from the Black Hills, and one from the west. The
sign [trail] was fresh and heavy, as though many lodges were
somewhere ahead of us. Near sundown our Wolves [scouts]
brought us word that there was a large village on Goose Creek.

And what a village it was! It reached from Goose Creek to
Tongue River. Five drums were going at once, and the big flat
was covered with horses. I could count more lodges than I had
ever seen before at one time. We should stand no chance against
such a village, but we could steal some horses. I looked at the
sky. The moon was already there waiting for night, and there
would be little darkness.

Our leaders were holding a council. By and by they stood up,
Bell-rock beckoning me, and Bear-in-the-water calling Covers-his-
face. We both went to them to get our orders. We, with several
others selected by Half-yellow-face and Fire-wind, were to go into
the village and cut as many horses as we could while the rest of the
party stood ready to cover our retreat when we should be discovered. My heart sang with pride.

Covers-his-face and I stole together to the edge of the village
and waited for darkness. But it did not come. Instead, the moon
grew brighter and brighter. But as though to reassure us the five
drums kept beating, telling us the enemy was dancing, and that

From Frank B. Linderman. *American: The Life Story of a Great Indian* (1930), pp. 125–33.

he was too busy with his pleasure to watch his horses. Nights in summer are very short, the light would come soon, and we dared not wait too long. "Let us go in," I whispered finally, and we tied our horses. I hated to leave mine. He was the best I had ever owned, but of course I could not take him with me.

Before I knew it Covers-his-face had disappeared. I was alone among the enemy lodges, and the nearest was a Striped-feathered-arrow [Cheyenne]! No wonder the village was so large. The Sioux were not alone. They had company, and this might make them stupid—sure that no enemy would dare attack them. So many lodges made me feel lonely, and I turned my course to where they were not so close together. My eyes could not look behind, ahead, and on both sides at once. I went away from the thickly pitched lodges until I reached a very tall one that stood a little apart. A fine bay horse was tied there. Immediately I set my heart on owning him. I saw I should have to be careful because the lodge-skin was raised from the ground. And next I made out that the lodge was an Arapahoe! The three worst enemies our people had were combined against us, with the intention, I believed, of making quick war on us. ["Arapahoe" in the Crow tongue means "Tattooed marks, plenty of."]

But my eyes were on the bay horse most of the time now. He was eating grass before the Arapahoe lodge, and the rope around his neck reached into it. Somebody loved him and slept with his hand on the rope. I could not blame him. I thought the bay might be as good as the Deer, my own good war-horse tied at the edge of the village. No Sioux owned a better horse than he. It occurred to me more than once that they might steal him while I was stealing one of their horses.

I crept a little closer. The lodge-skin was lifted in front, the rope going into the blackness inside. I tried to see under the lodge-skin, but the moonlight made a big, bright ring around it that stopped at the lodge-poles as though afraid to go farther. I could see nothing inside and there were no sounds. I would chance it! I was flat on the ground by the bay horse, my knife lifted to cut the rope, when somebody stirred, moved a bit inside the lodge. My hand with the knife came down to my side. The Arapahoe was awake and watching his horse!

The shadow of the bay was on me, and I dared not move. I heard the five drums, one beating in the middle of the village and two at either end, far off. I must not stay there too long. Even if the Arapahoe did not see me, the other Crows might be discovered, and then I should be caught and killed.

I crept out of the bay's shadow like a wolf until I had got his form between me and the eyes I felt sure were watching from the blackness of the Arapahoe lodge. Then I went swiftly until I came to another horse. He was a cream with white mane and tail, a good horse, but not so good as the bay. He was tied to a Sioux lodge that was dark and still. His owner was dancing, and while

he enjoyed himself I cut his horse's rope. But I wanted the bay.
I could not go away without him. I would have another try
anyway.

A cream-colored horse is difficult to see in the night, especially
in the moonlight. I would make him help me steal the bay. Leading
him, and yet crowding against his body to keep myself hidden
from the sharp eyes in the Arapahoe lodge, I managed to reach
the bay again, expecting to feel an arrow in my side or see the
flash of a gun out of the black hole beneath the lifted lodge-skin.
The horses, wondering what was going on, touched their noses
together, their warm bodies pressing against my naked sides,
while I stared into the black hole. Nothing stirred there. Perhaps
the man had gone to sleep. I would find out.

Instead of cutting the bay's rope I tied my own rope around
his neck. Dropping the coil at his feet, I kept hold of the other
end and slipped away, leading the cream till my rope was stretched.
Then the cream and I stood still while I began slowly to pull on
my rope. The bay, thinking somebody wanted him, began to come
toward me, and as he came I kept coiling my rope, until he stopped
short. He had reached the very end of the Arapahoe's rope, you see,
and could come no farther. I was very careful now to look and
listen. If the Arapahoe pulled in his rope, taking his bay back
with it, I would let him have my rope that was tied to his horse's
neck and go away from there with the cream. But he did not pull.
The bay horse, wondering what somebody was trying to do with
him, stood still with two ropes around his neck. The Arapahoe who
owned him was asleep!

I led the cream back to the bay and cut the other fellow's rope.
I knew it was time I was away from there now, so I hurried with
my two horses to the edge of the village where I had left the Deer.
But before I was halfway a shot cracked, then another. I sprang
upon the bay and, leading the cream, lashed them into a run,
wondering what had become of Covers-his-face.

The first Crow I met was Bell-rock. He was leading the Deer.
When I raced up to him he tossed me the rope. "Keep him," I
called. "Somebody will need him." The big village was aroused.
Guns were cracking. There was no time now to stop and change
horses, and I tossed the rope of the Deer back to Bell-rock. But
he did not catch it. The Deer was left behind; my wonderful war-
horse was mine no longer. The Sioux that got him was a lucky man.

I thought that Covers-his-face had been discovered and had
started the fight, but instead, those who stampeded the loose horses
just outside the village brought on the fighting. I saw that we had
a large number of horses, but did not wait to talk to anybody and
raced away for the place where we had left our clothes with two
men to watch them. It was on the right of Tongue River, just at
the canyon. We called it The-place-where-the-cranes-rest. The bay
horse was fast, and I reached the place first. "Get ready!" I cried,

springing from the bay and getting into my leggings and shirt, "our party is coming."

I could hear the pounding hoofs, even when my shirt was over my head. Before my clothes were decently on me I had seen the pointers [men in the lead to guide the running horses] and close behind them many frightened horses. The enemy was after them too. Guns flashed as our men turned on their horses to shoot back in the gray light of breaking day. There were four Crows in the lead, and they were riding like the wind toward a steep-cut bank, a regular canyon! Did they not know it was there? It seemed to jump up before my eyes and to run to meet my friends. What would they do?

Not knowing yet how I could help them I dashed for the river. I dared not call out or wave my arms to warn them, for fear I might turn the whole band and cause a stampede that would lose what we had gained. I stopped still, my breath nearly choking me, when the first horse went over the brink. They all went over—horses, riders, like a swirl of dry leaves in a gale of wind. And before I could take ten steps they were coming out—alive! I could not believe my eyes! Only one man was hurt. His face was smashed and his horse killed under him. I was happy again.

We soon reached the timber where we had the best of it and drove the enemy back easily. Three days later we rode into our village singing of victory, and our chiefs, Sits-in-the-middle-of-the-land and Iron-bull, came out to meet us, singing Praise Songs. My heart rejoiced when I heard them speak my own name. The village was on Arrow Creek, near the Gap, and was getting ready to move. But Iron-bull stopped all preparation until he could give us hot coffee to drink. It was the first I had ever tasted, and I shall never forget it, or how happy I felt because I had counted my first coup.

This is all of the story; but I left out something I ought to tell you. When we were in the timber where we drove back the enemy, Covers-his-face found that the animal he had stolen in the village was a mare. He felt disgusted and declared he would go back and steal a horse. We tried to talk him out of his plan, but he was determined. "I will wait here for you," said Bear in-the-water, who had given his horse to the man whose face had been smashed, and so was himself afoot.

"All right," said Bear-rears-up, "if Bear-in-the-water waits here I will wait with him." So we left them to do as they pleased and for ten days heard nothing more of them. We had begun to believe they had been killed, when one day the three came in, each riding a good horse that Covers-his-face had stolen from the Sioux. He told us he had found the lodge of a young man who was so jealous of his wife that he camped far from the nearest lodges of his friends. He had three very good horses tied to his tepee, just one apiece for Covers-his-face and his two friends waiting in the timber. This is what a man gets for being so jealous of a woman that he cannot be sociable with other men.

AN INDIAN DEER HUNT

James Paytiano, or
Flaming Arrow (Ácoma Pueblo)

First we get our men together. Four is enough in a bunch. We start out from home with a song. The song is translated:

> "From Acoma I am going to put the sewed-up moccasins on
>   my feet. I, the man, do put on the moccasin heel-piece.
> Painting my body with yellow, red, blue and white clay
>   color,
> Then clothing myself with an apron round my waist with
>   designs on,
> Then round my knee the colored yarn,
> Then the colored yarn around my wrist,
> Then around my arm green bands with fir tree branches
>   stuck in them.
> Next I paint my face red and black.
> I tie an eagle feather on top of my hair.
> I pick up my arrows. The bow made of a rainbow, and the
>   arrows representing the lightning flash.
> I travel sometimes with song to attract deer with my
>   singing."

After a whole day's travel we camp. For a whole day's trip I travel south from Acoma, and reach a place for my prayer-sticks [ceremonial twigs, painted and decorated with feathers, which are believed to possess magical powers]. I lay them down carefully, and

From James Paytiano (Flaming Arrow), *Flaming Arrow's People* (New York, 1932).

bury them, as if there were strange gods near to hear my prayers; and each one of the party does the same. After we bury our prayer-sticks, we all gather round the campfire.

We have started out with a supply of food and ready baked bread to last us for two weeks, the same amount of blue cornmeal to make our gravy, and such things as lard, onions, potatoes, coffee and sugar. We do not need any meat, as we will be killing rabbits on our way.

When we reach our camp, the first evening after dark, each one goes off in some direction by himself, to pray to strange gods. We pray towards any direction in which we think there may be some god listening to hear our prayers. We pray to the mountain lion, eagles, hawks, wolves, and other wild beasts. Then we bury our prayer-sticks and pick up a piece of log and sprinkle it with corn-meal, and say to it: "You be the deer which I expect to bring into camp," and then we carry this piece of wood in and place it on the campfire, and blow our breath on a pinch of cornmeal in our hands and throw it on the flames. Doing so we receive power, and hunt well.

Then each is seated on his rolled-up blanket around the campfire. The next thing we do is to choose our officers. First we choose the field chief, *Tsa-ta-ow-ho-tcha*. He has to see that all the hunters get their deer. If one of the hunters is unlucky enough not to get a deer, he has to divide up with him. Next we elect our governor, *Dta-po-po*. He is to see that the camp is in order, and keep peace in the camp. The youngest one is always elected as the cook, and also has to look after the horses and burros, and get wood for the fire. If he has any time, after the dishes are washed, and there is plenty of wood and water, and the stock has been watered, he can hunt right around the camp.

After these officers are elected, the field chief gives orders to put down as an altar, between us and the fire, the flint and other stone animals which every hunter carries with him to the hunt, and which are handed down in each family. After all of these little animals are placed on the level ground, they sprinkle white cornmeal over them, and around them, forming a circle of cornmeal. Then a song is sung which means: "We welcome this altar into our camp. Come and take a place with us." Then they sing to the mountain lion to take its place, then the wolf, then the man himself, then the owls, then the hawks. Song after song continues through the night until dawn. In the morning, each one picks up his little hunting animal, and ties it in the handkerchief around his neck, and takes his cornmeal from the little bag at his side. Praying to the strange gods, and breathing his breath on the cornmeal, he sprinkles it out to the east to the sun.

The hunters are ordered to pack up for another day's trip. All are feeling happy, and they are not supposed to make one complaint about anything, which is strict orders. They sing softly all the way they travel.

When an Indian has hit a deer, he runs to the fallen animal. First he takes a small branch of a tree and brushes him off, as he has a religious belief that the deer is made of sheets of clouds, and he has to brush off the clouds to get at him. Then he reaches down in his pocket for some yellow pollen he has collected from flowers, takes it between his thumb and forefinger, drops a little on the deer's mouth, then carries it to his own breath, and makes a sign with the pollen towards the hunter's camp, which is supposed to lead the spirit of the deer to the camp.

Then he pulls the deer around by the forelegs, until he lies with his head towards the camp. The next thing is to take the little flint animals in the shapes of lions, wolves and bears, as many as he carries, and place them on the deer to feed and get back the power they gave him. They always come first. While these animals are on the deer, the hunter rolls a cigarette of cornhusks, and while he smokes he talks to the dead creature just as if he were telling a human where to go. When he finishes he gathers his flint animals, carefully places them in his bag, and talks to them while he puts them in the bag, telling them that he hopes for the good luck of another deer. Then he ties the bag with these animals round his neck under his shirt.

He pulls out of his pocket a flint arrowhead, and, starting from the deer's neck pretends to cut it. In older days, they really cut with the spear head, instead of knives. Then he cuts off juniper pine twigs and lays them as thick as he can alongside of the deer, ready to be placed upon it after it is skinned, to keep the blood off the hide and the dirt off the meat.

After skinning the deer and placing the meat on these juniper twigs, the hunter starts to cut the animal into parts like a beef. He is always sure that he takes the entrails out first. He digs in the ground a shallow hole, and washes his hands. If there is no water nearby, he wipes his hands on a cloth. He reaches down with his hands into the blood and dips it up four times, and places it in the shallow hole on the earth. This is to feed the mother earth. Then he takes out the spleen, and places it nearby on a twig of a tree to feed the crow. Then he cuts him up.

The hind legs are taken off first, then the front quarters. Then he strips the meat off the bone from the hoofs to the first joint, and ties these muscles together, front and hind legs, so as to hang the deer over the saddle without any rope. Next the ribs are taken off in such a way as to hang over the saddle without being separated. This leaves the breast connected with the meat of the stomach, and in this way all the parts will balance on a burro's back, and the backbone and fur and head are still together, and are easily balanced on the saddle.

After each hunter gets one deer, they agree on a day to start home. Coming home they will all join in on their new songs, singing as loudly as they can, and if they camp again before reaching home, the burdens of the burros and horses are placed in line, so as to be easy to repack in line in the morning.

When they are within a mile from home, each of the hunters loads his gun with one shot, and they are fired off, one by one, so that each family by counting the shots, can tell which group of hunters is returning. As they come home each hunter makes a round circle from fir trees, to fit his head, puts evergreens on his horse's bridle, and around the deer heads. Even the burros' heads are decorated with fir twigs.

When they arrive home there will be relatives there to take charge of the meat, and see to the unsaddling and feeding of the animals. All the hunter does is to tell his wonderful story.

THE SUN DANCE
Chief Dick Washakie (Shoshone)

The sun dance, which perhaps some of the white people have witnessed or heard tell of, has always been considered one of the most heathenish and most barbarous and unchristian ceremonies ever participated in by the savages, as we red men have been termed by many of our white brothers, who, I must say, have failed to make themselves thoroughly acquainted with the sacred and religious beliefs of our so-called sun dance. We indians call it the "fasting dance." Our sun dance in reality, according to our indian beliefs, is in religious beliefs, the same as that of our white brothers. The indians pray to God, our Father above, or the Great Spirit, as some of our white brothers have termed it. Some white people have even accused the indian of worshipping the center sun dance pole, which is a great mistake. When the indian prays, he looks upward into the blue sky and says, "*Tomah-upah tomah-vond*, Our Father, who is above." He does not pray to the sun, or to the center sun dance pole as some white people would have it.

The reason the indian seems to worship the sun to some people is because the indian believes that the sun is a gift from God, our Father above, to enlighten the world and as the sun appears over the horizon they offer up a prayer in acceptance of our Father's gift. Then the medicine man, or the chief of the sun dance who acts similar to that of the priest or clergyman in a white man's church, offers up prayer beginning thus "*Tomah-upah, tomah-vond undidda-haidt soonda-hie*, Our Father who is above, have mercy upon your children."

From Grace Raymond Hebard, *Washakie* (Cleveland, 1930), pp. 292–96.

The sun dance hall (an out-of-doors structure) is constructed in a large circular corral perhaps some hundred feet in diameter, the circumference of which is lined on the outside with branches of trees to give shade to the dancers. Each dancer has a certain place in the dance hall which he must keep throughout the duration of the dance when he enters it. Two small poles or young saplings of pine or cottonwood are placed on each side of the dancer. The bark of these saplings may be peeled off or not, whichever the dancer may wish. If the dancer is a medicine man or has been wounded in battle sometime he should show this on the poles or saplings by painting them red, which signified his blood was lost in battle. The center pole which should always be a cottonwood was chosen by the originators of the dance because of its superiority over all other trees as a dry land tree growing with little or no water. This tree represents God. The twelve long poles that are placed from the top of the center pole down to the circumference of the dance hall represent, according to our indian beliefs, the twelve apostles of God, our Father.

The eagle feathers at the top of the poles above the center pole also represent the twelve apostles of our Father, or God, and also being a sacred bird of our race, we indians naturally regard the eagle with the highest esteem. The buffalo head in the crotch in the center pole represents a gift from God, our Father above, to his indian children for food and clothing.

The sun dance has been handed down to my people for generations as a sacred dance in which we may pray to God, our Father, for those who may be sick, that they may be healed. In many cases, I can truthfully state, many have been cured of long standing illnesses through their faith in prayer and fasting from food and water for the duration of the dance, which generally lasts three or four days. Many of our white brothers have condemned my people's sacred dance, and their form of worship. This form is, in the belief of my people, identical with that used by our white brothers in their christian church and in the form which they consider just and proper.

My people, the indians, worship this same Being as that worshipped by our white brothers, but only in our own way and in our beliefs, which I know is very strange to the white people. But this is the only form of worship the red man, my people, have known for generations past and is known throughout the indian race as the indians' church. Every indian tribe has its own form of worship which is somewhat different, but I wish to explain that they all worship the same Being, God, our Father above. I am told that many years ago some tribes of indians used drastic forms of worship in which they signified their bravery and fearlessness, but these forms of worship have long since vanished. We hear of them only through indian tradition.

Many years ago the sun dance among the Shoshone people was very plain. The worshippers were dressed in skins of animals. Today sun dance worshippers, though believing in the same form of worship as that of their forefathers of many years ago, wear gorgeous apparel, which is more for exhibition than true religion; with this exception, our form of worship is carried on identically in the same form as that of our forefathers.

The sun dance, according to the custom of my people in the past, is generally held once a year, about June or July. This is the season when grass and the trees are in their splendor and the weather is favorable. Before entering the sun dance hall the worshippers, or dancers, twice circle the hall. The chief of the sun dance or the medicine man is always in the lead. This is done merely according to our old indian customs, which according to our indian beliefs signifies that the dancers are all ready and willing to begin their dance or ceremony.

I shall state, though I know that it will sound very strange to some of our white brothers that of course they could not understand what was said in our prayers or otherwise they would have understood the meaning of our sacred dance. The indians believe in a Supreme Being, or God, our Father, as generally termed by many people, the creator of all things, and we worship and pray to God in our crude but comprehensive form as do our white brothers. It has been the custom of my people for generations past as well as at the present time to show our friendly relations, especially at the closing of our ceremonies of the sun dance, to give presents of some kind to some of our own people or visiting indians from other tribes which signifies that we have given these presents with a free and willing heart and all of our sins committed during the year past have been forgiven by our Father above.

I shall state here that the term "our Father" is used in place of God, as there is no Shoshone word which signifies the word "God." This word is an English word. Therefore, if an indian or interpreter must use this word he repeats the word "God" in English and not indian. Never once have I heard the indian tradition where there was any religious controversy as to the true form of worship of God or our Father. All indians, so far as I have ever heard, believe and worship in this one form.

HUMAN SACRIFICE
Eagle Chief (Pawnee)

[Tirawa, mentioned in
the following text, was the supreme deity of the Skidi Pawnee, the
god from whom all benefits in life and nature were considered to
have come.]

The Skidi alone of the Pawnees sacrificed human beings to *Ti-ra'-wa*.
When they had returned home from war successful, bringing cap-
tives with them, they selected one of these for the sacrifice. The
others were adopted into the tribe, but this one, who must be
young and stout, one who would fatten easily, was kept apart, eating by himself, fed on the best of food and treated with the
greatest kindness. No hint of the fate in store for him was given
until the day of the sacrifice. For four nights before that day the
people danced; and for four days they feasted. Each day after they had
got through feasting, the dishes were taken to their especial place.
Each woman, after she got through eating, rose, and said to the
prisoner, "I have finished eating, and I hope that I may be blessed
from *Ti-ra'-wa*; that he may take pity on me; that when I put my
seed in the ground they may grow, and that I may have plenty of
everything."

At the end of the four days two old men went, one to each end
of the village, and called aloud, directing every male person in the
village to make a bow and an arrow, and to be ready for the sacrifice. For every male child that had been born a bow and an
arrow was made; for the little boys small bows that they could

From George Bird Grinnell, *Pawnee Hero Stories and Folk-Tales* (New York, 1889), pp.
363–68.

77

bend and small arrows. The arrows must be feathered with the feathers of the eagle, or of some bird of prey, a hawk, an owl or an eagle. They must not cut the feathers nor burn them to make them low.

The next day, before daybreak, every one was ready. All of the warriors, who had led parties on the warpath, took from their sacred bundles their collars, made from the feathers of the bird they wore, and put them on their backs and tied them about their necks. They held their pipes in their left hands, to signify that they were warriors. Every male carried his bow and arrow. Every woman had a lance or a stick. Just before daylight they all went out to the west end of the village, and stood there looking for the prisoner to be brought. Here two stout posts had been set up, one of ash and the other of hackberry, and between these had been tied four cross-poles, the three lower ones to aid in climbing up to the highest of the four.

As day broke, the people, looking back toward the village, could see the captive being led toward them, bound hand and foot. Behind him, as he was led along, followed a warrior carrying the heart and tongue of a buffalo; after him came another, carrying a blazing stick, then one with a bow and arrow, and last a warrior with the stuffed skin of an owl.

They led the naked captive to the posts, and lifting him up, tied first the left hand and then the right to the top cross-pole, and afterward tied the feet below. Every one stood there silent, looking, waiting; the men holding their weapons and the women their sticks and lances. On the ground under the sacrifice was laid the wood for a great fire, which was now lighted. Then the man with the blazing stick stepped forward, but before he reached the captive, the warrior with the bow and arrow, he who had taken the captive, ran up close to the victim and shot him through from side to side, beneath the arms, with the sacred arrow, whose point was of flint, such as they used in the olden time. After the blood had run down upon the fire below, the warrior who carried the buffalo tongue and the heart, placed them on the fire beneath the body. When this had been done the man who carried the owl ran up, and seized the burning stick and burned the body, once under each arm, and once in each groin, in all four times. Then, at a given signal, the males all ran up, and shot their arrows into the body. If any male children were not large enough to shoot, some one shot for them. There were so many arrows that the body was stuck full of them; it bristled with them.

A man chosen for this purpose now climbed up, and pulled out all the arrows from the body, except the one which was first shot through the side of the sacrifice, and placed them together in a pile on the ground, where they were left. After pulling out the arrows, this man took his knife and cut open the breast of the captive, and putting his hand in the opening, took out a handful of blood, and smeared it over his face, and then jumped to the ground, and ran away as fast as he could. Each of the four men, after he had done his part, ran away very fast, and went down to the river and washed himself. When this had been done the women came with their sticks and spears and struck the body and counted *coup* on it. Even the little children struck it. After they had done this, they put their sticks together on the ground in a pile, and left them there. By this time the fire was burning up high and scorching the body, and it was kept up until the whole body was consumed. And while the smoke of the blood and the buffalo meat, and of the burning body, ascended to the sky, all the people prayed to *Ti-ra'-wa*, and walked by the fire and grasped handfuls of the smoke, and passed it over their bodies and over those of their children, and prayed *Ti-ra'-wa* to take pity on them, and to give them health, and success in war, and plenteous crops. The man who had killed the captive fasted and mourned for four days, and asked *Ti-ra'-wa* to take pity on him, for he knew that he had taken the life of a human being.

This sacrifice always seemed acceptable to *Ti-ra'-wa*, and when the Skidi made it they always seemed to have good fortune in war, and good crops, and they were always well.

After the sacrifice was over, then came the old women to rejoice over what had been done. They would act as the warriors used to do, when coming back from a war party. They carried the mother corn. They went to the body and counted *coup* on it, and then went back to the village. Some of them would take the large hollow stalks of the sunflower, and put dust in them, and then blow it out, pretending to shoot, the puff of dust standing for the smoke of a shot. They would go up to the secret lodge, and standing outside of it, would tell the story of how they came to go on their pretended war party, and what they did while they were gone, and what enemies they struck—the whole long story. The people meanwhile would stand about and laugh at them as they did these things. Imitating the warriors, the old women changed their names also. One of the leading old women once took the name "Mud on the Meat," another, "Skunk Skin Tobacco Pouch," another "Sitting Fish Old Man," another "Old Man Stepping on the Heart." The old men standing about would joke with the old women, and these would joke and make fun of each other.

"OUR PEOPLE ARE EBBING AWAY LIKE A RAPIDLY RECEDING TIDE:" A SPEECH TO GOVERNOR ISAAC STEVENS OF THE WASHINGTON TERRITORY, 1855

Chief Seattle (Puget Sound Tribes)

Yonder sky that has wept tears of compassion upon my people for centuries untold, and which to us appears changeless and eternal, may change. Today is fair. Tomorrow it may be overcast with clouds. My words are like the stars that never change. Whatever Seattle says the great chief at Washington can rely upon with as much certainty as he can upon the return of the sun or the seasons. The White Chief says that Big Chief at Washington sends us greetings of friendship and good will. This is kind of him for we know he has little need of our friendship in return. His people are many. They are like the grass that covers vast prairies. My people are few. They resemble the scattering trees of a storm-swept plain. The Great—and I presume—good White Chief sends us word that he wishes to buy our lands but is willing to allow us enough to live comfortably. This indeed appears just, even generous, for the Red Man no longer has rights that he need respect, and the offer may be wise also, as we are no longer in need of an extensive country.

From *The Washington Historical Quarterly*, October, 1931.

There was a time when our people covered the land as the waves of a wind-ruffled sea cover its shell-paved floor, but that time long since passed away with the greatness of tribes that are now but a mournful memory. I will not dwell on, nor mourn over, our untimely decay, nor reproach my pale face brothers with hastening it as we too may have been somewhat to blame.

Youth is impulsive. When our young men grow angry at some real or imaginary wrong, and disfigure their faces with black paint, it denotes that their hearts are black—and then they are often cruel and relentless, and our old men and old women are unable to restrain them. Thus it has ever been. Thus it was when the white man first began to push our forefathers westward. But let us hope that the hostilities between us may never return. We would have everything to lose and nothing to gain. Revenge by young braves is considered gain, even at the cost of their own lives, but old men who stay at home in times of war, and mothers who have sons to lose, know better.

Our good father at Washington—for I presume he is now our father as well as yours, since King George has moved his boundaries further north—our great and good father, I say, sends us word that if we do as he desires he will protect us. His brave warriors will be to us a bristling wall of strength, and his wonderful ships of war will fill our harbors so that our ancient enemies far to the northward—the Hidas and Timpsions, will cease to frighten our women, children and old men. Then in reality will he be our father and we his children. But can that ever be? Your God is not our God! Your God loves your people and hates mine. He folds his strong protecting arms lovingly about the pale face and leads him by the hand as a father leads his infant son—but He has forsaken His red children—if they are really His. Our God, the Great Spirit, seems also to have forsaken us. Your God makes your people wax strong every day. Soon they will fill all the land. Our people are ebbing away like a rapidly receding tide that will never return. The white man's God can not love our people or He would protect them. They seem to be orphans who can look nowhere for help. How then can we be brothers? How can your God become our God and renew our prosperity and awaken in us dreams of returning greatness. If we have a common Heavenly Father He must be partial—for He came to His pale-face children. We never saw Him. He gave you laws but had no word for His red children whose teeming multitudes once filled this vast continent as stars fill the firmament. No. We are two distinct races with separate origins and separate destinies. There is little in common between us.

To us the ashes of our ancestors are sacred and their resting place is hallowed ground. You wander far from the graves of your ancestors and seemingly without regret. Your religion was written on tables of stone by the iron finger of your God so that you could not forget. The Red Man could never comprehend nor remember it. Our religion is the traditions of our ancestors—the dreams of our old men, given them in the solemn hours of night by the Great Spirit; and the visions of our sachems, and is written in the hearts of our people.

Your dead cease to love you and the land of their nativity as soon as they pass the portals of the tomb and wander away beyond the stars. They are soon forgotten and never return. Our dead never forget the beautiful world that gave them being. They still love its verdant valleys, its murmuring rivers, its magnificent mountains, sequestered vales and verdant-lined lakes and bays, and ever yearn in tender, fond affection over the lonely hearted living, and often return from the Happy Hunting Ground to visit, guide, console and comfort them.

Day and night can not dwell together. The Red Man has ever fled the approach of the White Man as the morning mist flees before the rising sun.

However, your proposition seems fair, and I think that my folks will accept it and will retire to the reservation you offer them. Then we will dwell apart in peace for the words of the Great White Chief seem to be the voice of Nature speaking to my people out of dense darkness.

It matters little where we pass the remnant of our days. They will not be many. The Indian's night promises to be dark. Not a single star of hope hovers above his horizon. Sad-voiced winds moan in the distance. Grim Nemesis seems to be on the Red Man's trail, and wherever he goes he will hear the approaching footsteps of his fell destroyer and prepare to stolidly meet his doom, as does the wounded doe that hears the approaching footsteps of the hunter.

A few more moons. A few more winters—and not one of the descendants of the mighty hosts that once moved over this broad land or lived in happy homes, protected by the Great Spirit, will remain to mourn over the graves of a people—once more powerful and hopeful than yours. But why should I mourn at the untimely fate of my people? Tribe follows tribe, and nation follows nation, like the waves of the sea. It is the order of nature, and regret is useless. Your time of decay may be distant—but it will surely come, for even the White Man whose God walked and talked with him as friend with friend, can not be exempt from the common destiny. We may be brothers after all. We will see.

We will ponder your proposition and when we decide we will let you know. But should we accept it, I here and now make this condition—that we will not be denied the privilege without molestation, of visiting at any time the tombs of our ancestors, friends and children. Every part of this soil is sacred, in the estimation of my people. Every hillside, every valley, every plain and grove, has been hallowed by some sad or happy event in days long vanished. Even the rocks, which seem to be dumb and dead as they swelter in the sun along the silent shore thrill with memories of stirring events connected with the lives of my people, and the very dust upon which you now stand responds more lovingly to their footsteps than to yours, because it is rich with the dust of our ancestors and our bare feet are conscious of the sympathetic touch. Our departed braves, fond mothers, glad, happy-hearted maidens, and even the little children who lived here and rejoiced here for a brief season, still love these sombre solitudes and at eventide they grow shadowy of returning spirits. And when the last Red Man shall have perished, and the memory of my tribe shall have become a myth among the white man, these shores will swarm with the invisible dead of my tribe, and when your children's children think themselves alone in the field, the store, the shop, upon the highway, or in the silence of the pathless woods, they will not be alone. In all the earth there is no place dedicated to solitude. At night when the streets of your cities and villages are silent and you think them deserted, they will throng with the returning hosts that once filled them and still love this beautiful land. The White Man will never be alone.

Let him be just and deal kindly with my people, for the dead are not powerless. Dead—I say? There is no death. Only a change of worlds.

AN ACCOUNT
OF WOVOKA,
THE PAIUTE MESSIAH

Porcupine (Cheyenne)

[Around 1888 in
Nevada, a Paiute named Jack Wilson, or Wovoka, began to gain
fame among many western tribes as an Indian deliverer, or messiah.
He devised a doctrine composed of Indian and New Testament
sources that promised an imminent reconstitution of the world, in
which white men would have no place and all departed Indians
would return to life. This "Ghost Dance" religion gained a strong
following for a short time, notably among the Sioux.]

In November last [1889] I left the reservation with two other
Cheyennes. I went through [Fort] Washakie and took the Union
Pacific railroad at Rawlins. We got on early in the morning about
breakfast, rode all day on the railroad, and about dark reached a
fort [Bridger?]. I stayed there two days, and then took a passenger
train, and the next morning got to Fort Hall. I found some lodges
of Snakes and Bannocks there. I saw the agent here, and he told
me I could stay at the agency, but the chief of the Bannocks who
was there took me to his camp near by. The Bannocks told me
they were glad to see a Cheyenne and that we ought to make a
treaty with the Bannocks.

From *Fourteenth Annual Report of the Bureau of American Ethnology* (1896), Part 2,
pp. 793–96.

The chief told me he had been to Washington and had seen the President, and that we ought all to be friends with the whites and live at peace with them and with each other. We talked these matters over for ten days. The agent then sent for me and some of the Bannocks and Shoshones, and asked me where I was going. I told him I was just traveling to meet other Indians and see other countries; that my people were at peace with the whites, and I thought I could travel anywhere I wished. He asked me why I did not have a pass. I said because my agent would not give me one. He said he was glad to see me anyhow, and that the whites and Indians were all friends. Then he asked me where I wanted a pass to. I told him I wanted to go further and some Bannocks and Shoshones wanted to go along. He gave passes—five of them—to the chiefs of the three parties. We took the railroad to a little town near by, and then took a narrow-gauge road. We went on this, riding all night at a very fast rate of speed, and came to a town on a big lake [Ogden or Salt Lake City]. We stayed there one day, taking the cars at night, rode all night, and the next morning about 9 oclock saw a settlement of Indians. We traveled south, going on a narrow-gauge road. We got off at this Indian town. The Indians here were different from any Indians I ever saw. The women and men were dressed in white people's clothes, the women having their hair banged. These Indians had their faces painted white with black spots. We stayed with these people all day. We took the same road at night and kept on. We traveled all night, and about daylight we saw a lot of houses, and they told us there were a lot more Indians there; so we got off, and there is where we saw Indians living in huts of grass [tule?]. We stopped here and got something to eat. There were whites living near by. We got on the cars again at night, and during the night we got off among some Indians, who were fish-eaters [Paiute]. We stayed among the Fish-eaters till morning, and then got into a wagon with the son of the chief of the Fish-eaters, and we arrived about noon at an agency on a big river. There was also a big lake near the agency.

The agent asked us where we were from and said we were a long ways from home, and that he would write to our agent and let him know we were all right. From this agency we went back to the station, and they told us there were some more Indians to the south. One of the chiefs of the Fish-eaters then furnished us with four wagons. We traveled all day, and then came to another railroad. We left our wagons here and took the railroad, the Fish-eaters telling us there were some more Indians along the railroad who wanted to see us. We took this railroad about 2 oclock and about sun down got to another agency, where there were more Fish-eaters. [From diagrams drawn and explanations given of them in addition to the foregoing, there seems to be no doubt that the lakes visited are Pyramid and Walker lakes, western Nevada, and the agencies those of the same name.]

They told us they had heard from the Shoshone agency that the people in this country were all bad people, but that they were good people there. All the Indians from the Bannock agency down to where I finally stopped danced this dance [referring to the late religious dances at the Cheyenne agency], the whites often dancing it themselves. [It will be recollected that he traveled constantly through the Mormon country.] I knew nothing about this dance before going. I happened to run across it, that is all. I will tell you about it. [Here all the Indian auditors removed their hats in token that the talk to follow was to be on a religious subject.] I want you all to listen to this, so that there will be no mistake. There is no harm in what I am to say to anyone. I heard this where I met my friends in Nevada. It is a wonder you people never heard this before. In the dance we had there [Nevada] the whites and Indians danced together. I met there a great many kinds of people, but they all seemed to know all about this religion. The people there seemed all to be good. I never saw any drinking or fighting or bad conduct among them. They treated me well on the cars, without pay. They gave me food without charge, and I found that this was a habit among them toward their neighbors. I thought it strange that the people there should have been so good, so different from those here.

What I am going to say is the truth. The two men sitting near me were with me, and will bear witness that I speak the truth. I and my people have been living in ignorance until I went and found out the truth. All the whites and Indians are brothers, I was told there. I never knew this before.

The Fish-eaters near Pyramid lake told me that Christ had appeared on earth again. They said Christ knew he was coming; that eleven of his children were also coming from a far land. It appeared that Christ had sent for me to go there, and that was why unconsciously I took my journey. It had been foreordained. Christ had summoned myself and others from all heathen tribes, from two to three or four from each of fifteen or sixteen different tribes. There were more different languages than I ever heard before and I did not understand any of them. They told me when I got there that my great father was there also, but did not know who he was. The people assembled called a council, and the chief's son went to see the Great Father [messiah], who sent word to us to remain fourteen days in that camp and that he would come to see us. He sent me a small package of something white to eat that I did not know the name of. There were a great many people in the council, and this white food was divided among them. The food was a big white nut. Then I went to the agency at Walker lake and they told us Christ would be there in two days. At the end of two days, on the third morning, hundreds of people gathered at this place. They cleared off a place near the agency in the form of a circus ring and we all gathered there. This space was perfectly cleared of grass, etc. We waited there till late in the evening anxious to see Christ. Just before sundown I saw a great many people, mostly Indians, coming dressed in white men's clothes. The Christ was with them. They all formed in this ring around it. They put up sheets all around the circle, as they had no tents. Just after dark some of the Indians told me that the Christ [Father] was arrived. I looked around to find him, and finally saw him sitting on one side of the ring. They all started toward him to see him. They made a big fire to throw light on him. I never looked around, but went forward, and when I saw him I bent my head. I had always thought the Great Father was a white man, but this man looked like an Indian. He sat there a long time and nobody went up to speak to him. He sat with his head bowed all the time. After awhile he rose and said he was very glad to see his children. "I have sent for you and am glad to see you. I am going to talk to you awhile about your relatives who are dead and gone. My children, I want you to listen to all I have to say to you. I will teach you, too, how to dance a dance, and I want you to dance it. Get ready for your dance and then, when the dance is over, I will talk to you." He was dressed in a white coat with stripes. The rest of his dress was a white man's except that he had on a pair of moccasins. Then he commenced our dance, everybody joining in, the Christ singing while we danced. We danced till late in the night, when he told us we had danced enough.

The next morning, after breakfast was over, we went into the circle and spread canvas over it on the ground, the Christ standing in the midst of us. He told us he was going away that day, but would be back that next morning and talk to us.

In the night when I first saw him I thought he was an Indian, but the next day when I could see better he looked different. He was not so dark as an Indian, nor so light as a white man. He had no beard or whiskers, but very heavy eyebrows. He was a good-looking man. We were crowded up very close. We had been told that nobody was to talk, and even if we whispered the Christ would know it. I had heard that Christ had been crucified, and I looked to see, and I saw a scar on his wrist and one on his face, and he seemed to be the man. I could not see his feet. He would talk to us all day.

That evening we all assembled again to see him depart. When we were assembled, he began to sing, and he commenced to tremble all over, violently for a while, and then sat down. We danced all that night, the Christ lying down beside us apparently dead.

The next morning when we went to eat breakfast, the Christ was with us. After breakfast four heralds went around and called out that the Christ was back with us and wanted to talk with us. The circle was prepared again. The people assembled, and Christ came among us and sat down. He said he wanted to talk to us again and for us to listen. He said: "I am the man who made everything you see around you. I am not lying to you, my children. I made this earth and everything on it. I have been to heaven and seen your dead friends and have seen my own father and mother. In the beginning, after God made the earth, they sent me back to teach the people, and when I came back on earth the people were afraid of me and treated me badly. This is what they did to me [showing his scars]. I did not try to defend myself. I found my children were bad, so went back to heaven and left them. My father told me the earth was getting old and worn out, and the people getting bad, and that I was to renew everything as it used to be, and make it better."

He told us also that all our dead were to be resurrected; that they were all to come back to earth, and that as the earth was too small for them and us, he would do away with heaven, and make the earth itself large enough to contain us all; that we must tell all the people we meet about these things. He spoke to us about fighting, and said that was bad, and we must keep from it; that the earth was to be all good hereafter, and we must all be friends with one another. He said that in the fall of the year the youth of all the good people would be renewed, so that nobody would be more than 40 years old, and that if they behaved themselves well after this the youth of everyone would be renewed in the spring. He said if we were all good he would send people among us who could heal all our wounds and sickness by mere touch, and that we would live forever. He told us not to quarrel, or fight, nor strike each other, nor shoot one another; that the whites and Indians were to be all one people. He said if any man disobeyed what he ordered, his tribe would be wiped from the face of the earth; that we must believe everything he said, and that we must not doubt him, or say he lied; that if we did, he would know it; that he would know our thoughts and actions, in no matter what part of the world we might be.

When I heard this from the Christ, and came back home to tell it to my people, I thought they would listen. Where I went to there were lots of white people, but I never had one of them say an unkind word to me. I thought all of your people knew all of this I have told you of, but it seems you do not.

Ever since the Christ I speak of talked to me I have thought what he said was good. I see nothing bad in it. When I got back, I knew my people were bad, and had heard nothing of all this, so I got them together and told them of it and warned them to listen to it for their own good. I talked to them for four nights and five days. I told them just what I have told you here today. I told them what I said were the words of God Almighty, who was looking down on them. I wish some of you had been up in our camp here to have heard my words to the Cheyennes. The only bad thing that there has been in it at all was this: I had just told my people that the Christ would visit the sins of any Indian upon the whole tribe, when the recent trouble [killing of Ferguson] occurred. If any one of you think I am not telling the truth, you can go and see this man I speak of for yourselves. I will go with you, and I would like one or two of my people who doubt me to go with me.

The Christ talked to us all in our respective tongues. You can see this man in your sleep any time you want after you have seen him and shaken hands with him once. Through him you can go to heaven and meet your friends. Since my return I have seen him often in my sleep. About the time the soldiers went up to Rosebud I was lying in my lodge asleep, when this man appeared and told me that the Indians had gotten into trouble, and I was frightened. The next night he appeared to me and told me that everything would come out all right.

A DEFENSE OF THE GHOST DANCE RELIGION

Masse Hadjo (Sioux)

[The religion inspired by Wovoka, the Paiute messiah, found ready acceptance among many Sioux Indians, with whom it took on a militant spirit other western tribes did not share. Many white Americans, even far from the Sioux reservations, became alarmed over the prospect of an uprising, and the army was consequently called upon to put a stop to the new religion. This letter from a Sioux appeared in the *Chicago Tribune* in response to an earlier editorial.]

You say, "If the United States army would kill a thousand or so of the dancing Indians there would be no more trouble." I judge by the above language you are a "Christian," and are disposed to do all in your power to advance the cause of Christ. You are doubtless a worshiper of the white man's Saviour, but are unwilling that the Indians should have a "Messiah" of their own.

The Indians have never taken kindly to the Christian religion as preached and practiced by the whites. Do you know why this is the case? Because the Good Father of all has given us a better religion—a religion that is all good and no bad, a religion that is adapted to our wants. You say if we are good, obey the Ten Commandments and never sin any more, we may be permitted eventually to sit upon a white rock and sing praises to God forevermore, and look down upon our heathen fathers, mothers, brothers and sisters who are howling in hell.

From *Chicago Tribune*, December 5, 1890. "An Indian on the Messiah Craze."

It won't do. The code of morals as practiced by the white race will not compare with the morals of the Indians. We pay no lawyers or preachers, but we have not one-tenth part of the crime that you do. If our Messiah does come we shall not try to force you into our belief. We will never burn innocent women at the stake or pull men to pieces with horses because they refuse to join in our ghost dances. You white people had a Messiah, and if history is to be believed nearly every nation has had one. You had twelve Apostles; we have only eleven, and some of those are already in the military guard-house. We also had a Virgin Mary and she is in the guard-house. You are anxious to get hold of our Messiah, so you can put him in irons. This you may do—in fact, you may crucify him as you did that other one, but you cannot convert the Indians to the Christian religion until you contaminate them with the blood of the white man. The white man's heaven is repulsive to the Indian nature, and if the white man's hell suits you, why, you keep it. I think there will be white rogues enough to fill it.

AUTOBIOGRAPHY
Poor Wolf (Gros Ventre)

I was born on the Knife river in the middle of the three Grosventre villages near the mouth of that stream. The chief of this middle village was the Road Maker. His father's name was Buffalo-hide-tent. The Road Maker was my mother's brother. He was born 142 or 143 years ago. I have kept a record and know this. The Road Maker died when he was 78 years old. My father died the same year. I was then 22 years old. The Road Maker was 78. That was about 64 or 65 years ago. My father was a little the younger of the two. He died in the winter, and the Road Maker died the summer before, when the cherries were ripe.

When I was a child of five winters, perhaps only four, I prayed to the spirits of animals, to the stars, the sun and the moon. My words were not many, but I prayed. I was afraid of the enemy in the dark. My father had heard of the white man's God through a trader but nothing clearly. We sometimes prayed to the white man's God who made us and could make us grow.

We had female divinities above, and we prayed to the four winds, and to the earth that makes the corn grow. There are many songs concerning these things, some of the songs speak of the different colored flowers. These things were taught for a great price, by the priests of the tribe.

When I was about five winters old a white chief visited our village on the Knife river. He said that the Gros Ventres should obey the Great Father, and consider their hunting grounds as extending from Devil's lake to the Yellowstone river. I remember

From North Dakota State Historical Society, *Collections*, Vol. I (1906).

saying to my father: Will I be a white man now? And my father said, Yes. That was 77 years ago, and I have been a friend to the whites ever since.

These men had eight boats. They were drawn by ropes that the men pulled. They were soldiers with stripes on their breasts and arms. They returned down stream from the neighborhood of the Knife. One of the men in this company came to the Gros Ventre village just below the mouth of the Knife, where we were, and painted a picture of my uncle The Road Maker, the chief of our village. (Poor Wolf has a carefully preserved water color done by some amateur painter. It is in a little nest or round frame, covered with a cracked glass, and ornamented with some brass headed tacks, and hung up by a piece of raw hide. With the picture he had preserved the scalp locks of his father and younger brother.)

When I was 17 years of age I had the small pox. I was left alone in a lodge, helpless, weak, and my eyes nearly closed. A bear came in and walked up to where I was lying. He sat down with his back pressed against me, and began to scratch his breast with his fore paws. By and by he got up and walked out of the lodge. Was I dreaming or had it really happened? While I was thinking it over the bear returned, and while I trembled for fear, went through the same motions again, and then went off, leaving me unharmed. I thought surely the bear has had mercy on me. When my father came again we talked it over and agreed that the bear had pitied me. After that I worshiped the bear, and in the dance I wore anklets of bear's teeth.

When I was 19 or 20 years of age, I went fasting for 20 days. I would not eat anything nor smoke for four days. On the fifth day I would eat a little, and then fast again. My mother and friends would try to have me give up, but I persisted. I cried during this time, and then, for a year after, though I did not fast I kept on crying. After this I was tattooed on my arms and neck and other places on my body. This was done with great ceremony. Song was used in the performance. They would sing: Let his body be pictured, his face, his spirit also, and O! White Father in heaven, and ye four winds, make him blue. Let him not be bitten by rattle snakes. It was thought that the tattooing would give courage and afford protection; one would not be struck by bullets. One could suck out snake poison without harm. This last I did not like to try, but my father assured me it could be done. The tattooing left me sore-swollen, and itching. After a while I moved about slowly and painfully, and ate a little. I was rubbed with grease and then the sores healed and the blue patterns came out. In tattooing five little sharp instruments were fastened side by side. They were like needles, and pricked painfully into the flesh.

At the Knife river a party of Sioux once attacked us in the winter. The Gros Ventres were running away. I walked right up to the Sioux who were on horseback. They ran. Then two of them came against me on foot. They shot at me, but the bullets struck my beaded shirt and did no harm. I was then 21 years of age.

When I was 24 I came to the old Fort Berthold village. There they built a trading post. There were 50 warriors and 50 adults and children in the party. We put up a palisade round the post. We drew the logs with lariats of raw hide over our shoulders. We left the Knife because timber was scarce there and the Sioux were plenty. The Blackfeet (Hidu-sidi) also were troublesome.

There is a bluff in the "Six-Mile-creek," near the present stage-road crossing where they used to go to catch eagles. There my father used to worship when he was on such a hunt. They came from Knife river at that time. I once caught twelve eagles on one hunt. Three in one day was the most I ever caught. On another hunt I got seven. There are very strict rules for eagle hunting, but I did not think them correct and did not observe them all. One rule was that the successful hunter should return to camp with his eagles crying. I came back happy. If I cried over my success, I thought the eagles would not like it. If they cried because they did not catch an eagle, the rope might hear and help the next time. They prayed to the rope with which they caught the eagles. This was made of the fibre of a plant found in the woods. Two leaders of an eagle hunt wear eagle feathers round their necks, and sing songs in the night. There are other rules, but I liked to go about the business in my own way. I have an eagle claw tattooed on my right hand. My uncle put it on so that I could grab a Sioux.

Once one hundred warriors of us were out on a trip, and got very hungry. I had a piece of fat buffalo meat that I had hidden and carried along. This I roasted and gave to them and so kept them from starving. In consequence one of the warriors gave me my name "Poor Wolf." The warrior who gave the name had taken part in a sun dance. He had continued dancing four days till all the others had stopped, and then kept on four days more. Then he had a dream and saw a wolf that told him he would have a long life. So he gave the name of Poor, i.e. Lean, Wolf to me, because I had saved his life. Once when I first got a wagon and a span of mules, I hauled wood all winter for the people in our village who had no horses. One summer I killed buffalo when they were scarce, and brought in and divided the meat to the whole tribe. That same year I brought in two more pony loads of meat. I was alone. Once I gave away my meat and all my things, a nice horse, a war bonnet, a red blanket, a whet stone, a knife and sheath. I now enjoy thinking of these things.

Forty-four years ago when the Sioux made their last attack on the old Fort Berthold village. I was sick up river at our winter camp. The Sioux came from Poplar river and also from Standing Rock. They burnt a large part of the village, including my house, my big bell, and other things. They got some of the stores out of the cache holes. Pierre Garreau was in the village, and some of the Indians from the winter quarters had gone down to the village, and they helped defend the trader's corral, and block house. At this time Pierre scalped the Sioux whose body he hauled up from under the projecting upper story of the block house by a noose. After the fight Old-Knife, a Crow Indian, and a Sioux man living among us went as far as the Knife river and found two dead Sioux. These they scalped, and then returned having seen no more of the enemy. I was never wounded in a fight.

In the old time we had plenty to eat by hunting, but now we have cattle and big horses. In the old time there were many enemies everywhere, but now we are safe in any place. In the old time we prayed to everything, and dreamed, and conjured, and got horses for pay. Now we know that this is wrong, yet in that time we thought about what was right and wrong. We thought that a murderer or one who killed himself could not be in the happy place. . . .

I had a dried turtle shell, a muskrat skin, a mink skin, red muscles, a crane's head, an otter skin—six things, besides peppermint and other herbs. For these, and the songs and so forth connected with them, I paid eighty buffalo hides, besides guns, ponies, etc. I keep the turtle shell and the muscles yet, because they belong to my father; but I do not worship them. At one time, I paid one hundred and eighty buffalo hides, ten of which were decorated with porcupine work, and knives, and ponies, for a bear's arm, a crane's head, an owl's head, a buffalo skull, and a sweet-grass braid that represented a snake with two heads. There were other things. The long hair of the buffalo near the jaw, owl's claws, and an image of an owl in buffalo hair. Such things were used at the buffalo dance for conjuring. These things give the strength of the buffalo in fighting with the enemy. They also bring the buffalo when food is scarce. They also cure wounds. There is also corn in the ear, and in a basket; red foxes, swift foxes, arrow heads, and things to make the wind blow right. Such things as these I took out on to a hill talked to them, saying I do not need you any more, and threw them to the winds. For doing so Crow Breast, the Gros Ventre chief, called me a fool.

FUNERAL ORATION

You still sit among us, Brother, your person retains its usual resemblance, and continues similar to ours, without any visible deficiency, except that it has lost the power of action. But whither is that breath flown, which a few hours ago sent up smoke to the Great Spirit? Why are those lips silent, that lately delivered to us expressive and pleasing language? Why are those feet motionless, that a short time ago were fleeter than the deer on yonder mountains? Why useless hang those arms that could climb the tallest tree, or draw the toughest bow? Alas! Every part of that frame which we lately beheld with admiration and wonder, is now become as inanimate as it was three hundred years ago. We will not, however, bemoan thee as if thou was for ever lost to us, or that thy name would be buried in oblivion; thy soul yet lives in the great Country of Spirits, with those of thy nation that are gone before thee; and though we are left behind to perpetuate thy fame, we shall one day join thee. Actuated by the respect we bore thee while living, we now come to tender to thee the last act of kindness it is in our power to bestow: that thy body might not lie neglected on the plain, and become a prey to the beasts of the field, or the fowls of the air, we will take care to lay it with those of thy predecessors who are gone before thee; hoping at the same time, that thy spirit will feed with their spirits, and be ready to receive ours, when we also shall arrive at the great Country of Souls.

From Jonathan Carver, *Travels Through the Interior Parts of North America, in the Years 1767, and 1766, 1768* (London, 1778), Chapter 15.

THE END OF THE WORLD: A PAWNEE MYTH

Young Bull (Pitahaunat Pawnee)

Many years ago, when I was a little boy, I used to watch the old men sitting in the tipis, and sometimes in the lodges, rattling the gourds and singing. Several times I asked my father what the old men were singing about. My father would say: "Those old men are singing about Tirawa. When you grow up you will learn more about the songs of these old men." I was anxious to know more about the sacred bundle and the singing of the old men. When night came and I lay down with my grandmother, I said: "Grandmother, why do the old men sit in the lodges, rattle the gourds, and sing?" My grandmother then told me the following story:

My grandchild, many years ago, before we lived upon this earth, Tirawa placed wonderful human beings upon the earth. We knew of them as the wonderful beings or the large people. These people lived where the Swimming Mound is in Kansas. The bones of these large people were found upon the sides of the hill of the Swimming Mound. The old people told us that at this place the rain poured down from the heavens, and the water came from the northwest upon the earth so that it became deep and killed these wonderful beings. When these people were killed by the flood, Tirawa placed an old buffalo bull in the northwest, where the water had come in from the big water so that it over- flowed the land. The buffalo bull was put at this place to hold the water back, so that it would not overflow the land any more.

From George A. Dorsey, ed., *The Pawnee—Mythology*, Part 1 (Washington, D.C., 1906).

This buffalo was to remain at this place for many years. Each year this buffalo was to drop one hair. When all the hairs of the buffalo had come off then the people would not live upon the earth any more.

There were four things which Tirawa said he would do to kill the people, but he had promised that he would never send the flood upon the land any more. Tirawa said there were other ways of destroying the people on the earth. There were several ways of sending storms so that they would kill the people. There was one thing that Tirawa was not sure of doing, and that was sending fire from the sky to burn up the people. The gods in the heavens who were placed by Tirawa would have to sit in council and select a day when all things would end, and decide in what way all things should cease to be. We are told by the old people that the Morning-Star ruled over all the minor gods in the heavens; that the Morning-Star and the Evening-Star gave life to people on this earth. The Sun and the Moon also helped to give life to the people. The old people told us that the Morning-Star said that when the time came for the world to end the Moon would turn red; that if the Moon should turn black it would be a sign that some great chief was to die; that when the Moon should turn red the people would then know that the world was coming to an end. The Sun was also to shine bright and all at once that brightness would die out and the end would come.

The Morning-Star also said that the signs would be made; that as they gave life to the people they could also hold life back, for they had not the say as to when the world should end. The Morning-Star said further that in the beginning of all things they placed the North Star in the north, so that it should not move; it was to watch over the other stars and over the people. The North Star is the one which is to end all things. The Morning-Star told the people that the North Star stood in the north and to its left was a pathway which led from north to south; that when a person died they were taken by the North Star and they were placed upon the pathway which led to the Star of Death—the land of the spirits— the South Star.

The Morning-Star also said that in the beginning of all things they gave power to the South Star for it to move up close, once in a while, to look at the North Star to see if it were still standing in the north. If it were still standing there it was to move back to its place. The Morning-Star spoke to the people and said that in the first great councils when it was decided where each god should stand in the heavens, two of the people became sick. One was an old person and one a young person. They were placed upon stretchers, were carried by certain stars, and these two stretchers are tied on to the North Star. These two stretchers go around the North Star all the time. The North Star continued to tell the people that whenever the South Star came up from the south it would come up higher; that when the time approached for the world to end the South Star would come higher, until at last it would capture the people who were carrying the two people upon the stretchers; as soon as the South Star captured these two people upon the stretchers they were to die. The North Star would then disappear and move away and the South Star would take possession of the earth and of the people. The old people knew also that when the world was to come to an end there were to be many signs. Among the stars would be many signs. Meteors would fly through the sky. The Moon would change its color once in a while. The Sun would also show different colors, but the sign which was to be nearest to the people was that the rivers and the creeks were to rise. The animals, such as otter, beaver, and others, were to drift down the streams. While they were drifting down these animals were to cry out and their cry was to be like that of people. When the people would go swimming in these streams of water, clam shells were to cry out to them, and when the people should try to get away from the clam shells some of them would get on their clothing, and when they would see the clam shells they would be in the shape of birds. They would be, however, clam shells and would cry out like babies.

My grandchild, some of the signs have come to pass. The stars have fallen among the people, but the Morning-Star is still good to us, for we continue to live. The Moon has turned black several times, but we know that the Morning-Star said that whenever the Moon turned black it would be a sign that some great chief or warrior was to die. My grandchild, we are told by the old people that the Morning-Star and the Evening-Star placed people upon this earth. The North Star and the South Star will end all things. All commands were given in the west and these commands were carried out in the east. The command for the ending of all things will be given by the North Star, and the South Star will carry out the commands. Our people were made by the stars. When the time comes for all things to end our people will turn into small stars and will fly to the South Star, where they belong. When the time comes for the ending of the world the stars will again fall to the earth. They will mix among the people, for it will be a message to the people to get ready to be turned into stars.

Part Two

CAPTIVE NATIONS

What was wrought upon the American natives by European invaders over a period of four centuries was genocide, pure and simple. It was not called that, nor was there so systematic a policy as was operative in Germany from 1933 to 1945. But it was just as effective. The Indians of the Caribbean islands, Central America, Mexico, and North America were murdered by the millions. Spain was responsible for more deaths than any other country, because there were more Indians in its colonies. But the Anglo-Americans did their share, considering how few Indians there were to begin with in what is now the United States. When the English colonists first arrived in North America, there were about 800,000 Indians in approximately four hundred tribes scattered across the continent from east to west. By the end of the nineteenth century, there were about 200,000 left, penned up in concentration camps euphemistically called reservations.

The heart of the conflict between the white man and the Indian was, of course, land, and the wealth to be got from it. The history of how the white man acquired the land is an uninterrupted tale of war, massacre, violated treaties, unkept promises, murder, theft, and treachery of all kinds. It was not without wisdom that the Sioux called the white men "Wasichus"—the ones who take everything. Black Elk, an Oglala Sioux, summed it up neatly: "The Wasichus came, and they have made little islands for us and other little islands for the four-leggeds, and always the little islands are becoming smaller, for around them surges the gnawing flood of the Wasichu; and it is dirty with lies and greed." *

* John G. Neihardt, *Black Elk Speaks*, p. 9.

Under the United States Government, the Indians were unwelcome strangers in their own land, with few sympathizers and fewer protectors. Government itself became the chief predator, warring when it had to, stealing "legally" when it could. All the guarantees concerning liberty, justice, and rights, over which Americans boasted much, became one grand and shabby joke where the Indians were concerned.

Necessary and useful as it is to chronicle the wrongs done to American Indians by Anglo-Americans, one still must keep in mind the fact that the "Indian problem" was only one problem for a nation concerned with many other matters. The federal and state governments during the nineteenth century also dealt with foreign relations, international trade, agriculture, slavery, burgeoning industry, growing cities, labor movements, masses of immigrants, communications, and education. To characterize public officials and private persons as thoroughly preoccupied with oppressing the Indians would be to portray them as callous ogres. Only a few were actually that. It is a little more accurate to see them as members of a society that expanded rapidly, a society over which no one was exerting much control at any time. They were also men easily carried along on waves of public opinion and party spirit. Much of what we now deem policy was simply the result of expediency or poor judgment, combined with a prevailing racial arrogance that has always treated powerless ethnic minorities shabbily. Few of those who considered themselves friends of the Indian had any doubts about the mission, even duty, of the white race to control the Western World.

The selections in this section should be read against a background of the eighteenth- and nineteenth-century Indian wars, the hundreds of treaties made and broken, the emergence of the reservation system, and the creation of the federal Bureau of Indian Affairs to govern the tribal "wards" of the state. The term "wars" is perhaps a misnomer, for they were really skirmishes, small battles, and occasional massacres in which it was rare to find more than a few score men engaged on either side. But they were expensive wars, costing the government over $100 million—an expense that might have been considerably reduced by sound and consistent public policy combined with equitable treatment. The end of the Indian wars occurred simultaneously with the end of the frontier, in 1890, with the blow dealt the Sioux "ghost dance" religion by the massacre at Wounded Knee.

With the wars past, the troubles of the Indians enclosed on reservations were not over. In the 1830's, the federal govrepment had organized the Bureau of Indian Affairs. Ostensibly the Bureau was to aid, guide, and support the tribes as they sought to find a place for themselves in a rapidly changing America. Actually, the BIA became a tyrannical and paternalistic agency more eager to serve the wishes of predatory "Wasichus" than to protect and better the lives of the Indians. One writer on Indian history has this to say of the Bureau:

Almost completely unknown to most Americans, or of little interest to them, was the totalitarian state within a state . . . the Bureau of Indian Affairs and its empire of "wards." In the twentieth century many Americans have come to think of Nazi Germany and the Soviet Union of Stalin as prototypes of the all-embracing state, but Hitler and the Stalinists might well have been imitating the system of coercive culture change used earlier in the United States.*

What had been begun by the wars as a haphazard policy of extermination was translated by the BIA into a deliberate attempt at cultural genocide. One of America's leading cartoonists, Charles Schulz (in *Peanuts*, November 18, 1971) inadvertently gave an accurate summary of the Bureau's activities: "In all of mankind's history, there has never been more damage done by people who 'thought they were doing the right thing.' " The "right thing" was to civilize the Indians in the white man's terms, but even for that dubious enterprise adequate and decent means were never forthcoming.

Thus, by 1900, the American Indians, three-fourths wiped out, found themselves inhabitants of some of the most undesirable land in the nation and bereft of most of the constitutional and legal rights of other Americans. In fact, they were not really Americans at all, for citizenship was not granted them until 1924.

The following selections are arranged chronologically and cover a period of nearly three hundred years: from the early seventeenth century to the end of the nineteenth century. The story thus encompassed here is the whole span of the westward movement, from the years when the frontier was a few miles from the Atlantic seaboard until the Pacific Coast had been reached and most of the intervening territory had been conquered by Anglo-Americans. The overriding theme of this section, for all the suggestions of white ambivalence toward the tribes, is the submerging of the Indians by numerical forces, the gradual destruction of the bases of Indian livelihood, and the eventual relegation of these people to the status of aliens in their own country.

---

* Jack D. Forbes, *The Indian in America's Past*, p. 113.

EPIGRAPHS

The reason why the Christians have killed and destroyed such infinite numbers of souls, is solely because they have made gold their ultimate aim, seeking to load themselves with riches in the shortest time and to mount by high steps, disproportioned to their condition: namely by their insatiable avarice and ambition, the greatest, that could be on the earth. These lands, being so happy and so rich, and the people so humble, so patient, and so easily subjugated, they have had no more respect, nor consideration nor have they taken more account of them (I speak with truth of what I have seen during all the aforementioned time) than—I will not say of animals, for would to God they had considered and treated them as animals—but as even less than the dung in the streets.

—BARTOLOMÉ DE LAS CASAS. *A Very Brief Account of the Destruction of the Indies.* 1540

Unhappy people! to have lived in such times, and by such neighbors! We have seen that they would have been safer among the ancient heathens with whom the rites of hospitality were sacred. They would have been considered as guests of the public, and the religion of the country would have operated in their favor. But our frontier people call themselves Christians! They would have been safer if they had submitted to the Turks.

—BENJAMIN FRANKLIN. *A Narrative of the Late Massacres in Lancaster County.* 1764. Written following the murder of a band of Conestoga Indians by Scot-Irish settlers in Pennsylvania

Those that scaped the fire were slain with the sword, some hewed to pieces, others run through with their rapiers, so as they were quickly dispatched and very few escaped. It was conceived they thus destroyed about 400 at this time. It was a fearful sight to see them thus frying in the fire and the streams of blood quenching the same, and horrible was the stink and scent thereof; but the victory seemed a sweet sacrifice, and they gave the praise thereof to God, who had wrought so wonderfully for them, thus to enclose their enemies in their hands and give them so speedy a victory over so proud and insulting an enemy.

—WILLIAM BRADFORD. *Of Plymouth Plantation.*
On the burning of a Pequot village, 1637

You will do well to try to inoculate the Indians by means of blankets in which smallpox patients have slept, as well as by every other method that can serve to extirpate this execrable race. I should be very glad if your scheme of hunting them down by dogs could take effect.

—GENERAL JEFFREY AMHERST. Letter to a subordinate. 1732

It is necessary that we should not lose sight of an important truth which continually receives new confirmations, namely, that the provisions heretofore made with a view to the protection of the Indians from the violences of the lawless part of our frontier inhabitants are insufficient. It is demonstrated that these violences can now be perpetrated with impunity, and it can need no argument to prove that, unless the murdering of Indians can be restrained by bringing the murderers to condign punishment, all the exertions of the Government to prevent destructive retaliations by the Indians will prove fruitless and all our present agreeable prospects illusory. The frequent destruction of innocent women and children, who are chiefly the victims of retaliation, must continue to shock humanity.

—GEORGE WASHINGTON. Seventh Annual Message to Congress. 1795

If the savage resists, civilization, with the ten commandments in one hand and the sword in the other, demands his immediate extermination.

—ANDREW JOHNSON. Message to Congress. 1867

A crime is projected that confounds our understandings by its magnitude—a crime that really deprives us as well as the Cherokees of a country, for how could we call the conspiracy that should crush these poor Indians our government, or the land that was cursed by their parting and dying imprecations our country, any more? You, sir, will bring down that renowned chair in which you sit into infamy if your seal is set to this instrument of perfidy; and the name of this nation, hitherto the sweet omen of religion and liberty, will stink to the world.

—RALPH WALDO EMERSON. Letter to Martin Van Buren
on Indian removal. April 23, 1838

Anyone whom I have spoken to, whether officers or soldiers,

agree in the relation that the most fearful atrocities were committed that were ever heard of: women and children were killed and scalped, children shot at their mother's breast, and all the bodies mutilated in the most horrible manner.
　　　　　　　—MAJOR EDWARD W. WYNCOOP. Testimony on the
　　　　　　　　　　　Sand Creek Massacre. January 16, 1865

If the great family of North American Indians were all dying by a scourge or epidemic of the country, it would be natural, and a virtue, to weep for them; but merely to sympathise with them (and but partially to do that) when they are dying at our hands, and rendering their glebe to our possession, would be to subvert the simplest law of Nature, and turn civilised man, with all his boasted virtues, back to worse than savage barbarism.
　　　　　　　—GEORGE CATLIN. *The North American Indians.* 1841

Those who believe in the policy of the extermination of the Indians, and think the speedier the better its accomplishment, look upon the condition of war as inevitable, and are for pouring thousands of troops into the Indian country and giving them a terrible punishment. This class is small, even in the Army, where the policy of extermination is not popular save with a few high and restless officers.
　　　　　　　—*New York Times*, July 7, 1876. "Views at the War Department"

The only good Indians I ever saw were dead.
　　　　　　　—GENERAL PHILIP SHERIDAN. January, 1869

I should think it requisite that convenient tracts of land should be set out to them; and that by plain and natural boundaries, as much as may be—as lakes, rivers, mountains, rocks—upon which for any Englishman to encroach should be accounted a crime.
　　　　　　　—SAMUEL SEWALL. Letter to Sir William Ashurst. May 3, 1700

I hope too that your admonitions against encroachments on the Indian lands will have a beneficial effect—the U.S. find an Indian war too serious a thing, to risk incurring one merely to gratify a few intruders with settlements which are to cost the other inhabitants of the U.S. a thousand times their value in taxes for carrying on the war they produce. I am satisfied it will ever be preferred to send armed force and make war against the intruders as being more just & less expensive.
　　　　　　　—THOMAS JEFFERSON, to David Campbell, March 27, 1792

It is just and reasonable and essential to our interest and the security of our colonies that the several nations or tribes of Indians with whom we are connected, and who live under our protection, should not be molested or disturbed in the possession of such parts of our dominions and territories as, not having been ceded to or purchased by us, are reserved to them, or any of them, as their hunting grounds.

—Proclamation of 1763

The plan of collocating the Indians on suitable lands West of the Mississippi, contains the elements of their preservation; and will tend, if faithfully carried into effect, to produce the happiest benefits upon the Indian race. I have not been able to perceive in any other policy, principles which combine our own obligations to the Indians, in all that is humane and just, with effects so favorable to them, as is contained in this plan.

—SECRETARY OF WAR BARBOUR, to Congressman
William McLean, April 29, 1828

It may well be doubted whether those tribes which reside within the acknowledged boundaries of the United States can, with strict accuracy, be denominated foreign nations. They may more correctly, perhaps, be denominated domestic dependent nations.

—JOHN MARSHALL. *Cherokee Nation* v. *State of Georgia.* 1831

One great principle ought to govern all public negotiations—*a rigid adherence to truth*—a principle that is essential in negotiations with Indians if we would gain their permanent confidence and a useful influence over them. Jealousy is strongest in minds un-informed, so that the utmost purity and candor will hardly escape suspicion. Suspicions occasion delays, and issue in discontents, and these in depredations and war.

—TIMOTHY PICKERING. Letter to
General Anthony Wayne. April 8, 1795

The idea that a handful of wild, half-naked, thieving, plundering, murdering savages should be dignified with the sovereign attributes of nations, enter into solemn treaties, and claim a country five hundred miles wide by one thousand miles long as theirs in fee simple, because they hunted buffalo and antelope over it, might do for beautiful reading in Cooper's novels or Longfellow's *Hiawatha,* but is unsuited to the intelligence and justice of this age, or the natural rights of mankind.

—*United States* v. *Lucero.* 1869

It may be regarded as certain, that not a foot of land will ever be taken from the Indians, without their own consent. The sacredness of their rights is felt by all thinking persons in America as much as in Europe.

—THOMAS JEFFERSON. 1786

For a mighty nation like us to be carrying on a war with a few straggling nomads, under such circumstances, is a spectacle most humiliating, and injustice unparalleled, a national crime most revolting, that must, sooner or later, bring down upon us or our posterity the judgment of Heaven.

—GENERAL JOHN B. SANBORN to the Secretary of the Interior. 1867

The history of the government connections with the Indians is a shameful record of broken treaties and unfulfilled promises. The history of the border white man's connection with the Indians is a sickening record of murder, outrage, robbery, and wrongs committed by the former, as the rule, and occasional savage outbreaks and unspeakably barbarous deeds of retaliation by the latter, as the exception.

Taught by the government that they had rights entitled to respect, when those rights have been assailed by the rapacity of the white man, the arm which should have been raised to protect them has ever been ready to sustain the aggressor.

—Report of a Presidential commission on Indian affairs. 1869

Nowadays we undoubtedly ought to break up the great Indian reservations, disregard the tribal governments, allot the land in severalty (with, however, only a limited power of alienation), and treat the Indians as we do other citizens, with certain exceptions, for their sakes as well as ours.

—THEODORE ROOSEVELT. *The Winning of the West*, Vol. I. 1889

Gradually, as the tribes are able to stand alone, they should be turned over to their own resources. Most of the Indians are well-to-do. The lands reserved for them and the annuities due to them under treaties and bargains put them upon a good footing.

—JOHN WESLEY POWELL. *Forum*, May, 1893

When treaties were entered into between the United States and a tribe of Indians it was never doubted that the *power* to abrogate existed in Congress, and that in a contingency such power might be availed of from considerations of governmental policy, particularly if consistent with perfect good faith toward the Indians.

—*Lone Wolf* v. *Hitchcock*. January 5, 1903

The utmost good faith shall always be observed toward the Indians; their lands and property shall never be taken from them without their consent; and in their property, rights, and liberty they never shall be invaded or disturbed unless in just and lawful wars authorized by Congress; but laws founded in justice and humanity shall, from time to time, be made for preventing wrongs being done to them and for preserving peace and friendship with them.

—Northwest Ordinance. July 13, 1787

What use do these ringed, streaked, spotted, and speckled cattle make of the soil? Do they till it? Revelation said to man, "Thou

shalt till the ground." This alone is human life. It is favorable
to population, to science, to the information of a human mind
in the worship of God. Warburton has well said that before you
can make an Indian a Christian you must teach him agriculture
and reduce him to a civilized life.
—HUGH H. BRACKENRIDGE. *Indian Atrocities.* 1782

The hunter or savage state, requires, a greater extent of territory
to sustain it, than is compatible with the progress and just claims
of civilized life, and must yield to it. Nothing is more certain, than,
if the Indian tribes do not abandon that state, and become civilized,
that they will decline, and become extinct. The hunter state, tho
maintain'd by warlike spirits, presents but a feeble resistance to
the more dense, compact, and powerful population of civilized man.
—JAMES MONROE. Letter to Andrew Jackson. October 5, 1817

The tribes which occupied the countries now constituting the
Eastern states were annihilated or have melted away to make
room for the whites. The waves of population and civilization
are rolling to the westward, and we now propose to acquire the
countries occupied by the red men of the South and West by a
fair exchange, and, at the expense of the United States, to send
them to a land where their existence may be prolonged and perhaps
made perpetual.
—ANDREW JACKSON. Message to Congress. December 6, 1830

When we contemplate the change which has been wrought in this
one savage wilderness, by the arts, the industry, and the superior
knowledge of the new population; when we visit our thronged
cities, smiling fields, and happy habitations; when we contemplate
our numerous bays and harbors, once the resort only of the wild
fowl and the inhabitants of the deep; now studded with ships and
vessels of all sizes and nations, pouring upon these lands the rich
and extensive commerce of a whole world; when, instead of a roving
tribe of hunters, we behold a powerful nation of agriculturists,
as free in every desirable liberty, as their savage predecessors; when
our happy political institutions and the religion of the Bible, have
displaced their barbarous laws, and wretched superstitions; can
we wish these effects of civilization, religion, and the arts, to disappear, and the dark forests and roaming Indian again to possess
the land? Are we not compelled to admit that the superintending
providence of the Being who first formed the earth, is to be seen
in this mighty change?
—*Caldwell* v. *State of Alabama.* 1832

There is nothing which would be more gratifying to the people of
this state, and certainly there is, on my part, no desire affecting
the Indians more sincere, than to see the remnants of the Indian

tribes forsake entirely the manners and customs of their forefathers and adopt those of civilized life.

—WILLIAM SEWARD. June 15, 1841

There is no question of national dignity, be it remembered, involved in the treatment of savages by a civilized power. With wild men, as with wild beasts, the question whether in a given situation one shall fight, coax, or run is a question merely of what is easiest and safest.

—FRANCIS A. WALKER. Report of the Commissioner of Indian Affairs. 1873

When the Indians are individual owners of real property, and as individuals enjoy the protection of the laws, their tribal cohesion will necessarily relax and gradually disappear. They will have advanced an immense step in the direction of the "white man's way."

—CARL SCHURZ. *The North American Review*, July, 1881

This language which is good enough for a white man or a black man ought to be good enough for the red man. It is also believed that teaching an Indian youth in his own barbarous dialect is a positive detriment to him. The impractability, if not impossibility, of civilizing the Indians of this country in any other tongue than our own would seem obvious.

—Commissioner of Indian Affairs. 1887

These old, well-founded, historical hatreds have a savor of nobility for the independent. That the Jew should not love the Christian, nor the Irishman love the English, nor the Indian brave tolerate the thought of the American is not disgraceful to the nature of man; rather, indeed, honorable, since it depends on wrongs ancient, like the race, and not personal to him who cherishes the indignation.

—ROBERT LOUIS STEVENSON. *Longman's Magazine*, August, 1883

To civilize the Indian, make him a soldier. . . .

From the 250,000 Indians now living on reservations five regiments could easily be raised, which would take only about one-eighth of the men of military age. The advantages of giving employment (with an education and a career) to the young men of the tribes; the "bucks," who out of mere idleness now give the government no end of trouble, need not be dwelt upon; it is a proposition too clear for argument. We have our own Sikhs and Goorkhas in our Sioux and Apaches; an aboriginal military caste.

—JOHN T. BRAMHALL. *The Overland Monthly*, February, 1901

Kill the Indian and save the man!

—RICHARD H. PRATT, founder of the Carlisle Indian School

REMARKS TO CAPTAIN JOHN SMITH (c. 1609)

Powhatan (Powhatan Confederacy)

I am now grown old, and must soon die; and the succession must descend, in order, to my brothers, *Opitchapan, Opekankanough,* and *Catataugh,* and then to my two sisters, and their two daughters. I wish their experience was equal to mine; and that your love to us might not be less than ours to you. Why should you take by force that from us which you can have by love? Why should you destroy us, who have provided you with food? What can you get by war? We can hide our provisions, and fly into the woods; and then you must consequently famish by wronging your friends. What is the cause of your jealousy? You see us unarmed, and willing to supply your wants, if you will come in a friendly manner, and not with swords and guns, as to invade an enemy. I am not so simple, as not to know it is better to eat good meat, lie well, and sleep quietly with my women and children; to laugh and be merry with the English; and, being their friend, to have copper, hatchets, and whatever else I want, than to fly from all, to lie cold in the woods, feed upon acorns, roots, and such trash, and to be so hunted, that I cannot rest, eat, or sleep. In such circumstances, my men must watch, and if a twig should but break, all would cry out, *"Here comes Capt. Smith";* and so, in this miserable manner, to end my miserable life; and, Capt. Smith, this *might* be soon your fate too, through your rashness and unadvisedness. I, therefore, exhort you to peaceable councils; and, above all, I insist that the guns and swords, the cause of all our jealousy and uneasiness, be removed and sent away.

From Samuel G. Drake, *Biography and History of the Indians of North America,* 11th ed. (Boston, 1841), p. 353.

REASONS FOR THE PUEBLO REVOLT OF 1680 IN NEW MEXICO: TESTIMONY GIVEN TO SPANISH AUTHORITIES ON DECEMBER 19, 1681

Pedro Naranjo (Queres Pueblo)

In the said plaza de armas on the said day, month, and year, for the prosecution of the judicial proceedings of this case his lordship caused to appear before him an Indian prisoner named Pedro Naranjo, a native of the pueblo of San Felipe, of the Queres nation, who was captured in the advance and attack upon the pueblo of La Isleta. He makes himself understood very well in the Castilian language and speaks his mother tongue and the Tegua. He took the oath in due legal form in the name of God, our Lord, and a sign of the cross, under charge of which he promised to tell the truth concerning what he knows and as he might be questioned, and having understood the seriousness of the oath and so signified through the interpreters, he spoke as indicated by the contents of the *autos*.

Asked whether he knows the reason or motives which the Indians of this kingdom had for rebelling, forsaking the law of God and obedience to his Majesty, and committing such grave

From Charles Wilson Hackett, *Revolt of the Pueblo Indians of New Mexico and Otermin's Attempted Reconquest 1680–1682* (Albuquerque, 1942), pp. 245–49.

and atrocious crimes, and who were the leaders and principal
movers, and by whom and how it was ordered; and why they
burned the images, temples, crosses, rosaries, and things of divine
worship, committing such atrocities as killing priests, Spaniards,
women, and children, and the rest that he might know touching
the question, he said that since the government of Señor General
Hernando Ugarte y la Concha they have planned to rebel on
various occasions through conspiracies of the Indian sorcerers,
and that although in some pueblos the messages were accepted,
in other parts they would not agree to it; and that it is true
that during the government of the said señor general seven or
eight Indians were hanged for this same cause, whereupon the
unrest subsided. Some time thereafter they [the conspirators]
sent from the pueblo of Los Taos through the pueblos of the
custodia two deerskins with some pictures on them signifying
conspiracy after their manner, in order to convoke the people
to a new rebellion, and the said deerskins passed to the province
of Moqui, where they refused to accept them. The pact which
they had been forming ceased for the time being, but they always
kept in their hearts the desire to carry it out, so as to live as they
are living to-day. Finally, in the past years, at the summons of
an Indian named Popé who is said to have communication with
the devil, it happened that in an estufa of the pueblo of Los Taos
there appeared to the said Popé three figures of Indians who
never came out of the estufa. They gave the said Popé to understand that they were going underground to the lake of Copala.
He saw these figures emit fire from all the extremities of their
bodies, and that one of them was called Caudi, another Tilini,
and the other Tleume; and these three beings spoke to the said
Popé, who was in hiding from the secretary, Francisco Xavier,
who wished to punish him as a sorcerer. They told him to make
a cord of maguey fiber and tie some knots in it which would
signify the number of days that they must wait before the rebellion.
He said that the cord was passed through all the pueblos of
the kingdom so that the ones which agreed to it [the rebellion]
might untie one knot in sign of obedience, and by the other
knots they would know the days which were lacking; and this
was to be done on pain of death to those who refused to agree
to it. As a sign of agreement and notice of having concurred in
the treason and perfidy they were to send up smoke signals to
that effect in each one of the pueblos singly. The said cord was
taken from pueblo to pueblo by the swiftest youths under the
penalty of death if they revealed the secret. Everything being
thus arranged, two days before the time set for its execution,
bcause his lordship had learned of it and had imprisoned two
Indian accomplices from the pueblo of Tesuque, it was carried
out prematurely that night, because it seemed to them that they
were now discovered; and they killed religious, Spaniards, women,
and children. This being done, it was proclaimed in all the pueblos

that everyone in common should obey the commands of their
father whom they did not know, which would be given through
El Caydi or El Popé. This was heard by Alonso Catití, who came
to the pueblo of this declarant to say that everyone must unite
to go to the villa to kill the governor and the Spaniards who had
remained with him, and that he who did not obey would, on their
return, be beheaded; and in fear of this they agreed to it. Finally
the señor governor and those who were with him escaped from
the siege, and later this declarant saw that as soon as the
Spaniards had left the kingdom an order came from the said
Indian, Popé, in which he commanded all the Indians to break
the lands and enlarge their cultivated fields, saying that now they
were as they had been in ancient times, free from the labor they
had performed for the religious and the Spaniards, who could
not now be alive. He said that this is the legitimate cause and
the reason they had for rebelling, because they had always desired
to live as they had when they came out of the lake of Copala.
Thus he replies to the question.

Asked for what reason they so blindly burned the images,
temples, crosses, and other things of divine worship, he stated
that the said Indian, Popé, came down in person, and with him
El Saca and El Chato from the pueblo of Los Taos, and other
captains and leaders and many people who were in his train,
and he ordered in all the pueblos through which he passed that
they instantly break up and burn the images of the holy Christ,
the Virgin Mary and the other saints, the crosses, and everything
pertaining to Christianity, and that they burn the temples, break
up the bells, and separate from the wives whom God had given
them in marriage and take those whom they desired. In order
to take away their baptismal names, the water, and the holy oils,
they were to plunge into the rivers and wash themselves with
amole, which is a root native to the country, washing even their
clothing, with the understanding that there would thus be taken
from them the character of the holy sacraments. They did this,
and also many other things which he does not recall, given to
understand that this mandate had come from the Caydi and the
other two who emitted fire from their extremities in the said
estufa of Taos, and that they thereby returned to the state of
their antiquity, as when they came from the lake of Copala; that
this was the better life and the one they desired, because the God
of the Spaniards was worth nothing and theirs was very strong,
the Spaniard's God being rotten wood. These things were observed
and obeyed by all except some who, moved by the zeal of Christians,
opposed it, and such persons the said Popé caused to be killed
immediately. He saw to it that they at once erected and rebuilt
their houses of idolatry which they call estufas, and made very
ugly masks in imitation of the devil in order to dance the dance
of the cacina; and he said likewise that the devil had given them
to understand that living thus in accordance with the law of their

ancestors, they would harvest a great deal of maize, many beans, a great abundance of cotton, calabashes, and very large watermelons and cantaloupes; and that they could erect their houses and enjoy abundant health and leisure. As he has said, the people were very much pleased, living at their ease in this life of their antiquity, which was the chief cause of their falling into such laxity. Following what has already been stated, in order to terrorize them further and cause them to observe the diabolical commands, there came to them a pronouncement from the three demons already described, and from El Popé, to the effect that he who might still keep in his heart a regard for the priests, the governor, and the Spaniards would be known from his unclean face and clothes, and would be punished. And he stated that the said four persons stopped at nothing to have their commands obeyed. Thus he replies to the question.

Asked what arrangements and plans they had made for the contingency of the Spaniards' return, he said that what he knows concerning the question is that they were always saying they would have to fight to the death, for they do not wish to live in any other way than they are living at present; and the demons in the estufa of Taos had given them to understand that as soon as the Spaniards began to move toward this kingdom they would warn them so that they might unite, and none of them would be caught. He having been questioned further and repeatedly touching the case, he said that he has nothing more to say except that they should be always on the alert, because the said Indians were continually planning to follow the Spaniards and fight with them by night, in order to drive off the horses and catch them afoot, although they might have to follow them for many leagues. What he has said is the truth, and what happened, on the word of a Christian who confesses his guilt. He said that he has come to the pueblos through fear to lead in idolatrous dances, in which he greatly fears in his heart that he may have offended God, and that now having been absolved and returned to the fold of the church, he has spoken the truth in everything he has been asked.

SPEECHES TO THE GOVERNORS OF NEW YORK AND VIRGINIA, IN A COUNCIL ASSEMBLED AT ALBANY IN AUGUST, 1684

Onondaga, Cayuga, and Seneca Chiefs

Brother Corlear,

Your Sachem is a great Sachem, and we are but a small People; but when the English came first to Manhatan [New York], to Aragiske [Virginia] and to Yakokranagary [Maryland], they were then but a small People, and we were great. Then, because we found you a good People, we treated you kindly, and gave you Land; we hope therefore, now that you are great, and we small, you will protect us from the French. If you do not, we shall lose all our Hunting and Bevers: The French will get all the Bevers. The Reason they are now angry with us is, because we carry our Bever to our Brethren.

We have put our Lands and ourselves under the Protection of the great Duke of York, the Brother of your great Sachem, who is likewise a great Sachem.

We have annexed the Susquehana River, which we won with the Sword, to this Government; and we desire it may be a Branch of the great Tree that grows in this Place, the Top of which

From Cadwallader Colden, *The History of the Five Nations of Canada,* 3d ed. (London, 1755), Vol. I, pp. 46–51.

reaches the Sun, and its Branches shelter us from the French, and all other Nations. Our Fire burns in your Houses, and your Fire burns with us; we desire it may be so always. But we will not that any of the great Penn's People settle upon the Susquehana River, for we have no other Land to leave to our Children.

Our young Men are Soldiers, and when they are provoked, they are like Wolves in the Woods, as you, Sachem of Virginia, very well know.

We have put ourselves under the great Sachem Charles, that lives on the other Side the great Lake. We give you these two white dressed Deer-skins, to send to the great Sachem, that he may write on them, and put a great red Seal to them, to confirm what we now do; and put the Susquehana River above the Falls, and all the rest of our Land under the great Duke of York, and give that Land to none else. Our Brethren, his People, have been like Fathers to our Wives and Children, and have given us Bread when we were in Need of it; we will not therefore join ourselves, or our Land, to any other Government but this. We desire Corlear, our Governor, may send this our Proposition to the great Sachem Charles, who dwells on the other Side the great Lake, with this Belt of Wampum, and this other smaller Belt to the Duke of York his Brother: And we give you, Corlear, this Bever, that you may send over this Proposition.

You great Man of Virginia, we let you know, that great Penn did speak to us here in Corlear's House by his Agents, and desired to buy the Susquehana River of us, but we would not hearken to him, for we had fastened it to this Government.

We desire you therefore to bear witness of what we now do, and that we now confirm what we have done before. Let your Friend, that lives on the other Side the great Lake, know this, that we being a free People, though united to the English, may give our Lands, and be joined to the Sachem we like best. We give this Bever to remember what we say.

The Senekas arrived soon after, and, on the fifth of August, spoke to the Lord Howard in the following Manner:

We have heard and understood what Mischief hath been done in Virginia; we have it as perfect as if it were upon our Fingers Ends. O Corlear! we thank you for having been our Intercessor, so that the Axe has not fallen upon us.

And you Assarigoa, great Sachem of Virginia, we thank you for burying all Evil in the Pit. We are informed, that the Mohawks, Oneydoes, Onnondagas, and Cayugas, have buried the Axe already; now we that live remotest off, are come to do the same, and to include in this Chain the Cahnawaas, your Friends. We desire therefore, that an Axe, on our Part, may be buried with one of Assarigoa's. O Corlear! Corlear! we thank you for laying hold of one End of the Axe; and we thank you, great Governor of Virginia, not only for throwing aside the Axe, but more especially for your putting all Evil from your Heart. Now we have a new Chain, a strong and a straight Chain, that cannot be broken. The Tree of Peace is planted so firmly, that it cannot be moved, let us on both Sides hold the Chain fast.

We understand what you said of the great Sachem, that lives on the other Side the great Water.

You tell us, that the Cahnawaas will come hither, to strengthen the Chain. Let them not make any Excuse, that they are old and feeble, or that their Feet are sore. If the old Sachems cannot, let the young Men come. We shall not fail to come hither, tho' we live farthest off, and then the new Chain will be stronger and brighter.

We understand, that because of the Mischief that has been done to the People and Castles of Virginia and Maryland, we must not come near the Heads of your Rivers, nor near your Plantations; but keep at the Foot of the Mountains; for tho' we lay down our Arms, as Friends, we shall not be trusted for the future, but looked on as Robbers. We agree however to this Proposition, and shall wholly stay away from Virginia: And this we do in Gratitude to Corlear, who has been at so great Pains to persuade you, great Governor of Virginia, to forget what is past. You are wise in giving Ear to Corlear's good Advice, for we shall now go a Path which was never trod before.

We have now done speaking to Corlear, and the Governor of Virginia; let the Chain be for ever kept clean and bright by him, and we shall do the same.

The other Nations from the Mohawks Country to the Cayugas, have delivered up the Susquehana River, and all that Country, to Corlear's Government. We confirm what they have done by giving this Belt.

SPEECH IN BEHALF OF THE SIX NATIONS, TO PENNSYLVANIA OFFICIALS, JULY 7, 1742

Canassateego (Seneca)

Brethren, the governor and council, and all present,
According to our promise we now propose to return you an answer to the several things mentioned to us yesterday, and shall beg leave to speak to public affairs first, though they were what you spoke to last. On this head you yesterday put us in mind, first, of William Penn's early and constant care to cultivate friendship with all the Indians; of the treaty we held with one of his sons, about ten years ago; and of the necessity there is at this time of keeping the roads between us clear and free from all obstructions.

We are all very sensible of the kind regard that good man William Penn had for all the Indians, and cannot but be pleased to find that his children have the same. We well remember the treaty you mention held with his son on his arrival here, by which we confirmed our league of friendship, that is to last as long as the sun and moon endure. In consequence of this, we, on our part, shall preserve the road free from all encumbrances; in confirmation whereof we lay down this string of wampum.

You, in the next place, said you would enlarge the fire and make it burn brighter, which we are pleased to hear you mention; and

From Cadwallader Colden, *The History of the Five Nations of Canada*, 3d ed. (London, 1755), Vol. 2, pp. 18–24.

assure you we shall do the same by adding to it more fuel, that it may still flame out more strongly than ever.

In the last place, you were pleased to say that we are bound by the strictest leagues to watch for each others preservation; that we should hear with our ears for you, and you hear with your ears for us. This is equally agreeable to us; and we shall not fail to give you early intelligence, whenever anything of consequence comes to our knowledge. And to encourage you to do the same, and to nourish in your hearts what you have spoke to us with your tongues about the renewal of our amity and the brightening of the chain of friendship, we confirm what we have said with another belt of wampum.

Brethren, we received from the proprietors yesterday some goods in consideration of our release of the lands on the west side of Susquehanna. It is true, we have the full quantity according to agreement; but if the proprietor had been here himself, we think, in regard of our numbers and poverty, he would have made an addition to them. If the goods were only to be divided among the Indians present, a single person would have but a small portion; but if you consider what numbers are left behind, equally entitled with us to a share, there will be extremely little. We therefore desire, if you have the keys of the proprietor's chest, you will open it and take out a little more for us.

We know our lands are now become more valuable. The white people think we do not know their value; but we are sensible that the land is everlasting, and the few goods we receive for it are soon worn out and gone. For the future, we will sell no lands but when Brother Onas is in the country; and we will know beforehand the quantity of the goods we are to receive. Besides, we are not well used with respect to the lands still unsold by us. Your people daily settle on these lands, and spoil our hunting. We must insist on your removing them, as you know they have no right to settle to the northward of Kittochtinny Hills. In particular, we renew our complaints against some people who are settled at Juniata, a branch of Susquehanna, and all along the banks of that river, as far as Mahaniay; and desire they may be forthwith made to go off the land, for they do great damage to our cousins the Delawares.

We have further to observe, with respect to the lands lying on the west side of Susquehanna that though Brother Onas (meaning the proprietor) has paid us for what his people possess, yet some parts of that country have been taken up by persons whose place of residence is to the south of this province, from whom we have never received any consideration. This affair was recommended to you by our chiefs at our last treaty; and you then, at our earnest desire, promised to write a letter to that person who has the authority over those people, and to procure us his answer.

As we have never heard from you on this head, we want to know what you have done in it. If you have not done anything, we now renew our request, and desire you will inform the person whose people are seated on our lands that that country belongs to us, in right of conquest; we having bought it with our blood, and taken it from our enemies in fair war; and we expect, as owners of that land, to receive such a consideration for it as the land is worth. We desire you will press him to send a positive answer. Let him say Yes or No; if he says Yes, we will treat with him; if No, we are able to do ourselves justice, and we will do it by going to take payment ourselves.

It is customary with us to make a present of skins whenever we renew our treaties. We are ashamed to offer our brethren so few, but your horses and cows have eaten the grass our deer used to feed on. This has made them scarce, and will, we hope, plead in excuse for our not bringing a larger quantity. If we could have spared more, we would have given more; but we are really poor; and desire you'll not consider the quantity, but, few as they are, accept them in testimony of our regard.

ADDRESS TO AN ENGLISHMAN ON BRITISH-FRENCH RELATIONS WITH THE INDIANS, 1761

Minavavana (Chippewa)

[Many of the tribes in the Great Lakes region had long maintained friendly contact with the French. Consequently, they were much distressed by Britain's conquest of Canada in the Seven Years War. The Indians hoped that France would soon fight to regain Canada, restore trade, and halt the onrush of English colonists across the Alleghenies. The Englishman who is the object of Minavavana's remarks had inadvertently wandered into unfriendly Indian territory during his travels through Canada.]

Englishman!—It is to you that I speak, and I demand your attention!

Englishman!—You know that the French King is our father. He promised to be such; and we, in return, promised to be his children. This promise we have kept.

Englishman!—It is you that have made war with this our father. You are his enemy; and how then could you have the boldness to venture among us, his children? You know that his enemies are ours.

From B. B. Thatcher, *Indian Biography* (New York, 1841), Vol. 2, pp. 76–77.

Englishman!—We are informed that our father the king of France, is old and infirm; and that being fatigued with making war upon your nation, he is fallen asleep. During his sleep, you have taken advantage of him, and possessed yourselves of Canada. But his nap is almost at an end. I think I hear him already stirring, and inquiring for his children the Indians;—and, when he does awake, what must become of you? He will destroy you utterly!

Englishman!—Although you have conquered the French, you have not yet conquered us! We are not your slaves. These lakes, these woods and mountains, were left to us by our ancestors. They are our inheritance, and we will part with them to none. Your nation supposes that we, like the white people, cannot live without bread, and pork, and beef! But, you ought to know, that He—the Great Spirit and Master of Life—has provided food for us, in these broad lakes, and upon these mountains.

Englishman!—Our father, the king of France, employed our young men to make war upon your nation. In this warfare, many of them have been killed; and it is our custom to retaliate, until such time as the spirits of the slain are satisfied. Now the spirits of the slain are to be satisfied in either of two ways. The first is by the spilling of the blood of the nation by which they fell; the other, by *covering the bodies of the dead*, and thus allaying the resentment of their relations. This is done by making presents.

Englishman!—Your king has never sent us any presents, nor entered into any treaty with us. Wherefore he and we are still at war; and, until he does these things, we must consider that we have no other father, nor friend, among the white men, than the king of France. But, for you, we have taken into consideration, that you have ventured your life among us, in the expectation that we should not molest you. You do not come armed, with an intention to make war. You come in peace, to trade with us, and supply us with necessaries, of which we are much in want. We shall regard you, therefore, as a brother; and you may sleep tranquilly, without fear of the Chippewas. As a token of our friendship, we present you with this pipe, to smoke.

SPEECH TO THE FRENCH ON REASONS FOR MAKING WAR ON THE ENGLISH, MAY 25, 1763

Pontiac (Ottawa)

[Following the Seven Years War, the English failed to arrive at a firm and conciliatory Indian policy to replace the friendly relations the tribes had long sustained with the French. The fur trade was badly handled, and the Indians were generally mistreated. Resentment quickly built up among the trans-Allegheny tribes to the point where Pontiac was able to form a loose confederation in the hope of winning back Canada for the French.]

My brothers, we have never had in view to do you any evil. We have never intended that any should be done you. But amongst my young men there are, as amongst you, some who, in spite of all precautions which we take, always do evil. Besides, it is not only for my revenge that I make war upon the English, it is for you, my brothers, as for us. When the English, in their councils, which we have held with them, have insulted us, they have also insulted you, without your knowing anything about it, and as I know, and all our brothers know, the English have taken from you all means

From Pioneer Society of the State of Michigan, *Collections*, 2d ed. (Lansing, 1907), Vol. 8, pp. 300–301.

of avenging yourselves, by disarming you and making you write on a paper, which they have sent to their country, which they could not make us do; therefore, I will avenge you equally with us, and I swear their annihilation as long as any of them shall remain on our land. Besides, you do not know all the reasons which oblige me to act as I do. I have told you only that which regards you. You will know the rest in time. I know well that I pass amongst many of my brothers for a fool, but you will see in the future if I am such as is said, and if I am wrong. I also know well that there are amongst you, my brothers, some who take the part of the English, to make war against us, and that only pains me on their account. I know them well, and when our father shall have come, I will name them and point them out to him, and they will see whether they or we shall be the most content in the future.

I doubt not, my brothers, that this war tries you, on account of the movements of our brothers, who all the time go and come to your houses. I am sorry for it but do not believe, my brothers, that I instigate the wrong which is done to you, and for proof that I do not wish it, remember the war of the Foxes, and the manner in which I have behaved in your interest. It is now seventeen years that the Sauteux and Ottawas of Michelimakinak and all the nations of the north have come with the Takés [Sacs] and Foxes to annihilate you. Who has defended you? Was it not I and my people? When Mékinak, great chief of all the nations, said in his council that he would carry to his village the head of your commander, and eat his heart and drink his blood, have I not taken up your interest by going to his camp and telling him, if he wanted to kill the French, he must commence with me and my people? Have I not helped you to defeat them and drive them away? When or how came that? Would you, my brothers, believe that I to-day would turn my arms against you? No, my brothers, I am the same French Pondiak who lent you his hand seventeen years ago. I am a Frenchman, and I want to die a Frenchman! And I repeat to you they are both your interests and mine which I revenge. Let me go on. I don't ask your assistance, because I know you cannot give it. I only ask of you provisions for me and all my people. If, however, you would like to aid me, I would not refuse you. You would cause me pleasure, and you would the sooner be out of trouble. For I warrant you, when the English shall be driven from here or killed, we shall all retire to our villages according to our custom, and await the arrival of our father, the Frenchman. These, you see, my brothers, are my sentiments. Rest assured, my brothers, I will watch that no more wrong shall be done to you by my people, nor by other Indians. What I ask of you is that our women be allowed to plant our corn on the fallows [clearings] of your lands. We shall be obliged to you for that.

SPEECH AT THE END OF LORD DUNMORE'S WAR

Logan (Mingo)

[There is some doubt concerning the authenticity of this speech, but the following version, as transcribed by Thomas Jefferson in the *Notes on Virginia*, is traditionally dated 1774. The murder of virtually all of Logan's family by Colonel Cresap and his followers is what had initiated the war in the first place.]

I appeal to any white to say, if ever he entered Logan's cabin hungry, and he gave him not meat: if ever he came cold and naked and he clothed him not.

During the course of the last long bloody war, Logan, remained idle in his cabin, an advocate for peace. Such was my love for the whites, that my countrymen pointed as they passed, and said, "Logan is the friend of white men."

I had even thought to have lived with you, but for the injuries of one man. Col. Cresap, the last spring, in cold blood, and unprovoked, murdered all the relations of Logan; not even sparing my women and children.

There runs not a drop of my blood in the veins of any living creature. This called on me for revenge. I have sought it. I have killed many. I have fully glutted my vengeance. For my country, I rejoice at the beams of peace. But do not harbor a thought that mine is the joy of fear. Logan never felt fear. He will not turn on his heel to save his life. Who is there to mourn for Logan?—Not one!

From Samuel G. Drake, *Indian Biography* (Boston, 1832), pp. 163–64.

SPEECH TO THE BRITISH AT A COUNCIL IN DETROIT, NOVEMBER, 1781

Captain Pipe (Delaware)

"Father!"—he began; and here he paused, turned round to the audience with a most sarcastic look, and then proceeded in a lower tone, as addressing *them*—"I have said *father*, though indeed I do not know why I should call *him* so—I have never known any father but the French —I have considered the English only as brothers. But as this name is imposed upon us, I shall make use of it and say—

"Father"—fixing his eyes again on the Commandant.—"Some time ago you put a war-hatchet into my hands, saying, 'take this weapon and try it on the heads of my enemies, the Long-Knives, and let me know afterwards if it was sharp and good.'

"Father!—At the time when you gave me this weapon, I had neither cause nor wish to go to war against a foe who had done me no injury. But you say you are my father—and call me your child—and in obedience to you I received the hatchet. I knew that if I did not obey you, you would withhold from me the necessaries of life, which I could procure nowhere but here.

"Father! You may perhaps think me a fool, for risking my life at your bidding—and that in a cause in which I have no prospect of gaining any thing. For it is your cause, and not mine—you have raised a quarrel among yourselves—and you ought to fight it out— It is *your* concern to fight the Long-Knives—You should not compel

From B. B. Thatcher, *Indian Biography* (New York, 1845), Vol. 2, pp. 146-48.

your children, the Indians, to expose themselves to danger for your sake.

"Father!—Many lives have already been lost on *your account*—The tribes have suffered, and been weakened—Children have lost parents and brothers—Wives have lost husbands—It is not known how many more may perish before *your* war will be at an end.

"Father!—I have said, you may perhaps think me a fool, for thus thoughtlessly rushing on your enemy! Do not believe this, Father: Think not that I want sense to convince me, that although you now pretend to keep up a perpetual enmity to the Long-Knives, you may, before long, conclude a peace with them.

"Father! You say you love your children, the Indians.—This you have often told them; and indeed it is your interest to say so to them, that you may have them at your service.

"But, Father! Who of us can believe that you can love a people of a different colour from your own, better than those who have a white skin, like yourselves?

"Father! Pay attention to what I am going to say. While you, Father, are setting me on your enemy, much in the same manner as a hunter sets his dog on the game; while I am in the act of rushing on that enemy of yours, with the bloody destructive weapon you gave me, I may, perchance, happen to look back to the place from whence you started me, and what shall I see? Perhaps I may see my father shaking hands with the Long-Knives; yes, with those very people he now calls his enemies. I may *then* see him laugh at my folly for having obeyed his orders; and yet I am now risking my life at his command!—Father! keep what I have said in remembrance.

"Now, Father! here is what has been done with the hatchet you gave me" [handing the stick with the scalps on it]. "I have done with the hatchet what you ordered me to do, and found it sharp. Nevertheless, I did not do all that I might have done. No, I did not. My heart failed within me. I felt compassion for your enemy. Innocence had no part in your quarrels; therefore I distinguished—I spared. I took some live flesh, which, while I was bringing to you, I spied one of your large canoes, on which I put it for you. In a few days you will receive this flesh, and find that the skin is of the same color with your own.

"Father! I hope you will not destroy what I have saved. You, Father, have the means of preserving that which would perish with us from want. The warrior is poor, and his cabin is always empty; but your house, Father, is always full."

LETTER TO PRESIDENT WASHINGTON, 1790

Big Tree, Cornplanter, and Half-Town (Seneca)

Father: **The voice** of the Seneca nations speaks to you; the great counsellor, in whose heart the wise men of all the *thirteen fires* [13 U.S.] have placed their wisdom. It may be very small in your ears, and we, therefore, entreat you to hearken with attention; for we are able to speak of things which are to us very great.

When your army entered the country of the Six Nations, we called you the *town destroyer;* to this day, when your name is heard, our women look behind them and turn pale, and our children cling close to the necks of their mothers.

When our chiefs returned from Fort Stanwix, and laid before our council what had been done there, our nation was surprised to hear how great a country you had compelled them to give up to you, without your paying to us any thing for it. Every one said, that your hearts were yet swelled with resentment against us for what had happened during the war, but that one day you would consider it with more kindness. We asked each other, *What have we done to deserve such severe chastisement?*

Father: when you kindled your 13 fires separately, the wise men assembled at them told us that you were all brothers; the children of one great father, who regarded the red people as his children. They called us brothers, and invited us to his protection. They told

From Samuel G. Drake, *Biography and History of the Indians of North America,* 11th ed. (Boston, 1841), pp. 609–11.

us that he resided beyond the great water where the sun first rises; and that he was a king whose power no people could resist, and that his goodness was as bright as the sun. What they said went to our hearts. We accepted the invitation, and promised to obey him. What the Seneca nation promises, they faithfully perform. When you refused obedience to that king, he commanded us to assist his beloved men in making you sober. In obeying him, we did no more than yourselves had led us to promise. We were deceived; but your people teaching us to confide in that king, had helped to deceive us; and we now appeal to your breast. *Is all the blame ours?*

Father: when we saw that we had been deceived, and heard the invitation which you gave us to draw near to the fire you had kindled, and talk with you concerning peace, we made haste towards it. You told us you could crush us to nothing; and you demanded from us a great country, as the price of that peace which you had offered to us: *as if our want of strength had destroyed our rights.* Our chiefs had felt your power, and were unable to contend against you, and they therefore gave up that country. What they agreed to has bound our nation, but your anger against us must by this time be cooled, and although our strength is not increased, nor your power become less, we ask you to consider calmly—*Were the terms dictated to us by your commissioners reasonable and just? . . .*

Father: you have said that we were in your hand, and that by closing it you could crush us to nothing. Are you determined to crush us? If you are, tell us so; that those of our nation who have become your children, and have determined to die so, may know what to do. In this case, one chief has said, he would ask you to put him out of his pain. Another, who will not think of dying by the hand of his father, or his brother, has said he will retire to the Chataughque, eat of the fatal root, and sleep with his fathers in peace.

All the land we have been speaking of belonged to the Six Nations. No part of it ever belonged to the king of England, and he could not give it to you.

Hear us once more. At Fort Stanwix we agreed to deliver up those of our people who should do you any wrong, and that you might try them and punish them according to your law. We delivered up two men accordingly. But instead of trying them according to your law, the lowest of your people took them from your magistrate, and put them immediately to death. It is just to punish the murder with death; but the Senecas will not deliver up their people to men who disregard the treaties of their own nation.

RELATIONS WITH THE UNITED STATES AND BRITAIN

Blue Jacket (Shawnee)

[During President Thomas Jefferson's second administration (1805–9), relations with Britain worsened rapidly, and the Indians of the Great Lakes region found themselves, as during the Revolution, caught between two hostile white camps, both seeking their allegiance. All the while they were being overrun by American settlers who had little regard for what land they seized or how they went about it. Tecumseh and his brother, the Prophet, had gained a wide and restless following among many tribes, causing much apprehension among frontier communities. The governor of Ohio sought to learn the intentions of the Indians through commissioners sent to a council at Greenville in September, 1807. Blue jacket gave the following reply to the commissioners' inquiries.]

Brethren—We are seated who heard you yesterday. You will get a true relation, as far as we and our connections can give it, who are as follows: Shawanoes, Wyandots, Potawatamies, Tawas, Chippewas, Winnepaus, Malominese, Malockese, Secawgoes, and one more from the north of the Chippewas. *Brethren*—you see all these men sitting before you, who now speak to you.

About eleven days ago we had a council, at which the tribe of Wyandots (the elder brother of the red people) spoke and said God had kindled a fire and all sat around it. In this council we

From Benjamin Drake, *Life of Tecumseh, and of His Brother, the Prophet* (Cincinnati, 1841), pp. 94–96.

talked over the treaties with the French and the Americans. The Wyandot said, the French formerly marked a line along the Alleghany mountains, southerly, to Charleston, (S.C.) No man was to pass it from either side. When the Americans came to settle over the line, the English told the Indians to unite and drive off the French, until the war came on between the British and the Americans, when it was told them that king George, by his officers, directed them to unite and drive the Americans back.

After the treaty of peace between the English and Americans, the summer before Wayne's army came out, the English held a council with the Indians, and told them if they would turn out and unite as one man, they might surround the Americans like deer in a ring of fire and destroy them all. The Wyandot spoke further in the council. We see, said he, there is like to be war between the English and our white brethren, the Americans. Let us unite and consider the sufferings we have undergone, from interfering in the wars of the English. They have often promised to help us, and at last, when we could not withstand the army that came against us, and went to the English fort for refuge, the English told us, "I cannot let you in; you are painted too much, my children." It was then we saw the British dealt treacherously with us. We now see them going to war again. We do not know what they are going to fight for. Let us, my brethren, not interfere, was the speech of the Wyandot.

Further, the Wyandot said, I speak to you, my little brother, the Shawanoes at Greenville, and to you, our little brothers all around. You appear to be at Greenville to serve the *Supreme Ruler* of the universe. Now send forth your speeches to all our brethren far around us, and let us unite to seek for that which shall be for our eternal welfare; and unite ourselves in a band of perpetual brotherhood. These, brethren, are the sentiments of all the men who sit around you: they all adhere to what the elder brother, the Wyandot, has said, and these are their sentiments. It is not that they are afraid of their white brethren, but that they desire peace and harmony, and not that their white brethren could put them to great necessity, for their former arms were bows and arrows, by which they got their living.

SPEECH TO GOVERNOR WILLIAM HENRY HARRISON AT VINCENNES, AUGUST 12, 1810

Tecumseh (Shawnee)

[Callous indifference to Indian affairs by the Jefferson and Madison administrations, together with the brutality of frontier whites, enabled Tecumseh and the Prophet to gain numerous adherents among trans-Allegheny tribes in a loose confederation aimed at curbing white settlement. His contention was that all the tribes held the land in common, and therefore the common heritage could not be bartered away piecemeal by any one tribe.]

It is true I am a Shawanee. My forefathers were warriors. Their son is a warrior. From them I only take my existence; from my tribe I take nothing. I am the maker of my own fortune; and oh! that I could make that of my red people, and of my country, as great as the conceptions of my mind, when I think of the Spirit that rules the universe. I would not then come to Governor Harrison, to ask him to tear the treaty, and to obliterate the landmark; but I would say to him, Sir, you have liberty to return to your own country. The being within, communing with past ages, tells me,

From Samuel G. Drake, *Biography and History of the Indians of North America*, 11th ed. (Boston, 1841), pp. 617–18.

that once, nor until lately, there was no white man on this continent. That it then all belonged to red men, children of the same parents, placed on it by the Great Spirit that made them, to keep it, to traverse it, to enjoy its productions, and to fill it with the same race. Once a happy race. Since made miserable by the white people, who are never contented, but always encroaching. The way, and the only way to check and stop this evil, is, for all the red men to unite in claiming a common and equal right in the land, as it was at first, and should be yet; for it never was divided, but belongs to all, for the use of each. That no part has a right to sell, even to each other, much less to strangers; those who want all, and will not do with less. The white people have no right to take the land from the Indians, because they had it first; it is theirs. They may sell, but all must join. Any sale not made by all is not valid. The late sale is bad. It was made by a part only. Part do not know how to sell. It requires all to make a bargain for all. All red men have equal rights to the unoccupied land. The right of occupancy is as good in one place as in another. There cannot be two occupations in the same place. The first excludes all others. It is not so in hunting or travelling; for there the same ground will serve many, as they may follow each other all day; but the camp is stationary, and that is occupancy. It belongs to the first who sits down on his blanket or skins, which he has thrown upon the ground, and till he leaves it no other has a right.

REFUSAL OF A LAND-PURCHASE OFFER, IN A SPEECH MADE AT BUFFALO CREEK, NEW YORK, IN MAY, 1811

Red Jacket (Seneca)

Brother!—We opened our ears to the talk you lately delivered to us, at our council-fire. In doing important business it is best not to tell long stories, but to come to it in a few words. We therefore shall not repeat your talk, which is fresh in our minds. We have well considered it, and the advantages and disadvantages of your offers. We request your attention to our answer, which is not from the speaker alone, but from all the Sachems and Chiefs now around our council-fire.

Brother!—We know that great men, as well as great nations, have different interests and different minds, and do not see the same light—but we hope our answer will be agreeable to you and your employers.

Brother!—Your application for the purchase of our lands is to our minds very extraordinary. It has been made in a crooked manner. You have not walked in the straight path pointed out by the great Council of your nation. You have no writings from your great Father, the President. In making up our minds we have looked back, and remembered how the Yorkers purchased our lands in former times. They bought them, piece after piece—for a little money paid to a few men in our nation, and not to all our

From B. B. Thatcher, *Indian Biography* (New York, 1845), Vol. 2, pp. 282–84.

brethren—until our planting and hunting-grounds have become very small, and if we sell *them*, we know not where to spread our blankets.

Brother!—You tell us your employers have purchased of the Council of Yorkers, a right to buy our lands. We do not understand how this can be. The lands do not belong to the Yorkers; they are ours, and were given to us by the Great Spirit.

Brother!—We think it strange that you should jump over the lands of our brethren in the East, to come to our council-fire so far off, to get our lands. When we sold our lands in the East to the white people, we determined never to sell those we kept, which are as small as we can comfortably live on.

Brother!—You want us to travel with you and look for new lands. If we should sell our lands and move off into a distant country towards the setting sun, we should be looked upon in the country to which we go, as foreigners and strangers. We should be despised by the red, as well as the white men, and we should soon be surrounded by the white people, who will there also kill our game, and come upon our lands and try to get them from us.

Brother!—We are determined not to sell our lands, but to continue on them. We like them. They are fruitful, and produce us corn in abundance for the support of our women and children, and grass and herbs for our cattle.

Brother!—At the treaties held for the purchase of our lands, the white men, with sweet voices and smiling faces, told us they loved us, and that they would not cheat us, but that the king's children on the other side of the lake would cheat us. When we go on the other side of the lake, the king's children tell us *your* people will cheat us. These things puzzle our heads, and we believe that the Indians must take care of themselves, and not trust either in your people, or in the king's children.

Brother!—At a late council we requested our agents to tell you that we would not sell our lands, and we think you have not spoken to our agents, or they would have told you so, and we should not have met you at our council-fire at this time.

Brother!—The white people buy and sell false rights to our lands, and your employers have, you say, paid a great price for their rights. They must have a plenty of money, to spend it in buying false rights to lands belonging to Indians. The loss of it will not hurt them, but our lands are of great value to us, and we wish you to go back with our talk to your employers, and tell them and the Yorkers that they have no right to buy and sell false rights to our lands.

Brother!—We hope you clearly understand the ideas we have offered. This is all we have to say.

LETTER TO WILLIAM EUSTIS, SECRETARY OF WAR, DECEMBER 19, 1811

Farmers-Brother (Seneca)

To the Honorable William Eustis, secretary at war.

The sachems and chief warriors of the Seneca nation of Indians, understanding you are the person appointed by the great council of your nation to manage and conduct the affairs of the several nations of Indians with whom you are at peace and on terms of friendship, come, at this time, as children to a father, to lay before you the trouble which we have on our minds.

Brother, we do not think it best to multiply words: we will, therefore, tell you what our complaint is.—Brother, listen to what we say: Some years since, we held a treaty at Bigtree, near the Genesee River. This treaty was called by our great father, the president of the United States. He sent an agent, Col. Wadsworth, to attend this treaty, for the purpose of advising us in the business, and seeing that we had justice done us. At this treaty we sold to Robert Morris the greatest part of our country; the sum he gave us was 100,000 dollars. The commissioners who were appointed on your part, advised us to place this money in the hands of our great father, the president of the United States. He told us our father loved his red children, and would take care of our money, and plant it in a field where it would bear seed forever, as long as trees grow, or waters run. Our money has heretofore been of great

From Samuel G. Drake, *Biography and History of the Indians of North America*, 11th ed. (Boston, 1841), pp. 605–6.

service to us; it has helped us to support our old people, and our women and children; but we are told the field where our money was planted is become barren.—Brother, we do not understand your way of doing business. This thing is very heavy on our minds. We mean to hold our white brethren of the United States by the hand; but this weight lies heavy; we hope you will remove it.—We have heard of the bad conduct of our brothers towards the setting sun. We are sorry for what they have done; but you must not blame us; we have had no hand in this bad business. They have had bad people among them. It is your enemies have done this.— We have persuaded our agent to take this talk to your great council. He knows our situations, and will speak our minds.

SPEECH ON THE FUTILITY OF FIGHTING THE AMERICANS IN THE WAR OF 1812

Between-the-Logs (Wyandot)

Brothers!—I am directed by my American father to inform you, that if you reject the advice given you, he will march here with a large army, and if he should find any of the red people opposing him in his passage through this country, he will trample them under his feet. You cannot stand before him.

And now for myself, I earnestly intreat you to consider the good talk I have brought, and listen to it. Why would you devote yourselves, your women, and your children, to destruction? Let me tell you, if you should defeat the American army this time, you have not done. Another will come on, and if you defeat that, still another will appear that you cannot withstand; one that will come like the waves of the great water, and overwhelm you, and sweep you from the face of the earth. If you doubt the account I give of the force of the Americans, you can send some of your people in whom you have confidence, to examine their army and navy. They shall be permitted to return in safety. The truth is, your British father tells you lies, and deceives you. He boasts of the few victories he gains, but he never tells you of his defeats, of his armies being slaughtered, and his vessels taken on the big water. He keeps all these things to himself.

And now, father, let me address a few words to you. Your re-

From B. B. Thatcher, *Indian Biography* (New York, 1845), Vol. 2, pp. 218–19.

quest shall be granted. I will bear your message to my American father. It is true none of your children appear willing to forsake your standard, and it will be the worse for them. You compare the Americans to ground-hogs, and complain of their mode of fighting. I must confess that a ground-hog is a very difficult animal to contend with. He has such sharp teeth, such an inflexible temper, and such an unconquerable spirit, that he is truly a dangerous enemy, especially when he is in his own hole. But, father, let me tell you, you can have your wish. Before many days, you will see the ground-hog floating on yonder lake, paddling his canoe towards your hole; and then, father, you will have an opportunity of attacking your formidable enemy in any way you may think best.

SPEECH TO AMERICAN COMMISSIONERS IN RESPONSE TO THE ALLEGATION THAT INDIANS HAD BROKEN TREATY OBLIGATIONS, JULY, 1815

Black Thunder (Fox)

My father, restrain your feelings, and hear calmly what I shall say. I shall say it plainly. I shall not speak with fear and trembling. I have never injured you, and innocence can feel no fear. I turn to you all, red-skins and white-skins—where is the man who will appear as my accuser? Father, I understand not clearly how things are working. I have just been set at liberty. Am I again to be plunged into bondage? Frowns are all around me; but I am incapable of change. You, perhaps, may be ignorant of what I tell you; but it is a truth, which I call heaven and earth to witness. It is a fact which can easily be proved, that I have been assailed in almost every possible way that pride, fear, feeling, or interest, could touch me—that I have been pushed to the last to raise the tomahawk against you; but all in vain. I never could be made to feel that you were my enemy. *If this be the conduct of an enemy, I shall never be your friend.* You are acquainted with my removal above Prairie des Chiens. I went, and formed a settlement, and called my warriors around me.

From Samuel G. Drake, *Biography and History of the Indians of North America*, 11th ed. (Boston, 1841), p. 632.

We took counsel, and from that counsel we never have departed. We smoked, and resolved to make common cause with the U.States. I sent you the pipe—it resembled this—and I sent it by the Missouri, that the Indians of the Mississippi might not know what we were doing. You received it. I then told you that your friends should be my friends—that your enemies should be my enemies—and that I only awaited your signal to make war. *If this be the conduct of an enemy, I shall never be your friend.*—Why do I tell you this? Because it is a truth, and a melancholy truth, that the good things which men do are often buried in the ground, while their evil deeds are stripped naked, and exposed to the world. When I came here, I came to you in friendship. I little thought I should have had to defend myself. I have no defence to make. If I were guilty, I should have come prepared; but I have ever held you by the hand, and I am come without excuses. If I had fought against you, I would have told you so: but I have nothing now to say here in your councils, except to repeat what I said before to my great father, the president of your nation. You heard it, and no doubt remember it. It was simply this. My lands can never be surrendered; I was cheated, and basely cheated, in the contract; I will not surrender my country but with my life. Again I call heaven and earth to witness, and I smoke this pipe in evidence of my sincerity. If you are sincere, you will receive it from me. My only desire is, that we should smoke it together—that I should grasp your sacred hand, and I claim for myself and my tribe the protection of your country. When this pipe touches your lip, may it operate as a blessing upon all my tribe.—*May the smoke rise like a cloud, and carry away with it all the animosities which have arisen between us.*

LETTER TO THE GOVERNOR OF PENNSYLVANIA, FEBRUARY, 1822

Cornplanter (Seneca)

I feel it my duty to send a speech to the Governor of Pennsylvania at this time, and inform him of the place where I was from—which was at Connewaugus on the Genesee River.

When I was a child I played with the butterfly, the grasshopper, and the frogs; and as I grew up I began to pay some attention, and play with the Indian boys in the neighbourhood, and they took notice of my skin being of a different colour from theirs, and spoke about it. I inquired of my mother the cause, and she told me that my father was a residenter in Albany. I still eat my victuals out of a bark dish. I grew up to be a young man, and married me a wife, and I had no kettle nor gun. I then knew where my father lived, and went to see him, and found he was a white man, and spoke the English language. He gave me victuals while I was at his house, but when I started home, he gave me no provision to eat on the way. He gave me neither kettle nor gun, neither did he tell me that the United States were about to rebel against the Government of England.

I will now tell you, brothers, who are in session of the Legislature of Pennsylvania, that the Great Spirit has made known to me that I have been wicked; and the cause thereof has been the

From Samuel G. Drake, *Biography and History of the Indians of North America*, 11th ed. (Boston, 1841), pp. 611–13.

revolutionary war in America. The cause of Indians being led into sin at that time, was that many of them were in the practice of drinking and getting intoxicated. Great Britain requested us to join with them in the conflict against the Americans, and promised the Indians land and liquor. I myself was opposed to joining in the conflict, as I had nothing to do with the difficulty that existed between the two parties. I have now informed you how it happened that the Indians took a part in the revolution, and will relate to you some circumstances that occurred after the close of the war. General Putnam, who was then at Philadelphia, told me there was to be a council at Fort Stanwix; and the Indians requested me to attend on behalf of the Six Nations, which I did, and there met with three commissioners who had been appointed to hold the council. They told me that they would inform me of the cause of the revolution, which I requested them to do minutely. They then said that it originated on account of the heavy taxes that had been imposed upon them by the British Government, which had been for fifty years increasing upon them; that the Americans had grown weary thereof, and refused to pay, which affronted the king. There had likewise a difficulty taken place about some tea which they wished me not to use, as it had been one of the causes that many people had lost their lives. And the British Government now being affronted, the war commenced, and the cannons began to roar in our country.

General Putnam then told me at the council at Fort Stanwix, that by the late war the Americans had gained two objects: they had established themselves an independent nation, and had obtained some land to live upon, the division line of which from Great Britain run through the Lakes. I then spoke, and said I wanted some land for the Indians to live on, and General Putnam said that it should be granted, and I should have land in the State of New York for the Indians. He then encouraged me to use my endeavours to pacify the Indians generally; and as he considered it an arduous task, wished to know what pay I would require. I replied, that I would use my endeavours to do as he requested with the Indians, and for pay therefor I would take land. I told him not to pay me money or dry goods, but land. And for having attended thereto I received the tract of land on which I now live, which was presented to me by Governor Mifflin. I told General Putnam that I wished the Indians to have the exclusive privilege of the deer and wild game, to which he assented; I also wished the Indians to have the privilege of hunting in the woods and making fires, which he likewise assented to.

The treaty that was made at the aforementioned council has been broken by some of the white people, which I now intend acquainting the Governor with. Some white people are not willing that Indians should hunt any more, whilst others are satisfied therewith; and those white people who reside near our reservation tell us that the woods are theirs, and they have obtained them

America before Columbus—Burial Ground of the Algonquins.

The town of Secota
in the present
Beaufort County,
North Carolina,
around 1500.

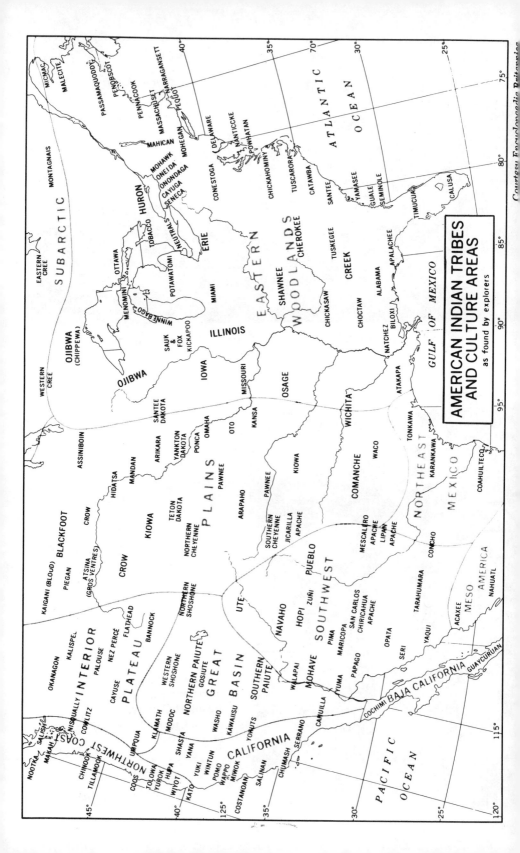

AMERICAN INDIAN TRIBES
AND CULTURE AREAS

as found by explorers

Courtesy Encyclopaedia Britannica

Two Creeks who visited George Washington in New York in 1790 to discuss land cessions. Drawings by John Trumbull.

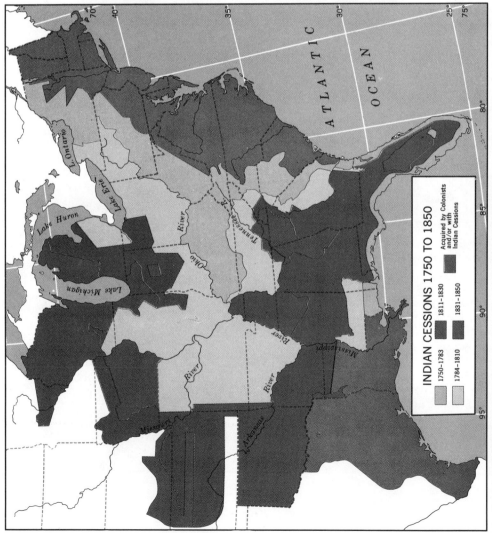

INDIAN CESSIONS 1750 TO 1850

1750-1783

1784-1810

1811-1830

1831-1850

Acquired by Colonists
and/or with
Indian Cessions

A Comanche capturing a wild horse. Drawing by George Catlin.

Drawing by George Catlin of a Plains Indian's horse being charged by a bison. Catlin lived among the Indians in the 1830's.

INDIAN CESSIONS 1850 TO 1900

Land ceded
prior to 1850

Ceded by Indians
1850-1870

Land taken by U.S. Govt.
without Indian Cession

Ceded by Indians
1871-1890

Land to which Indians possessed
original title 1890

Courtesy
Encyclopaedia
Britannica

Captain Jack, Chief of the Modocs, *ca.* 1897.

Old Joseph, father of the famous
Chief Joseph who led the 1877
Nez Percé retreat.

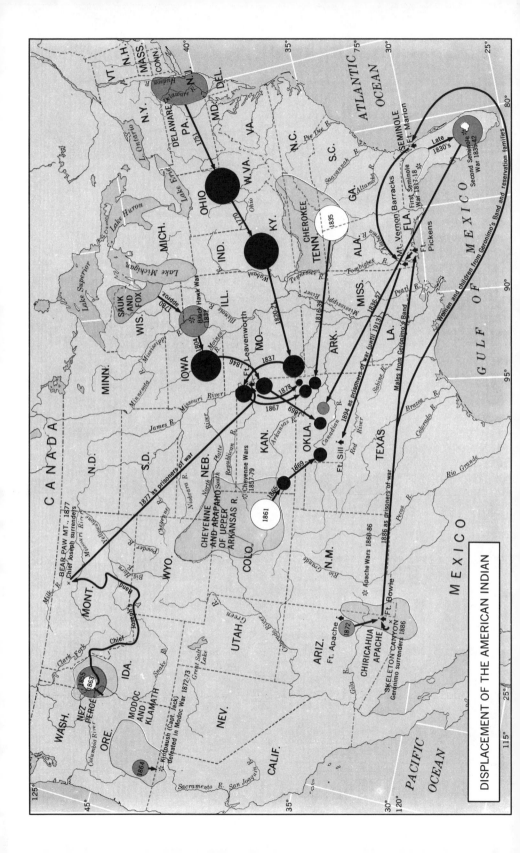

DISPLACEMENT OF THE AMERICAN INDIAN

from the Governor. The treaty has also been broken by the white people using their endeavours to destroy all the wolves, which was not spoken about in the council at Fort Stanwix by General Putnam, but has originated lately.

It has been broken again, which is of recent origin. White people get credit from Indians, and do not pay them honestly according to agreement. In another respect also, it has been broken by white people residing near my dwelling; for when I plant melons and vines in my field, they take them as their own. It has been broken again, by white people using their endeavours to obtain our pine trees from us. We have very few pine trees on our land in the State of New York; and whites and Indians often get into dispute respecting them. There is also a great quantity of whisky brought near our reservation, and the Indians obtain it and become drunken.

Another circumstance has taken place which is very trying to me, and I wish for the interference of the Governor. The white people who live at Warren, called upon me some time ago to pay taxes for my land, which I objected to, as I never had been called upon for that purpose before; and having refused to pay, they became irritated, called upon me frequently, and at length brought four guns with them and seized our cattle. I still refused to pay, and was not willing to let the cattle go. After a time of dispute they returned home, and I understood the militia was ordered out to enforce the collection of the tax. I went to Warren, and, to avert the impending difficulty, was obliged to give my note for the tax, the amount of which was forty-three dollars and seventy-nine cents. It is my desire that the Governor will exempt me from paying taxes for my land to white people; and also to cause that the money I am now obliged to pay be refunded to me, as I am very poor. The Governor is the person who attends to the situation of the people, and I wish him to send a person to Alleghany, that I may inform him of the particulars of our situation, and he be authorised to instruct the white people in what manner to conduct themselves towards the Indians.

The Government has told us that, when difficulties arose between the Indians and the white people, they would attend to having them removed. We are now in a trying situation, and I wish the Governor to send a person authorised to attend thereto, the fore part of next summer, about the time that the grass has grown big enough for pasture.

The Governor formerly requested me to pay attention to the Indians, and take care of them. We are now arrived at a situation in which I believe the Indians cannot exist unless the Governor should comply with my request, and send a person authorised to treat between us and the white people, the approaching summer. I have now no more to speak.

WHY THE INDIANS WILL NOT GIVE UP THEIR LAND, 1827

Känakûk (Kickapoo)

[In 1815, the Kickapoo tribe had ceded its traditional lands in Illinois to the United States. But as the years passed, they proved reluctant to move to their proposed new home in Missouri, as it was located among their long-time enemies, the Osage. One of the more persuasive voices urging them to remain in Illinois was the prophet Känakûk, who had attracted a devoted following owing to the revelations he claimed to have received directly from the "Great Spirit." In the following remarks to General William Clark at St. Louis, he explains the position of his people.]

My father, you call all the redskins your children. When we have children, we treat them well. That is the reason I make this long talk to get you to take pity on us and let us remain where we are.

My father, I wish after my talk is over you would write to my Great Father, the president, that we have a desire to remain a little longer where we now are. I have explained to you that we have thrown all our badness away and keep the good path. I wish our Great Father could hear that. I will now talk to my Great Father, the president.

My Great Father, I don't know if you are the right chief, because

From *Fourteenth Annual Report of the Bureau of American Ethnology* (1896), Part 2, pp. 685–96.

I have heard some things go wrong. I wish you to reflect on our situation and let me know. I want to talk to you mildly and in peace, so that we may understand each other. When I saw the Great Spirit, he told me to throw all our bad acts away. We did so. Some of our chiefs said the land belonged to us, the Kickapoos; but this is not what the Great Spirit told me—the lands belong to him. The Great Spirit told me that no people owned the lands—that all was his, and not to forget to tell the white people that when we went into council. When I saw the Great Spirit, he told me, Mention all this to your Great Father. He will take pity on your situation and let you remain on the lands where you are for some years, when you will be able to get through all the bad places (the marks in the figure), and where you will get to a clear piece of land where you will all live happy. When I talked to the Great Spirit, he told me to make my warriors throw their tomahawks in the bad place. I did so, and every night and morning I raise my hands to the Great Spirit and pray to him to give us success. I expect, my father, that God has put me in a good way—that our children shall see their sisters and brothers and our women see their children. They will grow up and travel and see their totems. The Great Spirit told me, "Our old men had totems. They were good and had many totems. Now you have scarcely any. If you follow my advice, you will soon have totems again." Say this to my Great Father for me.

My father, since I talked with the Great Spirit, our women and children and ourselves, we have not such good clothes, but we don't mind that. We think of praying every day to the Great Spirit to get us safe to the good lands, where all will be peace and happiness.

My father, the Great Spirit holds all the world in his hands. I pray to him that we may not be removed from our land until we can see and talk to all our totems. . . .

My father, when I left my women and children, they told me, "As you are going to see our Great Father, tell him to let us alone and let us eat our victuals with a good heart."

My father, since my talk with the Great Spirit we have nothing cooked until the middle of the day. The children get nothing in the morning to eat. We collect them all to pray to the Great Spirit to make our hearts pure, and then eat. We bring our children up to be good.

My father, I will tell you all I know. I will put nothing on my back. God told me, Whenever you make a talk, tell everything true. Keep nothing behind, and then you will find everything go right.

My father, when I talked with the Great Spirit, he did not tell me to sell my lands, because I did not know how much was a dollar's worth, or the game that run on it. If he told me so, I would tell you to-day.

My father, you have heard what I have said. I have represented to you our situation, and ask you to take pity on us and let us remain where we are. . . .

My father, I have shown you in the lines I have made the bad places. Our warriors even are afraid of those dark places you see there. That is the reason they threw their tomahawks aside and put up their hands to the Great Spirit.

My father, every time we eat we raise our hands to the Great Spirit to give us success.

My father, we are sitting by each other here to tell the truth. If you write anything wrong, the Great Spirit will know it. If I say anything not true, the Great Spirit will hear it.

My father, you know how to write and can take down what is said for your satisfaction. I can not; all I do is through the Great Spirit for the benefit of my women and children.

My father, everything belongs to the Great Spirit. If he chooses to make the earth shake, or turn it over, all the skins, white and red, can not stop it. I have done. I trust to the Great Spirit.

RESPONSE TO A MESSAGE FROM PRESIDENT ANDREW JACKSON CONCERNING INDIAN REMOVAL, 1830

Speckled Snake (Cherokee)

Brothers! We have heard the talk of our great father; it is very kind. He says he loves his red children. *Brothers!* When the white man first came to these shores, the Muscogees gave him land, and kindled him a fire to make him comfortable; and when the pale faces of the south made war on him, their young men drew the tomahawk, and protected his head from the scalping knife. But when the white man had warmed himself before the Indian's fire, and filled himself with the Indian's hominy, he became very large; he stopped not for the mountain tops, and his feet covered the plains and the valleys. His hands grasped the eastern and the western sea. Then he became our great father. He loved his red children; but said, "You must move a little farther, lest I should, by accident, tread on you." With one foot he pushed the red man over the Oconee, and with the other he trampled down the graves of his fathers. But our great father still loved his red children, and he soon made them another talk. He said much; but it all meant nothing, but "move a little farther; you are too near me." I have heard a great many talks from our great father, and they all begun and ended the same. *Brothers!* When he made us a talk on a former occasion, he said,

From Samuel G. Drake, *Biography and History of the Indians of North America*, 11th ed. (Boston, 1841), p. 450.

"Get a little farther; go beyond the Oconee and the Oakmulgee; there is a pleasant country." He also said, "It shall be yours forever." Now he says, "The land you live on is not yours; go beyond the Mississippi; there is game; there you may remain while the grass grows or the water runs." *Brothers!* Will not our great father come there also? He loves his red children, and his tongue is not forked.

FAREWELL LETTER TO THE AMERICAN PEOPLE, 1832

George W. Harkins (Choctaw)

[In December, 1830, the Choctaws had signed away their last remaining territory in the state of Mississippi and faced the prospect of moving west to Indian Territory. It was with much regret that the tribe members left their old homes; and the move, ill-provided for by the U.S. Government, came in midwinter. As the journey was about to take place, one of the tribal leaders voiced the sentiments of his people regarding the treaty and the decision to go west.]

To the American People.

It is with considerable diffidence that I attempt to address the American people, knowing and feeling sensibly my incompetency; and believing that your highly and well improved minds could not be well entertained by the address of a Choctaw. But having determined to emigrate west of the Mississippi river this fall, I have thought proper in bidding you farewell, to make a few remarks of my views and the feelings that actuate me on the subject of our removal.

Believing that our all is at stake and knowing that you readily sympathize with the distressed of every country, I confidently throw myself on your indulgence and ask you to listen patiently. I do not arrogate to myself the prerogative of deciding upon the expediency of the late treaty, yet I feel bound as a Choctaw, to

From *The American Indian*, December, 1926.

give a distinct expression of my feelings on that interesting, (and to the Choctaws) all important subject.

We were hedged in by two evils, and we chose that which we thought least. Yet we could not recognize the right that the state of Mississippi had assumed to legislate for us. Although the legislature of the state were qualified to make laws for their own citizens, that did not qualify them to become law makers to a people who were so dissimilar in manners and customs as the Choctaws are to the Mississippians. Admitting that they understood the people, could they remove that mountain of prejudice that has ever obstructed the streams of justice, and prevented their salutary influence from reaching my devoted countrymen? We as Choctaws rather chose to suffer and be free, than live under the degrading influence of laws, where our voice could not be heard in their formation.

Much as the state of Mississippi has wronged us, I cannot find in my heart any other sentiment than an ardent wish for her prosperity and happiness.

I could cheerfully hope that those of another age and generation may not feel the effects of those oppressive measures that have been so illiberally dealt out to us; and that peace and happiness may be their reward. Amid the gloom and honors of the present separation, we are cheered with a hope that ere long we shall reach our destined home, and that nothing short of the basest acts of treachery will ever be able to wrest it from us, and that we may live free. Although your ancestors won freedom on the fields of danger and glory, our ancestors owned it as their birthright, and we have had to purchase it from you as the vilest slaves buy their freedom.

Yet it is said that our present movements are our own voluntary acts—such is not the case. We found ourselves like a benighted stranger, following false guides, until he was surrounded on every side, with fire or water. The fire was certain destruction, and feeble hope was left him of escaping by water. A distant view of the opposite shore encourages the hope; to remain would be utter annihilation. Who would hesitate, or would say that his plunging into the water was his own voluntary act? Painful in the extreme is the mandate of our expulsion. We regret that it should proceed from the mouth of our professed friend, and for whom our blood was commingled with that of his bravest warriors, on the field of danger and death.

But such is the instability of professions. The man who said that he would plant a stake and draw a line around us, that never should be passed, was the first to say he could not guard the lines, and drew up the stake and wiped out all traces of the line. I will not conceal from you my fears, that the present grounds may be removed—I have my foreboding—who of us can tell after witnessing what has already been done, what the next force may be.

I ask you in the name of justice, for repose for myself and my injured people. Let us alone—we will not harm you, we want rest. We hope, in the name of justice, that another outrage may never be committed against us, and that we may for the future be cared for as children, and not driven about as beasts, which are benefitted by a change of pasture.

Taking an example from the American government, and knowing the happiness which its citizens enjoy, under the influence of mild republican institutions, it is the intention of our countrymen to form a government assimilated to that of our white breathern in the United States, as nearly as their condition will permit.

We know that in order to protect the rights and secure the liberties of the people, no government approximates so nearly to perfection as the one to which we have alluded. As east of the Mississippi we have been friends, so west we will cherish the same feelings with additional fervor; and although we may be removed to the desert, still we shall look with fine regard, upon those who have promised us their protection. Let that feeling be reciprocated.

Friends, my attachment to my native land is strong—that cord is now broken; and we must go forth as wanderers in a strange land! I must go—let me entreat you to regard us with feelings of kindness, and when the hand of oppression is stretched against us, let me hope that every part of the United States, filling the mountains and valleys, will echo and say stop, you have no power, we are the sovereign people, and our friends shall no more be disturbed. We ask you for nothing that is incompatible with your other duties.

We go forth sorrowful, knowing that wrong has been done. Will you extend to us your sympathizing regards until all traces of disagreeable oppositions are obliterated, and we again shall have confidence in the professions of our white brethern.

Here is the land of our progenitors, and here are their bones; they left them as a sacred deposit, and we have been compelled to venerate its trust; it is dear to us yet we cannot stay, my people are dear to me, with them I must go. Could I stay and forget them and leave them to struggle alone, unaided, unfriended, and forgotten by our great father? I should then be unworthy the name of a Choctaw, and be a disgrace to my blood. I must go with them; my destiny is cast among the Choctaw people. If they suffer, so will I; if they prosper, then I will rejoice. Let me again ask you to regard us with feelings of kindness.

FAREWELL SPEECH AT PRAIRIE DU CHIEN, WISCONSIN, AT THE END OF THE BLACK HAWK WAR, AUGUST 1835

Black Hawk (Sac-Potawatomi)

You have taken me prisoner with all my warriors. I am much grieved, for I expected, if I did not defeat you, to hold out much longer, and give you more trouble before I surrendered. I tried hard to bring you into ambush, but your last general understands Indian fighting. The first one was not so wise. When I saw that I could not beat you by Indian fighting, I determined to rush on you, and fight you face to face. I fought hard. But your guns were well aimed. The bullets flew like birds in the air, and whizzed by our ears like the wind through the trees in the winter. My warriors fell around me; it began to look dismal. I saw my evil day at hand. The sun rose dim on us in the morning, and at night it sunk in a dark cloud, and looked like a ball of fire. That was the last sun that shone on Black-hawk. His heart is dead, and no longer beats quick in his bosom.—He is now a prisoner to the white men; they will do with him as they wish. But he can stand torture, and is not afraid of death. He is no coward. Black-hawk is an Indian.

He has done nothing for which an Indian ought to be ashamed. He has fought for his countrymen, the squaws and papooses, against

From Samuel G. Drake, *Biography and History of the Indians of North America*, 11th ed. (Boston, 1841), p. 657.

white men, who came, year after year, to cheat them and take away their lands. You know the cause of our making war. It is known to all white men. They ought to be ashamed of it. The white men despise the Indians, and drive them from their homes. But the Indians are not deceitful. The white men speak bad of the Indian, and look at him spitefully. But the Indian does not tell lies; Indians do not steal.

An Indian, who is as bad as the white men, could not live in our nation; he would be put to death, and eat up by the wolves. The white men are bad schoolmasters; they carry false looks, and deal in false actions; they smile in the face of the poor Indian to cheat him; they shake them by the hand to gain their confidence, to make them drunk, to deceive them, and ruin our wives. We told them to let us alone, and keep away from us; but they followed on, and beset our paths, and they coiled themselves among us, like the snake. They poisoned us by their touch. We were not safe. We lived in danger. We were becoming like them, hypocrites and liars, adulterers, lazy drones, all talkers, and no workers.

We looked up to the Great Spirit. We went to our great father. We were encouraged. His great council gave us fair words and big promises; but we got no satisfaction. Things were growing worse. There were no deer in the forest. The opossum and beaver were fled; the springs were drying up, and our squaws and papooses without victuals to keep them from starving; we called a great council, and built a large fire. The spirit of our fathers arose and spoke to us to avenge our wrongs or die. We all spoke before the council fire. It was warm and pleasant. We set up the war-whoop, and dug up the tomahawk; our knives were ready, and the heart of Black-hawk swelled high in his bosom, when he led his warriors to battle. He is satisfied. He will go to the world of spirits contented. He has done his duty. His father will meet him there, and commend him.

Black-hawk is a true Indian, and disdains to cry like a woman. He feels for his wife, his children and friends. But he does not care for himself. He cares for his nation and the Indians. They will suffer. He laments their fate. The white men do not scalp the head; but they do worse—they poison the heart; it is not pure with them.—His countrymen will not be scalped, but they will, in a few years, become like the white men, so that you can't trust them, and there must be, as in the white settlements, nearly as many officers as men, to take care of them and keep them in order.

Farewell, my nation! Black-hawk tried to save you, and avenge your wrongs. He drank the blood of some of the whites. He has been taken prisoner, and his plans are stopped. He can do no more. He is near his end. His sun is setting, and he will rise no more. Farewell to Black-hawk.

SURRENDER OF A SEMINOLE BAND, 1841

Coacooche (Seminole)

[In mid-1841, the fifth year of the Seminole War in Florida, Coacooche, one of the chiefs and a few of his warriors were captured and brought in chains to Fort Brooke in Tampa Bay. In an interview with Colonel William Worth on July 4, he was persuaded to send some of his men to urge the remainder of the band to surrender or forfeit the chief's life. It was felt that if Coacooche, one of the more aggressive chiefs, gave in, others would soon follow suit. Within the forty days allotted, the rest of the band—about three hundred in all—began to come in. The first paragraph, below, was spoken to Colonel Worth. On hearing the colonel's reply that he must remain hostage, Coacooche directed the remaining remarks to his warriors.]

Coacooche rose, evidently struggling to suppress a feeling which made his manly form quiver with excitement: "I was once a boy," said he, in a subdued tone; "then I saw the white man afar off. I hunted in these woods, first with a bow and arrow; then with a rifle. I saw the white man, and was told he was my enemy. I could not shoot him as I would a wolf or a bear; yet like these he came upon me; horses, cattle, and fields, he took from me. He said he was my friend; he abused our women and children, and told us to go from the land. Still he gave me his hand in friendship; we took it; whilst taking it, he had a snake in the other;

From John T. Sprague, *The Origin, Progress, and Conclusion of the Florida War* (New York, 1848), Chapter 6.

his tongue was forked; he lied, and stung us. I asked but for a
small piece of these lands, enough to plant and to live upon, far
south, a spot where I could place the ashes of my kindred, a spot
only sufficient upon which I could lay my wife and child. This was
not granted me. I was put in prison; I escaped. I have been again
taken; you have brought me back; I am here; I feel the irons
in my heart. I have listened to your talk; you and your officers
have taken us by the hand in friendship. I thank you for bringing
me back; I can now see my warriors, my women and children;
the Great Spirit thanks you; the heart of the poor Indian thanks
you. We know but little; we have no books which tell all things;
but we have the Great Spirit, moon, and stars; these told me, last
night, you would be our friend. I give you my word; it is the word
of a warrior, a chief, a brave, it is the word of Coacooche. It is
true I have fought like a man, so have my warriors; but the whites
are too strong for us. I wish now to have my band around me and
go to Arkansas. You say I *must* end the war! Look at these irons!
can I go to my warriors? Coacooche chained! No; do not ask me
to see them. I never wish to tread upon my land unless I am free.
If I can go to them *unchained*, they will follow me in; but I fear
they will not obey me when I talk to them in irons. They will say
my heart is weak, I am afraid. Could I go free, they will surrender
and emigrate."

"Has not Coacooche," said he [to his warriors], "sat with you
by the council-fire at midnight, when the wolf and white man were
around us? Have I not led the war-dance, and sung the song of
the Seminole? Did not the spirits of our mothers, our wives, and
our children stand around us? Has not my scalping-knife been
red with blood, and the scalps of our enemy been drying in our
camps? Have I not made the war-path red with blood, and has
not the Seminole always found a home in my camp? Then, will
the warriors of Coacooche desert him? No! If your hearts are
bad, let me see them now; take them in your hands, and let me
know they are dark with bad blood; but do not, like a dog, bite
me, so soon as you turn your backs. If Coacooche is to die, he
can die like a man. It is not my heart that shakes; no, it never
trembles; but I feel for those now in the woods, pursued night and
day by the soldiers; for those who fought with us, until we were
weak. The sun shines bright to-day, the day is clear; so let your
hearts be: the Great Spirit will guide you. At night, when you camp,
take these pipes and tobacco, build a fire when the moon is up
and bright, dance around it, then let the fire go out, and just before
the break of day, when the deer sleeps, and the moon whispers
to the dead, you will hear the voices of those who have gone to
the Great Spirit; they will give you strong hearts and heads to
carry the talk of Coacooche. Say to my band that my feet are
chained. I cannot walk, yet I send them my word as true from
the heart, as if I was on the war-path or in the deer-hunt. I am not

a boy; Coacooche can die, not with a shivering hand, but as when grasping the rifle with my warriors around me.

"My feet are chained, but the head and heart of Coacooche reaches you. The great white chief (Po-car-ger) will be kind to us. He says, when my band comes in I shall again walk my land free, with my band around me. He has given you forty days to do this business in; If you want more, say so; I will ask for more; if not, be true to the time. Take these sticks; here are thirty-nine, one for each day; *this,* much larger than the rest, with blood upon it, is the fortieth. When the others are thrown away, and this only remains, say to my people, that with the setting sun Coacooche hangs like a dog, with none but white men to hear his last words. Come then; come by the stars, as I have led you to battle! Come, for the voice of Coacooche speaks to you!"

A PORTION OF A SPEECH TO A MEETING OF THE NEW YORK HISTORICAL SOCIETY, MAY, 1847

Peter Wilson (Cayuga)

The Empire State, as you love to call it, was once laced by our trails from Albany to Buffalo—trails that we had trod for centuries—trails worn so deep by the feet of the Iroquois, that they became your roads of travel, as your possessions gradually eat into those of my people. Your roads still traverse those same lines of communication, which bound one part of the Long House to the other. Have we, the first holders of this prosperous region, no longer a share in your history? Glad were your fathers to sit down upon the threshold of the Long House. Had our forefathers spurned you from it, when the French were thundering at the opposite side to get a passage through, and drive you into the sea, whatever has been the fate of other Indians, the Iroquois might still have been a nation, and I, instead of pleading here for the privilege of living within your borders, I—might have had a country.

From Lewis H. Morgan, *League of the Hodensaunec or Iroquois* (New York, 1901), pp. 104–5.

SPEECH TO CANADIAN OFFICIALS ON LAND-PURCHASE POLICY, GIVEN AT A COUNCIL AT THE SAULT STE. MARIE, AUGUST 9, 1848

Peau de Chat (Ojibway)

Father, do you ask how we possess this land? It is well known that 4,000 years have passed since the Great Spirit first placed us here, and you white skins ought to know, as we red skins do know it. He gave to us this country. At that time we spoke but one language; since then a great change has taken place, for we have become a divided people, and we speak many. From the time that our ancestors thus obtained it, it has been truly deemed ours only. This land where lie the bones of our ancestors, is ours. We have never sold it, nor has it been taken from us by conquest, or by any other means. When the Great Spirit placed us here, long before the whites came from where the sun so often sets upon them in its wrath, the red man was living at his ease. He roved the forests, independent of famine or want, because he had the animals of the woods for his food and their furs for his dress. But now, wherever we turn our eyes, we behold nothing but poverty, trouble and sorrow.

When the white man came here a stranger from beyond the great salt lake, and found this portion of the world peopled, he saw

From Green Bay (Wisconsin) *Advocate*, November 30, 1848.

that the furs worn by our nations were valuable, and he showed to our ancestors many goods which he had brought with him over the big water, and these were very tempting to our old ancestors. The white man said, "Will you not sell the skins of your animals for the goods I bring?" Our ancestors replied, "We will buy your goods, and you will buy our furs." The whites proposed nothing more; our ancestors acceded to nothing else. The man did not say, come, I will buy your land, and everything that is upon it, and under it. The white man never made any contract about this: he only asked for the skins we had to sell him. These are the reasons I have to show that we own and possess up to this moment this country. Can you tell me, Father, how, when or where, we lost, or surrendered our right to it?

Such was the agreement made by the red skins, my ancestors, with the white man. They hunted for the white man, and before many years the game grew scarce, and the benefits we derive from this agreement are these: Instead of using a stone to cut my wood, I used a sharp axe. Instead of being clothed in my own warm ancient clothing, I use that which comes from across the big water. Instead of having plenty of food, I am always hungry. And instead of being sober, the Indians are drunk. This last is a misery unknown to our ancestors.

When the white man came to the country, the red men were very numerous; they were strong; they were powerful. The white men were but few, and they were weak. But whilst the red man had the power to crush, he had the humanity to save and protect the white man, who became his brother. The red men have now become but few, and are weak. You have grown to be many and are strong. Have the humanity to guard and protect the rights of your red children.

When the English came across the waters of the rising sun to fight the French and said to our ancestors: "Come, be allied to us; become our children, and we will drive the French from out the land"; then you did not say to us, "The time will come when we will take your land from you." When you raised the war cry against the Long Knives (the Americans), you sent to us red skins to assist you. We sent you many warriors, and you became very strong. This man (pointing to Shingwawkonce) and his warriors were with you, and they served you long, they served you well and truly, they served you with a warrior's faith, whilst they suffered much misery and lost many of their kindred upon the field of battle *for you*. At that time, nor when the war was over, the English did not say, "We will take your lands from you," nor did we say, "You may have them." And, Father, this you know. I have shown a long possession; I have shown that the English never doubted, but always recognized our right to it.

You ask in what instance the whites prevent our farming. There are a people upon our lands, a bad people. These people are ever saying to us, "Do not farm, live as the Indians always did. You will be unhappy if you turn to cultivate the lands. Take your gun, go and hunt, and bring the skins to us, and abandon the idea of tilling the ground." But there are others again who say to us, "Become Christians." But when these bad men see me they say, "Leave it alone, and do as you formerly did." And this is the way they destroy both our religion and our farming. It is thus I explain the question you ask me.

The miners burn and destroy the land, and drive away the game upon which we subsist. We can neither eat the flesh for food, nor can we procure their skins, wherewith to buy subsistence. I begin to think that the white man, having driven away the game, will steal our land too, and we must perish. I will not make reflections upon his conduct. We are not unwilling to sell our lands; we will sell both lands and minerals; but give us good pay for it. It is not for me to go to you and say, come buy my land: I expect you to ask for it; send someone to make us an offer for it and we will let it go. I believe it would be good for my people—yes, very good. The Great Spirit, we think, placed these rich mines in our lands for the benefit of his red children, so that their rising generation might get support from them when the animals of the woods shall have grown scarce for subsistence. We will carry out therefore the good object of our Father, the Great Spirit. We will sell these lands, if you will give us what is right. At the same time we want pay for the mineral which has been taken away, as well as for that which shall hereafter be carried away.

AN INTERVIEW WITH GOVERNOR ALEXANDER RAMSEY OF MINNESOTA, DECEMBER, 1852

Red Iron (Sisseton Sioux)

[One of the hazards Indians continually faced was dealing with dishonest traders who, in collusion with public officials, sought to obtain money due the tribes from the federal government. Treatment of the Sioux similar to that described in the following selection led eventually to the Great Sioux Uprising of 1862.]

Governor Ramsey asked: "What excuse have you for not coming to the council when I sent for you?"

The chief rose to his feet with native grace and dignity, his blanket falling from his shoulders, and purposely dropping the pipe of peace, he stood erect before the governor with his arms folded, and right hand pressed on the sheath of his scalping-knife; with firm voice he replied:

"I started to come, but your braves drove me back."

Gov. "What excuse have you for not coming the second time I sent for you?"

Red Iron. "No other excuse than I have given you."

Gov. "At the treaty I thought you a good man, but since you have acted badly, and I am disposed to break you. I do break you."

Red Iron. "You break me! My people made me a chief. My people love me. I will still be their chief. I have done nothing wrong."

From Helen Hunt Jackson, *A Century of Dishonor* (Boston, 1893), Appendix 6.

Gov. "Why did you get your braves together and march around here for the purpose of intimidating other chiefs, and prevent their coming to the council?"

Red Iron. "I did not get my braves together, they got together themselves to prevent boys going to council to be made chiefs, to sign papers, and to prevent single chiefs going to council at night, to be bribed to sign papers for money we have never got. We have heard how the Medewakantons were served at Mendota; that by secret councils you got their names on paper, and took away their money. We don't want to be served so. My braves wanted to come to council in the daytime, when the sun shines, and we want no councils in the dark. We want all our people to go to council together, so that we can all know what is done."

Gov. "Why did you attempt to come to council with your braves, when I had forbidden your braves coming to council?"

Red Iron. "You invited the chiefs only, and would not let the braves come too. This is not the way we have been treated before; this is not according to our customs, for among Dakotas chiefs and braves go to council together. When you first sent for us, there were two or three chiefs here, and we wanted to wait till the rest would come, that we might all be in council together and know what was done, and so that we might all understand the papers, and know what we were signing. When we signed the treaty the traders threw a blanket over our faces and darkened our eyes, and made us sign papers which we did not understand, and which were not explained or read to us. We want our Great Father at Washington to know what has been done."

Gov. "Your Great Father has sent me to represent him, and what I say is what he says. He wants you to pay your old debts, in accordance with the paper you signed when the treaty was made, and to leave that money in my hands to pay these debts. If you refuse to do that I will take the money back."

Red Iron. "You can take the money back. We sold our land to you, and you promised to pay us. If you don't give us the money I will be glad, and all our people will be glad, for we will have our land back if you don't give us the money. That paper was not interpreted or explained to us. We are told it gives about 300 boxes ($300,000) of our money to some of the traders. We don't think we owe them so much. We want to pay all our debts. We want our Great Father to send three good men here to tell us how much we do owe, and whatever they say we will pay; and that's what all these braves say. Our chiefs and all our people say this." All the Indians present responded, "Ho! ho!"

Gov. "That can't be done. You owe more than your money will pay, and I am ready now to pay your annuity, and no more; and when you are ready to receive it, the agent will pay you."

Red Iron. "We will receive our annuity, but we will sign no papers for anything else. The snow is on the ground, and we have been waiting a long time to get our money. We are poor; you have plenty. Your fires are warm. Your tepees keep out the cold. We have nothing to eat. We have been waiting a long time for our moneys. Our hunting-season is past. A great many of our people are sick, for being hungry. We may die because you won't pay us. We may die, but if we do we will leave our bones on the ground, that our Great Father may see where his Dakota children died. We are very poor. We have sold our hunting-grounds and the graves of our fathers. We have sold our own graves. We have no place to bury our dead, and you will not pay us the money for our lands."

FOURTH OF JULY ADDRESS AT REIDSVILLE, NEW YORK, 1854

John Quinney (Mahican)

It may appear to those whom I have the honor to address a singular taste for me, an Indian, to take an interest in the triumphal days of a people who occupy, by conquest or have usurped, the possessions of my fathers and have laid and carefully preserved a train of terrible miseries to end when my race ceased to exist.

But thanks to the fortunate circumstances of my life I have been taught in the schools and been able to read your histories and accounts of Europeans, yourselves and the Red Man; which instruct me that while your rejoicings today are commemorative of the free birth of this giant nation, they simply convey to my mind the recollection of a transfer of the miserable weakness and dependence of my race from one great power to another.

My friends, I am getting old and have witnessed for many years your increase in wealth and power while the steady consuming decline of my tribe admonishes me that their extinction is inevitable. They know it themselves and the reflection teaches them humility and resignation, directing their attention to the existence of those happy hunting grounds which the Great Father has prepared for all his red children.

In this spirit, my friends, as a Muh-he-con-new, and now standing upon the soil which once was and now ought to be the property of this tribe, I have thought for once and certainly the last time I would shake you by the hand and ask you to listen for a little while to what I have to say.

From *The American Indian*, January, 1928.

About the year 1645, when King Ben the last of the hereditary chiefs of the Muh-he-con-new nation was in his prime, grand council was convened of the Muh-he-con-new tribe for the purpose of conveying from the old to the young men a knowledge of the past.

Councils for this object especially had been held. Here for the space of two moons, the stores of memory were dispensed; corrections and comparisons made and the results committed to faithful breasts to be transmitted again to succeeding posterity.

Many years after, another and last council of this kind was held; and the traditions reduced to writing, by two of our young men who had been taught to read and write in the school of the Rev. John Sargent of Stockbridge, Mass. They were obtained in some way by a white man for publication, who soon after dying, all trace of them became lost. The traditions of the tribe, however, have mainly been preserved, of which I give you substantially, the following:

A great people from the northwest crossed over the salt water, and after long and weary pilgrimage, planting many colonies on their track, took possession of and built their fires upon the Atlantic coast, extending from the Delaware on the south to the Penobscott on the north. They became in process of time different tribes and interests; all, however, speaking one common dialect.

This great confederacy, Pequots, Penobscotts, and many others (Delawares, Mohegans, Munsees, Narragansetts) held its council fires once a year to deliberate on the general welfare.

Patriarchial delegates from each tribe attended, assisted by the priests and the wise men, who communicated the will and invoked the blessing of the Great and Good Spirit. The policies and decisions of this council were everywhere respected, and inviolably observed. Thus contentment smiled upon their existence and they were happy.

Their religion communicated by priest and prophet, was simple and true. The manner of worship is imperfectly transmitted; but their reverence for a Great Spirit, the observance of feasts each year, the offering of beasts in thanksgiving and atonement is clearly expressed.

They believed the soul to be immortal—in the existence of a happy land beyond the view, inhabited by those whose lives had been blameless. While for the wicked had been reserved a region of misery covered with thorns and thistles, where comfort and pleasure were unknown. Time was divided into years and seasons; twelve moons for a year, a number of years by so many winters.

The tribe to which your speaker belongs and of which there were many bands, occupied and possessed the country from the sea-shore at Manhattan to Lake Champlain. Having found the ebb and flow of the tide, they said: "This is Muh-he-con-new," "Like our waters which are never still." From this expression and by this name they were afterwards known, until their removal to Stockbridge in the year 1630.

Housatonic river Indians, Mohegans, Manhattans, were all names
of bands in different localities, but bound together as one family
by blood and descent.

At a remote period, before the advent of the European their
wise men foretold the coming of a strange race from the sunrise,
as numerous as the leaves upon the trees, who would eventually
crowd them from their fair land possessions. But apprehension
was mitigated by the knowledge and belief at that time entertained,
that they originally were not there, and after a period of years
they would return to the west from which they had come. And
they moreover said all Red Men are sprung from a common
ancestor, made by the Great Spirit from red clay, who will unite
their strength to avert a common calamity. This tradition is confirmed by the common belief, which prevails in our day with all
the Indian tribes; for they recognize one another by their color,
as brothers and acknowledge one Great Creator.

Two hundred and fifty winters ago, this prophecy was verified
and the Muh-he-con-new for the first time beheld the paleface.
Their number was small, but their canoes were big.

In the select and exclusive circles of your rich men of the
present day I should encounter the gaze of curiosity, but not such
as overwhelmed the senses of the Aborigines, my ancestors. Our
visitors were white and must be sick. They asked for rest and
kindness; we gave them both. They were strangers, and we took
them in; naked and we clothed them.

The first impression of astonishment and pity was succeeded by
awe and admiration of superior intelligence and address.

A passion for information and improvement possessed the
Indians. A residence was given—territory offered—and covenants
of friendship exchanged.

Your written accounts of events at this period are familiar to you,
my friends. Your children read them every day in their school
books; but they do not read—no mind at this time can conceive,
and no pen record, the terrible story of recompense for kindness,
which for two hundred years has been paid the simple, guileless
Muh-he-con-new.

I have seen much myself—I have been connected with more—and
I tell you I know all. The tradition of the wise men is figuratively
true—that our home at last will be found in the west; for another
tradition informs us that far beyond the setting sun, upon the
smiling happy lands, we shall be gathered with our fathers, and
be at rest.

Promises and professions were freely given and ruthlessly and
intentionally broken. To kindle your fires was sought as a privilege;
and yet at that moment you were transmitting to your kings
intelligence of our possessions, "by right of discovery," and demanding assistance to assert your hold.

Where are the 25,000 in number, and the 4,000 warriors, who

constituted the power and population of the great Muh-he-con-new nation in 1604?

They have been victims to vice and disease, which the white men imported. Smallpox, measles and firewater have done the work of annihilation. Divisions and feuds were insidiously promoted between the several bands. They were induced to thin each others ranks without just cause; and subsequently were defeated and disorganized in detail.

It is curious, the history of my tribe, in its decline, in the last two centuries and a half. Nothing that deserved the name of purchase was made. From various causes, they were induced to abandon their territory at intervals and retire farther inland. Deeds were given indifferently to the government by individuals, for which little or no compensation was paid.

The Indians were informed, in many instances, that they were selling one piece of land when they were conveying another and much larger limits. Should a particular band, for purposes of hunting or fishing, for a time leave its usual place of residence, the land was said to be abandoned, and the Indian claim extinguished. To legalize and confirm titles thus acquired, laws and edicts were subsequently passed, and these laws were said then to be, and are now called, justice.

Oh, what mockery to confound justice with law! Will you look steadily at the intrigues, bargains, corruptions and log rollings of your present legislatures, and see any trace of justice? And by what test shall be tried the acts of the colonial courts and councils?

Let it not surprise you, my friends, when I say that the spot upon which I stand has never been rightly purchased or obtained. And by justice, human and Divine, is the property of the remnant of the great people from whom I am descended. They left it in the tortures of starvation and to improve their miserable existence; but a cession was never made, and their title was never extinguished.

The Indian is said to be the ward of the white man, and the negro his slave. Has it ever occurred to you, my friend, that while the negro is increasing and increased by every appliance, the Indian is left to rot and die before the inhumanities of this model republic?

You have your tears and groans and mobs and riots for the individuals of the former, while your indifference of purpose and vacillation of policy is hurrying to extinction whole communities of the latter.

What are the treaties of the general government? How often and when has its plighted faith been kept? Indian occupation is forever next year, or one removal follows another; or by the next commissioner, more wise than his predecessor, repurchased, and thus your sympathies and justice are evinced in speedily fulfilling the terrible destinies of our race.

My friends, your Holy Book, the Bible, teaches us that individual offenses are punished in an existence—when time shall be no more—and the annals of the earth are equally instructive that national wrongs are avenged, and national crimes atoned for in this world to which alone the conformation of existence adapts them.

These events are above our comprehension, and for a wise purpose; for myself and for my tribe I ask for justice—I believe it will sooner or later occur, and may the Great Spirit enable me to die in hope.

SPEECH TO COUNCIL OF WAR ON THE EVE OF THE SIOUX UPRISING IN MINNESOTA, AUGUST 18, 1862

Little Crow (Santee Sioux)

Taoyateduta is not a coward, and he is not a fool! When did he run away from his enemies? When did he leave his braves behind him on the warpath and turn back to his tepee? When he ran away from your enemies, he walked behind on your trail with his face to the Ojibways and covered your backs as a she-bear covers her cubs! Is Taoyateduta without scalps? Look at his war feathers! Behold the scalp locks of your enemies hanging there on his lodgepoles! Do they call him a coward? Taoyateduta is not a coward, and he is not a fool. Braves, you are like little children: you know not what you are doing.

You are full of the white man's devil water. You are like dogs in the Hot Moon when they run mad and snap at their own shadows. We are only little herds of buffalo left scattered; the great herds that once covered the prairies are no more. See!—the white men are like the locusts when they fly so thick that the whole sky is a snowstorm. You may kill one—two—ten; yes, as many as the leaves in the forest yonder, and their brothers will not miss them. Kill one—two—ten, and ten times ten will come to kill you. Count

From "Taoyateduta is not a coward," in *Minnesota History*, September, 1962.

your fingers all day long and white men with guns in their hands will come faster than you can count.

Yes; they fight among themselves—away off. Do you hear the thunder of their big guns? No; it would take you two moons to run down to where they are fighting, and all the way your path would be among white soldiers as thick as tamaracks in the swamps of the Ojibways. Yes; they fight among themselves, but if you strike at them they will all turn on you and devour you and your women and little children just as the locusts in their time fall on the trees and devour all the leaves in one day.

You are fools. You cannot see the face of your chief; your eyes are full of smoke. You cannot hear his voice; your ears are full of roaring waters. Braves, you are little children—you are fools. You will die like the rabbits when the hungry wolves hunt them in the Hard Moon (January).

Taoyateduta is not a coward: he will die with you.

THE GREAT SIOUX UPRISING OF 1862

Big Eagle (Santee Sioux)

[This selection is part of a memoir dictated by Big Eagle in the summer of 1894 to interpreters John Eastman and Nancy Huggan at Flandreau, South Dakota. It was subsequently edited and published by R. I. Holcombe in the St. Paul *Pioneer Press*.]

Of the causes that led to the outbreak of August, 1862, much has been said. Of course it was wrong, as we all know now, but there were not many Christians among the Indians then, and they did not understand things as they should. There was great dissatisfaction among the Indians over many things the whites did. The whites would not let them go to war against their enemies. This was right, but the Indians did not then know it. Then the whites were always trying to make the Indians give up their life and live like white men—go to farming, work hard and do as they did—and the Indians did not know how to do that, and did not want to anyway. It seemed too sudden to make such a change. If the Indians had tried to make the whites live like them, the whites would have resisted, and it was the same way with many Indians. The Indians wanted to live as they did before the treaty of Traverse des Sioux—go where they pleased and when they pleased; hunt game wherever they could find it, sell their furs to the traders and live as they could.

From "A Sioux Story of the War," in Minnesota Historical Society *Collections*, Vol. 6 (1894).

Then the Indians did not think the traders had done right. The Indians bought goods of them on credit, and when the government payments came the traders were on hand with their books, which showed that the Indians owed so much and so much, and as the Indians kept no books they could not deny their accounts, but had to pay them, and sometimes the traders got all their money. I do not say that the traders always cheated and lied about these accounts. I know many of them were honest men and kind and accommodating, but since I have been a citizen I know that many white men, when they go to pay their accounts, often think them too large and refuse to pay them, and they go to law about them and there is much bad feeling. The Indians could not go to law, but there was always trouble over their credits. Under the treaty of Traverse des Sioux the Indians had to pay a very large sum of money to the traders for old debts, some of which ran back fifteen years, and many of those who had got the goods were dead and others were not present, and the traders' books had to be received as to the amounts, and the money was taken from the tribe to pay them. Of course the traders often were of great service to the Indians in letting them have goods on credit, but the Indians seemed to think the traders ought not to be too hard on them about the payments, but do as the Indians did among one another, and put off the payment until they were better able to make it.

Then many of the white men often abused the Indians and treated them unkindly. Perhaps they had excuse, but the Indians did not think so. Many of the whites always seemed to say by their manner when they saw an Indian, "I am much better than you," and the Indians did not like this. There was excuse for this, but the Dakotas did not believe there were better men in the world than they. Then some of the white men abused the Indian women in a certain way and disgraced them, and surely there was no excuse for that.

All these things made many Indians dislike the whites. Then a little while before the outbreak there was trouble among the Indians themselves. Some of the Indians took a sensible course and began to live like white men. The government built them houses, furnished them tools, seed, etc., and taught them to farm. At the two agencies, Yellow Medicine and Redwood, there were several hundred acres of land in cultivation that summer. Others staid in their tepees. There was a white man's party and an Indian party. We had politics among us and there was much feeling. A new chief speaker for the tribe was to be elected. There were three candidates—Little Crow, myself and Wa-sui-hi-ya-ye-dan ("Traveling Hail"). After an exciting contest Traveling Hail was elected. Little Crow felt sore over his defeat. Many of our tribe believed him responsible for the sale of the north ten-mile strip, and I think this was why he was defeated. I did not care much about it. Many whites think that Little Crow was the principal chief of the Dakotas at this time, but he was not. Wabasha was the principal chief, and he was of the white man's party; so was I; so was old Shakopee, whose band was very large. Many think if old Shakopee had lived there would have been no war, for he was for the white men and had great influence. But he died that summer, and was succeeded by his son, whose real name was Ea-to-ka ("Another Language"), but when he became chief he took his father's name, and was afterwards called "Little Shakopee," or "Little Six," for in the Sioux language "Shakopee" means six. This Shakopee was against the white men. He took part in the outbreak, murdering women and children, but I never saw him in a battle, and he was caught in Manitoba and hanged in 1864. My brother, Medicine Bottle, was hanged with him.

As the summer advanced, there was great trouble among the Sioux—troubles among themselves, troubles with the whites, and one thing and another. The war with the South was going on then, and a great many men had left the state and gone down there to fight. A few weeks before the outbreak the president called for many more men, and a great many of the white men of Minnesota and some half-breeds enlisted and went to Fort Snelling to be sent South. We understood that the South was getting the best of the fight, and it was said that the North would be whipped. The year before the new president had turned out Maj. Brown and Maj. Cullen, the Indian agents, and put in their places Maj. Galbraith and Mr. Clark Thompson, and they had turned out the men under them and put in others of their own party. There were a great many changes. An Indian named Shonka-sha ("White Dog"), who had been hired to teach the Indians to farm, was removed and another Indian named Ta-opi ("The Wounded Man"), a son of old Betsy, of St. Paul, put in his place. Nearly all of the men who were turned out were dissatisfied, and the most of the Indians did not like the new men. At last Maj. Galbraith went to work about the agencies and recruited a company of soldiers to go South. His men were nearly all half-breeds. This was the company called the Renville Rangers, for they were mostly from Renville county. The Indians now thought the whites must be pretty hard up for men to fight the South, or they would not come so far out on the frontier and take half-breeds or anything to help them.

It began to be whispered about that now would be a good time to go to war with the whites and get back the lands. It was believed that the men who had enlisted last had all left the state, and that before help could be sent the Indians could clean out the country, and that the Winnebagoes, and even the Chippewas, would assist the Sioux. It was also thought that a war with the whites would cause the Sioux to forget the troubles among themselves and enable many of them to pay off some old scores. Though I took part in the war, I was against it. I knew there was no good cause for it, and I had been to Washington and knew the power of the whites and that they would finally conquer us. We might succeed for a time, but we would be overpowered and defeated at last. I said all this and many more things to my people, but many of my own bands were against me, and some of the other chiefs put words in their mouths to say to me. When the outbreak came Little Crow told some of my band that if I refused to lead them to shoot me as a traitor who would not stand up for his nation, and then select another leader in my place.

But after the first talk of war the counsels of the peace Indians prevailed, and many of us thought the danger had all blown over. The time of the government payment was near at hand, and this may have had something to do with it. There was another thing that helped to stop the war talk. The crops that had been put in by the "farmer" Indians were looking well, and there seemed to be a good prospect for a plentiful supply of provisions for them the coming winter without having to depend on the game of the country or without going far out to the west on the plains for buffalo. It seemed as if the white men's way was certainly the best. Many of the Indians had been short of provisions that summer and had exhausted their credits and were in bad condition. "Now," said the farmer Indians, "if you had worked last season you would not be starving now and begging for food." The "farmers" were favored by the government in every way. They had houses built for them, some of them even had brick houses, and they were not allowed to suffer. The other Indians did not like this. They were envious of them and jealous, and disliked them because they had gone back on the customs of the tribe and because they were favored. They called them "farmers," as if it was disgraceful to be a farmer. They called them "cut-hairs," because they had given up the Indian fashion of wearing the hair, and "breeches men," because they wore pantaloons, and "Dutchmen," because so many of the settlers on the north side of the river and elsewhere in the country were Germans. I have heard that there was a secret organization of the Indians called the "Soldiers' Lodge," whose object was to declare war against the whites, but I knew nothing of it.

At last the time for the payment came and the Indians came in to the agencies to get their money. But the paymaster did not come, and week after week went by and still he did not come. The payment was to be in gold. Somebody told the Indians that the payment would never be made. The government was in a great war, and gold was scarce, and paper money had taken its place, and it was said the gold could not be had to pay us. Then the trouble began again and the war talk started up. Many of the Indians who had gathered about the agencies were out of provisions and were easily made angry. Still, most of us thought the trouble would pass, and we said nothing about it. I thought there might be trouble, but I had no idea there would be such a war. Little Crow and other chiefs did not think so. But it seems some of the tribe were getting ready for it.

You know how the war started—by the killing of some white people near Acton, in Meeker county. I will tell you how this was done, as it was told me by all of the four young men who did the killing. These young fellows all belonged to Shakopee's band. Their names were Sungigidan ("Brown Wing"), Ka-om-de-i-ye-ye-dan ("Breaking Up"), Nagi-wi-cak-te ("Killing Ghost"), and Pa-zo-i-yo-pa ("Runs against Something when Crawling"). I do not think their names have ever before been printed. One of them is yet living. They told me they did not go out to kill white people. They said they went over into the Big Woods to hunt; that on Sunday, Aug. 17, they came to a settler's fence, and here they found a hen's nest with some eggs in it. One of them took the eggs, when another said: "Don't take them, for they belong to a white man and we may get into trouble." The other was angry, for he was very hungry and wanted to eat the eggs, and he dashed them to the ground and replied: "You are a coward. You are afraid of the white man. You are afraid to take even an egg from him, though you are half-starved. Yes, you are a coward, and I will tell everybody so." The other replied: "I am not a coward. I am not afraid of the white man, and to show you that I am not I will go to the house and shoot him. Are you brave enough to go with me?" The one who had called him a coward said: "Yes, I will go with you, and we will see who is the braver of us two." Their two companions then said: "We will go with you, and we will be brave, too." They all went to the house of the white man (Mr. Robinson Jones), but he got alarmed and went to another house (that of his son-in-law, Howard Baker), where were some other white men and women. The four Indians followed them and killed three men and two women (Jones, Baker, a Mr. Webster, Mrs. Jones and a girl of fourteen). Then they hitched up a team belonging to another settler and drove to Shakopee's camp (six miles above Redwood agency), which they reached late that night and told what they had done, as I have related.

The tale told by the young men created the greatest excitement. Everybody was waked up and heard it. Shakopee took the young men to Little Crow's house (two miles above the agency), and he sat up in bed and listened to their story. He said war was now declared. Blood had been shed, the payment would be stopped, and the whites would take a dreadful vengeance because women had been killed. Wabasha, Wacouta, myself and others still talked for peace, but nobody would listen to us, and soon the cry was "Kill the whites and kill all these cut-hairs who will not join us." A council was held and war was declared. Parties formed and dashed away in the darkness to kill settlers. The women began to run bullets and the men to clean their guns. Little Crow gave orders to attack the agency early next morning and to kill all the traders. When the Indians first came to him for counsel and advice he said to them, tauntingly: "Why do you come to me for advice? Go to the man you elected speaker (Traveling Hail) and let him tell you what to do"; but he soon came around all right and somehow took the lead in everything, though he was not head chief, as I have said.

At this time my village was upon Crow creek, near Little Crow's. I did not have a very large band—not more than thirty or forty fighting men. Most of them were not for the war at first, but nearly all got into it at last. A great many members of the other bands were like my men; they took no part in the first movements, but afterward did. The next morning, when the force started down to attack the agency, I went along. I did not lead my band, and I took no part in the killing. I went to save the lives of two particular friends if I could. I think others went for the same reason, for nearly every Indian had a friend that he did not want killed; of course he did not care about anybody else's friend. The killing was nearly all done when I got there. Little Crow was on the ground directing operations. The day before, he had attended church there and listened closely to the sermon and had shaken hands with everybody. So many Indians have lied about their saving the lives of white people that I dislike to speak of what I did. But I did save the life of George H. Spencer at the time of the massacre. I know that his friend, Chaska, has always had the credit of that, but Spencer would have been a dead man in spite of Chaska if it had not been for me. I asked Spencer about this once, but he said he was wounded at the time and so excited that he could not remember what I did. Once after that I kept a half-breed family from being murdered; these are all the people whose lives I claim to have saved. I was never present when the white people were willfully murdered. I saw all the dead bodies at the agency. Mr. Andrew Myrick, a trader, with an Indian wife, had refused some hungry Indians credit a short time before when they asked him for some provisions. He said to them: "Go and eat grass." Now he was lying on the ground dead, with his mouth stuffed full of grass, and the Indians were saying tauntingly: "Myrick is eating grass himself."

When I returned to my village that day I found that many of my band had changed their minds about the war, and wanted to get into it. All the other villages were the same way. I was still of the belief that it was not best, but I thought I must go with my band and my nation, and I said to my men that I would lead them into the war, and we would all act like brave Dakotas and do the best we could. All my men were with me; none had gone off on raids, but we did not have guns for all at first.

That afternoon word came to my village that soldiers were coming to the agency from Fort Snelling. (These were Capt. Marsh and his men.) At once I mounted the best horse I had, and, with some of my men, rode as fast as I could to meet them at the ferry. But when I got there the fight was over, and I well remember that a cloud of powder smoke was rising slowly from the low, wet ground where the firing had been. I heard a few scattering shots down the river, where the Indians were still pursuing the soldiers, but I took no part. I crossed the river and saw the bodies of the soldiers that had been killed. I think Mr. Quinn, the interpreter, was shot several times after he had been killed. The Indians told me that the most of them who fired on Capt. Marsh and his men were on the same side of the river; that only a few shots came from the opposite or south side. They said that White Dog did not tell Mr. Quinn to come over, but told him to go back. Of course I do not know what the truth is about this. White Dog was the Indian head farmer who had been replaced by Taopi and who was hanged at Mankato.

I was not in the first fight at New Ulm nor the first attack on Fort Ridgely. Here let me say that the Indian names of these and other places in Minnesota are different from the English names. St. Paul is the "White Rock"; Minneapolis is "the Place Where the Water Falls"; New Ulm is "the Place Where There Is a Cottonwood Grove on the River"; Fort Ridgely was "the Soldiers' House"; Birch Coulie was called "Birch Creek," etc. I was in the second fight at New Ulm and in the second attack on Fort Ridgely. At New Ulm I had but a few of my band with me. We lost none of them. We had but few, if any, of the Indians killed; at least I did not hear of but a few. A half-breed named George Le Blanc, who was with us, was killed. There was no one in chief command of the Indians at New Ulm. A few sub-chiefs, like myself, and the head soldiers led them, and the leaders agreed among themselves what was to be done. I do not think there was a chief present at the first fight. I think that attack was made by marauding Indians from several bands, every man for himself, but when we heard they were fighting we went down to help them. I think it probable that the first attack on Fort Ridgely was made in the same way; at any rate, I do not remember that there was a chief there.

The second fight at Fort Ridgely was made a grand affair. Little Crow was with us. Mr. Good Thunder, now at Birch Coulie agency, was with us. He counted the Indians as they filed past him on the march to the attack, and reported that there were 800 of us. He acted very bravely in the fight, and distinguished himself by running close up to the fort and bringing away a horse. He is now married to the former widow of White Dog, and both he and his wife are good Christian citizens. We went down determined to take the fort, for we knew it was of the greatest importance to us to have it. If we could take it we would soon have the whole Minnesota valley. But we failed, and of course it was best that we did fail.

Though Little Crow was present, he did not take a very active part in the fight. As I remember, the chief leaders in the fight were "The Thief," who was the head soldier of Mankato's band, and Mankato ("Blue Earth") himself. This Mankato was not the old chief for whom the town was named, but a sub-chief, the son of old Good Road. He was a very brave man and a good leader. He was killed at the battle of Wood lake by a cannon ball. We went down to the attack on both sides of the river. I went down on the south side with my men, and we crossed the river in front of the fort and went up through the timber and fought on that side next the river. The fight commenced about noon on Friday after the out-

break. We had a few Sissetons and Wakpatons with us, and some
Winnebagoes, under the "Little Priest," were in this fight and at
New Ulm. I saw them myself. But for the cannon I think we would
have taken the fort. The soldiers fought us so bravely we thought
there were more of them than there were. The cannons disturbed
us greatly, but did not hurt many. We did not have many Indians
killed. I think the whites put the number too large, and I think
they overestimated the number killed in every battle. We seldom
carried off our dead. We usually buried them in a secluded place
on the battle-field when we could. We always tried to carry away
the wounded. When we retreated from Ridgely I recrossed the
river opposite the fort and went up on the south side. All our army
but the scouts fell back up the river to our villages near Redwood
agency, and then on up to the Yellow Medicine and the mouth of
the Chippewa.

Our scouts brought word that our old friend Wapetonhonska
("The Long Trader"), as we called Gen. Sibley, was coming up
against us, and in a few days we learned that he had come to Fort
Ridgely with a large number of soldiers. Little Crow, with a strong
party, went over into the Big Woods, towards Forest City and
Hutchinson. After he had gone, I and the other sub-chiefs concluded to go down and attack New Ulm again and take the town
and cross the river to the east, or in the rear of Fort Ridgely, where
Sibley was, and then our movements were to be governed by circumstances. We had left our village near the Redwood in some
haste and alarm, expecting to be followed after the defeat at
Ridgely, and had not taken all our property away. So we took many
of our women with us to gather up the property and some other
things, and we brought along some wagons to haul them off.

We came down the main road on the south side of the river, and
were several hundred strong. We left our camps in the morning
and got to our old villages in the afternoon. When the men in
advance reached Little Crow's village—which was on the high bluff
on the south side of the Minnesota, below the mouth of the Redwood—they looked to the north across the valley, and up on the
high bluff on the north side, and out on the prairie some miles
away, they saw a column of mounted men and some wagons coming out of the Beaver creek timber on the prairie and going eastward. We also saw signs in Little Crow's village that white men
had been there only a few hours before, and judging from the trail
they had made when they left, these were the men we now saw to
the northward. There was, of course, a little excitement, and the
column halted. Four or five of our best scouts were sent across the
valley to follow the movements of the soldiers, creeping across the
prairie like so many ants. It was near sundown, and we knew they
would soon go into camp, and we thought the camping ground
would be somewhere on the Birch Coulie, where there was wood
and water. The women went to work to load the wagons. The scouts
followed the soldiers carefully, and a little after sundown returned

with the information that they had gone into camp near the head of Birch Coulie. At this time we did not know there were two companies there. We thought the company of mounted men (Capt. Anderson's) was all, and that there were not more than seventy-five men.

It was concluded to surround the camp that night and attack it at daylight. We felt sure we could capture it, and that 200 men would be enough for the undertaking. So about that number was selected. There were four bands—my own, Hu-sha-sha's ("Red Legs"), Gray Bird's and Mankato's. I had about thirty men. Nearly all the Indians had double-barreled shotguns, and we loaded them with buckshot and large bullets called "traders' balls." After dark we started, crossed the river and valley, went up the bluffs and on the prairie, and soon we saw the white tents and the wagons of the camp. We had no difficulty in surrounding the camp. The pickets were only a little way from it. I led my men up from the west through the grass and took up a position 200 yards from the camp, behind a small knoll or elevation. Red Legs took his men into the coulie east of the camp. Mankato ("Blue Earth") had some of his men in the coulie and some on the prairie. Gray Bird and his men were mostly on the prairie.

Just at dawn the fight began. It continued all day and the following night until late the next morning. Both sides fought well. Owing to the white men's way of fighting they lost many men. Owing to the Indians' way of fighting they lost but few. The white men stood up and exposed themselves at first, but at last they learned to keep quiet. The Indians always took care of themselves. We had an easy time of it. We could crawl through the grass and into the coulie and get water when we wanted it, and after a few hours our women crossed the river and came up near the bluff and cooked for us, and we could go back and eat and then return to the fight. We did not lose many men. Indeed, I only saw two dead Indians, and I never heard that any more were killed. The two I saw were in the coulie and belonged to Red Legs' band. One was a Wakpaton named Ho-ton-na ("Animal's Voice") and the other was a Sisseton. Their bodies were taken down the coulie and buried during the fight. I did not see a man killed on the prairie. We had several men wounded, but none very badly. I did not see the incident which is related of an Indian, a brother of Little Crow, who, it is said, rode up on a white horse near the camp with a white flag and held a parley and had his horse killed as he rode away. That must have happened while I was absent from the field eating my dinner. Little Crow had no brother there. The White Spider was not there. I think Little Crow's brothers were with him in the Big Woods at this time. The only Indian horse I saw killed that I remember was a bay. Buffalo Ghost succeeded in capturing a horse from the camp. Late in the day some of the men who had been left in the villages came over on their horses to see what the trouble was that the camp had not been taken, and they rode about the prairie for a time, but I don't think many of them got into the fight. I do not remember that we got many re-enforcements that day. If we got any, they must have come up the coulie and I did not see them. Perhaps some horsemen came up on the east side of the coulie, but I knew nothing about it. I am sure no re-enforcements came to me. I did not need any. Our circle about the camp was rather small and we could only use a certain number of men.

About the middle of the afternoon our men became much dissatisfied at the slowness of the fight, and the stubbornness of the whites, and the word was passed around the lines to get ready to charge the camp. The brave Mankato wanted to charge after the first hour. There were some half-breeds with the whites who could speak Sioux well, and they heard us arranging to assault them. Jack Frazer told me afterward that he heard us talking about it very plainly. Alex Faribault was there and heard the talk and called out to us: "You do very wrong to fire on us. We did not come out to fight; we only came out to bury the bodies of the white people you killed." I have heard that Faribault, Frazer and another half-breed dug a rifle pit for themselves with bayonets, and that Faribault worked so hard with his bayonet in digging that he wore the flesh from the inside of his hand. One half-breed named Louis Bourier attempted to desert to us, but as he was running towards us some of our men shot and killed him. We could have taken the camp, I think. During the fight the whites had thrown up breastworks, but they were not very high and we could easily have jumped over them. We did not know that Maj. Joe Brown was there; if we had, I think some of our men would have charged anyhow, for they wanted him out of the way. Some years ago I saw Capt. Grant in St. Paul and he told me he was in command of the camp at Birch Coulie.

Just as we were about to charge word came that a large number of mounted soldiers were coming up from the east toward Fort Ridgely. This stopped the charge and created some excitement. Mankato at once took some men from the coulie and went out to meet them. He told me he did not take more than fifty, but he scattered them out and they all yelled and made such a noise that the whites must have thought there were a great many more, and they stopped on the prairie and began fighting. They had a cannon and used it, but it did no harm. If the Indians had any men killed in the fight I never heard of it. Mankato flourished his men around so, and all the Indians in the coulie kept up a noise, and at last the whites began to fall back, and they retreated about two miles and began to dig breastworks. Mankato followed them and left about thirty men to watch them, and returned to the fight at the coulie with the rest. The Indians were laughing when they came back at the way they had deceived the white men, and we were all glad that the whites had not pushed forward and driven us away. If any more Indians went against this force than the fifty or possibly seventy-five that I have told you of I never heard of it. I was not with them and cannot say positively, but I do not think there were. I went out to near the fortified camp during the night, and there was no large force of Indians over there, and I know there were not more than thirty of our men watching the camp. When the men of this force began to fall back, the whites in the camp hallooed and made a great commotion, as if they were begging them to return and relieve them, and seemed much distressed that they did not.

The next morning Gen. Sibley came with a very large force and drove us away from the field. We took our time about getting away. Some of our men said they remained till Sibley got up and that they fired at some of his men as they were shaking hands with some of the men of the camp. Those of us who were on the prairie went back to the westward and on down the valley. Those in the coulie went down back southward to where their horses were, and then mounted and rode westward across the prairie about a mile south of the battle-field. There was no pursuit. The whites fired their cannons at us as we were leaving the field, but they might as well have beaten a big drum for all the harm they did. They only made a noise. We went back across the river to our camps in the old villages, and then on up the river to the Yellow Medicine and the mouth of the Chippewa, where Little Crow joined us.

For some time after the fight at Birch Coulie the greater part of the Indians remained in the camps about the Yellow Medicine and the mouth of the Chippewa. At last the word came that Sibley with his army was again on the move against us. Our scouts were very active and vigilant, and we heard from him nearly every hour. He had left a letter for Little Crow in a split stick on the battle-field of Birch Coulie, and some of our men found it and brought it in, and correspondence had been going on between us ever since. Tom Robinson and Joe Campbell, half-breed prisoners, wrote the letters for Little Crow. It seems that some letters were written to Gen. Sibley by the half-breeds which Little Crow never saw. I and others understood from the half-breeds that Gen. Sibley would treat with all of us who had only been soldiers and would surrender as prisoners of war, and that only those who had murdered people in cold blood, the settlers and others, would be punished in any way. There was great dissatisfaction among us at our condition. Many wanted to surrender; others left us for the West. But Sibley came on and on, and at last came the battle of Wood lake.

When we learned that Sibley had gone into camp at the Wood lake, a council of the sub-chiefs and others was held and it was determined to give him a battle near there. I think the lake now called Battle lake was the old-time Wood lake. As I understand it, there once were some cottonwoods about it, and the Indians called it "M'da-chan"—Wood lake. The larger lake, two miles west, now called Wood lake, was always known to me by the Indian name of "Hinta hauk-pay-an wo-ju," meaning literally, "the Planting Place of the Man who ties his Moccasins with Basswood Bark." We soon learned that Sibley had thrown up breastworks and it was not deemed safe to attack him at the lake. We concluded that the fight should be about a mile or more to the northwest of the lake, on the road along which the troops would march. This was the road leading to the upper country, and of course Sibley would travel it. At the point determined on we planned to hide a large number of men on the side of the road. Near the lake, in a ravine formed by the outlet, we were to place another strong body. Behind a hill to the west were to be some more men. We thought that when Sibley marched out along the road and when the head of his column had reached the farther end of the line of our first division, our men would open fire. The men in the ravine would then be in the rear of the whites and would begin firing on that end of the column. The men from behind the hill would rush out and attack the flank, and then we had horsemen far out on the right and left who would come up. We expected to throw the whole white force into confusion by the sudden and unexpected attack and defeat them before they could rally.

I think this was a good plan of battle. Our concealed men would not have been discovered. The grass was tall and the place by the road and the ravine were good hiding places. We had learned that Sibley was not particular about sending out scouts and examining the country before he passed it. He had a number of mounted men, but they always rode together, at the head of the columns, when on a march, and did not examine the ground at the sides of the road. The night he lay at Wood lake his pickets were only a short distance from camp—less than half a mile. When we were putting our men into position that night we often saw them plainly. I worked hard that night fixing the men. Little Crow was on the field, too. Mankato was there. Indeed, all our fighting chiefs were present and all our best fighting Indians. We felt that this would be the deciding fight of the war. The whites were unconscious. We could hear them laughing and singing. When all our preparations were made Little Crow and I and some other chiefs went to the mound or hill to the west so as to watch the fight better when it should commence. There were numbers of other Indians there.

The morning came and an accident spoiled all our plans. For some reason Sibley did not move early as we expected he would. Our men were lying hidden waiting patiently. Some were very near the camp lines in the ravine, but the whites did not see a man of all our men. I do not think they would have discovered our ambuscade. It seemed a considerable time after sun-up when some four or five wagons with a number of soldiers started out from the camp in the direction of the old Yellow Medicine agency. We learned afterwards that they were going without orders to dig potatoes over at the agency, five miles away. They came on over the prairie, right where part of our line was. Some of the wagons were not in the road, and if they had kept straight on would have driven right over our men as they lay in the grass. At last they came so close that our men had to rise up and fire. This brought on the fight, of course, but not according to the way we had planned it. Little Crow saw it and felt very badly.

Of course you know how the battle was fought. The Indians that were in the fight did well, but hundreds of our men did not get into it and did not fire a shot. They were out too far. The men in the ravine and the line connecting them with those on the road did most of the fighting. Those of us on the hill did our best, but we were soon driven off. Mankato was killed here, and we lost a very good and brave war chief. He was killed by a cannon ball that was so nearly spent that he was not afraid of it, and it struck him in the back, as he lay on the ground, and killed him. The whites drove our men out of the ravine by a charge and that ended the battle. We retreated in some disorder, though the whites did not offer to pursue us. We crossed a wide prairie, but their horsemen did not follow us. We lost fourteen or fifteen men killed and quite a number wounded. Some of the wounded died afterwards, but I do not know how many. We carried off no dead bodies, but took away all our wounded. The whites scalped all our dead men—so I have heard.

Soon after the battle I, with many others who had taken part in the war, surrendered to Gen. Sibley. Robinson and the other half-breeds assured us that if we would do this we would only be held as prisoners of war a short time, but as soon as I surrendered I was thrown into prison. Afterwards I was tried and served three years in the prison at Davenport and the penitentiary at Rock Island for taking part in the war. On my trial a great number of the white prisoners, women and others were called up, but not one of them could testify that I had murdered any one or had done anything to deserve death, or else I would have been hanged. If I had known that I would be sent to the penitentiary I would not have surrendered, but when I had been in the penitentiary three years and they were about to turn me out, I told them they might keep me another year if they wished, and I meant what I said. I did not like the way I had been treated. I surrendered in good faith, knowing that many of the whites were acquainted with me and that I had not been a murderer, or present when a murder had been committed, and if I had killed or wounded a man it had been in fair, open fight.

LETTER TO GENERAL ULYSSES S. GRANT, JANUARY 24, 1864

Ely S. Parker or Donehogawa (Seneca)

[Nine years after Parker wrote this letter, he became the first Indian commissioner of Indian affairs.]

GENERAL: In compliance with your request, I have the honor to submit the following proposed plan for the establishment of a permanent and perpetual peace, and for settling all matters of differences between the United States and the various Indian tribes.

First. The transfer of the Indian bureau from the Interior Department back to the War Department, or military branch of the government, where it originally belonged, until within the last few years.

The condition and disposition of all the Indians west of the Mississippi river, as developed in consequence of the great and rapid influx of immigration by reason of the discovery of the precious metals throughout the entire west, renders it of the utmost importance that military supervision should be extended over the Indians. Treaties have been made with a very large number of the tribes, and generally reservations have been provided as homes for them. Agents appointed from civil life have generally been provided to protect their lives and property, and to attend to the prompt and faithful observance of treaty stipulations. But as the hardy pioneer and adventurous miner advanced into the inhos-

From Senate Executive Document No. 13, 40th Congress, 1st Session, pp. 42-47.

pitable regions occupied by the Indians in search of the precious metals, they found no rights possessed by the Indians that they were bound to respect. The faith of treaties solemnly entered into were totally disregarded, and Indian territory wantonly violated. If any tribe remonstrated against the violation of their natural and treaty rights, members of the tribe were inhumanly shot down and the whole treated as mere dogs. Retaliation generally followed, and bloody Indian wars have been the consequence, costing many lives and much treasure. In all troubles arising in this manner the civil agents have been totally powerless to avert the consequences, and when too late the military have been called in to protect the whites and punish the Indians; when if, in the beginning, the military had had the supervision of the Indians, their rights would not have been improperly molested, or if disturbed in their quietude by any lawless whites, a prompt and summary check to any further aggressions could have been given. In cases where the government promises the Indians the quiet and peaceable possession of a reservation, and precious metals are discovered or found to exist upon it, the military alone can give the Indians the needed protection and keep the adventurous miner from encroaching upon the Indians until the government has come to some understanding with them. In such cases the civil agent is absolutely powerless.

Most of Indian treaties contain stipulations for the payment annually to Indians of annuities, either in money or goods, or both, and agents are appointed to make these payments whenever government furnishes them the means. I know of no reason why officers of the army could not make all these payments as well as civilians. The expense of agencies would be saved, and, I think, the Indians would be more honestly dealt by. An officer's honor and interest is at stake, which impels him to discharge his duty honestly and faithfully, while civil agents have none of those incentives, the ruling passion with them being generally to avoid all trouble and responsibility, and to make as much money as possible out of their offices.

In the retransfer of this bureau I would provide for the complete abolishment of the system of Indian traders, which, in my opinion, is a great evil to Indian communities. I would make government the purchaser of all articles usually brought in by Indians, giving them a fair equivalent for the same in money or goods at cost prices. In this way it would be an easy matter to regulate the sale of issue of arms and ammunition to Indians, a question which of late has agitated the minds of the civil and military authorities. If the entry of large numbers of Indians to any military post is objectionable, it can easily be arranged that only limited numbers shall be admitted daily. . . .

Second. The next measure I would suggest is the passage by Congress of a plan of territorial government for the Indians, as was submitted last winter, or a similar one. When once passed it should remain upon the statute-books as the permanent and settled policy

of the government. The boundaries of the Indian territory or territories should be well defined by metes and bounds, and should
remain inviolate from settlement by any except Indians and government employés.

The subject of the improvement and civilization of the Indians,
and the maintenance of peaceful relations with them, has engaged
the serious consideration of every administration since the birth of
the American republic; and, if I recollect aright, President Jefferson was the first to inaugurate the policy of the removal of the
Indians from the States to the country west of the Mississippi; and
President Monroe, in furtherance of this policy, recommended that
the Indians be concentrated, as far as was practicable, and civil
governments established for them, with schools for every branch
of instruction in literature and the arts of civilized life. The plan
of removal was adopted as the policy of the government, and, by
treaty stipulation, affirmed by Congress; lands were set apart for
tribes removing into the western wilds, and the faith of a great
nation pledged that the homes selected by the Indians should be
and remain their homes forever, unmolested by the hand of the
grasping and avaricious white man; and, in some cases, the government promised that the Indian homes and lands should never be
incorporated within the limits of any new State that might be
organized. How the pledges so solemnly given and the promises
made were kept, the history of the western country can tell. It is
presumed that humanity dictated the original policy of the removal
and concentration of the Indians in the west to save them from
threatened extinction. But to-day, by reason of the immense aug-
mentation of the American population, and the extension of their
settlements throughout the entire west, covering both slopes of the
Rocky mountains, the Indian races are more seriously threatened
with a speedy extermination than ever before in the history of the
country. And, however much such a deplorable result might be
wished for by some, it seems to me that the honor of a Christian
nation and every sentiment of humanity dictate that no pains
should be spared to avert such an appalling calamity befalling a
portion of the human race. The establishment of the Indians upon
any one territory is perhaps impracticable, but numbers of them
can, without doubt, be consolidated in separate districts of country,
and the same system of government made to apply to each. By the
concentration of tribes, although in several and separate districts,
government can more readily control them and more economically
press and carry out plans for their improvement and civilization,
and a better field be offered for philanthropic aid and Christian
instruction. Some system of this kind has, at different periods in
the history of our government, been put forward, but never successfully put into execution. A renewal of the attempt, with proper
aids, it seems to me cannot fail of success.

Third. The passage by Congress of an act authorizing the appointment of an inspection board, or commission, to hold office

during good behavior, or until the necessity for their services is terminated by the completion of the retransfer of the Indian Bureau to the War Department. It shall be the duty of this board to examine the accounts of the several agencies, see that every cent due the Indians is paid to them promptly as may be promised in treaties, and that proper and suitable goods and implements of agriculture are delivered to them when such articles are due; to make semi-annual reports, with such suggestions as, in their judgment, might seem necessary to the perfect establishment of a permanent and friendly feeling between the people of the United States and the Indians.

This commission could undoubtedly be dispensed with in a few years, but the results of their labors might be very important and beneficial, not only in supervising and promptly checking the delinquencies of incompetent and dishonest agents, but it would be a most convincing proof to the Indians' mind that the government was disposed to deal honestly and fairly by them. Such a commission might, indeed, be rendered wholly unnecessary if Congress would consent to the next and fourth proposition which I submit in this plan.

Fourth. The passage of an act authorizing the appointment of a permanent Indian commission, to be a mixed commission, composed of such white men as possessed in a large degree the confidence of their country, and a number of the most reputable educated Indians, selected from different tribes. The entire commission might be composed of ten members, and, if deemed advisable, might be divided so that five could operate north and five south of a given line, but both to be governed by the same general instructions, and impressing upon the Indians the same line of governmental policy. It shall be made their duty to visit all the Indian tribes within the limits of the United States, whether, to do this, it requires three, five, or ten years. They shall hold talks with them, setting forth the great benefits that would result to them from a permanent peace with the whites, from their abandonment of their nomadic mode of life, and adopting agricultural and pastoral pursuits, and the habits and modes of civilized communities. Under the directions of the President the commission shall explain to the various tribes the advantages of their consolidation upon some common territory, over which Congress shall have extended the aegis of good, wise, and wholesome laws for their protection and perpetuation. It would be wise to convince the Indians of the great power and number of the whites; that they cover the whole land, to the north, south, east, and west of them. I believe they could easily understand that although this country was once wholly inhabited by Indians, the tribes, and many of them once powerful, who occupied the countries now constituting the States east of the Mississippi, have, one by one, been exterminated in their abortive attempts to stem the western march of civilization.

They could probably be made to comprehend that the waves of

population and civilization are upon every side of them; that it is too strong for them to resist; and that, unless they fall in with the current of destiny as it rolls and surges around them, they must succumb and be annihilated by its overwhelming force. In consequence of the gradual extinction of the Indian races, and the failure of almost every plan heretofore attempted for the amelioration of their condition, and the prolongation of their national existence, and also because they will not abandon their savage tastes and propensities, it has of late years become somewhat common, not only for the press, but in the speeches of men of intelligence, and some occupying high and responsible positions, to advocate the policy of their immediate and absolute extermination. Such a proposition, so revolting to every sense of humanity and Christianity, it seems to me could not for one moment be entertained by any enlightened nation. On the contrary, the honor of the national character and the dictates of a sound policy, guided by the principles of religion and philanthropy, would urge the adoption of a system to avert the extinction of a people, however unenlightened they may be. The American government can never adopt the policy of a total extermination of the Indian race within her limits, numbering, perhaps, less than four hundred thousand, without a cost of untold treasure and lives of her people, besides exposing herself to the abhorrence and censure of the entire civilized world.

AN EYEWITNESS REPORT OF THE SAND CREEK MASSACRE, NOVEMBER 28, 1864

George Bent (Cheyenne)

[A variety of Indian hostilities occurred during the Civil War, when the bulk of the U.S. Army was occupied elsewhere. One especially destructive episode involved the combined forces of Arapahos, Southern Cheyenne, and Sioux who raided trails and wagon trains in the Colorado area in the summer of 1863. Through the efforts of Major Edward W. Wyncoop, some of the Cheyenne and Arapahos stopped fighting and set up camps to await peace negotiations. One such camp was at Sand Creek, forty miles from Fort Lyon, under Black Kettle and White Hand (both Cheyenne) and Left Hand (Arapaho). There were about 700 people at the site, of whom 500 were women and children. On November 28, 1864, troops under Colonel John Chivington and Major Scott J. Anthony undertook a deliberate, surprise massacre of the encampment.]

When I looked toward the chief's lodge, I saw that Black Kettle had a large American flag up on a long lodgepole as a signal to the troop that the camp was friendly. Part of the warriors were running out toward the pony herds and the rest of the people were rushing about the camp in great fear. All the time Black Kettle kept calling out not to be frightened; that the camp was under protection and there was no danger. Then suddenly the troops

From George Bird Grinnell, *The Fighting Cheyennes* (Norman, Okla., 1956), pp. 177–80.

opened fire on this mass of men, women, and children, and all
began to scatter and run.

The main body of Indians rushed up the bed of the creek, which
was dry, level sand with only a few little pools of water here and
there. On each side of this wide bed stood banks from two to ten
feet high. While the main body of the people fled up this dry bed,
a part of the young men were trying to save the herd from the
soldiers, and small parties were running in all directions toward
the sand hills. One of these parties, made up of perhaps ten mid-
dle-aged Cheyenne men, started for the sand hills west of the creek,
and I joined them. Before we had gone far, the troops saw us and
opened a heavy fire on us, forcing us to run back and take shelter
in the bed of the creek. We now started up the stream bed, following the main body of Indians and with a whole company of cavalry
close on our heels shooting at us every foot of the way. As we went
along we passed many Indians, men, women, and children, some
wounded, others dead, lying on the sand and in the pools of water.
Presently we came to a place where the main party had stopped,
and were now hiding in pits that they had dug in the high bank
of the stream. Just as we reached this place, I was struck by a ball
in the hip and badly wounded, but I managed to get into one of
the pits. About these pits nearly all Chivington's men had gathered
and more were continually coming up, for they had given up the
pursuit of the small bodies of Indians who had fled to the sand
hills.

The soldiers concentrated their fire on the people in the pits,
and we fought back as well as we could with guns and bows, but
we had only a few guns. The troops did not rush in and fight hand
to hand, but once or twice after they had killed many of the men
in a certain pit, they rushed in and finished up the work, killing
the wounded and the women and children that had not been hurt.
The fight here was kept up until nearly sundown, when at last the
commanding officer called off his men and all started back down
the creek toward the camp that they had driven us from. As they
went back, the soldiers scalped the dead lying in the bed of the
stream and cut up the bodies in a manner that no Indian could
equal. Little Bear told me recently that after the fight he saw the
soldiers scalping the dead and saw an old woman who had been
scalped by the soldiers walk about, but unable to see where to go.
Her whole scalp had been taken and the skin of her forehead fell
down over her eyes.

At the beginning of the attack Black Kettle, with his wife and
White Antelope, took their position before Black Kettle's lodge and
remained there after all others had left the camp. At last Black
Kettle, seeing that it was useless to stay longer, started to run,
calling out to White Antelope to follow him, but White Antelope
refused and stood there ready to die, with arms folded, singing
his death song:

> *Nothing lives long,*
> *Except the earth and the mountains,*

until he was shot down by the soldiers.

Black Kettle and his wife followed the Indians in their flight up the dry bed of the creek. The soldiers pursued them, firing at them constantly, and before the two had gone far, the woman was shot down. Black Kettle supposed she was dead and, the soldiers being close behind him, continued his flight. The troops followed him all the way to the rifle pits, but he reached them unhurt. After the fight he returned down the stream looking for his wife's body. Presently he found her alive and not dangerously wounded. She told him that after she had fallen wounded, the soldiers had ridden up and again shot her several times as she lay there on the sand. Black Kettle put her on his back and carried her up the stream until he met a mounted man, and the two put her on the horse. She was taken to the Cheyenne camp on Smoky Hill. When she reached there, it was found that she had nine wounds on her body. My brother Charlie was in the camp, and he and Jack Smith, another half blood, were captured. After the fight the soldiers took Jack Smith out and shot him in cold blood. Some of the officers told Colonel Chivington what the men were about and begged him to save the young man, but he replied curtly that he had given orders to take no prisoners and that he had no further orders to give. Some of the soldiers shot Jack and were going to shoot my brother also, but fortunately among the troops there were a number of New Mexican scouts whom Charlie knew, and these young fellows protected him. A few of our women and children were captured by the soldiers, but were turned over to my father at the fort, with the exception of two little girls and a boy, who were taken to Denver and there exhibited as great curiosities.

Soon after the troops left us, we came out of the pits and began to move slowly up the stream. More than half of us were wounded and all were on foot. When we had gone up the stream a few miles, we began to meet some of our men who had left camp at the beginning of the attack and tried to save the horses which were being driven off by the soldiers. None of these men had more than one rope, so each one could catch only a single horse. As they joined us, the wounded were put on these ponies' backs. Among these men was my cousin, a young Cheyenne, from whom I secured a pony. I was so badly wounded that I could hardly walk.

When our party had gone about ten miles above the captured camp, we went into a ravine and stopped there for the night. It was very dark and bitterly cold. Very few of us had warm clothing, for we had been driven out of our beds and had had no time to dress. The wounded suffered greatly. There was no wood to be had, but the unwounded men and women collected grass and made fires. The wounded were placed near the fires and covered with grass to keep them from freezing. All night long the people kept up a constant hallooing to attract the attention of any Indians who might be wandering about in the sand hills. Our people had been scattered all over the country by the troops, and no one knows how many of them may have been frozen to death in the open country that night.

We left this comfortless ravine before day and started east toward a Cheyenne camp on the Smoky Hill, forty or fifty miles away. The wounded were all very stiff and sore, and could hardly mount. My hip was swollen with the cold, and I had to walk a long way before I could mount my horse. Not only were half our party wounded, but we were obliged also to look out for a large number of women and little children. In fact, it was on the women and children that the brunt of this terrible business fell. Over three-fourths of the people killed in the battle were women and children.

We had not gone far on our way before we began to meet Indians from the camp on the Smoky Hill. They were coming, bringing us horses, blankets, cooked meat, and other supplies. A few of our people had succeeded in getting horses when the soldiers began the attack, and these men had ridden to the Smoky Hill River and sent aid back to us from the camp there. Almost everyone in that camp had friends or relatives in our camp, and when we came in sight of the lodges, everyone left the camp and came out to meet us, wailing and mourning in a manner that I have never heard equaled.

A year after this attack on our camp a number of investigations of the occurrence were made. Colonel Chivington's friends were then extremely anxious to prove that our camp was hostile, but they had no facts in support of their statements. It was only when these investigations were ordered that they began to consider the question; at the time of the attack it was of no interest to them whether we were hostiles or friendlies. One of Chivington's most trusted officers recently said: "When we came upon the camp on Sand Creek we did not care whether these particular Indians were friendly or not." It was well known to everybody in Denver that the Colonel's orders to his troops were to kill Indians, to "kill all, little and big."

HOW THE INDIANS ARE VICTIMIZED BY GOVERNMENT AGENTS AND SOLDIERS

Palaneapope (Yankton Sioux)

[The following testimony was given in August, 1865, to a commissioner of Indian affairs, A. W. Hubbard, at the Yankton agency in South Dakota.]

I cannot say much. The Great Spirit knows that I speak the truth; knows what I say. When I went to see my grandfather, he told me I should have my reserve; that I should have fifty miles up and down the Missouri river for fifty years, and I might become rich and high up; but I am like one on a high snow bank; the sun shines and continually melts it away, and it keeps going down and down until there is nothing left. When I went to make my treaty, my grandfather agreed, if I would put three young men to work, he would put one white laborer with them to learn them; that I should put three young men to learn ploughing, and he would put one white man to learn them; also, three to sow, three to learn the carpenter's trade, three to learn the blacksmith's trade, and such other trades as we should want; and my great grandfather was to furnish one white man for each trade to learn the young men. My grandfather also said that a school should be established for the nation to learn them to read and write; that the young boys and girls should go to school, and that the young men who worked should have the same pay as the whites. My grandfather told me

From Senate Report No. 156, 39th Congress, 2d Session, pp. 366–72.

if my young men would go to work that the money going to those
who would not work should be given to those who would work.
None of these things have been fulfilled. If my grandfather had
told me that I must split rails, I could have tried it, and then perhaps my young men would have tried; but they would say, how
could I learn them when I did not know how myself. If I try to
get my young men to plough, they would say, if you cannot plough
how can we; there is no one to learn them, and the same thing
would be true if I should try to get the young men to run the
saw-mill or work at any other trade; if I do not know myself, how
can I learn the young men; and the same thing would be the case
if I try to get the young men to build a house; if I don't know
myself, how can I learn them. If I should get all the young men,
half-breeds and Indians, and put them in a room, and pick out
those who have big arms and hands, and take a big bar of iron
and tell them to work it, they would not know how. If I were to
take all the young men and girls, half-breeds and Indians, and tell
them that we will go in that house and take pen and ink and write,
how could I make letters as they ought to be made; I never learned
myself.

My friend, I think if my young men knew how to sow, farm,
carpenter, and do everything else, I could send the white men
away; we ourselves should have the money paid the white men, and
we should have plenty of money. If we had been learned all these
things we could support ourselves, have plenty of money, have
schools, and I could have written my great grandfather, and have
got a letter from him; I could have written him myself what I
wanted.

My grandfather sent me two agents, and I understood the governor was over them. I came down here (Yankton) and the governor was gone to Washington. I staid three days, and then went
back home.

I think I gave my land to my grandfather. When I signed the
treaty I told them I never would sign for the pipestone quarry.
I wanted to keep it myself; but I understand white men are going
there and getting and breaking up the stone.

I would have to tell my grandfather that I made a treaty with
him, and I would have to ask him how many goods he is going to
give me; and I would tell him that I want him to give me the
invoices of my goods, that I may know what I am entitled to. I do
not want corn thrown to me the same as to hogs. If I could get
my invoices I should always know what belongs to me. Every time
our goods come I have asked the agent for the invoices, but they
never show me the invoices; they can write what they please, and
they go and show it to my grandfather, and he thinks it all right. I
think, my friend, my grandfather tells me lies. My friend, what I
give a man I don't try to take back. I think, my friend, there is a
great pile of money belonging to us which we never yet have
received.

I think the Great Spirit hears what I say. When they bring the goods to the agency, my goods are all mixed up with the agent's goods; I can't tell my goods from the trader's goods. I think if you go to all the nations, you will not find any who has been used as I have been. My grandfather told me I should have a warehouse separate from the agents; he told me I should take one hundred and sixty acres of land for my own use, and that I should have plenty of land to raise hay for the stock. All the hay on my bottom land is cut by the white man to sell. I asked for hay, but I can get none—white man cut it; I can't tell who gets the money for the hay, but I think Redfield got some money for hay; my ponies can have no hay. I think, my friend, if you go up to my agency you will have a bad feeling; you will feel bad for me to see the situation I am in, and to see my buildings, after what my grandfather told me.

The first agent was Redfield; and when he came there he borrowed blankets from me to sleep upon, and agreed to return them, but never did, though I asked for them. Goods have been stored up stairs in the warehouse, and have all disappeared; perhaps the rats eat them; I don't know what became of them. If they bring any goods for the Indians to eat and put them in the warehouse, the agents live out of them, and the mess-house where travellers stop has been supplied from the Indians' goods, and pay has been taken by the agents, and they have put the money in their pockets and taken it away with them. I have seen them take the goods from the storehouse of the Indians and take them to the mess-house, and I have had to pay for a meal for myself at the mess-house, and so have others of our Indians had to pay for meals at the mess-house, prepared from their own goods.

I understand that the agents are allowed fifteen hundred dollars per year for salary. I think fifteen hundred dollars is not much—not more than enough to last a month, the way they live; they bring all their families there, and friends also. When the agents have been there one, two and three years, their property increases—the goods in their house and their household furniture increase. When Redfield left the agency, a steamboat came in the night and took away fifteen boxes of goods, so that the Indians would not know it; but the Indians were too sharp for him. When Redfield came up he brought his nephew to be trader for the Indians, and one night he took a load of flour out of the shed where the Indians' flour was, and carried it to his store to sell out to the Indians. My friend, what I say about his taking the flour I did not see with my own eyes, but my young men came and told me so. Because I wanted the blankets that I loaned Redfield, he got mad and never answered me, and never gave me the blankets.

My friend, a great many things have been going on, but they do them in the night, so as to blind me. What I say I see myself. After Redfield took away the fifteen boxes he sent back and took away more. I think all these young chiefs have eyes, the same as I, and that they have seen these things. I went down to Washington twice to see my grandfather, and the third time I went I came back by the Missouri. When I went down I saw many stores full of goods; the suttlers come to our agency and make money and then go off. I think if we had two stores it would be better for us. If I had understood from what my grandfather told me, that I was to be treated as I have been, I would never have done as I have done; I never would have signed the treaty. Mr. Redfield said to me, "when I am gone you will meet with a great many agents; but you will never meet one like me." I think I never want to see one like him.

When I made my treaty these young men (chiefs) were there, and my grandfather told me that the half-breeds should have some portion of the money. When I was making the treaty the half-breeds were all about me, my body was sweet, and my grandfather told me that I could give the money to any I pleased. These white men had Indian women for wives; and they came with their accounts against the Indians and gave them to Redfield. They told me if I would help them get the money I should always have plenty of money myself; they would always assist me. I told them I did not believe what they said; that if I should give them the money and should come into their house they would tell me to go out of their house. After I gave them the money they all scattered, and I cannot see them. After what I have done for them, given them the money, these white men have gone away and left their half-breed children for me to support and take care of. But when the agents come with money, the white men come from every direction and get the money, and then go away and spend the money at groceries. I think, after I have paid them so much, they ought to treat me better. I do not want any more of the half-breed money paid Joseph Lionais, Eli Bedard, Charles Ruleoux, August Trovercier, John B. La Plant, Bruno Coneyer, Theophile Bruginer, and Joseph Preoux. The half-breeds that live with the Indians are poor, and I want the money that has been paid the above-named half-breeds retained hereafter and paid over to the tribe towards supporting the poor half-breeds with the Indians. According to the treaty, there is $20,000 belonging to the poor orphan children, but I don't know what has become of it. If the white men should get their money again they would spend it for whiskey, and I want their shares of the money stopped. The reason I am saying this is, the white men and half-breeds, whom we did not provide for by treaty, are displeased with us because we did not give them a share of the money.

Among our nations there are a great many tribes come every year. The Tetons and others come down, and sometimes steal horses, and then the white men lay it to the Yanktons, and come to us to get pay for the stolen horses because we have got a treaty. They came last fall with their claim for stolen horses to the agent, and the agent showed it to the interpreter, and he told the agent that the Indians who stole the horses did not belong to the Yanktons; and the whites said if we had another interpreter they could collect their claims. Our grandfather has given this young man, Charles Pecout, a medal and made him a chief.

I am now done with the management of Agent Redfield and the half-breeds, and now commence upon other matters. . . .

My grandfather, Mr. Redfield, the first agent, did not tell me the same things that my grandfather told me, neither did Agent Burleigh, but both of them told me lies; they filled my belly with lies. Everybody has got a copy of the treaty I made with my grandfather, I suppose. I suppose you are sent by my grandfather to represent the great council. I am here to represent my great council. The money my grandfather sent me has been thrown away. You know who threw it away. The guns, ammunition, wagons, horses, and everything have been thrown away. I can tell who threw them away. The reason the whites have trouble with the Indians is on account of the agents. When the goods come they are not according to the treaty; they never fulfill the treaty. When the agent goes away he says he is going to leave these things to be done by his successor. When Agent Burleigh came he made fine promises of what he would do. I asked for my invoice, but he would not let me have it; and I told him what my grandfather told me. I think the agents are all alike. The agent puts his foot on me as though I were a skunk. And the agents are all getting rich and we are getting poor.

My friend, what I am telling you is the truth, and what I have seen. What the agents have done in the night, I cannot tell. That is the reason I am telling you this; I want you to report it to my grandfather. I want to go to Washington; and I wish you to do all you can with my grandfather to induce him to let me come there next winter. I want to see my grandfather to ascertain how much money and goods have been sent me, and that I may know how much has been stolen and who stole it. I would like to have the agents there with my grandfather when I talk to him, that they may hear what I have to say. If there was a bible there for them to swear upon, they could not swear that they had not stolen the goods.

My friend, I feel glad to see you; and if I could see my grandfather I should feel better.

When Burleigh brought the goods the first time he put the goods on the bank of the river; and there was one bale of fine goods with them, and Burleigh said the goods belonged to the Indians; and one of my young men come and told me about the fine bale of goods, and I went and examined it, and it was fine goods, and would have made nice breech-clouts; but we received none of it, and don't know what become of it. This was the second year Burleigh was there. The first year Burleigh was there, Redfield brought and distributed the goods. The first goods Burleigh undertook to bring there was the first fall of his agency, but the goods were sunk. For my part, I don't wish to hide anything. My friend, if you had come to see me, I could have gone into a council-house with you, and could have said what I wanted to say to you without any one being round to fill my ears. My friend, I know what matters you want to inquire about. I think you are the man to try and do some good to my nation, and my heart feels good. I do not speak a lie. They have got my head so turned that I cannot say what I want to say now, and I will stop now and come and talk more this afternoon.

A steamboat arrived with our goods, and the goods were put out; Burleigh said they were our goods, and they were marked for us; there were five boxes. There were some officers and soldiers there. The boxes remained there on the bank until the next day. At night somebody scratched the marks off and put on other marks. (This statement was witnessed by Medicine Cow and Walking Elk.) They saw it done. The soldiers told the Indians that the goods belonged to the Indians. At another time, Doctor Burleigh had some calico for us, and said he would take it to his house, so that the Indian girls could learn to sew. My daughter went and made one dress, which was given her for making it. Five or six Indian girls went and sewed there, and all got dresses. They were two days there. After the young girls sewed two days apiece and got a dress apiece, they never saw anything more of the calico, and never got any more. Another time, Doctor Burleigh told us he had some ploughs for us. After that I saw one of them at Booge's store. We never had any of them. I told Charles Lamont's wife to take good care of that plough; that the whites might come round and, seeing it, take it. That is the way our property goes. . . .

My friend, we are now done with the agent, and we will now commence with the soldiers. The first year they came up in this country, I think my grandfather must have told them to commence on me, and that is the reason I commence thus with them. I would like to know if my grandfather told them to commence against me first; I should think so, the way they treated us. The first time they came up our young men had nothing to eat, and had gone over the Missouri river to hunt, and the soldiers killed seven of them. The Two-Kettle band and the Low Yanktonais were friendly, and were then on my reservation at the time, and some of them went out with my young men to hunt, and were among the seven that were killed; they were all friendly to the whites. When General Sully returned from his expedition, and was crossing my reserve, there were some of the Indian women married to half-breeds, and they had houses, and the soldiers went in and drove all the persons in them out, and robbed the houses of all there was in them. I would like to know if my grandfather told them to do so. I do not think he did. (All the chiefs present assent to this.) One of my chiefs, Little Swan, now here, had a house, and the soldiers broke in and destroyed all his goods, furniture, utensils and tools, and all the property of his band, the same being stored there. I would like to know if my grandfather told the soldiers when they returned from the expedition with their horses worn out, lost or stolen, to take horses from the Yanktons, in place of those they had lost or had worn out and broken down; I don't believe he did, but that is the way the soldiers did. I think the way the white men treated us is worse than the wolves do. We have a way in the winter of putting our dead up on scaffolds up from the ground, but the soldiers cut down the scaffolds and cut off the hair of the dead, and if they had good teeth they pulled them out, and some of them cut off the heads of the dead and carried them away. One time one of my young men and two squaws went over the river to Fort Randall, and a soldier wanted one of the squaws to do something with; he wanted to sleep with her, and she refused to sleep with him; one of the Indians asked the other squaw if she would sleep with the soldier, and she said she would; but the soldier would not have her, but wanted the other squaw, and claimed that the Indian was trying to prevent him from sleeping with his (the Indian's) squaw, his wife, and the Indian, fearing trouble, started for the ferry, and the soldier shot the Indian, though the Indian got over it. Another time when General Sully came up he passed through the middle of our field, turned all his cattle and stock into our corn and destroyed the whole of it. The ears of some were then a foot long; the corn was opposite Fort Randall, and they not only destroyed the corn but burnt up the fence. I think no other white man would do so; I do not think my grandfather told them to do so. The soldiers set fire to the prairie and burnt up four of our lodges and all there was in them, and three horses. When my corn is good to eat they cross the river from Fort Randall and eat it, and when it is not good they throw it in the river. I think my reserve is very small; the soldiers cut all my wood and grass, and I think this is bad treatment. The above in regard to the soldiers applies to my three chiefs on the reserve opposite Fort Randall, and I will now speak of things at my agency when the soldiers came down from the expedition last fall. At that time myself and others were out on a hunt, and had put our goods under the floors; but when the expedition came down the soldiers broke open the houses, destroyed our pans and kettles, and fired into the stoves and kettles. The soldiers are very drunken and come to our place—they have arms and guns; they run after our women and fire into our houses and lodges; one soldier came along and wanted one of our young men to drink, but he would not, and turned to go away, and the soldier shot at him. Before the soldiers came along we had good health; but once the soldiers come along they go to my squaws and want to sleep with them, and the squaws being hungry will sleep with them in order to get something to eat, and will get a bad disease, and then the squaws turn to their husbands and give them the bad disease.

I would like to know if my grandfather tells the soldiers to get all my hay. Every year great contracts are made for cutting hay for Fort Randall, and they cut the hay all off our land, and I would like to know if my grandfather gave them permission to cut all the hay and take the money. I never see any of the money myself. They take all my mowing machines, bought with my money, to cut hay to sell to the soldiers, and I cannot get the mowing machines to cut anything for ourselves, and I have no use of them. I think the agents are in partnership with these men cutting hay to sell to the soldiers. The reason I think the agent had a hand in cutting hay for the soldiers is, because one year Burleigh gave all of us chiefs fifty dollars each for the hay cut upon the contract. Last spring I asked him for the money for the hay he cut last year, and he told me he could not give it to me, because he had spent it last winter to get us something to eat; but I do not know whether he did or not. I hope you will report these things to my grandfather, and have him stop those men from cutting the hay right off. I think if they would return me my mowing machines I could cut part of the hay on the contract, and I must have some for my ponies; I wish you would attend to it. When I started to come down here they were getting ready to cut hay on another contract for the soldiers at Fort Randall. If they would return our mowing machines we could take the contract ourselves; we have some white men and half-breeds who could assist us, but they want it all themselves. The reason I talk thus is, I think all is wrong. I know the young man who has the contract; I think he has had it two years before. When he breaks any part of the mowing machine he goes to my blacksmith shop and carpenter shop to repair it; it is all paid for out of my annuity fund. It is Hedges who has the contract. Thompson, our blacksmith, has had charge of cutting the hay on the contracts for the past two years, and is getting ready to cut it this year. . . .

Since I made the treaty I am an American. My new agent told me the other day that the old Commissioner of Indian Affairs had been stealing part of the annuities, and that a better man had been put in his place. At this I felt good, and I put on my hat, I felt so good, my heart so big. My new agent is an entirely different man; he shows me the invoices, and I think he is a good man for us. He hired a blacksmith right off. My friend, what I am going to tell you is the truth. We only get five dollars apiece; we have only had one trader; he often makes us feel bad; he sells us goods so high it makes us cry; I think there ought to be two traders; I want two traders. I think if you come up to our agency you will laugh in the first place, and then be mad to see our storehouse in the same building with the trader's store. I want the store moved away a mile, so that it won't be so handy to our goods; I want you to have this changed. I hope my grandfather will see that the store is moved away from my warehouse, because the trader's store is under the floor where my goods are stored. I sometimes have bad dreams; I feel that there may be cracks that my goods may fall through.

I am done. Again I say, my friend, I am glad you have come to see us, and I hope will report all I have said to the Great Father, and that you will do us good. The Great Spirit knows that I have spoken the truth.

THE CONDITION OF THE WINNEBAGO INDIANS IN NEBRASKA, OCTOBER 3, 1865

Little Hill (Winnebago)

You are one of our friends, as it appears. We are very glad to meet you here. Here are some of our old chiefs with me, but not all. And we will tell you something about how we have lived for the four years past. Now, you see me here to-day. Formerly I did not live as I do now. We used to live in Minnesota. While we lived in Minnesota we used to live in good houses, and always take our Great Father's advice, and do whatever he told us to do. We used to farm and raise a crop of all we wanted every year. While we lived there we had teams of our own. Each family had a span of horses or oxen to work, and had plenty of ponies; now, we have nothing. While we lived in Minnesota another tribe of Indians committed depredations against the whites, and then we were compelled to leave Minnesota. We did not think we would be removed from Minnesota; never expected to leave; and we were compelled to leave so suddenly that we were not prepared; not many could sell their ponies and things they had. The superintendent of the farm for the Winnebagoes was to take care of the ponies we left there and bring them on to us wherever we went; but he only brought to Crow Creek about fifty, and the rest we do not know what became of them. Most all of us had put in our crops that spring before we left, and we had to go and leave everything but our clothes and

From Senate Report No. 156, 39th Congress 2d Session, pp. 416–17.

household things; we had but four days' notice. Some left their houses just as they were, with their stoves and household things in them. They promised us that they would bring all our ponies, but they only brought fifty, and the hostile Sioux came one night and stole all of them away. In the first place, before we started from Minnesota, they told us that they had got a good country for us, where they were going to put us. The interpreter here with me now (Bradford L. Porter) was appointed interpreter, on the first boat that came round, to see to things for the Indians on the trip round. After we got on the boat we were as though in a prison. We were fed on dry stuff all the time. We started down the Mississippi river, and then up the Missouri to Dakota Territory, and there we found our superintendent, and stopped there, (at Crow Creek.) Before we left Minnesota they told us that the superintendent had started on ahead of us, and would be there before us, and that he had plenty of Indians, and would have thirty houses built for us before we got there. After we got there they sometimes give us rations, but not enough to go round most of the time. Some would have to go without eating two or three days. It was not a good country; it was all dust. Whenever we cooked anything it would be full of dust. We found out after a while we could not live there. Sometimes the women and children were sick, and some of them died; and we think many of them died because they could not get enough to eat while they were sick. We don't know who was to blame for our bad treatment—whether it was our superintendent, Thompson, or whether it was our agent. We don't blame our agent, Balcombe. He used to treat us very well while we were in Minnesota, and we cannot say who was to blame at Crow Creek. For the past three years we suppose our Great Father has sent us enough goods, provisions, and money, but we do not think we have got half of it. Sometimes some of the women and children don't get much of what they ought to have, only a piece of calico, or something like that. After we had remained at Crow Creek awhile we discovered, or found out, that the whole tribe could not stay there. There was not enough to eat. The first winter one party (Minnesheik's gang) started down the Missouri river as far as Fort Randall, where they wintered. Before Clark Thompson, the superintendent, left us, (the first fall after we went there,) he had a cottonwood trough made and put beef in it, and sometimes a whole barrel of flour and a piece of pork, and let it stand a whole night, and the next morning, after cooking it, would give us some of it to eat. We tried to use it, but many of us got sick on it and died. I am telling nothing but the truth now. They also put in the unwashed intestines of the beeves and the liver and lights, and, after dipping out the soup, the bottom would be very nasty and offensive. Some of the old women and children got sick on it and died.

Now, I will speak about our annuity goods. I think some of our goods—I know pretty near where they have gone to. One time

Major Balcombe told me to take some goods in the store.
Major B. went into our storehouse and got the goods and gave
them to me, and told me to take them in the store and leave them,
and I did. There were six pieces of calico that I carried into the
store. One time I went in the store, and the storekeeper told me
they would have goods to-morrow. Next morning I went in again
and saw some goods there, and I think the goods belonged to
the Winnebagoes, because no teams came there that night from
no way. What I have told you, not only I know, but some of these
chiefs know also. I know one thing certain, that the pork and flour
we left in Minnesota, that belonged to us, was brought over to
Crow Creek and sold to us by Hawley & Hubbell, our storekeepers
at Crow Creek. I will pass and not say more about the provision,
and say of things since we left Crow Creek. For myself, in the first
place, I thought I could stay there for a while and see the country.
But I found out it wasn't a good country. I lost six of my children,
and so I came down the Missouri river. When I got ready to start,
some soldiers came there and told me if I started they would fire
at me. I had thirty canoes ready to start. No one interceded with
the soldiers to permit me to go; but the next night I got away and
started down the river, and when I got down as far as the town
of Yankton I found a man there and got some provisions; then
came on down further and got more provisions of the military
authorities, and then went on to the Omahas. After we got to the
Omahas, somebody gave me a sack of flour; and some one told
us to go to the other side of the Missouri and camp, and we did so.
We thought we would keep on down the river, but some one came
and told us to stay, and we have been there ever since. Since that
time Mr. Graff has been finding rations for us; and I have been
chief thirty years, and have never seen such a man. He is a good
man. He has been feeding us good beef, flour, and sometimes corn,
ever since we have been down there. There is another good man
close by us, and that is Colonel Furnas. We the chiefs have no
particular complaint to make against our present agent. It is some
of our young men that speak against him. We are very glad that
Mr. Graff feeds us, and hope he will keep on. We don't know
how long he will feed us. You see us here now. We are most all
naked; the whole tribe. Some of the tribe are more destitute of
clothing than we are. We got some goods here now which the
Great Father sent us. They are lying in the Omaha warehouse, and
we don't know but that the rats have eat them. There are a good
many women and children that are naked and cannot come out
of their tents. Some of the young men work out and get something
for some of them to wear. The time I went to Washington last
winter I asked the commissioner about my goods, and he said
the goods had already been sent, and when I got back the agent
would give them to us. But when we ask our agent for them he will
not give them to us. The reason, I suppose, he will not give us our
goods, he is mad with us, because our young men have been talking

that the major would be removed and a new agent appointed; and we suppose he was mad about it, and when we went and asked for the goods he told us to go to our new agent. That is the last word I have heard from the agent. Would like you to see about it. We left a good country in Minnesota. We like our present place on the Omaha reservation very well, and, if our treaty is ratified, we shall be well satisfied.

SPEECH AT THE MEDICINE LODGE INDIAN COUNCIL, ADDRESSED TO THE INDIAN COMMISSIONER, NATHANIEL G. TAYLOR, OCTOBER 20, 1867

Ten Bears (Comanche)

My heart is filled with joy when I see you here, as the brooks fill with water when the snow melts in the spring; and I feel glad as the ponies do when the fresh grass starts in the beginning of the year. I heard of your coming when I was many sleeps away, and I made but few camps when I met you. I know that you had come to do good to me and to my people. I looked for benefits which would last forever, and so my face shines with joy as I look upon you.

My people have never first drawn a bow or fired a gun against the whites. There has been trouble on the line between us, and my young men have danced the war-dance. But it was not begun by us. It was you [white men] to send the first soldier and we who sent out the second. Two years ago I came upon this road, following the buffalo, that my wives and children might have their cheeks plump and their bodies warm. But the soldiers fired on us, and since that time there has been a noise like that of a thunderstorm, and we have not known which way to go. So it was upon the Canadian.

From *The American Indian*, February, 1930.

Nor have we been made to cry once alone. The blue dressed soldiers and the Utes came from out of the night when it was dark and still, and for campfires they lit our lodges. Instead of hunting game they killed my braves, and the warriors of the tribe cut short their hair for the dead. So it was in Texas. They made sorrow come into our camps, and we went out like the buffalo bulls when the cows are attacked. When we found them, we killed them, and their scalps hang in our lodges.

The Comanches are not weak and blind, like the pups of the dog when seven sleeps old. They are strong and farsighted, like grown horses. We took their road and we went on it. The white women cried and our women laughed.

But there are things which you have said to me which I do not like. They were not sweet like sugar, but bitter like gourds. You said that you wanted to put us upon a reservation, to build our houses and make us medicine lodges. I do not want them. I was born upon the prairie where the wind blew free and there was nothing to break the light of the sun.

I was born where there were no inclosures and where everything drew a free breath. I want to die there and not within walls. I know every stream and every wood between the Rio Grande and the Arkansas, I have hunted and lived over that country. I lived like my fathers before me, and, like them, I lived happily.

When I was at Washington the Great Father told me that all the Comanches' land was ours and that no one should hinder us in living upon it. So why do you ask us to leave the rivers and the sun and the wind and live in houses? Do not ask us to give up the buffalo for the sheep. The young men have heard talk of this, and it has made them sad and angry. Do not speak of it more. I love to carry out the talk I get from the Great Father. When I get goods and presents I and my people feel glad, since it shows that he holds us in the eye.

If Texans had kept out of my country there might have been peace. But that which you now say we must live on is too small. The Texans have taken away the places where the grass grew the thickest and the timber the best. Had we kept that, we might have done the things you ask. But it is too late. The white man has the country which we loved, and we only wish to wander on the prairies until we die. Any good thing you say to me shall not be forgotten. I shall carry it as near to my heart as my children, and it shall be as often on my tongue as the name of the Great Father. I want no blood upon my land to stain the grass. I want it all clear and pure, and I wish it so that all who go through among my people may find peace when they come in and leave it when they go out.

The commissioners have come afar to listen to our grievances. My heart is glad, and I shall hide nothing from you. I understood that you were coming down here to see us. I moved away from those disposed to war, and I also came from afar to see you. The

Kiowas and Comanches have not been fighting. We were away down south when we heard that you were coming to see us.

The Cheyennes are those that have been fighting you. They did it in broad daylight, so that all could see them. If I had been fighting I would have done so also. Two years ago I made peace with General Harney, Sanborn, and Colonel Leavenworth at the mouth of the Little Arkansas. That peace I have never broken. When the grass was growing this spring a large body of soldiers came along on the Santa Fe road. I had not done anything and therefore was not afraid.

All the chiefs of the Kiowas, Comanches, and Arapahoes are here today. They have come to listen to the good word. We have been waiting here a long time to see you, and we are getting tired. All the land south of the Arkansas belongs to the Kiowas and Comanches, and I don't want to give away any of it. I love the land and the buffalo, and will not part with any. I want you to understand also that the Kiowas do not want to fight and have not been fighting since we made the treaty. I hear a good deal of fine talk from these gentlemen, but they never do what they say. I don't want any of these medicine homes built in the country; I want the papooses brought up just exactly like I am. When I make peace, it is a long and lasting one; there is no end to it. We thank you for your presents.

All these chiefs and headmen feel happy. They will do what you want. They know that you are doing the best you can. I and they will do so also. There is one big chief lately died—Jim Pockmark, of the Caddoes—he was a great peacemaker, and we are sorry he is dead.

When I look upon you I know you are all big chiefs. While you are in the country we go to sleep happy and are not afraid. I have heard that you intend to settle us on a reservation near the mountains. I don't want to settle there. I love to roam over the wide prairie, and when I do it I feel free and happy, but when we settle down we grow pale and die.

Hearken well to what I say. I have laid aside my lance, my bow, and my shield, and yet I feel safe in your presence. I have told you the truth. I have no little lies hid about me, but I don't know how it is with the commissioners; are they as clear as I am? A long time ago this land belonged to my fathers, but when I go up to the river I see a camp of soldiers, and they are cutting my wood down or killing my buffalo. I don't like that, and when I see it my heart feels like bursting with sorrow. I have spoken.

SPEECH AT COOPER UNION, NEW YORK, JULY 16, 1870

Red Cloud (Oglala Sioux)

[As one of the most influential of the Sioux chiefs, Red Cloud had been on a tour of the East to visit President Grant. While in New York, he was persuaded to speak at the Cooper Union, one of the popular lyceums in the United States at the time. He was given a warm welcome and standing ovation by the New York audience.]

My brethren and my friends who are here before me this day, God Almighty has made us all, and He is here to bless what I have to say to you today. The Good Spirit made us both. He gave you lands and He gave us lands; He gave us these lands; you came in here, and we respected you as brothers. God Almighty made you but made you all white and clothed you; when He made us He made us with red skins and poor; now you have come.

When you first came we were very many, and you were few; now you are many, and we are getting very few, and we are poor. You do not know who appears before you today to speak. I am a representative of the original American race, the first people of this continent. We are good and not bad. The reports that you hear concerning us are all on one side. We are always well disposed to them. You are here told that we are traders and thieves, and it is not so. We have given you nearly all our lands, and if we had any more land to give we would be very glad to give it. We have nothing more. We are driven into a very little land, and we

From *New York Times*, July 17, 1870.

want you now, as our dear friends, to help us with the government of the United States.

The Great Father made us poor and ignorant—made you rich
and wise and more skillful in these things that we know nothing
about. The Great Father, the Good Father in heaven, made you
all to eat tame food—made us to eat wild food—gives us the wild
food. You ask anybody who has gone through our country to
California; ask those who have settled there and in Utah, and you
will find that we have treated them always well. You have children;
we have children. You want to raise your children and make them
happy and prosperous; we want to raise [ours] and make them
happy and prosperous. We ask you to help us to do it.

At the mouth of the Horse Creek, in 1852, the Great Father
made a treaty with us by which we agreed to let all that country
open for fifty-five years for the transit of those who were going
through. We kept this treaty; we never treated any man wrong;
we never committed any murder or depredation until afterward
the troops were sent into that country, and the troops killed our
people and ill-treated them, and thus war and trouble arose; but
before the troops were sent there we were quiet and peaceable,
and there was no disturbance. Since that time there have been
various goods sent from time to time to us, the only ones that
ever reached us, and then after they reached us (very soon after)
the government took them away. You, as good men, ought to
help us to these goods.

Colonel Fitzpatrick of the government said we must all go to
farm, and some of the people went to Fort Laramie and were
badly treated. I only want to do that which is peaceful, and the
Great Fathers know it, and also the Great Father who made us both.
I came to Washington to see the Great Father in order to have
peace and in order to have peace continue. That is all we want,
and that is the reason why we are here now.

In 1868 men came out and brought papers. We are ignorant
and do not read papers, and they did not tell us right what was
in these papers. We wanted them to take away their forts, leave
our country, would not make war, and give our traders something.
They said we had bound ourselves to trade on the Missouri, and
we said, no, we did not want that. The interpreters deceived us.
When I went to Washington I saw the Great Father. The Great
Father showed me what the treaties were; he showed me all these
points and showed me that the interpreters had deceived me and
did not let me know what the right side of the treaty was. All I
want is right and justice. . . . I represent the Sioux Nation; they
will be governed by what I say and what I represent. . . .

Look at me. I am poor and naked, but I am the chief of the
Nation. We do not want riches, we do not ask for riches, but
we want our children properly trained and brought up. We look
to you for your sympathy. Our riches will . . . do us no good; we
cannot take away into the other world anything we have—we

want to have love and peace. . . . We would like to know why commissioners are sent out there to do nothing but rob [us] and get the riches of this world away from us?

I was brought up among the traders and those who came out there in those early times. I had a good time for they treated us nicely and well. They taught me how to wear clothes and use tobacco, and to use firearms and ammunition, and all went on very well until the Great Father sent out another kind of men—men who drank whisky. He sent out whiskymen, men who drank and quarreled, men who were so bad that he could not keep them at home, and so he sent them out there.

I have sent a great many words to the Great Father, but I don't know that they ever reach the Great Father. They were drowned on the way, therefore I was a little offended with it. The words I told the Great Father lately would never come to him, so I thought I would come and tell you myself.

And I am going to leave you today, and I am going back to my home. I want to tell the people that we cannot trust his agents and superintendents. I don't want strange people that we know nothing about. I am very glad that you belong to us. I am very glad that we have come here and found you and that we can understand one another. I don't want any more such men sent out there, who are so poor that when they come out there their first thoughts are how they can fill their own pockets.

We want preserves in our reserves. We want honest men, and we want you to help to keep us in the lands that belong to us so that we may not be a prey to those who are viciously disposed. I am going back home. I am very glad that you have listened to me, and I wish you good-bye and give you an affectionate farewell.

REMARKS MADE TO GENERAL GORDON GRANGER DURING A CONFERENCE ON THE MATTER OF GOING TO A RESERVATION, 1871

Cochise (Apache)

The sun has been very hot on my head and made me as in a fire; my blood was on fire, but now I have come into this valley and drunk of these waters and washed myself in them and they have cooled me. Now that I am cool I have come with my hands open to you to live in peace with you. I speak straight and do not wish to deceive or be deceived. I want a good, strong and lasting peace. When God made the world he gave one part to the white man and another to the Apache. Why was it? Why did they come together? Now that I am to speak, the sun, the moon, the earth, the air, the waters, the birds and beasts, even the children unborn shall rejoice at my words. The white people have looked for me long. I am here! What do they want? They have looked for me long; why am I worth so much? If I am worth so much why not mark when I set my foot and look when I spit? The coyotes go about at night to rob and kill; I can not see them; I am not God. I am no longer chief of all the Apaches. I am no longer rich; I am but a poor man. The world was not always this way. I can not command the animals; if I would they would not obey me. God made us not as you; we were born like the animals, in the dry grass, not on beds like you.

From Kansas State Historical Society *Collections*, Vol. 13, pp. 391–92.

This is why we do as the animals, go about of a night and rob and steal. If I had such things as you have, I would not do as I do, for then I would not need to do so. There are Indians who go about killing and robbing. I do not command them. If I did, they would not do so. My warriors have been killed in Sonora. I came in here because God told me to do so. He said it was good to be at peace —so I came! I was going around the world with the clouds, and the air, when God spoke to my thought and told me to come in here and be at peace with all. He said the world was for us all; how was it? When I was young I walked all over this country, east and west, and saw no other people than the Apaches. After many summers I walked again and found another race of people had come to take it. How is it? Why is it that the Apaches wait to die—that they carry their lives on their finger nails? They roam over the hills and plains and want the heavens to fall on them. The Apaches were once a great nation; they are now but few, and because of this they want to die and so carry their lives on their finger nails. Many have been killed in battle. You must speak straight so that your words may go as sunlight to our hearts. *Tell me, if the Virgin Mary has walked throughout all the land, why has she never entered the wigwam of the Apache? Why have we never seen or heard her?*

I have no father nor mother; I am alone in the world. No one cares for Cochise; that is why I do not care to live, and wish the rocks to fall on me and cover me up. If I had a father and a mother like you, I would be with them and they with me. When I was going around the world, all were asking for Cochise. Now he is here—you see him and hear him—are you glad? If so, say so. Speak, Americans and Mexicans, I do not wish to hide anything from you nor have you hide anything from me; I will not lie to you; do not lie to me. I want to live in these mountains; I do not want to go to Tularosa. That is a long ways off. The flies on those mountains eat out the eyes of the horses. The bad spirits live there. I have drunk of these waters and they have cooled me; I do not want to leave here.

EVENTS LEADING UP TO THE MODOC WAR, 1873

Captain Jack (Modoc)

[In 1864, the Modoc tribe had ceded their land in California to the United States and had gone to live on a reservation in Oregon with the Klamaths. Being unhappy there among this hostile tribe, many of the Modocs returned to their old home in 1870 under the leadership of Captain Jack. When the U.S. Army tried to force them to return to Oregon, they fled to the lava beds near Tule Lake, where they could not be easily attacked. A few of their leaders, including Captain Jack, were induced to attend a conference with General Edward R. S. Canby and three other commissioners in April, 1873. However, the Indians killed Canby and one other commissioner, and escaped. After a year of fighting large army contingents, the Modocs finally surrendered. Captain Jack, a part of whose testimony appears below, and three others were tried and hanged for the murders. Most of the Modocs were then sent to Indian Territory.]

CAPTAIN JACK. I have always told white men when they came to my country, that if they wanted a home to love there they could have it; and I never asked them for any pay for living there as my people lived. I liked to have them come there and live. I liked to be with white people. I didn't know anything about the war—when it was going to commence. Major Jackson came down there and commended on me while I was in bed asleep. When Meacham came to talk to me he always came and talked good to me. He never talked about shooting, or anything of that kind. It was my understanding that Ivon Applegate was to come and have a talk with me, and

From House Executive Document No. 122, 43d Congress, 1st Session, pp. 173–78.

not to bring any soldiers, but to come alone. I was ready to have a talk with any man that would come to talk peace with me. The way I wanted that council with Applegate to come off, was, I wanted Henry Miller to be there and hear it. He always talked good to me and gave me good advice. Miller told me he wanted to talk with me, and wanted to be there when Applegate met me, and wanted to talk for me and with me. Dennis Crawley told me he wanted to be there to talk with me when Applegate came. He told me I was a good man, and he wanted to see me get my rights. It scared me when Major Jackson came and got there just at daylight, and made me jump out of my bed without a shirt or anything else on. I didn't know what it meant, his coming at that time of day. When Major Jackson and his men came up to my camp, they surrounded it, and I hollered to Major Jackson for them not to shoot, that I would talk. I told Bogus Charley to go and talk, until I could get my clothes on. He went and told them that he wanted to talk; that he didn't want them to shoot. Then they all got down off their horses, and I thought then we were going to have a talk; and I went into another tent. I thought, then, why were they mad with me; what had they found out about me, that they came here to fight me. I went into my tent then and sat down and they commenced shooting. My people were not all there; there were but a few of us there. Major Jackson shot my men while they were standing round. I ran off; I did not fight any. I threw my people away that they had shot and wounded. I did not stop to get them. I ran off, and did not want to fight. They shot some of my women, and they shot my men. I did not stop to inquire anything about it, but left and went away. I went then into the lava-beds. I had very few people, and did not want to fight. I thought I had but few people, and it was not of any use for me to fight, and so I went to the lava-beds. While I was on my way to the cave, there was a white man came to my camp. I told him the soldiers had pitched onto me, and fired into me while I was asleep, but I would not hurt him—for him to go back to town, home. I went into the lava-beds and staid there. I didn't go to any place, I did not want to fight, and I did not think about fighting any more. I didn't see any white men for a long time. I didn't want to kill anybody. I went to my cave and there I staid. John Fairchild came to my house, and asked me if I wanted to fight, and I said no, I had quit fighting, that I did not want to fight any more—him nor anybody. The Hot Creek Indians then started for the reservation and got as far as Bob Whittle's, on Klamath River, and there the Linkville men scared them and they ran back. They were going to kill them. Then the Hot Creeks came to my camp and told me the whites were going to kill them all. They got scared by what the white men had told them, that they were going to kill them all.

There were some of the Indians I left at Fairchild's; they were talking about bringing them by the way of Lost River. They ran off too. When they all got to my place I told some of them to go back to Fairchild's. The Hot Creek Indians came from the other side and came to my place. Hooker Jim came from this side, the east side of Lost River or Tule Lake, and they came around the lower end of Tule Lake and came to my place. I didn't know anything of any settlers being killed until Hooker Jim came with his band and told me. I didn't think that they would kill the whites when they went around that way. I did not believe it. I did not want them to stay with me. None of my people had killed any of the whites, and I had never told Hooker Jim and his party to murder any settlers; and I did not want them to stay with me. I don't know who told them to kill the settlers. I always advised them not to kill white people. I told Hooker that I never had killed any white person, and never had advised him to kill them; that he killed them of his own accord, not from my advice. I thought all of the white men liked me that was living in my country. I always thought they did. They always treated me well. (To Hooker Jim:) What did you kill those people for? I never wanted you to kill my friends. You have done it on your own responsibility.

Then I thought that, after hearing that those white people had been killed that the whites would all be mad at me. And it troubled me and made me feel bad. I told them it was bad, and they ought not to have done it. I knew that the white people would be mad at me just on account of this Hooker Jim killing so many white people when he had no business to do it. After I had left Lost River, I had quit then, and I had not fought any, and did not intend to fight any more. Fairchilds told me that that was bad; that they had killed the settlers; that it was wrong; and if they did not quit fighting there, the chances were the soldiers would all come on us again and kill us all, if we did not make peace then. I told Fairchilds that I did not want to fight any more; that I was willing to quit if the soldiers would quit. Fairchilds then never came to my house any more for a long time after the Indians that were stopping with him had run off. He was afraid to come then any more. It was a long time that I heard nothing from him. Nobody came to my place, and I could not get any news. After a great while Fairchilds came again with a squaw, and told me I had better make peace, for the white people were all mad at us. For a good while then there was nothing going on, and again the soldiers came there. When the soldiers came they came fighting and fought all day. The first day the soldiers got there they fought a little; the next day, all day. The soldiers came and they fought a part of two days and then went away again.

Link River John came and told me not to be mad at them. I told them that I never had killed anybody and never wanted to. When Fairchilds came in to see me I told him I was not mad at anybody, and did not want to fight, and did not want any more war. I told Fairchilds I did not know what they were mad with me about;

that I was willing to quit fighting; willing for both sides to quit it and live again in peace. I told him that I did not want the Lost River country any more; that as there had been trouble about that, I wanted to go to some place else and live, and did not want to live there any more. I told them there had been blood spilt there on Lost River, and that I did not want to live there; that I would hunt some other place and live; and that I was willing to quit fighting if they would let me alone. I do not deny telling Fairchilds, or anybody else, that I wanted to talk good talk. I always wanted to talk good talk. I wanted to quit fighting. My people were all afraid to leave the cave. They had been told that they were going to be killed, and they were afraid to leave there; and my women were afraid to leave there. While the peace talk was going on there was a squaw came from Fairchilds and Dorris's, and told us that the peace commissioners were going to murder us. That they were trying to get us out to murder us. A man by the name of Nate Beswick told us so. There was an old Indian man came in the night and told us again.

The INTERPRETER. That is one of those murdered in the wagon while prisoners by the settlers.

CAPTAIN JACK (continuing). This old Indian man told me that Nate Beswick told him that that day Meacham, General Canby, Dr. Thomas, and Dyer were going to murder us if we came at the council. All of my people heard this old man tell us so. And then there was another squaw came from Fairchilds and told me that Meacham and the peace commissioners had a pile of wood ready built up, and were going to burn me on this pile of wood; that when they brought us into Dorris's they were going to burn me there. All of the squaws about Fairchilds's and Dorris's told me the same thing. After hearing all this news I was afraid to go, and that is the reason I did [not] come in to make peace.

Riddle and his woman always told me the truth, and advised me to do good, but I have never taken their advice. If I had listened to them instead of to the squaws, that were lying all of the time, I would not have been in the fix that I am in now.

The reason that I did not come when the wagons came after me was, this squaw had come the night before and told me they were going to burn me, and I was afraid to come. I can see now that the squaws at Fairchilds's and Dorris's were lying to me all the time; and Bob Whittles's wife lied to me. If I had listened to Riddle I would have been a heap better off. Bob Whittles's came to see me and she told me that I was not her people, and she did not want to talk anything good to me. She always gave me bad advice. She told me that if she did not come back again right straight, that I might know the soldiers would be on to me the next day to fight me.

I have told you about the advice that I heard and the main cause of my never coming in and making peace. I was afraid to come. I don't consider myself, when you came to have a talk with me, the chief then. When you, and the reporters came in the cave with you, I didn't know what to say; I didn't know anything about fighting then, and didn't want to fight. Your chief makes his men mind him and listen to him, and they do listen to what he tells them, and they believe him; but my people won't. My men would not listen to me. They wanted to fight. I told them not to fight. I wanted to talk and make peace and live right; but my men would not listen to me. The men that were in the cave with me never listened to what I said; and they cannot one of them say, and tell the truth, that I ever advised them to fight. I have always told my people to keep out of trouble; that when I met in council I wanted to meet in peace and in a friendly way. I told them when they would not listen to me, that if they wanted to fight, and would fight, they would have to fight; but they would not do so from anything that I told them; that it was against my will to fight.

By my being the chief of the Modoc tribe, I think that the white people all think that I raised the fight and kept it going. I have told my people that I thought the white people would think that about me; and I didn't want to have anything to do with it; that if they wanted to fight they would have to go on their own hook.

Hooker Jim was one that agitated the fighting: that wanted to fight all of the time. I sat over to one side with my few men and did not say anything about fighting. Now I have to bear the blame for him and the rest of them.

Schonchis was with Hooker Jim; he was on Hooker Jim's side. I was by myself with my few men that I had, and did not have anything to say. They were all mad at me. Then I would think that the white people would think that I was the cause of all this fuss; and then I would think again that they surely could not think so, when they knew that these other men had committed these murders. I would talk to them, but they would not listen to me. I told them that I liked my wife and my children, and I did not want any trouble, but wanted to live in peace; but they would not listen to what I would say. I had not done anything. I had not shot anybody. I never commenced the fight. Hooker Jim is the one that always wanted to fight, and commenced killing and murdering. When I would get to talking they would tell me to hush! that I didn't know anything; that I was nothing more than an old squaw. I and Hooker Jim had a fuss, and I told him that I had not done anything mean; that he had been murdering the settlers. And I got my revolver, and if I could have seen him through the canvas I would have killed him. I thought that I would kill him; and I wanted to kill him, for he is the one that murdered the settlers on Tule Lake. I thought that the white people were mad because I was living on Lost River, and that they wanted that land there; that is what I thought when the fight commenced. I then had a fuss with another Indian because I got mad at Hooker Jim—an Indian called George. George and I had a quarrel, and he told me I was nothing but an old squaw; that I never had killed anybody; that he had killed white people and had killed lots of soldiers—him and Hooker Jim. Hooker Jim said, "You are like an old squaw; you have never done any fighting yet; we have done the fighting, and you are our chief. You are not fit to be a chief." I told him that I was not ashamed of it; that I knew I had not killed anybody, and I did not want to kill anybody, and I would have felt sorry if I had killed any white people. They told me that I was laying around in camp and did not do anything, but lay there like a log, and they were traveling around and killing people and stealing things. That they, Hooker and George, were not afraid to travel. They said "What do you want with a gun? you don't shoot anything with it. You don't go any place to do anything. You are sitting around on the rocks." I told them that I knew and was not ashamed to be called an old squaw; that I thought I done my duty by telling them to keep the peace; but they would not listen to me. I told them that they run around and committed these murders against my will. Scar-faced Charley told me that he would go with Hooker and them; that he could fight with them; that I was nothing but an old squaw. I told them then if that was what they were going to do, why they could go on their own responsibility; that I did not want to go with them; that I did not want to live with them. Scar-faced Charley will tell everything that he knows. He don't want to keep anything back; neither do I want to keep anything back. . . .

The four scouts have told you they didn't know anything about the murder of General Canby; and they advocated the murder of General Canby with me. The Indians that told that the talk took place in my house about the murder of General Canby, lie. It was their own house it took place in. I don't want to keep anything back. I do not want to tell a lie about it. I would like to know why they told that they did not want to fight; or didn't say anything in regard to fighting. They all talked to me and were all in with it, because we didn't want to move off to any country that we didn't know anything about. I would like to know why Hooker Jim could not tell who he wanted to kill when he went out there. He says he went there to kill a man; but he would not tell the man he wanted to kill. Meacham was the man that he wanted to kill. Them four scouts knew all about it; and they were in our councils when we were holding councils, and they all wanted to kill the peace commissioners; they all advised me to do it. I thought that it would all be laid on to me, and I wondered to myself if there could be any other man that it could be laid upon.

Another thing that made me afraid to meet the commissioners, the Indians lied to me and told me that Dr. Thomas and the other peace commissioners had pistols with them, and wanted to kill us. I told them that I didn't see any pistols with anybody, and they surely must have lied. I told them that I did not want to have any trouble with the peace commissioners; that I did not want to kill them. Hooker Jim, he said that he wanted to kill Meacham, and we must do it. That is all I have to say.

TESTIMONY ABOUT THE WHITE MAN'S PROMISES AND INTENTIONS, AUGUST 11, 1873
Blackfoot (Crow)

I went to Fort Laramie; the old Indians signed the treaty. We came back to the camp and told the young men, and they said we had done wrong and they did not want to have anything to do with it. They said, "We love the Great Father, and hold on to the hands of our white friend. All the other Indian tribes fight the whites; we do not do so. We love the whites, and we want them to leave us a big country."

All the other Indians go and talk with the Great Father; you take them to Washington; they are bad; they hide their hearts; but they talk good to the Great Father, and you do more for them than for us. This I want to tell you; yesterday you spoke to us and we listened to you. If you wish to have peace with all the Indians get them all together and make peace with them. Then I will make peace with them, too.

The Great Spirit made these mountains and rivers for us, and all this land. We were told so, and when we go down the river hunting for food we come back here again. We cross over to the other river, and we think it is good. Many years ago the buffalo got sick and died, and Mr. Maldron gave us annuity goods, and since then they have given us something every year. The guns you give us we do not point at the whites. We do not shoot our white friends. We are

From House Executive Document No. 89, 43d Congress, 1st Session, pp. 28–42.

true when we look in your face. On our hands is no white man's blood. When you give us arms to go and fight the Sioux, we fight them to keep our lands from them. When we raise our camp and go for buffalo, some white men go with us; they see what we are doing; they see that we jump over the places that are bloody. On the other side of the river below there are plenty of buffalo; on the mountains are plenty of elk and black-tail deer, and white-tail deer are plenty at the foot of the mountain. All the streams are full of beaver. In the Yellowstone River the whites catch trout; there are plenty of them. The white men give us food; we know nothing about it. Do not be in a hurry; when we are poor, we will tell you of it. At Laramie we went to see the commissioners. Now commissioners come to see us, and we listen to what you say. The commissioners told us at Laramie if we remained good friends of the whites we would be taken care of for forty years. Since we made that treaty it is only five years. You are in a hurry to quit giving us food. I am a young man yet; my teeth are all good. They told us at Laramie we would get food till we were old, and our children after us. This is not the place for the agency, on this point of rocks. We would like to know who built the agency here. They told us they would give us our food. They promised to send a good agent and good traders, and if they were not good they would be taken away. Pease never treated us wrong; the young men and the children he always treated right; all that was sent for us he gave us; he was not a thief; he treated us well, and we do not want him to go away from us. On Sheep Mountain white men come; they are my friends; they marry Crow women, they have children with them; the men talk Crow. When we come from hunting we get off at their doors, and they give us something to eat. We like it. We raised Shane, (the interpreter;) he was a boy when he came here. You ask us what we have to say, and that is what we tell you. Here is the doctor; when our people are sick he doctors them. He has two children by a Crow woman; we like him. Here are our traders; when we go hunting they give us ammunition; they gave me a revolver to kill buffalo. We do not know anything about Cross, (a new trader;) we do not know his face. We want the soldiers at Ellis to take the part of the Crows. When they come here to see the giving of annuity goods we give them robes to take with them, and when they hear bad talk about the Crows we want them to speak well of us. When we camp here some of the whites run off with our horses into the mountains. We know about it, but we do not say anything. We have a strong heart, as firm as a rock, and we say nothing about it, but you want to hear what we have to say and I tell you. In Gallatin valley the Cheyennes, Arapahoes and Sioux made a raid and the people blamed the Crows with it. We want them to quit speaking bad about us. On the Missouri River, the whites have married into all the different Indian tribes; their brothers-in-law, the white men, come here and steal our horses. We follow them and find who have them. Some of the Crows went to the Missouri River and got some

Crow horses. The white people sent word they were their horses, and we sent them all back. We claim our horses, but they are not brought back.

When we set up our lodge-poles, one reaches to the Yellowstone, the other is on White River; another one goes to Wind River; the other lodges on the Bridger mountains. This is our land and so we told the commissioners at Fort Laramie, but all kinds of white people come over it and we tell you of it, though we say nothing to them. On this side of the Yellowstone there is a lake; about it are buffalo. It is a rich country; the whites are on it; they are stealing our quartz; it is ours, but we say nothing to them. The whites steal a great deal of our money. We do not want them to go into our country. . . .

The first time I went to Fort Laramie and met the peace commissioners, what each said to the other, we said "Yes, yes." The second time we went we signed the treaty; but neither of us, my white friends nor the Indian chiefs, said "Yes, yes," to what is in that treaty. What we said to them, and what they said to us, was "Good." We said, "Yes, yes," to it; but it is not in the treaty. Shane was there the first time, and what he interpreted to us are not the words that are in the treaty. The first time we went we did not sign the treaty; we only said "Yes, yes," to each other. The Indian way of making a treaty is to light a pipe, and the Indians and their white friends smoke it. When we were in council at Laramie we asked whether we might eat the buffalo for a long time. They said yes. That is not in the treaty. We told them we wanted a big country. They said we should have it; and that is not in the treaty. They promised us plenty of goods, and food for forty years—plenty for all the Crows to eat; but that is not in the treaty. Listen to what I say. We asked "Shall we and our children get food for forty years?" They said "Yes;" but it is not that way in the treaty. They told us when we got a good man for agent he should stay with us; but it is not so in the treaty. We asked that the white man's road along Powder River be abandoned, and that the grass be permitted to grow in it. They said "Yes, yes;" but it is not in the treaty. The land that we used to own we do not think of taking pay for. We used to own the land in the Mud River Valley. These old Crows you see here were born there. We owned Horse Creek, the Stinking Water, and Heart's Mountains. Many of these Indians were born there. So we owned the country about Powder River and Tongue River, and many of our young men were born there. So we owned the mouth of Muscleshell, and Crazy Mountain, and Judith Basin; many of our children were born there. So we told the commissioners. They said "Yes, yes;" but there is nothing about it in the treaty. We told them there were many bad Indians, but that we would hold on to the hands of the white man, and would love each other. We told them the Piegans, the Sioux, and other tribes, have killed white men. We told them the whites were afraid of them. I asked them to look at us; that we had no arms, and they should not be afraid of the Crows. They said "Yes, yes;" but it is not so written in the treaty. The treaty, you say, has bought all our land except on this side of the river; and what do we get for it? I am ashamed about it. We sell our land, and what do we get for it? We get a pair of stockings, and when we put them on they go to pieces. They get some old shirts, and have them washed, and give them to us; we put them on, and our elbows go right through them. They send us tin kettles; we go to get water to carry to our lodges; we dip the water up, but it all runs out again. That is what we get for our land. Why do they send us annuity goods? We go to the buffalo country and get skins; our wives dress them, and we give them to our friends. We give more presents to our white friends than all the annuity goods we get are worth. And this is what we get for our lands. What goods are given us are no better than we give the whites, and I do not see what we are getting for our lands. We told the commission at Laramie that the Sioux were in our country on Tongue River. The Sioux and the Crows were at war, yet I went into the Sioux camp alone. They offered to give us two hundred and sixty horses and mules, all taken from white men, if we would join them, but we refused to do so. They took me by the arm and asked me to stay with them and fight the whites, but I pulled loose from them and would not do so. I told the commission that I was asked to hold the whites with my left hand and the Sioux with my right hand; but now I gave my right hand to the whites and would hold on to them; they said "Yes, yes." But none of this is in the treaty. We told them we had plenty of fish and game, and when they got scarce we would tell them, and ask help from them.

They said "Will you sell the Powder River country, Judith Basin, and Wind River country?" I told them "No;" but that is not in the treaty. When Major Camp came here as agent we gave him a present of a large number of robes to send to the Great Father. We never heard that the Great Father got those robes; we would like to hear about them. The Crow tribe want Major Pease to remain with us as our agent. Some of the young men want him to take them to see the Great Father at Washington. You ask us to tell you what we want. We want Mexican blankets, elk-teeth, beads, eagle-feathers, and panther and otter skins. We like fine horses and needle-guns; these things are to us what money is to you.

THE BATTLE OF THE LITTLE BIGHORN, NARRATED BY AN INDIAN WHO FOUGHT IN IT, JUNE 25, 1876

Two Moons (Cheyenne)

[The Black Hills region of the Dakotas was recognized as inviolable Indian land by the federal government. But the onset of a gold rush there in 1874–75 led the administration of President Ulysses S. Grant to decide that it would be easier to contrive a war against the Indians and seize the land than it would be to oust the white intruders. The campaign of 1876 was commanded by Generals George Crook and Alfred Terry. General George A. Custer and his 7th Cavalry arrived at the huge Sioux encampment in eastern Montana, and there he hoped to achieve fame and advancement by defeating the Indians.]

That spring [1876] I was camped on Powder River with fifty lodges of my people—Cheyennes. The place is near what is now Fort Mc-Kenney. One morning soldiers charged my camp. They were in command of Three Fingers [Colonel McKenzie]. We were surprised and scattered, leaving our ponies. The soldiers ran all our horses off. That night the soldiers slept, leaving the horses one side; so we crept up and stole them back again, and then we went away.

We traveled far, and one day we met a big camp of Sioux at Charcoal Butte. We camped with the Sioux, and had a good time, plenty grass, plenty game, good water. Crazy Horse was head chief of the camp. Sitting Bull was camped a little ways below, on the Little Missouri River.

From *McClure's Magazine*, September, 1898.

Crazy Horse said to me, "I'm glad you are come. We are going to fight the white man again."

The camp was already full of wounded men, women, and children.

I said to Crazy Horse, "All right. I am ready to fight. I have fought already. My people have been killed, my horses stolen; I am satisfied to fight."

[Here the old man paused a moment, and his face took on a lofty and somber expression.]

I believed at that time the Great Spirits had made Sioux, put them there [he drew a circle to the right], and white men and Cheyennes here [indicating two places to the left], expecting them to fight. The Great Spirits I thought liked to see the fight; it was to them all the same like playing. So I thought then about fighting. [As he said this, he made me feel for one moment the power of a sardonic god whose drama was the wars of men.]

About May, when the grass was tall and the horses strong, we broke camp and started across the country to the mouth of the Tongue River. Then Sitting Bull and Crazy Horse and all went up the Rosebud. There we had a big fight with General Crook, and whipped him. Many soldiers were killed—few Indians. It was a great fight, much smoke and dust.

"From there we all went over the divide, and camped in the valley of Little Horn. Everybody thought, "Now we are out of the white man's country. He can live there, we will live here." After a few days, one morning when I was in camp north of Sitting Bull, a Sioux messenger rode up and said, "Let everybody paint up, cook, and get ready for a big dance."

Cheyennes then went to work to cook, cut up tobacco, and get ready. We all thought to dance all day. We were very glad to think we were far away from the white man.

I went to water my horses at the creek, and washed them off with cool water, then took a swim myself. I came back to the camp afoot. When I got near my lodge, I looked up the Little Horn towards Sitting Bull's camp. I saw a great dust rising. It looked like a whirlwind. Soon Sioux horseman came rushing into camp shouting: "Soldiers come! Plenty white soldiers."

I ran into my lodge, and said to my brother-in-law, "Get your horses; the white man is coming. Everybody run for horses."

Outside, far up the valley, I heard a battle cry, *Hay-ay, hay-ay!* I heard shooting, too, this way [clapping his hands very fast]. I couldn't see any Indians. Everybody was getting horses and saddles. After I had caught my horse, a Sioux warrior came again and said, "Many soldiers are coming."

Then he said to the women, "Get out of the way, we are going to have hard fight."

I said, "All right, I am ready."

I got on my horse, and rode out into my camp. I called out to the people all running about: "I am Two Moon, your chief. Don't run

away. Stay here and fight. You must stay and fight the white soldiers. I shall stay even if I am to be killed."

I rode swiftly toward Siting Bull's camp. There I saw the white
soldiers fighting in a line [Reno's men]. Indians covered the flat.
They began to drive the soldiers all mixed up—Sioux, then soldiers,
then more Sioux, and all shooting. The air was full of smoke and
dust. I saw the soldiers fall back and drop into the river-bed like
buffalo fleeing. They had no time to look for a crossing. The Sioux
chased them up the hill, where they met more soldiers in wagons,
and then messengers came saying more soldiers were going to kill
the women, and the Sioux turned back. Chief Gall was there fighting, Crazy Horse also.

I then rode toward my camp, and stopped squaws from carrying
off lodges. While I was sitting on my horse I saw flags come up
over the hill to the east like that [he raised his finger-tips]. Then
the soldiers rose all at once, all on horses, like this [he put his
fingers behind each other to indicate that Custer appeared march-
ing in columns of fours]. They formed into three bunches [squad-
rons] with a little ways between. Then a bugle sounded, and they
all got off horses, and some soldiers led the horses back over the
hill.

Then the Sioux rode up the ridge on all sides, riding very fast.
The Cheyennes went up the left way. Then the shooting was quick,
quick. Pop—pop—pop very fast. Some of the soldiers were down
on their knees, some standing. Officers all in front. The smoke was
like a great cloud, and everywhere the Sioux went the dust rose
like smoke. We circled all round him—swirling like water round a
stone. We shoot, we ride fast, we shoot again. Soldiers drop, and
horses fall on them. Soldiers in line drop, but one man rides up and
down the line—all the time shouting. He rode a sorrel horse with
white face and white fore-legs. I don't know who he was. He was
a brave man.

Indians keep swirling round and round, and the soldiers killed
only a few. Many soldiers fell. At last all horses killed but five.
Once in a while some man would break out and run toward the
river, but he would fall. At last about a hundred men and five
horsemen stood on the hill all bunched together. All along the
bugler kept blowing his commands. He was very brave too. Then
a chief was killed. I hear it was Long Hair [Custer], I don't know;
and then the five horsemen and the bunch of men, may be so
forty, started toward the river. The man on the sorrel horse led
them, shouting all the time. He wore a buckskin shirt, and had
long black hair and mustache. He fought hard with a big knife.
His men were all covered with white dust. I couldn't tell whether
they were officers or not. One man all alone ran far down toward
the river, then round up over the hill. I thought he was going to
escape, but a Sioux fired and hit him in the head. He was the last
man. He wore braid on his arms [sergeant].

All the soldiers were now killed, and the bodies were stripped.

After that no one could tell which were officers. The bodies were left where they fell. We had no dance that night. We were sorrowful.

Next day four Sioux chiefs and two Cheyennes and I, Two Moon, went upon the battlefield to count the dead. One man carried a little bundle of sticks. When we came to dead men, we took a little stick and gave it to another man, so we counted the dead. There were 388. There were thirty-nine Sioux and seven Cheyennes killed, and about a hundred wounded.

Some white soldiers were cut with knives, to make sure they were dead; and the war women had mangled some. Most of them were left just where they fell. We came to the man with the big mustache; he lay down the hills towards the river. The Indians did not take his buckskin shirt. The Sioux said, "That is a big chief. That is Long Hair." I don't know. I had never seen him. The man on the white-faced horse was the bravest man.

That day as the sun was getting low our young men came up the Little Horn riding hard. Many white soldiers were coming in a big boat, and when we looked we could see the smoke rising. I called my people together, and we hurried up the Little Horn, into Rotten Grass Valley. We camped there three days, and then rode swiftly back over our old trail to the east. Sitting Bull went back into the Rosebud and down the Yellowstone, and away to the north. I did not see him again.

THE BLACK HILLS IS OUR COUNTRY: TESTIMONY TO A FEDERAL COMMISSION, SEPTEMBER, 1876

Black Coal (Arapahoe)

My friends, you that have come here to counsel with the Indians at this agency, I remember the same thing that took place with my father at the treaty at Horse Creek, when the Arapahoes, Cheyennes, Ogallallas, and Brûlés were all represented. You have come here to speak to us about the Black Hills, and, without disguising anything that we say, and without changing anything that we say, we wish you to tell the Great Father when you get back that this is the country in which we were brought up, and it has also been given to us by treaty by the Great Father, and I am here to take care of the country, and, therefore, not only the Dakota Indians, but my people have an interest in the Black Hills that we have come to speak about to-day. This is my country, and the Great Father has allowed the Arapahoe people to live here, and he told them that they must not be foolish, and they have never been foolish or behaved badly since they have been in this country, and, therefore, they have an interest in whatever becomes of it, the sale of it. You have come here from the Great Father to speak to us about our country here, desiring to get it from us, and I, together with the other people that are here, have said yes in answer to that question, that we will give it up; but we consider that we have the same interest in it that the Ogallallas have, and therefore whatever they receive for

From Senate Executive Document No. 9, 44th Congress, 2d Session, pp. 34–35.

the country our people expect to receive in like proportion; and the expectation of both tribes is that we will receive such help that we and our children will live comfortably like white men. We do not wish you to hurry us in our decision about the country, but we will all consider the matter together after our men have returned from the journey to the South.

This place here is the agency of the Government, a place of peace, where we and our people have lived together happily, and behaved ourselves, and we do not understand why so many soldiers have come here among us. We have never had any trouble and have behaved ourselves, and wish to have the soldiers sent away as soon as possible, and leave us in peace. The people that live here have both minds and hearts and good sense, but it seems as if the Great Father all at once thought differently, and speaks of us as people that are very bad. Our only idea has been to live here in peace and do that which is good for the future of our people.

INDIAN CONDITIONS FOR TREATY RENEWAL, OCTOBER 11, 1876

John Grass (Blackfoot Sioux)

My friends, this day I behold you, and I behold you with a glad heart. We are going this day to renew a treaty; that is why my heart is glad. You saw me and you pray to the Great Spirit, which pleases me very much. The Great Spirit made this earth for me and He raised me on it; you brought this to my mind and I am thankful. Our Great Father selected this commission from just and kind-hearted men. Look well at me with both eyes and listen to me with both ears. What I am looking forward to in the future I want you to remember always. The white people look for a country that pleases them; they find one, make a selection, locate themselves there, and consider that as an inheritance for their children; the Indians do the same. The different countries that the Great Spirit has made, the people inhabiting these countries, are bargaining with each other for land. You come here from the Great Father to inquire of me about my land. I will never find another land better than the one I have. I cannot look upon my land as cheap and valueless. You speak to us about a strange country. We want you to strike that out. My father had the white people for friends. Our grandfathers, our fathers, and all of our kindred were raised on the Missouri River. I told my grandchildren that I would never leave the land on the Missouri River. Red Cloud and Spotted Tail's people are not pleased to live on the Missouri River, hence you take them off to look at other countries, but we are not displeased with this country; we are

From Senate Executive Document No. 9, 44th Congress, 2d Session, pp. 47–48.

pleased with the country on the Missouri River, and consequently we wish to remain here. You have come to us with the words from other agencies. If the majority of Indians desire to remain on the Missouri River I wish the commission would decide that Red Cloud and Spotted Tail should also be brought to the Missouri River. I am going to say something that will not please you before I sign the agreement: I desire to know whether the commissioners are willing to erase that part of the propositions where you ask the Indians to go to a strange country? . . .

My friends, I have considered the words you have brought me, and I am ready to answer you. The chiefs you see here have all come to the same conclusion. You have brought words to the chiefs here that will bring life to their children; that will make their children live; they answer *how* [signifying their approval] to that. And now since they have ceded their country to you, they ʾvant to tell you of certain things that they shall want for their families, and people, and children in the future. What we shall need for our children to succeed in life, to instruct our children so that they will become self-supporting—the things you have spoken to us about. The affairs at this agency are allotted to a society of Christians. They are to think for our people, and to instruct our people in the way they should live. I want them to live in this country with us and instruct our children. We want wagons that are good wagons, and will last for ten years; and we want some light wagons so that I can ride over the country rapidly. We want cows and bulls for breeding purposes. We want some sheep and hogs. We want mares and stallions for breeding purposes. We want mowing-machines, and large plows; we also want small plows, and cultivators, and harrows. We want yokes of heavy cattle for plowing. I want a house with at least three rooms in it. I want furniture for the house— stoves, tables and other house furniture. We have not seen the Great Father and discussed this matter with him. I wish that I could see him and talk these matters over with him. If I could see him, I think he would have a reply for me in regard to these things that I am asking for. I wish when the Great Father buys anything for my people—provisions, annuity, goods, etc.—that he would send me a list of the articles purchased. I want this list to be sent to me every year, for all goods purchased. I also want a copy of this agreement left with me. Is the present President the one that has been buying goods and annuities for the Indians? Are the men that have been our agents here, from time to time, still living? The Great Father has not been respected nor obeyed; I have not been respected, I have been abused together with the Great Father. The Great Father thinks that I have received all that has been pur- chased for me, but that which I have received is the smallest part of what has been provided for us. Notwithstanding that I did not receive them, they are mine still; they were all for me, and are still mine, and I expect to get them, and shall look for them. I want the Great Father to look these things up, and make the men that have made away with them pay for them. These things have been made away with, and I am an Indian, and am not able to tell the Great Father. I meet these just men, and hope you will tell a straight story to the Great Father. The things that would enable me to become self-supporting on this river, this day you remind me of them, but they are all gone. This day I want to learn something, to learn a lesson, to learn how to do something. You have talked to me well, spoken to me well, and I am going to state in what way I can learn something to-day. You are writing here [referring to the stenographer], and you have a paper underneath the one upon which you are writing that is not written on. In times past we used to know such things as that; we have seen business done the same way in past times—a blank paper underneath the one we sign. I wish the Great Father would select a physician, a man who is capable of treating sick Indians, and who can cure them, and send him to us. I want a sawyer, a blacksmith, and a man that can work in tin to make pans, kettles, cups, etc., I also want an expert carpenter. I want a trader that will trade with us at the same prices that he trades with the whites, one that will not charge an Indian more than he does a white man. I have a trader here, but he treats me badly. He has a bad way of trading. Tell the Great Father to take him away and send a man in his place who is acquainted with Indians and with Indian ways, a man who can live with the Indians and be their friend. I wish they would send me three or four traders. We want you to consider our half-breeds and the white men who are married to our women as a part of our people.

A PROTEST TO GOVERNOR JOHN W. HOYT OF THE WYOMING TERRITORY, 1878

Washakie (Shoshone)

We are right glad, sir, that you have so bravely and kindly come among us. I shall, indeed, speak to you freely of the many wrongs we have suffered at the hands of the white man. They are things to be noted and remembered. But I cannot hope to express to you the half that is in our hearts. They are too full for words.

Disappointment; then a deep sadness; then a grief inexpressible; then, at times, a bitterness that makes us think of the rifle, the knife and the tomahawk, and kindles in our hearts the fires of desperation—that, sir, is the story of our experience, of our wretched lives.

The white man, who possesses this whole vast country from sea to sea, who roams over it at pleasure, and lives where he likes, cannot know the cramp we feel in this little spot, with the undying remembrance of the fact, which you know as well as we, that every foot of what you proudly call America, not very long ago belonged to the red man. The Great Spirit gave it to us. There was room enough for all his many tribes, and all were happy in their freedom. But the white man had, in ways we know not of, learned some things we had not learned; among them, how to make superior tools and terrible weapons, better for war than bows and arrows; and there seemed no end to the hordes of men that followed them from other lands beyond the sea.

From Grace Raymond Hebard, *Washakie* (Cleveland, 1930), pp. 212–13.

And so, at last, our fathers were steadily driven out, or killed, and we, their sons, but sorry remnants of tribes once mighty, are cornered in little spots of the earth all ours of right—cornered like guilty prisoners, and watched by men with guns, who are more than anxious to kill us off.

Nor is that all. The white man's government promised that if we, the Shoshones, would be content with the little patch allowed us, it would keep us well supplied with everything necessary to comfortable living, and would see that no white man should cross our borders for our game, or for anything that is ours. *But it has not kept its word!* The white man kills our game, captures our furs, and sometimes feeds his herds upon our meadows. And your great and mighty government—Oh sir, I hesitate, for I cannot tell the half! It does not protect us in our rights. It leaves us without the promised seed, without tools for cultivating the land, without implements for harvesting our crops, without breeding animals better than ours, without the food we still lack, after all we can do, without the many comforts we cannot produce, without the schools we so much need for our children.

I say again, *the government does not keep its word!* And so, after all we can get by cultivating the land, and by hunting and fishing, we are sometimes nearly starved, and go half naked, as you see us!

Knowing all this, do you wonder, sir, that we have fits of desperation and think to be avenged?

THE FATE OF THE NEZ PERCÉS TRIBE, 1879

Chief Joseph (Nez Percés)

My friends, I have been asked to show you my heart. I am glad to have a chance to do so. I want the white people to understand my people. Some of you think an Indian is like a wild animal. This is a great mistake. I will tell you all about our people, and then you can judge whether an Indian is a man or not. I believe much trouble and blood would be saved if we opened our hearts more. I will tell you in my way how the Indian sees things. The white man has more words to tell you how they look to him, but it does not require many words to speak the truth. What I have to say will come from my heart, and I will speak with a straight tongue. Ah-cum-kin-i-ma-me-hut (The Great Spirit) is looking at me, and will hear me.

My name is In-mut-too-yah-lat-lat (Thunder traveling over the Mountains). I am chief of the Wal-lam-wat-kin band of Chute-pa-lu, or Nez Percés (nose-pierced Indians). I was born in eastern Oregon, thirty-eight winters ago. My father was chief before me. When a young man, he was called Joseph by Mr. Spaulding, a missionary. He died a few years ago. There was no stain on his hands of the blood of a white man. He left a good name on the earth. He advised me well for my people.

Our fathers gave us many laws, which they had learned from their fathers. These laws were good. They told us to treat all men as they treated us; that we should never be the first to break a bargain; that it was a disgrace to tell a lie; that we should speak only the truth; that it was a shame for one man to take from another his wife, or his property without paying for it. We were

From *North American Review*, April, 1879.

taught to believe that the Great Spirit sees and hears everything, and that he never forgets; that hereafter he will give every man a spirit-home according to his deserts: if he has been a good man, he will have a good home; if he has been a bad man, he will have a bad home. This I believe, and all my people believe the same.

We did not know there were other people besides the Indian until about one hundred winters ago, when some men with white faces came to our country. They brought many things with them to trade for furs and skins. They brought tobacco, which was new to us. They brought guns with flint stones on them, which frightened our women and children. Our people could not talk with these white-faced men, but they used signs which all people understand. These men were Frenchmen, and they called our people "Nez Percés," because they wore rings in their noses for ornaments. Although very few of our people wear them now, we are still called by the same name. These French trappers said a great many things to our fathers, which have been planted in our hearts. Some were good for us, but some were bad. Our people were divided in opinion about these men. Some thought they taught more bad than good. An Indian respects a brave man, but he despises a coward. He loves a straight tongue, but he hates a forked tongue. The French trappers told us some truths and some lies.

The first white men of your people who came to our country were named Lewis and Clarke. They also brought many things that our people had never seen. They talked straight, and our people gave them a great feast, as a proof that their hearts were friendly. These men were very kind. They made presents to our chiefs and our people made presents to them. We had a great many horses, of which we gave them what they needed, and they gave us guns and tobacco in return. All the Nez Percés made friends with Lewis and Clarke, and agreed to let them pass through their country, and never to make war on white men. This promise the Nez Percés have never broken. No white man can accuse them of bad faith, and speak with a straight tongue. It has always been the pride of the Nez Percés that they were the friends of the white men. When my father was a young man there came to our country a white man [Rev. Mr. Spaulding] who talked spirit law. He won the affections of our people because he spoke good things to them. At first he did not say anything about white men wanting to settle on our lands. Nothing was said about that until about twenty winters ago, when a number of white people came into our country and built houses and made farms. At first our people made no complaint. They thought there was room enough for all to live in peace, and they were learning many things from the white men that seemed to be good. But we soon found that the white men were growing rich very fast, and were greedy to possess everything the Indian had. My father was the first to see through the schemes of the white men, and he warned his tribe to be careful about trading with them. He had suspicion of men who seemed so anxious to make money. I was a boy then, but I remember well my father's caution. He had sharper eyes than the rest of our people.

Next there came a white officer [Governor Stevens], who invited all the Nez Percés to a treaty council. After the council was opened he made known his heart. He said there were a great many white people in the country, and many more would come; that he wanted the land marked out so that the Indians and white men could be separated. If they were to live in peace it was necessary, he said, that the Indians should have a country set apart for them, and in that country they must stay. My father, who represented his band, refused to have anything to do with the council, because he wished to be a free man. He claimed that no man owned any part of the earth, and a man could not sell what he did not own.

Mr. Spaulding took hold of my father's arm and said, "Come and sign the treaty." My father pushed him away, and said: "Why do you ask me to sign away my country? It is your business to talk to us about spirit matters, and not to talk to us about parting with our land." Governor Stevens urged my father to sign his treaty, but he refused. "I will not sign your paper," he said; "you go where you please, so do I; you are not a child, I am no child; I can think for myself. No man can think for me. I have no other home than this. I will not give it up to any man. My people would have no home. Take away your paper. I will not touch it with my hand."

My father left the council. Some of the chiefs of the other bands of the Nez Percés signed the treaty, and then Governor Stevens gave them presents of blankets. My father cautioned his people to take no presents, for "after a while," he said, "they will claim that you have accepted pay for your country." Since that time four bands of the Nez Percés have received annuities from the United States. My father was invited to many councils, and they tried hard to make him sign the treaty, but he was firm as the rock, and would not sign away his home. His refusal caused a difference among the Nez Percés.

Eight years later (1863) was the next treaty council. A chief called Lawyer, because he was a great talker, took the lead in this council, and sold nearly all the Nez Percés country. My father was not there. He said to me: "When you go into council with the white man, always remember your country. Do not give it away. The white man will cheat you out of your home. I have taken no pay from the United States. I have never sold our land." In this treaty Lawyer acted without authority from our band. He had no right to sell the Wallowa [winding water] country. That had always belonged to my father's own people, and the other bands had never disputed our right to it. No other Indians ever claimed Wallowa.

In order to have all people understand how much land we owned, my father planted poles around it and said:

"Inside is the home of my people—the white man may take the land outside. Inside this boundary all our people were born. It circles around the graves of our fathers, and we will never give up these graves to any man."

The United States claimed they had bought all the Nez Percés country outside of Lapwai Reservation, from Lawyer and other chiefs, but we continued to live in this land in peace until eight years ago, when white men began to come inside the bounds my father had set. We warned them against this great wrong, but they would not leave our land, and some bad blood was raised. The white men represented that we were going upon the war-path. They reported many things that were false.

The United States Government again asked for a treaty council. My father had become blind and feeble. He could no longer speak for his people. It was then that I took my father's place as chief. In this council I made my first speech to white men. I said to the agent who held the council:

"I did not want to come to this council, but I came hoping that we could save blood. The white man has no right to come here and take our country. We have never accepted any presents from the Government. Neither Lawyer nor any other chief had authority to sell this land. It has always belonged to my people. It came unclouded to them from our fathers, and we will defend this land as long as a drop of Indian blood warms the hearts of our men."

The agent said he had orders, from the Great White Chief at Washington, for us to go upon the Lapwai Reservation, and that if we obeyed he would help us in many ways. "You *must* move to the agency," he said. I answered him: "I will not. I do not need your help; we have plenty and we are contented and happy if the white man will let us alone. The reservation is too small for so many people with all their stock. You can keep your presents; we can go to your towns and pay for all we need; we have plenty of horses and cattle to sell, and we won't have any help from you; we are free now; we can go where we please. Our fathers were born here. Here they lived, here they died, here are their graves. We will never leave them." The agent went away, and we had peace for a little while.

Soon after this my father sent for me. I saw he was dying. I took his hand in mine. He said: "My son, my body is returning to my mother earth, and my spirit is going very soon to see the Great Spirit Chief. When I am gone, think of your country. You are the chief of these people. They look to you to guide them. Always remember that your father never sold his country. You must stop your ears whenever you are asked to sign a treaty selling your home. A few years more, and white men will be all around you. They have their eyes on this land. My son, never forget my dying words. This country holds your father's body. Never sell the bones of your father and your mother." I pressed my father's hand and told him I would protect his grave with my life. My father smiled and passed away to the spirit-land.

I buried him in that beautiful valley of winding waters. I love that land more than all the rest of the world. A man who would not love his father's grave is worse than a wild animal.

For a short time we lived quietly. But this could not last. White men had found gold in the mountains around the land of winding water. They stole a great many horses from us, and we could not get them back because we were Indians. The white men told lies for each other. They drove off a great many of our cattle. Some white men branded our young cattle so they could claim them. We had no friend who would plead our cause before the law councils. It seemed to me that some of the white men in Wallowa were doing these things on purpose to get up a war. They knew that we were not strong enough to fight them. I labored hard to avoid trouble and bloodshed. We gave up some of our country to the white men, thinking that then we could have peace. We were mistaken. The white man would not let us alone. We could have avenged our wrongs many times, but we did not. Whenever the Government has asked us to help them against other Indians, we have never refused. When the white men were few and we were strong we could have killed them all off, but the Nez Percés wished to live at peace.

If we have not done so, we have not been to blame. I believe that the old treaty has never been correctly reported. If we ever owned the land we own it still, for we never sold it. In the treaty councils the commissioners have claimed that our country had been sold to the Government. Suppose a white man should come to me and say, "Joseph, I like your horses, and I want to buy them." I say to him, "No, my horses suit me, I will not sell them." Then he goes to my neighbor, and says to him: "Joseph has some good horses. I want to buy them, but he refuses to sell." My neighbor answers, "Pay me the money, and I will sell you Joseph's horses." The white man returns to me, and says, "Joseph, I have bought your horses, and you must let me have them." If we sold our lands to the Government, this is the way they were bought.

On account of the treaty made by the other bands of the Nez Percés, the white men claimed my lands. We were troubled greatly by white men crowding over the line. Some of these were good men, and we lived on peaceful terms with them, but they were not all good.

Nearly every year the agent came over from Lapwai and ordered us on to the reservation. We always replied that we were satisfied to live in Wallowa. We were careful to refuse the presents or annuities which he offered.

Through all the years since the white men came to Wallowa we have been threatened and taunted by them and the treaty Nez Percés. They have given us no rest. We have had a few good friends among white men, and they always advised my people to bear

these taunts without fighting. Our young men were quick-tem-
pered, and I have had great trouble in keeping them from doing
rash things. I have carried a heavy load on my back ever since I
was a boy. I learned then that we were but few, while the white
men were many, and that we could not hold our own with them.
We were like deer. They were like grizzly bears. We had a small
country. Their country was large. We were contented to let things
remain as the Great Spirit Chief made them. They were not; and
would change the rivers and mountains if they did not suit them.

Year after year we have been threatened, but no war was made
upon my people until General Howard came to our country two
years ago and told us that he was the white war-chief of all that
country. He said: "I have a great many soldiers at my back. I
am going to bring them up here, and then I will talk to you again.
I will not let white men laugh at me the next time I come. The
country belongs to the Government, and I intend to make you go
upon the reservation."

I remonstrated with him against bringing more soldiers to the
Nez Percés country. He had one house full of troops all the time
at Fort Lapwai.

The next spring the agent at Umatilla agency sent an Indian
runner to tell me to meet General Howard at Walla Walla. I
could not go myself, but I sent my brother and five other head men
to meet him, and they had a long talk.

General Howard said: "You have talked straight, and it is all
right. You can stay in Wallowa." He insisted that my brother
and his company should go with him to Fort Lapwai. When the
party arrived there General Howard sent out runners and called all
the Indians in to a grand council. I was in that council. I said to
General Howard, "We are ready to listen." He answered that he
would not talk then, but would hold a council next day, when he
would talk plainly. I said to General Howard: "I am ready to talk
to-day. I have been in a great many councils, but I am no wiser.
We are all sprung from a woman, although we are unlike in many
things. We can not be made over again. You are as you were
made, and as you were made you can remain. We are just as we
were made by the Great Spirit, and you can not change us; then
why should children of one mother and one father quarrel—why
should one try to cheat the other? I do not believe that the Great
Spirit Chief gave one kind of men the right to tell another kind of
men what they must do."

General Howard replied: "You deny my authority, do you? You
want to dictate to me, do you?"

Then one of my chiefs—Too-hool-hool-suit—rose in the council
and said to General Howard: "The Great Spirit Chief made the
world as it is, and as he wanted it, and he made a part of it for us
to live upon. I do not see where you get authority to say that we
shall not live where he placed us."

General Howard lost his temper and said: "Shut up! I don't

want to hear any more of such talk. The law says you shall go upon the reservation to live, and I want you to do so, but you persist in disobeying the law" (meaning the treaty). "If you do not move, I will take the matter into my own hand, and make you suffer for your disobedience."

Too-hool-hool-suit answered: "Who are you, that you ask us to talk, and then tell me I sha'n't talk? Are you the Great Spirit? Did you make the world? Did you make the sun? Did you make the rivers to run for us to drink? Did you make the grass to grow? Did you make all these things, that you talk to us as though we were boys? If you did, then you have the right to talk as you do."

General Howard replied, "You are an impudent fellow, and I will put you in the guard-house," and then ordered a soldier to arrest him.

Too-hool-hool-suit made no resistance. He asked General Howard: "Is that your order? I don't care. I have expressed my heart to you. I have nothing to take back. I have spoken for my country. You can arrest me, but you can not change me or make me take back what I have said."

The soldiers came forward and seized my friend and took him to the guard-house. My men whispered among themselves whether they should let this thing be done. I counseled them to submit. I knew if we resisted that all the white men present, including General Howard would be killed in a moment, and we would be blamed. If I had said nothing, General Howard would never have given another unjust order against my men. I saw the danger, and, while they dragged Too-hool-hool-suit to prison, I arose and said: "*I am going to talk now.* I don't care whether you arrest me or not." I turned to my people and said: "The arrest of Too-hool-hool-suit was wrong, but we will not resent the insult. We were invited to this council to express our hearts, and we have done so." Too-hool-hool-suit was prisoner for five days before he was released.

The council broke up for that day. On the next morning General Howard came to my lodge, and invited me to go with him and White-Bird and Looking-Glass, to look for land for my people. As we rode along we came to some good land that was already occupied by Indians and white people. General Howard, pointing to this land, said: "If you will come on to the reservation, I will give you these lands and move these people off."

I replied: "No. It would be wrong to disturb these people. I have no right to take their homes. I have never taken what did not belong to me. I will not now."

We rode all day upon the reservation, and found no good land unoccupied. I have been informed by men who do not lie that General Howard sent a letter that night, telling the soldiers at Walla Walla to go to Wallowa Valley, and drive us out upon our return home.

In the council, next day, General Howard informed me, in a haughty spirit, that he would give my people *thirty days* to go back home, collect all their stock, and move on to the reservation, saying, "If you are not here in that time, I shall consider that you want to fight, and will send my soldiers to drive you on."

I said: "War can be avoided, and it ought to be avoided. I want no war. My people have always been the friends of the white man. Why are you in such a hurry? I can not get ready to move in thirty days. Our stock is scattered, and Snake River is very high. Let us wait until fall, then the river will be low. We want time to hunt up our stock and gather supplies for winter."

General Howard replied, "If you let the time run over one day, the soldiers will be there to drive you on to the reservation, and all your cattle and horses outside of the reservation at that time will fall into the hands of the white men."

I knew I had never sold my country, and that I had no land in Lapwai; but I did not want bloodshed. I did not want my people killed. I did not want anybody killed. Some of my people had been murdered by white men, and the white murderers were never punished for it. I told General Howard about this, and again said I wanted no war. I wanted the people who lived upon the lands I was to occupy at Lapwai to have time to gather their harvest.

I said in my heart that, rather than have war, I would give up my country. I would give up my father's grave. I would give up everything rather than have the blood of white men upon the hands of my people.

General Howard refused to allow me more than thirty days to move my people and their stock. I am sure that he began to prepare for war at once.

When I returned to Wallowa I found my people very much excited upon discovering that the soldiers were already in the Wallowa Valley. We held a council, and decided to move immediately, to avoid bloodshed.

Too-hool-hool-suit, who felt outraged by his imprisonment, talked for war, and made many of my young men willing to fight rather than be driven like dogs from the land where they were born. He declared that blood alone would wash out the disgrace General Howard had put upon him. It required a strong heart to stand up against such talk, but I urged my people to be quiet, and not to begin a war.

We gathered all the stock we could find, and made an attempt to move. We left many of our horses and cattle in Wallowa, and we lost several hundred in crossing the river. All of my people succeeded in getting across in safety. Many of the Nez Percés came together in Rocky Cañon to hold a grand council. I went with all my people. This council lasted ten days. There was a great deal of war-talk, and a great deal of excitement. There was one young brave present whose father had been killed by a white man five years before. This man's blood was bad against white men, and he left the council calling for revenge.

Again I counseled peace, and I thought the danger was past. We had not complied with General Howard's order because we could not, but we intended to do so as soon as possible. I was leaving the council to kill beef for my family, when news came that the young man whose father had been killed had gone out with several other hot-blooded young braves and killed four white men. He rode up to the council and shouted: "Why do you sit here like women? The war has begun already." I was deeply grieved. All the lodges were moved except my brother's and my own. I saw clearly that the war was upon us when I learned that my young men had been secretly buying ammunition. I heard then that Too-hool-hool-suit, who had been imprisoned by General Howard, had succeeded in organizing a war-party. I knew that their acts would involve all my people. I saw that the war could not then be prevented. The time had passed. I counseled peace from the beginning. I knew that we were too weak to fight the United States. We had many griev-ances, but I knew that war would bring more. We had good white friends, who advised us against taking the war-path. My friend and brother, Mr. Chapman, who has been with us since the surrender, told us just how the war would end. Mr. Chapman took sides against us, and helped General Howard. I do not blame him for doing so. He tried hard to prevent bloodshed. We hoped the white settlers would not join the soldiers. Before the war commenced we had discussed this matter all over, and many of my people were in favor of warning them that if they took no part against us they should not be molested in the event of war being begun by General Howard. This plan was voted down in the war-council.

There were bad men among my people who had quarreled with white men, and they talked of their wrongs until they roused all the bad hearts in the council. Still I could not believe that they would begin the war. I know that my young men did a great wrong, but I ask, Who was first to blame? They had been insulted a thousand times; their fathers and brothers had been killed; their mothers and wives had been disgraced; they had been driven to madness by whisky sold to them by white men; they had been told by General Howard that all their horses and cattle which they had been unable to drive out of Wallowa were to fall into the hands of white men; and, added to all this, they were homeless and des-perate.

I would have given my own life if I could have undone the killing of white men by my people. I blame my young men and I blame the white men. I blame General Howard for not giving my people time to get their stock away from Wallowa. I do not acknowledge that he had the right to order me to leave Wallowa at any time. I deny that either my father or myself ever sold that land. It is still our land. It may never again be our home, but my father sleeps there, and I love it as I love my mother. I left there, hoping to avoid bloodshed.

If General Howard had given me plenty of time to gather up my stock, and treated Too-hool-hool-suit as a man should be treated, there *would have been no war*.

My friends among white men have blamed me for the war. I am not to blame. When my young men began the killing, my heart was hurt. Although I did not justify them, I remembered all the insults I had endured, and my blood was on fire. Still I would have taken my people to the buffalo country without fighting, if possible.

I could see no other way to avoid a war. We moved over to White Bird Creek, sixteen miles away, and there encamped, intending to collect our stock before leaving; but the soldiers attacked us, and the first battle was fought. We numbered in that battle sixty men, and the soldiers a hundred. The fight lasted but a few minutes, when the soldiers retreated before us for twelve miles. They lost thirty-three killed, and had seven wounded. When an Indian fights, he only shoots to kill; but soldiers shoot at random. None of the soldiers were scalped. We do not believe in scalping, nor in killing wounded men. Soldiers do not kill many Indians unless they are wounded and left upon the battle-field. Then they kill Indians.

Seven days after the first battle, General Howard arrived in the Nez Percés country, bringing seven hundred more soldiers. It was now war in earnest. We crossed over Salmon River, hoping General Howard would follow. We were not disappointed. He did follow us, and we got back between him and his supplies, and cut him off for three days. He sent out two companies to open the way. We attacked them, killing one officer, two guides, and ten men.

We withdrew, hoping the soldiers would follow, but they had got fighting enough for that day. They intrenched themselves, and next day we attacked them again. The battle lasted all day, and was renewed next morning. We killed four and wounded seven or eight.

About this time General Howard found out that we were in his rear. Five days later he attacked us with three hundred and fifty soldiers and settlers. We had two hundred and fifty warriors. The fight lasted twenty-seven hours. We lost four killed and several wounded. General Howard's loss was twenty-nine men killed and sixty wounded.

The following day the soldiers charged upon us, and we retreated with our families and stock a few miles, leaving eighty lodges to fall into General Howard's hands.

Finding that we were outnumbered, we retreated to Bitter Root Valley. Here another body of soldiers came upon us and demanded our surrender. We refused. They said, "You can not get by us." We answered, "We are going by you without fighting if you will let us, but we are going by you anyhow." We then made a treaty with these soldiers. We agreed not to molest any one, and they agreed that we might pass through the Bitter Root country in peace. We bought provisions and traded stock with white men there.

We understood that there was to be no more war. We intended

to go peaceably to the buffalo country, and leave the question of returning to our country to be settled afterward.

With this understanding we traveled on for four days, and, thinking that the trouble was all over, we stopped and prepared tentpoles to take with us. We started again, and at the end of two days we saw three white men passing our camp. Thinking that peace had been made, we did not molest them. We could have killed or taken them prisoners, but we did not suspect them of being spies, which they were.

That night the soldiers surrounded our camp. About daybreak one of my men went out to look after his horses. The soldiers saw him and shot him down like a coyote. I have since learned that these soldiers were not those we had left behind. They had come upon us from another direction. The new white war-chief's name was Gibbon. He charged upon us while some of my people were still asleep. We had a hard fight. Some of my men crept around and attacked the soldiers from the rear. In this battle we lost nearly all our lodges, but we finally drove General Gibbon back.

Finding that he was not able to capture us, he sent to his camp a few miles away for his big guns (cannons), but my men had captured them and all the ammunition. We damaged the big guns all we could, and carried away the powder and lead. In the fight with General Gibbon we lost fifty women and children and thirty fighting men. We remained long enough to bury our dead. The Nez Percés never make war on women and children; we could have killed a great many women and children while the war lasted, but we would feel ashamed to do so cowardly an act.

We never scalp our enemies, but when General Howard came up and joined General Gibbon, their Indian scouts dug up our dead and scalped them. I have been told that General Howard did not order this great shame to be done.

We retreated as rapidly as we could toward the buffalo country. After six days General Howard came close to us, and we went out and attacked him, and captured nearly all his horses and mules (about two hundred and fifty head). We then marched on to the Yellowstone Basin.

On the way we captured one white man and two white women. We released them at the end of three days. They were treated kindly. The women were not insulted. Can the white soldiers tell me of one time when Indian women were taken prisoners, and held three days and then released without being insulted? Were the Nez Percés women who fell into the hands of General Howard's soldiers treated with as much respect? I deny that a Nez Percé was ever guilty of such a crime.

A few days later we captured two more white men. One of them stole a horse and escaped. We gave the other a poor horse and told him he was free.

Nine days' march brought us to the mouth of Clarke's Fork of the Yellowstone. We did not know what had become of General Howard, but we supposed that he had sent for more horses and mules. He did not come up, but another new war-chief (General Sturgis) attacked us. We held him in check while we moved all our women and children and stock out of danger, leaving a few men to cover our retreat.

Several days passed, and we heard nothing of General Howard, or Gibbon, or Sturgis. We had repulsed each in turn, and began to feel secure, when another army, under General Miles, struck us. This was the fourth army, each of which outnumbered our fighting force, that we had encountered within sixty days.

We had no knowledge of General Miles's army until a short time before he made a charge upon us, cutting our camp in two, and capturing nearly all of our horses. About seventy men, myself among them, were cut off. My little daughter, twelve years of age, was with me. I gave her a rope, and told her to catch a horse and join the others who were cut off from the camp. I have not seen her since, but I have learned that she is alive and well.

I thought of my wife and children, who were now surrounded by soldiers, and I resolved to go to them or die. With a prayer in my mouth to the Great Spirit Chief who rules above, I dashed unarmed through the line of soldiers. It seemed to me that there were guns on every side, before and behind me. My clothes were cut to pieces and my horse was wounded, but I was not hurt. As I reached the door of my lodge, my wife handed me my rifle, saying: "Here's your gun. Fight!"

The soldiers kept up a continuous fire. Six of my men were killed in one spot near me. Ten or twelve soldiers charged into our camp and got possession of two lodges, killing three Nez Percés and losing three of their men, who fell inside our lines. I called my men to drive them back. We fought at close range, not more than twenty steps apart, and drove the soldiers back upon their main line, leaving their dead in our hands. We secured their arms and ammunition. We lost, the first day and night, eighteen men and three women. General Miles lost twenty-six killed and forty wounded. The following day General Miles sent a messenger into my camp under protection of a white flag. I sent my friend Yellow Bull to meet him.

Yellow Bull understood the messenger to say that General Miles wished me to consider the situation; that he did not want to kill my people unnecessarily. Yellow Bull understood this to be a demand for me to surrender and save blood. Upon reporting this message to me, Yellow Bull said he wondered whether General Miles was in earnest. I sent him back with my answer, that I had not made up my mind, but would think about it and send word soon. A little later he sent me some Cheyenne scouts with another message. I went out to meet them. They said they believed that General Miles was sincere and really wanted peace. I walked on to

General Miles's tent. He met me and we shook hands. He said, "Come, let us sit down by the fire and talk this matter over." I remained with him all night; next morning Yellow Bull came over to see if I was alive, and why I did not return.

General Miles would not let me leave the tent to see my friend alone.

Yellow Bull said to me: "They have got you in their power, and I am afraid they will never let you go again. I have an officer in our camp, and I will hold him until they let you go free."

I said: "I do not know what they mean to do with me, but if they kill me you must not kill the officer. It will do no good to avenge my death by killing him."

Yellow Bull returned to my camp. I did not make any agreement that day with General Miles. The battle was renewed while I was with him. I was very anxious about my people. I knew that we were near Sitting Bull's camp in King George's land, and I thought maybe the Nez Percés who had escaped would return with assistance. No great damage was done to either party during the night.

On the following morning I returned to my camp by agreement, meeting the officer who had been held a prisoner in my camp at the flag of truce. My people were divided about surrendering. We could have escaped from Bear Paw Mountain if we had left our wounded, old women, and children behind. We were unwilling to do this. We have never heard of a wounded Indian recovering while in the hands of white men.

On the evening of the fourth day General Howard came in with a small escort, together with my friend Chapman. We could now talk understandingly. General Miles said to me in plain words, "If you will come out and give up your arms, I will spare your lives and send you to your reservation." I do not know what passed between General Miles and General Howard.

I could not bear to see my wounded men and women suffer any longer; we had lost enough already. General Miles had promised that we might return to our own country with what stock we had left. I thought we could start again. I believed General Miles, or *I never would have surrendered.* I have heard that he has been censured for making the promise to return us to Lapwai. He could not have made any other terms with me at that time. I would have held him in check until my friends came to my assistance, and then neither of the generals nor their soldiers would have ever left Bear Paw Mountain alive.

On the fifth day I went to General Miles and gave up my gun, and said, "From where the sun now stands I will fight no more." My people needed rest—we wanted peace.

I was told we could go with General Miles to Tongue River and stay there until spring, when we would be sent back to our country. Finally it was decided that we were to be taken to Tongue River.

We had nothing to say about it. After our arrival at Tongue River, General Miles received orders to take us to Bismarck. The reason given was, that subsistence would be cheaper there.

General Miles was opposed to this order. He said: "You must not blame me. I have endeavored to keep my word, but the chief who is over me has given the order, and I must obey it or resign. That would do you no good. Some other officer would carry out the order."

I believe General Miles would have kept his word if he could have done so. I do not blame him for what we have suffered since the surrender. I do not know who is to blame. We gave up all our horses—over eleven hundred—and all our saddles—over one hundred—and we have not heard from them since. Somebody has got our horses.

General Miles turned my people over to another soldier, and we were taken to Bismarck. Captain Johnson, who now had charge of us, received an order to take us to Fort Leavenworth. At Leavenworth we were placed on a low river bottom, with no water except river-water to drink and cook with. We had always lived in a healthy country, where the mountains were high and the water was cold and clear. Many of my people sickened and died, and we buried them in this strange land. I can not tell how much my heart suffered for my people while at Leavenworth. The Great Spirit Chief who rules above seemed to be looking some other way, and did not see what was being done to my people.

During the hot days (July, 1878) we received notice that we were to be moved farther away from our own country. We were not asked if we were willing to go. We were ordered to get into the railroad-cars. Three of my people died on the way to Baxter Springs. It was worse to die there than to die fighting in the mountains.

We were moved from Baxter Springs (Kansas) to the Indian Territory, and set down without our lodges. We had but little medicine, and we were nearly all sick. Seventy of my people have died since we moved there.

We have had a great many visitors who have talked many ways. Some of the chiefs (General Fish and Colonel Stickney) from Chief (General Butler), and many other law chiefs (Congressmen), and they all say they are my friends, and that I shall have justice, but while their mouths all talk right I do not understand why nothing is done for my people. I have heard talk and talk, but nothing is done. Good words do not last long unless they amount to something. Words do not pay for my dead people. They do not pay for my country, now overrun by white men. They do not protect my father's grave. They do not pay for all my horses and cattle. Good words will not give me back my children. Good words will not make good the promise of your War Chief General Miles. Good words will not give my people good health and stop them from dying. Good words will not get my people a home where they can live in peace and take care of themselves. I am tired of talk that comes to nothing. It makes my heart sick when I remember all the good words and all the broken promises. There has been too much talking by men who had no right to talk. Too many misrepresentations have been made, too many misunderstandings have come up between the white men about the Indians. If the white man wants to live in peace with the Indian he can live in peace. There need be no trouble. Treat all men alike. Give them all the same law. Give them all an even chance to live and grow. All men were made by the same Great Spirit Chief. They are all brothers. The earth is the mother of all people, and all people should have equal rights upon it. You might as well expect the rivers to run backward as that any man who was born a free man should be contented when penned up and denied liberty to go where he pleases. If you tie a horse to a stake, do you expect he will grow fat? If you pen an Indian up on a small spot of earth, and compel him to stay there, he will not be contented, nor will he grow and prosper. I have asked some of the great white chiefs where they get their authority to say to the Indian that he shall stay in one place, while he sees white men going where they please. They can not tell me.

I only ask of the Government to be treated as all other men are treated. If I can not go to my own home, let me have a home in some country where my people will not die so fast. I would like to go to Bitter Root Valley. There my people would be healthy; where they are now they are dying. Three have died since I left my camp to come to Washington.

When I think of our condition my heart is heavy. I see men of my race treated as outlaws and driven from country to country, or shot down like animals.

I know that my race must change. We can not hold our own with the white men as we are. We only ask an even chance to live as other men live. We ask to be recognized as men. We ask that the same law shall work alike on all men. If the Indian breaks the law, punish him by the law. If the white man breaks the law, punish him also.

Let me be a free man—free to travel, free to stop, free to work, free to trade where I choose, free to choose my own teachers, free to follow the religion of my fathers, free to think and talk and act for myself—and I will obey every law, or submit to the penalty.

Whenever the white man treats the Indian as they treat each other, then we will have no more wars. We shall all be alike—brothers of one father and one mother, with one sky above us and one country around us, and one government for all. Then the Great Spirit Chief who rules above will smile upon this land, and send rain to wash out the bloody spots made by brothers' hands from the face of the earth. For this time the Indian race are waiting and praying. I hope that no more groans of wounded men and women will ever go to the ear of the Great Spirit Chief above, and that all people may be one people.

A MESSAGE FOR THE PRESIDENT OF THE UNITED STATES, 1881

Sitting Bull (Hunkpapa Sioux)

[No Indian was better known among the American public in his lifetime than Sitting Bull, owing largely to his brief travels with the Buffalo Bill "Wild West" show. Among his own people, he was a revered leader and one who was thoroughly reluctant to compromise with white officialdom. In 1877, subsequent to the Custer affair, he and his band went to live in Canada rather than settle on a reservation. Finding Canada less than hospitable after four years, he returned with his followers to settle at the Standing Rock agency. Shortly before, the following message was sent via Mr. William Selwyn, a Sioux Indian employed as government census taker.]

I am the son of the He-Topa (Four Horns, late a chief of the Unk-pa-pas), and it is said that he was one of your relatives; so, then, you are a younger brother to me (sunkachiye). You are a full-blooded Dakota, but you adopt the ways of the whites, and I hear that you have been employed by the Great Father.

For the last few years I have been in the North, where there are plenty of buffalo, for the buffalo were my means of living. God made me to live on the flesh of the buffalo, so I thought I would stay out there as long as there were buffalo enough for us. But the Great Father sent for me several times, and although I did not know why he wanted me to come down, at last I consented to do so. I never, myself, made war against the children of the Great Father,

From W. Fletcher Johnson, *Life of Sitting Bull* (1891), pp. 162–67.

and I never sought a fight with them. While I was looking for buffalo, they would attack and shoot at me, and of course I had to defend myself or else I should die. But all the blame is put on me. I have always thought that the Dakotas were all one body, and I wanted to make an agreement with them to come and settle down. While I have been in the North, here and there, a good many little things have happened, and I have been blamed for them; but I know that I am innocent. Those men who have made the trouble ought to be blamed. Everybody knows that I was not going to stay at the North any longer, but that when the buffalo disappeared I should make up my mind to come down.

Although you are a Dakota, you are employed by the Great Father; therefore I want you to let him hear my words. When I first came down, white men came to me almost every day to get some words out of me, but I said: "No! When I settle down I shall say some words to the Great Father." I know that some white rascals have dealt with the Dakotas, and by their foolish ways have ruined them. As for myself, I do not want any one to do mischievously or deceitfully. So I do not want to let any ordinary man hear my words. I tell the whites that my words are worth something; and even if they were willing to pay me for it, I never made any reply. But as soon as I saw you I was well pleased. Although you are a Dakota, you have gathered up many good words and put them into my ears. To-day I was wishing that some one would come in and advise me, and as you have done so, it pleases me very much. All this people here belong to me and I hope that the Great Father will treat them kindly. I always thought that when we came back, and any of my relatives came to me with good words, I should reply, "Yes, yes." To-day you have put good words into my ears, and I save said, "Yes." In the future I hope I shall have some good, honest, reliable man with me. Interpreters have come to me often, following me up, and I have said, "No. I am not a child; if I want to do anything, I shall take time to think it over." It is said Spotted Tail was killed by getting mixed up with bad men. Oftentimes a man has lost his life by being mixed up with bad men. But I wish that my people may be treated well, so that they may do rightly. I am the last one that has come in from the North, and yet I want to surpass the old agency Dakotas in what is right, and I wish that the Great Father would furnish me with farming implements, so that I can till the ground.

My brother, I wish you would send this message to the Great Father right away, so that he will help me. Now I have confidence in you that you will be able to send off my message. I am glad that you came to see me. It is a good thing for relatives to see each other. I have no objections to your numbering the people.

THE KILLING OF BIG SNAKE, A PONCA CHIEF, OCTOBER 31, 1879

Hairy Bear (Ponca)

I was present when the officer tried to arrest Big Snake. I stood by the door of the office, inside the door. The officer was in about the middle of the room. He told Big Snake, "I have come to arrest you." Big Snake said he did not want to go without an interpreter went; then he would go along. Big Snake said, "If the interpreter don't go, I want to take one of my wives along." The officer said he could not do that; that he came to arrest only him. The agent told Big Snake he had better go, and said he would give him a blanket to sleep on. The officer told Big Snake to come along, to get up and come. Big Snake would not get up, and told the officer he wanted him to tell him what he had done. He said he had killed no one, stolen no horses, and that he had done nothing wrong. After Big Snake said that the officer spoke to the agent, and then told Big Snake he had tried to kill two men, and had been pretty mean. Big Snake denied it. The agent then told him he had better go, and could then learn all about it down there. Big Snake said he had done nothing wrong; that he carried no knife; and threw off his blanket and turned around to show he had no weapon. The officer again told him to come along. Big Snake said he had done nothing wrong, and that he would die before he would go. I then went up to Big Snake and told him this man (the officer) was not going to arrest him for nothing, and that he had better go along, and that perhaps he would come back all right; I coaxed all I could to get him to go;

From Senate Executive Document No. 14, 46th Congress, 3d Session, p. 13.

told him that he had a wife and children, and to remember them and not get killed. Big Snake then got up and told me that he did not want to go, and that if they wanted to kill him they could do it, right there. Big Snake was very cool. Then the officer told him to get up, and told him that if he did not go, there might something happen. He said there is no use in talking; I came to arrest you, and want you to go. The officer went for the handcuffs, which a soldier had, and brought them in. The officer and a soldier then tried to put them on him, but Big Snake pushed them both away. Then the officer spoke to the soldiers, and four of them tried to put them on, but Big Snake pushed them all off. One soldier, who had stripes on his arms, also tried to put them on, but Big Snake pushed them all off. They tried several times, all of them, to get hold of Big Snake and hold him. But Big Snake was sitting down, when six soldiers got hold of him. He raised up and threw them off. Just then one of the soldiers, who was in front of him, struck Big Snake in the face with his gun, another soldier struck him along side the head with the barrel of his gun. It knocked him back to the wall. He straightened up again. The blood was running down his face. I saw the gun pointed at him, and was scared, and did not want to see him killed. So I turned away. Then the gun was fired and Big Snake fell down dead on the floor.

"THE AMERICAN NATION IS TOO POWERFUL FOR US TO FIGHT"

Manuelito (Navajo)

[After a series of Navajo raids in 1863–64, the U.S. Army defeated the tribe and gradually brought all of its members (about 8,000 persons) to the Bosque Redonde reservation in eastern New Mexico. Conditions there were so deplorable, however, that in June, 1868, a treaty was signed allowing the Navajos to return to their desert homeland in Arizona and western New Mexico. Manuelito, one of the Navajo chiefs, recounted this bit of tribal history for William Parsons, special agent for the Indian bureau, on February 25, 1886.]

Manuelito is the head chief of the east side of the reservation, and Ganada-Mucho is head chief of the western side. You have already heard some of the history of the tribe. When our fathers lived they heard that the Americans were coming across the great river westward. Now we are settling among the powerful people. We heard of the guns and powder and lead—first flint locks, then percussion caps, and now repeating rifles. We first saw the Americans at Cottonwood Wash. We had wars with the Mexicans and Pueblos. We captured mules from the Mexicans, and had many mules. The Americans came to trade with us. When the Americans first came we had a big dance, and they danced with our women. We also traded. The Americans went back to Santa Fe, which the Mexicans then held. Afterwards we heard that the Mexicans had reached Santa Fe, and that the Mexicans had disarmed them and made

From House Executive Document No. 263, 49th Congress, 1st Session, pp. 14–15.

them prisoners. This is how the Mexican war began. Had the Mexicans let the Americans alone they would not have been defeated by the Americans. Then there were many soldiers at Santa Fe, and the Mexican governor was driven away. They did not kill the governor. Therefore we like the Americans. The Americans fight fair, and we like them. Then the soldiers built the fort here, and gave us an agent who advised us to behave well. He told us to live peaceably with the whites; to keep our promises. They wrote down promises, and so always remember them. From that on we had sheep and horses. We had lots of horses, and felt good; we had a fight with the Americans, and were whipped. At that time we thought we had a big country, extending over a great deal of land. We fought for that country because we did not want to lose it, but we made a mistake. We lost nearly everything, but we had some beads left, and with them we thought we were rich. I have always advised the young men to avoid war. I am ashamed for having gone to war. The American nation is too powerful for us to fight. When we had a fight for a few days we felt fresh, but in a short time we were worn out, and the soldiers starved us out. Then the Americans gave us something to eat, and we came in from the mountains and went to Texas. We were there for a few years; many of our people died from the climate. Then we became good friends with the white people. The Comanches wanted us to fight, but we would not join them. One day the soldiers went after the Comanches. I and the soldiers charged on the Comanches, but the Comanches drove us back, and I was left alone to fight them; so the white men came in twelve days to talk with us, as our people were dying off. People from Washington held a council with us. He explained how the whites punished those who disobeyed the law. We promised to obey the laws if we were permitted to get back to our own country. We promised to keep the treaty you read to us to-day. We promised four times to do so. We all said "yes" to the treaty, and he gave us good advice. He was General Sherman. We told him we would try to remember what he said. He said: "I want all you people to look at me." He stood up for us to see him. He said if we would do right we could look people in the face. Then he said: "My children, I will send you back to your homes." The nights and days were long before it came time for us to go to our homes. The day before we were to start we went a little way towards home, because we were so anxious to start. We came back and the Americans gave us a little stock to start with and we thanked them for that. We told the drivers to whip the mules, we were in such a hurry. When we saw the top of the mountain from Albuquerque we wondered if it was our mountain, and we felt like talking to the ground, we loved it so, and some of the old men and women cried with joy when they reached their homes. The agent told us here how large our reservation was to be. A small piece of land was surveyed off to us, but we think we ought to have had more. Then we began to talk about more land, and we went to Washington to see about our land.

Some backed out of going for fear of strange animals and from bad water, but I thought I might as well die there as here. I thought I could do something at Washington about the land. I had a short talk with the Commissioner. We were to talk with him the next day, but the agent brought us back without giving us a chance to say what we wanted. I saw a man whom I called my younger brother; he was short and fat; and we came back on foot. So Ganada-Mucho thought he would go on to Washington and fix things up, and he got sick and couldn't stand it, and came back without seeing the Commissioner. I tell these things in order that you might know what troubles we have had, and how little satisfaction we got. Therefore we have told you that the reservation was not large enough for our sheep and horses; what the others have told you is true. It is true about the snow on the mountains in the center of the reservation. It is nice there in the summer, but we have to move away in the winter. But we like to be at the mountains in the summer because there is good water and grass there, but in the winter we always move our camps. We like the southern part of the country because the land is richer. We can have farms there. We want the reservation to be extended below the railroad on the south, and also in an easterly direction.

We all appreciate the goods issued to us by the Government. At first we did not understand, now we know how to use plows and scrapers. We have good use for these things and wagons. We can then make new farms and raise crops. We are thankful for what the Government sends. We give nothing back to the whites. When we make blankets our women sell them. They look well in white men's rooms on the beds or walls. If I had a good house I would keep the blankets myself. When any man comes from the East we tell him our troubles. There are some bad men, both whites and Indians, whom we cannot keep from doing mischief. The whites control them by laws, and we talk ours into being good. I am glad the young men have freed their minds; now we old men have our say.

REASONS FOR LEAVING THE RESERVATION

Geronimo (Chiracahua Apache)

[Geronimo and other Apaches had fled the reservation on several occasions since 1876, mostly out of fear of the U.S. Army. The instance of the flight in 1885, however, was the result of boredom and alcohol. The Apaches may also have been afraid, justifiably, of being arrested and confined to the guard house, an army tactic frequently used to intimidate the tribe. In March, 1886, General George Crook, one of the more successful negotiators of Indian affairs in the army, went to Mexico to meet with Geronimo, the Apache leader, and after three days of talks the Indians agreed to surrender and return. During the discussions, Geronimo made the following statement to General Crook.]

I want to talk first of the causes which led me to leave the reservation. I was living quietly and contented, doing and thinking of no harm, while at the Sierra Blanca. I don't know what harm I did to those three men, Chatto, Mickey Free, and Lieutenant Davis. I was living peaceably and satisfied when people began to speak bad of me. I should be glad to know who started those stories. I was living peaceably with my family, having plenty to eat, sleeping well, taking care of my people, and perfectly contented. I don't know where those bad stories first came from. There we were doing well and my people well. I was behaving well. I hadn't killed a horse or man, American or Indian. I don't know what was the

From Senate Executive Document No. 88, 51st Congress, 1st Session, pp. 11–12.

matter with the people in charge of us. They knew this to be so, and yet they said I was a bad man and the worst man there; but what harm had I done? I was living peaceably and well, but I did not leave on my own accord. Had I so left it would have been right to blame me; but as it is, blame those men who started this talk about me. Some time before I left an Indian named Wadiskay had a talk with me. He said, "they are going to arrest you," but I paid no attention to him, knowing that I had done no wrong; and the wife of Magnus, "Huera," told me that they were going to seize me and put me and Magnus in the guard-house, and I learned from the American and Apache soldiers, from Chatto, and Mickey Free, that the Americans were going to arrest me and hang me, and so I left. I would like to know now who it was that gave the order to arrest me and hang me. I was living peaceably there with my family under the shade of the trees, doing just what General Crook had told me I must do and trying to follow his advice. I want to know now who it was ordered me to be arrested. I was praying to the light and to the darkness, to God and to the sun, to let me live quietly there with my family. I don't know what the reason was that people should speak badly of me. I don't want to be blamed. The fault was not mine. Blame those three men. With them is the fault, and find out who it was that began that bad talk about me.

I have several times asked for peace, but trouble has come from the agents and interpreters. I don't want what has passed to happen again. Now, I am going to tell you something else. The Earth-Mother is listening to me and I hope that all may be so arranged that from now on there shall be no trouble and that we shall always have peace. Whenever we see you coming to where we are, we think that it is God—you must come always with God. From this on I do not want that anything shall be told you about me even in joke. Whenever I have broken out, it has always been on account of bad talk. From this on I hope that people will tell me nothing but the truth. From this on I want to do what is right and nothing else and I do not want you to believe any bad papers about me. I want the papers sent you to tell the truth about me, because I want to do what is right. Very often there are stories put in the newspapers that I am to be hanged. I don't want that any more. When a man tries to do right, such stories ought not to be put in the newspapers. There are very few of my men left now. They have done some bad things but I want them all rubbed out now and let us never speak of them again. There are very few of us left. We think of our relations, brothers, brothers-in-law, father-in-law, etc., over on the reservation, and from this on we want to live at peace just as they are doing, and to behave as they are behaving. Sometimes a man does something and men are sent out to bring in his head. I don't want such things to happen to us. I don't want that we should be killing each other. . . .

I have not forgotten what you told me, although a long time has passed. I keep it in my memory. I am a complete man. Nothing has gone from my body. From here on I want to live at peace. Don't believe any bad talk you hear about me. The agents and the interpreter hear that somebody has done wrong, and they blame it all on me. Don't believe what they say. I don't want any of this bad talk in the future. I don't want those men who talked this way about me to be my agents any more. I want good men to be my agents and interpreters; people who will talk right. I want this peace to be legal and good. Whenever I meet you I talk good to you, and you to me, and peace is soon established; but when you go to the reservation you put agents and interpreters over us who do bad things. Perhaps they don't mind what you tell them, because I do not believe you would tell them to do bad things to us. In the future we don't want these bad men to be allowed near where we are to live. We don't want any more of that kind of bad talk. I don't want any man who will talk bad about me, and tell lies, to be there, because I am going to try and live well and peaceably. I want to have a good man put over me. While living I want to live well. I know I have to die some time, but even if the heavens were to fall on me, I want to do what is right. I think I am a good man, but in the papers all over the world they say I am a bad man; but it is a bad thing to say so about me. I never do wrong without a cause. Every day I am thinking, how am I to talk to you to make you believe what I say; and, I think, too, that you are thinking of what you are to say to me. There is one God looking down on us all. We are all children of the one God. God is listening to me. The sun, the darkness, the winds, are all listening to what we now say.

To prove to you that I am telling you the truth, remember I sent you word that I would come from a place far away to speak to you here, and you see us now. Some have come on horseback and some on foot. If I were thinking bad, or if I had done bad I would never have come here. If it had been my fault, would I have come so far to talk to you?

KEEPING TREATIES
Sitting Bull (Hunkpapa Sioux)

What treaty that the whites have kept has the red man broken? Not one. What treaty that the whites ever made with us red men have they kept? Not one. When I was a boy the Sioux owned the world. The sun rose and set in their lands. They sent 10,000 horsemen to battle. Where are the warriors to-day? Who slew them? Where are our lands? Who owns them? What white man can say I ever stole his lands or a penny of his money? Yet they say I am a thief. What white woman, however lonely, was ever when a captive insulted by me? Yet they say I am a bad Indian. What white man has ever seen me drunk? Who has ever come to me hungry and gone unfed? Who has ever seen me beat my wives or abuse my children? What law have I broken? Is it wrong for me to love my own? Is it wicked in me because my skin is red; because I am a Sioux; because I was born where my fathers lived; because I would die for my people and my country?

From W. Fletcher Johnson, *Life of Sitting Bull* (1891), p. 201.

REASONS FOR THE TROUBLE BETWEEN THE INDIANS AND THE GOVERNMENT DURING THE GHOST DANCE EXCITEMENT OF 1890

Red Cloud (Oglala Sioux)

[The religious fervor aroused by Jack Wilson, or Wovoka, the Paiute Messiah, in 1888 caught on among several of the western tribes, and nowhere more strongly than among the Sioux. The military as well as many civilians viewed the new religion as a source of potential trouble. The following statement by Red Cloud sought to point out for the whites that the many unresolved grievances among the Indians were more troublesome than the new religion.]

Everybody seems to think that the belief in the coming of the Messiah has caused all the trouble. This is a mistake. I will tell you the cause.

When we first made treaties with the Government, this was our position: Our old life and our old customs were about to end; the game upon which we lived was disappearing; the whites were closing around us, and nothing remained for us but to adopt their ways and have the same rights with them if we wished to save ourselves. The Government promised us all the means necessary to make our living out of our land, and to instruct us how to do

From W. Fletcher Johnson, *Life of Sitting Bull* (1891), pp. 461–67.

it, and abundant food to support us until we could take care of ourselves. We looked forward with hope to the time when we could be as independent as the whites, and have a voice in the Government.

The officers of the army could have helped us better than any others, but we were not left to them. An Indian Department was made, with a large number of agents and other officials drawing large salaries, and these men were supposed to teach us the ways of the whites. Then came the beginning of trouble. These men took care of themselves but not of us. It was made very hard for us to deal with the Government except through them. It seems to me that they thought they could make more by keeping us back than by helping us forward. We did not get the means to work our land. The few things given were given in such a way as to do us little or no good. Our rations began to be reduced. Some said that we were lazy and wanted to live on rations, and not to work. That is false. How does any man of sense suppose that so great a number of people could get to work at once, unless they were at once supplied with means to work, and instructors enough to teach them how to use them?

Remember that even our little ponies were taken away under the promise that they would be replaced by oxen and large horses, and that it was long before we saw any, and then we got very few. We tried, even with the means we had, but on one pretext or another we were shifted from place to place or were told that such a transfer was coming. Great efforts were made to break up our customs, but nothing was done to introduce the customs of the whites. Everything was done to break the power of the real chiefs, who really wished their people to improve, and little men, so-called chiefs, were made to act as disturbers and agitators. Spotted Tail wanted the ways of the whites, and a cowardly assassin was found to remove him. This was charged upon the Indians, because an Indian did it, but who set on the Indian?

I was abused and slandered, to weaken my influence for good and make me seem like one who did not want to advance. This was done by the men paid by the Government to teach us the ways of the whites. I have visited many other tribes, and find that the same things were done among them. All was done to discourage and nothing to encourage. I saw the men paid by the Government to help us all very busy making money for themselves, but doing nothing for us.

Now, don't you suppose we saw all this? Of course we did, but what could we do? We were prisoners, not in the hands of the army, but in the hands of robbers. Where was the army? Set by the Government to watch us, but having no voice in setting things right, so that they would not need to watch us. They could not speak for us, though we wished it very much. Those who held us pretended to be very anxious about our welfare, and said our condition was a great mystery. We tried to speak and clear up this mystery, but were laughed at and treated as children. So things went on from year to year. Other treaties were made, and it was all the same. Rations were further reduced, and we were starving, sufficient food not given us, and no means to get food from the land were provided. Rations were still further reduced. A family got for two weeks what was not enough for one week.

What did we eat when that was gone? The people were desperate from starvation—they had no hope. They did not think of fighting. What good would it do? They might die like men, but what would the women and children do? Some say they saw the son of God. All did not see Him. I did not see Him. If He had come He would do some great thing as He did before. We doubted it, because we saw neither Him nor His works. Then Gen. Crook came. His words sounded well; but how could we know that a new treaty would be kept any better than the old one? For that reason we did not care to sign. He promised to see that his promises would be kept. He, at least, had never lied to us. His words gave the people hope. They signed. They hoped. He died. Their hope died with him. Despair came again. The people were counted, and wrongly counted. Our rations were again reduced. The white men seized on the land we sold them through Gen. Crook, but our pay was as distant as ever. The man who counted us told all over that we were feasting and wasting food. Where did he see this?

How can we eat or waste what we have not? We felt that we were mocked in our misery. We had no newspapers, and no one to speak for us. We had no redress. Our rations were again reduced. You who eat three times each day, and see your children well and happy around you, can't understand what starving Indians feel. We were faint with hunger and maddened by despair. We held our dying children, and felt their little bodies tremble as their souls went out and left only a dead weight in our hands. They were not very heavy, but we ourselves were very faint, and the dead weighed us down. There was no hope on earth, and God seemed to have forgotten us. Some one had again been talking of the Son of God, and said He had come. The people did not know; they did not care. They snatched at the hope. They screamed like crazy men to Him for mercy. They caught at the promises they heard He had made.

The white men were frightened, and called for soldiers. We had begged for life, and the white men thought we wanted theirs. We heard that soldiers were coming. We did not fear. We hoped that we could tell them our troubles and get help. A white man said the soldiers meant to kill us. We did not believe it, but some were frightened and ran away to the Bad Lands. The soldiers came. They said: "Don't be afraid; we come to make peace, and not war." It was true. They brought us food, and did not threaten us. If the Messiah has really come, it must be in this way. The people prayed for life, and the army brought it. The Black Robe, Father Jule, went to the Bad Lands and brought in some Indians to talk to Gen. Brooke. The General was very kind to them, and quieted their fears, and was a real friend. He sent out Indians to call in the other Indians from the Bad Lands. I sent all my horses and all my young men to help Gen. Brooke save the Indians. Am I not right when I say that he will know how to settle this trouble? He has settled it.

The Indian Department called for soldiers to shoot down the Indians whom it had starved into despair. Gen. Brooke said, "No, what have they done? They are dying. They must live." He brought us food. He gave us hope. I trust to him now to see that we will be well treated. I hope that the despair that he has driven away will never return again. If the army had been with us from the first there never would have been any trouble. The army will, I hope, keep us safe and help us to become as independent as the whites.

[What do you think of the killing of Sitting Bull?]

Sitting Bull was nothing but what the white men made him. He was a conceited man who never did anything great, but wanted to get into notice, and white men who had something to make by it, encouraged him and used him. When they had made him as great as they could they killed him to get a name by it. The fight at his arrest would have been made for any one arrested in the same way. If he was a little man, he was a man, and should not have been murdered uselessly. What is worse, many good men were killed also. The soldiers came in time to prevent more murders, but too late to save all. If the army had wanted to arrest him they knew how to do it, and never would have done it in that way. You see how they are doing here. The agent does not interfere with the army, and the army saves lives and does not do anything foolish. No Indian wants to fight; they want to eat, and work, and live; and as the soldiers are peace-makers there will be no trouble here.

The Indian Department has almost destroyed us. Save us from it. Let the army take charge of us. We know it can help us. Let it manage our affairs in its own way. If this can be done I will think that all this late trouble has been only a storm that broke the clouds. Let the sun shine on us again.

THE MASSACRE AT WOUNDED KNEE, SOUTH DAKOTA, ON DECEMBER 29, 1890

Turning Hawk, Captain Sword, Spotted Horse, and American Horse (Sioux)

[The furor that the appearance of the ghost dance religion created among the Sioux brought about a concomitant hysteria in the white community, even far from Indian country. There were numerous public demands that the whole thing be stopped by the army. On December 14, 1890, Sioux police were sent to arrest Sitting Bull, and in the ensuing fracas the old chief was killed. Some of Sitting Bull's followers fled and joined a band of Sioux under Big Foot. A few days later, in this emotionally charged situation, the appearance of soldiers caused the band to flee toward the Pine Ridge reservation. At Wounded Knee Creek, they were surrounded by army troops, and surrendered. This was on the evening of December 28, ironically enough, the day on which the Christian church has long celebrated the festival of the Massacre of the Holy Innocents. The following morning, in a search for weapons, shooting started, whereupon ensued the indiscriminate slaughter of Indians by members of the 7th Cavalry, Custer's old regiment. The following account is taken from reports given to the Commissioner of Indian Affairs on February 11, 1891.]

TURNING HAWK, Pine Ridge (Mr Cook, interpreter). Mr Commissioner, my purpose to-day is to tell you what I know of the condi-

From *Fourteenth Annual Report of the Bureau of American Ethnology* (1896), Part 2, pp. 884–86.

tion of affairs at the agency where I live. A certain falsehood came to our agency from the west which had the effect of a fire upon the Indians, and when this certain fire came upon our people those who had farsightedness and could see into the matter made up their minds to stand up against it and fight it. The reason we took this hostile attitude to this fire was because we believed that you yourself would not be in favor of this particular mischief-making thing; but just as we expected, the people in authority did not like this thing and we were quietly told that we must give up or have nothing to do with this certain movement. Though this is the advice from our good friends in the east, there were, of course, many silly young men who were longing to become identified with the movement, although they knew that there was nothing absolutely bad, nor did they know there was anything absolutely good, in connection with the movement.

In the course of time we heard that the soldiers were moving toward the scene of trouble. After awhile some of the soldiers finally reached our place and we heard that a number of them also reached our friends at Rosebud. Of course, when a large body of soldiers is moving toward a certain direction they inspire a more or less amount of awe, and it is natural that the women and children who see this large moving mass are made afraid of it and be put in a condition to make them run away. At first we thought that Pine Ridge and Rosebud were the only two agencies where soldiers were sent, but finally we heard that the other agencies fared likewise. We heard and saw that about half our friends at Rosebud agency, from fear at seeing the soldiers, began the move of running away from their agency toward ours (Pine Ridge), and when they had gotten inside of our reservation they there learned that right ahead of them at our agency was another large crowd of soldiers, and while the soldiers were there, there was constantly a great deal of false rumor flying back and forth. The special rumor I have in mind is the threat that the soldiers had come there to disarm the Indians entirely and to take away all their horses from them. That was the oft-repeated story.

So constantly repeated was this story that our friends from Rosebud, instead of going to Pine Ridge, the place of their destination, veered off and went to some other direction toward the "Bad Lands." We did not know definitely how many, but understood there were 300 lodges of them, about 1,700 people. Eagle Pipe, Turning Bear, High Hawk, Short Bull, Lance, No Flesh, Pine Bird, Crow Dog, Two Strike, and White Horse were the leaders.

Well, the people after veering off in this way, many of them who believe in peace and order at our agency, were very anxious that some influence should be brought upon these people. In addition to our love of peace we remembered that many of these people were related to us by blood. So we sent out peace commissioners to the people who were thus running away from their agency.

I understood at the time that they were simply going away from fear because of so many soldiers. So constant was the word of these good men from Pine Ridge agency that finally they succeeded in getting away half of the party from Rosebud, from the place where they took refuge, and finally were brought to the agency at Pine Ridge. Young-Man-Afraid-of-his-Horses, Little Wound, Fast Thunder, Louis Shangreau, John Grass, Jack Red Cloud, and myself were some of these peacemakers.

The remnant of the party from Rosebud not taken to the agency finally reached the wilds of the Bad Lands. Seeing that we had succeeded so well, once more we sent to the same party in the Bad Lands and succeeded in bringing these very Indians out of the depths of the Bad Lands and were being brought toward the agency. When we were about a day's journey from our agency we heard that a certain party of Indians (Big Foot's band) from the Cheyenne River agency was coming toward Pine Ridge in flight.

CAPTAIN SWORD. Those who actually went off of the Cheyenne River agency probably number 303, and there were a few from the Standing Rock reserve with them, but as to their number I do not know. There were a number of Ogalallas, old men and several school boys, coming back with that very same party, and one of the very seriously wounded boys was a member of the Ogalalla boarding school at Pine Ridge agency. He was not on the warpath, but was simply returning home to his agency and to his school after a summer visit to relatives on the Cheyenne river.

TURNING HAWK. When we heard that these people were coming toward our agency we also heard this. These people were coming toward Pine Ridge agency, and when they were almost on the agency they were met by the soldiers and surrounded and finally taken to the Wounded Knee creek, and there at a given time their guns were demanded. When they had delivered them up, the men were separated from their families, from their tipis, and taken to a certain spot. When the guns were thus taken and the men thus separated, there was a crazy man, a young man of very bad influence and in fact a nobody, among that bunch of Indians fired his gun, and of course the firing of a gun must have been the breaking of a military rule of some sort, because immediately the soldiers returned fire and indiscriminate killing followed.

SPOTTED HORSE. This man shot an officer in the army; the first shot killed this officer. I was a voluntary scout at that encounter and I saw exactly what was done, and that was what I noticed; that the first shot killed an officer. As soon as this shot was fired the Indians immediately began drawing their knives, and they were exhorted from all sides to desist, but this was not obeyed. Consequently the firing began immediately on the part of the soldiers.

TURNING HAWK. All the men who were in a bunch were killed right there, and those who escaped that first fire got into the ravine, and as they went along up the ravine for a long distance they were pursued on both sides by the soldiers and shot down, as the dead bodies showed afterwards. The women were standing off at a different place from where the men were stationed, and when the firing began, those of the men who escaped the first onslaught went in one direction up the ravine, and then the women, who were bunched together at another place, went entirely in a different direction through an open field, and the women fared the same fate as the men who went up the deep ravine.

AMERICAN HORSE. The men were separated, as has already been said, from the women, and they were surrounded by the soldiers. Then came next the village of the Indians and that was entirely surrounded by the soldiers also. When the firing began, of course the people who were standing immediately around the young man who fired the first shot were killed right together, and then they turned their guns, Hotchkiss guns, etc., upon the women who were in the lodges standing there under a flag of truce, and of course as soon as they were fired upon they fled, the men fleeing in one direction and the women running in two different directions. So that there were three general directions in which they took flight.

There was a women with an infant in her arms who was killed as she almost touched the flag of truce, and the women and children of course were strewn all along the circular village until they were dispatched. Right near the flag of truce a mother was shot down with her infant; the child not knowing that its mother was dead was still nursing, and that especially was a very sad sight. The women as they were fleeing with their babes were killed together, shot right through, and the women who were very heavy with child were also killed. All the Indians fled in these three directions, and after most all of them had been killed a cry was made that all those who were not killed or wounded should come forth and they would be safe. Little boys who were not wounded came out of their places of refuge, and as soon as they came in sight a number of soldiers surrounded them and butchered them there.

Of course we all feel very sad about this affair. I stood very loyal to the government all through those troublesome days, and believing so much in the government and being so loyal to it, my disappointment was very strong, and I have come to Washington with a very great blame on my heart. Of course it would have been all right if only the men were killed; we would feel almost grateful for it. But the fact of the killing of the women, and more especially the killing of the young boys and girls who are to go to make up the future strength of the Indian people, is the saddest part of the whole affair and we feel it very sorely.

I was not there at the time before the burial of the bodies, but I did go there with some of the police and the Indian doctor and a great many of the people, men from the agency, and we went through the battlefield and saw where the bodies were from the track of the blood.

TURNING HAWK. I had just reached the point where I said that the women were killed. We heard, besides the killing of the men, of the onslaught also made upon the women and children, and they were treated as roughly and indiscriminately as the men and boys were.

Of course this affair brought a great deal of distress upon all the people, but especially upon the minds of those who stood loyal to the government and who did all that they were able to do in the matter of bringing about peace. They especially have suffered much distress and are very much hurt at heart. These peacemakers continued on in their good work, but there were a great many fickle young men who were ready to be moved by the change in the events there, and consequently, in spite of the great fire that was brought upon all, they were ready to assume any hostile attitude. These young men got themselves in readiness and went in the direction of the scene of battle so they might be of service there. They got there and finally exchanged shots with the soldiers. This party of young men was made up from Rosebud, Ogalalla (Pine Ridge), and members of any other agencies that happened to be there at the time. While this was going on in the neighborhood of Wounded Knee—the Indians and soldiers exchanging shots—the agency, our home, was also fired into by the Indians. Matters went on in this strain until the evening came on, and then the Indians went off down by White Clay creek. When the agency was fired upon by the Indians from the hillside, of course the shots were returned by the Indian police who were guarding the agency buildings.

Although fighting seemed to have been in the air, yet those who believed in peace were still constant at their work. Young-Man-Afraid-of-his-Horses, who had been on a visit to some other agency in the north or northwest, returned, and immediately went out to the people living about White Clay creek, on the border of the Bad Lands, and brought his people out. He succeeded in obtaining the consent of the people to come out of their place of refuge and return to the agency. Thus the remaining portion of the Indians who started from Rosebud were brought back into the agency. Mr. Commissioner, during the days of the great whirlwind out there, those good men tried to hold up a counteracting power, and that was "Peace." We have now come to realize that peace has prevailed and won the day. While we were engaged in bringing about peace our property was left behind, of course, and most of us have lost everything, even down to the matter of guns with which to kill ducks, rabbits, etc, shotguns, and guns of that order. When Young-Man-Afraid brought the people in and their guns were asked for, both men who were called hostile and men who stood loyal to the government delivered up their guns.

Part Three

HEADING TOWARD THE MAINSTREAM

It is fair to say that, for the American Indian, the beginning of the twentieth century foreboded a second "century of dishonor." The frontier wars and skirmishes were over, but Anglo-American attitudes had not markedly changed. White predators still gazed longingly at any plot of ground the Indian was forced to call home. The problem of making a living was crucial, since most Indians were, until after World War II, living on reservations, and most reservation land was only marginally useful, save for untapped mineral wealth. The Bureau of Indian Affairs still maintained a stranglehold on nearly all aspects of Indian life, especially in its control of the disbursement of government money to the tribes. On the part of Congress, there was, as there always had been, much talk and little action for the benefit of the Indians. The free enterprise–oriented American might ask, "Why couldn't the Indians help themselves?" But, when hundreds of thousands of persons, through public policy and private lawlessness, have been systematically deprived of their ordinary ways of making a living, much help should have been forthcoming.

The Indians found themselves in an increasingly urban and industrial society, with few means to cope with it and fewer of the ordinary opportunities. Indian leaders in all parts of the nation were aware of the problems, and many of them had learned enough in the white man's world to seek workable solutions. So the twentieth century became for the Indians, as for several other ethnic groups, an era of organization, a time for getting together to seek redress from the majority population, even though the minority could not present itself as a political or economic power bloc.

Many organizations for Indian betterment have been formed since 1900: the Society of American Indians, the National Council of American Indians, the National Congress of American Indians, the National Indian Youth Council, the American Indian Movement, Americans for Indian Opportunity, and a number of others. Indians did learn that, to bring effective pressure to bear, they had to organize. They also learned that organization without voter-power and economic muscle does not get very far in this country. It was only after 1924, when Indians were granted citizenship and voting rights, that their real (though sometimes almost imperceptible) progress in this century began.

The best years for the American Indian since 1900 were during the Roosevelt New Deal, when John Collier was Commissioner of Indian Affairs and the Wheeler-Howard Indian Reorganization Act (1934) was passed. Some of the worst years have been since 1945, when, as part of the reaction against the entire New Deal program, Congress seemed to turn upon the Indian with a vengeance. During the Eisenhower Administration the policy of "termination" was inaugurated. This meant relieving the federal government of jurisdiction over (and fiscal responsibility for) the tribes and turning them over to the states. Euphemistically, this venture was called "bringing the Indians into the mainstream" or "granting the Indians first-class citizenship." Actually, it was for the most part a throwing of the tribes to the wolves of private interest and local corruption. Fortunately, Collier had seen bad days coming as early as the mid-1940's and had encouraged the tribes to organize to meet the approaching onslaught.

One of the least beneficial trends among Indians in the past quarter-century has been the schism within tribal life itself. Perhaps half of today's nearly 800,000 Indians live in urban areas, have learned urban ways, and have received better educations than their reservation counterparts. Many such urban Indians have never lived on reservations at all and have little feeling for the mystique of tribal life as expressed in such a setting. On the other hand, the older leaders and reservation Indians have equally little feeling for city life, whatever its opportunities. Such a schism was not only bound to divide Indian organizations; it also confused the goals at which Indians were aiming. The "Red Power" movement since 1966 has mainly obtained among younger, better educated Indians. This does not mean that Indians are turning away from "Indian-ness" and becoming assimilated. It does mean that the determination to express their identity has been at least bifurcated. What Indians do want is to be American, but not necessarily in the same way others are. Such is their natural right, if we admit the possibility of diversity in unity.

The selections in this section, arranged chronologically from about 1900 to 1970, focus on three issues: the grievances of the Indians in the twentieth century; the pan-Indian efforts at cooperative problem-solving; and the complexities of adjusting to urbanization, technology, the political power structures, and the modern economy.

EPIGRAPHS

The allotment of lands in severalty, which began in land lust and is being carried to the bitter end by those who believe a Stone Age man can be developed into a citizen of the United States in a single generation, is in violent antagonism to every wish and innate desire of the red man, and has failed of expected results, even among the Southern Cheyennes, where the land is rich and climate mild, because it presents a somber phase of civilized life.

The attempt to make the Sioux a greedy landowner, content to live the lonely life of the poor Western rancher, cut off from daily association with his fellows, is to me uselessly painful. If we would convert the primitive man to our ways, we must make our ways alluring.

—HAMLIN GARLAND. *The North American Review.* April, 1902

It is probably true that the majority of our wild Indians have no inherited tendencies whatever toward morality or chastity, according to an enlightened standard. Chastity and morality among them must come from education and contact with the better element of the whites.

—W. A. JONES, Commissioner of Indian Affairs. 1903

Let us not make the mistake, in the process of absorbing them, of washing out whatever is distinctly Indian. Our aboriginal brother brings, as his contribution to the common store of character, a great deal which is admirable, and which only needs to be developed along the right line. Our proper work is improvement, not transformation.

—FRANCIS LEUPP, Commissioner of Indian Affairs. 1905

The dominant factor in each Indian athlete's success, aside from

his natural physical adaptability to the sport, has been a coolness
under fire that amounts almost to carelessness, a quick unerring
eye, craftiness, cool, calculating judgment under the most trying
conditions, an absolute lack of nervous system, and a stoicism that
refuses to be shaken in the most crucial situations.

—*Literary Digest.* May 27, 1922

No longer can we naively talk of or think of the "Indian problem."
Our task is to help Indians meet the myriad of complex, interre-
lated, mutually dependent situations which develop among them
according to the very best light we can get on those happenings—
much as we deal with our own perplexities and opportunities.

—JOHN COLLIER, Commissioner of Indian Affairs. 1938

While white Americans by the thousands enjoy the romance and
color of the Indians, and love to sentimentalize about them, they
do not give a whoop in hell whether they live well, die in misery,
or just drag along in weary, broken despair.

—OLIVER LaFARGE. *Harper's Magazine.* November, 1947

The dominant white society insists on conformity. It applauds the
melting pot concept, and discriminates against those who do not, or
cannot, fit exactly into the popular mold. Indians, like members of
other ethnic groups, bitterly resent discrimination, whether it
comes in the form of unequal job opportunities or in the unthink-
ing stereotypes of Hollywood movies; but many accept it as the price
they must pay for holding on to some vestiges of their culture.

The Spirit They Live In. Published by the American Friends
Service Committee. 1956

The Oglala Sioux are regarded as the great masters of passive resistance. They pay no attention to foolish ideas coming from outside. A local schoolteacher took charge of the local civil defense
effort and tried to get the Indians to build bomb shelters; they
paid little heed. In a fury, he put around the story that while one
in every seventeen Americans was a Communist, the rate at the
reservation was considerably higher. His efforts ended in failure.

JAMES RIDGEWAY. *New Republic.* December 11, 1965

It is long past time that the Indian policies of the Federal government began to recognize and build upon the capacities and insights
of the Indian people. Both as a matter of justice and as a matter of
enlightened social policy, we must begin to act on the basis of what
the Indians themselves have long been telling us. The time has come
to break decisively with the past and to create the conditions for a
new era in which the Indian future is determined by Indian acts
and Indian decisions.

RICHARD M. NIXON. *The American Indians,* Message to Congress,
July 8, 1970

It is ironic that after almost 500 years of attempting to destroy both
the American earth and the civilization of the American Indian, the
oppressors are discovering that they now need the Indian to save
them from themselves. America still has national forests, parks,
and wilderness areas, but everywhere they are under growing pressures of destruction. Excessive timber cutting, reckless mineral ex-
ploitation, damming and pollution of wild rivers, extinction of wildlife—all proceed apace. If the Government could persuade various
Indian tribes to take over protection of these last natural paradises,
perhaps they could be saved.

DEE BROWN. "The First Environmentalists." *New York Times.*
June 15, 1971

THE RESERVATION SCHOOL (c. 1900)

Don C. Talayesva (Hopi)

I grew up believing that Whites are wicked, deceitful people. It seemed that most of them were soldiers, government agents, or missionaries, and that quite a few were Two-Hearts. The old people said that the Whites were tough, possessed dangerous weapons, and were better protected than we were from evil spirits and poison arrows. They were known to be big liars too. They sent Negro soldiers against us with cannons, tricked our war chiefs to surrender without fighting, and then broke their promises. Like Navahos, they were proud and domineering—and needed to be reminded daily to tell the truth. I was taught to mistrust them and to give warning whenever I saw one coming.

Our chief had to show respect to them and pretend to obey their orders, but we knew that he did it halfheartedly and that he put his trust in our Hopi gods. Our ancestors had predicted the coming of these Whites and said that they would cause us much trouble. But it was understood that we had to put up with them until our gods saw fit to recall our Great White Brother from the East to deliver us. Most people in Oraibi argued that we should have nothing to do with them, accept none of their gifts, and make no use of their building materials, medicine, food, tools, or clothing—but we did want their guns. Those who would have nothing to do with Whites were called "Hostiles" and those who would cooperate a little were called "Friendlies." These two groups were quarreling over the subject from my earliest memories and sometimes their arguments spoiled the ceremonies and offended the Six-Point-Cloud-

From Leo W. Simmons, ed., *Sun Chief: The Autobiography of a Hopi Indian* (New Haven, 1942), Chapter 5.

People, our ancestral spirits, who held back the rain and sent droughts and disease. Finally the old chief, with my grandfather and a few others, became friendly with the Whites and accepted gifts, but warned that we would never give up our ceremonies or foresake our gods. But it seemed that fear of Whites, especially of what the United States Government could do, was one of the strongest powers that controlled us, and one of our greatest worries.

A few years before my birth the United States Government had built a boarding school at the Keams Canyon Agency. At first our chief, Lolulomai, had not wanted to send Oraibi children, but chiefs from other villages came and persuaded him to accept clothes, tools, and other supplies, and to let them go. Most of the people disliked this and refused to cooperate. Troops came to Oraibi several times to take the children by force and carry them off in wagons. The people said that it was a terrible sight to see Negro soldiers come and tear children from their parents. Some boys later escaped from Keams Canyon and returned home on foot, a distance of forty miles.

Some years later a day school was opened at the foot of the mesa in New Oraibi, where there were a trading post, a post office, and a few government buildings. Some parents were permitted to send their children to this school. When my sister started, the teacher cut her hair, burned all her clothes, and gave her a new outfit and a new name, Nellie. She did not like school, stopped going after a few weeks, and tried to keep out of sight of the Whites who might force her to return. About a year later she was sent to the New Oraibi spring to fetch water in a ceremonial gourd for the Ooqol society and was captured by the school principal who permitted her to take the water up to the village, but compelled her to return to school after the ceremony was over. The teachers had then forgotten her old name, Nellie, and called her Gladys. Although my brother was two years older than I, he had managed to keep out of school until about a year after I started, but he had to be careful not to be seen by Whites. When finally he did enter the day school at New Oraibi, they cut his hair, burned his clothes, and named him Ira.

In 1899 it was decided that I should go to school. I was willing to try it but I did not want a policeman to come for me and I did not want my shirt taken from my back and burned. So one morning in September I left it off, wrapped myself in my Navaho blanket, the one my grandfather had given me, and went down the mesa barefoot and bareheaded.

I reached the school late and entered a room where boys had bathed in tubs of dirty water. Laying aside my blanket, I stepped into a tub and began scrubbing myself. Suddenly a white woman entered the room, threw up her hands, and exclaimed, "On my life!" I jumped out of the tub, grabbed my blanket, darted through the door, and started back up the mesa at full speed. But I was never a swift runner. Boys were sent to catch me and take me back. They told me that the woman was not angry and that "On my life!" meant that she was surprised. They returned with me to the building, where the same woman met me with kind words which I could not understand. Sam Poweka, the Hopi cook, came and explained that the woman was praising me for coming to school without a policeman. She scrubbed my back with soap and water, patted me on the shoulder, and said, "Bright boy." She dried me and dressed me in a shirt, underwear, and very baggy overalls. Then she cut my hair, measured me for a better-fitting suit, called me Max, and told me through an interpreter to leave my blanket and go out to play with the other boys.

The first thing I learned in school was "nail," a hard word to remember. Every day when we entered the classroom a nail lay on the desk. The teacher would take it up and say, "What is this?" Finally I answered "nail" ahead of the other boys and was called "bright."

At first I went to school every day, not knowing that Saturday and Sunday were rest days. I often cut wood in order to get candy and to be called a "smart boy." I was also praised again and again for coming to school without a policeman.

At Christmas we had two celebrations, one in the school and another in the Mission Church. Ralph of the Masau'u Clan and I each received a little painted wagon as a reward for good attendance. Mine was about fifteen inches long with two shafts and a beautiful little gray horse.

I learned little at school the first year, except "bright boy," "smart boy," "yes" and "no," "nail," and "candy." Just before Christmas we heard that a disease, smallpox, was coming west from First Mesa. Within a few weeks news came to us that on Second Mesa the people were dying so fast that the Hopi did not have time to bury them, but just pitched their bodies over the cliff. The government employees and some of the schoolteachers fled from Oraibi, leaving only the principal and missionaries, who said that they would stay. About this time my mother had a new baby, named Perry much later.

During the month of January I danced for the first time as a real Katcina. One evening I entered the Howeove kiva, to which both my father and grandfather belonged, and found the men painting for a dance. Even though I had not practiced I decided to paint myself and dance with them. When my father and grandfather arrived, they discouraged me, but the kind old man who had promised to protect me from the Giant Katcinas in the same kiva about a year before was an important man and insisted that I could dance. When I finished painting, my grandfather gave me a small black blanket to use as a sash, and, since there were not enough gourd rattles, someone gave me an inflated and dried bull scrotum which contained a few small stones and made a good rattle. We left the kiva for the women to enter and then one of

the Katcinas carried me down the ladder on his back which made
the people laugh. I was at the end of the line and danced well
enough for an old woman to pull me over by the stove so that
all could see me. Then I went with the Katcinas to the other kivas.
The people praised me and said that my reward might be a nice
girl for a wife.

One day when I was playing with the boys in the plaza in Oraibi, the school principal and the missionary came to vaccinate
us. My mother brought me in to the principal who was holding a
knife in his hand. Trembling, I took hold of his arm which caused
him to laugh. They had a small bottle of soaplike liquid which
they opened, and placed a little on my arm. After it had dried,
they rubbed my arm with a cloth and the missionary took a
sharp instrument and stuck it into my skin three times. I proved
myself brave enough to take it and set a good example for the
rest of the family who were vaccinated in their turn. It was spring
when the disease disappeared. We were lucky. The old people said
that the vaccinations were all nonsense but probably harmless, and
that by our prayers we had persuaded the spirits to banish the
disease—that it was Masau'u, who guards the village with his fire-
brand, who had protected us. . . .

That autumn some of the people took their children to Keams
Canyon to attend the boarding school. Partly because I was tired
of working and herding sheep and partly because my father was
poor and I could not dress like some of the other boys, I was
persuaded to go to the Agency school to learn to read and cipher
—and to get clothes. My mother and father took three burros
and accompanied me to Keams Canyon. When we arrived at the
end of two days, the matron, Mrs. Weans, took me into the building
and gave me a bath, clipped my hair, and dressed me in clean
clothes.

I ate my supper in the dining room with the other children.
My father and mother ate outside in a camp. That night I slept
in the dormitory on a bed. This was something new for me and
felt pretty good. I was eleven, and the biggest boy in that dormitory; I did not cry. The next morning I had breakfast with the
other children. My father and mother went to the kitchen, where
the cook fed them. For breakfast we had coffee, oatmeal, fried
bacon, fried potatoes, and syrup. The bacon was too salty and
the oatmeal too sloppy.

After breakfast we were all told to go to the office and see the
superintendent of the Reservation, Mr. Burton, for whom my
parents would have to sign their names, or make their marks,
before going home. There were a great many of us and we had
to stand in line. The agent shook hands with us and patted us
on the head, telling us through an interpreter that we had come
to be educated. Then he told us to pass into another room where
we would receive some gifts. They gave my mother fifteen yards
of dress cloth and presented an axe, a claw hammer, and a small

brass lamp to my father. Then they asked him to choose between a shovel and a grubbing hoe. He took the hoe.

We did not go to school that day. We returned to the kitchen, where the cook gave my parents two loaves of bread and some bacon, syrup, and meat. Then we went to the camp, where my father saddled a burro and told my mother to mount. "Well, son," they advised me, "don't ever try to run away from here. You are not a good runner, and you might get lost and starve to death. We would not know where to find you, and the coyotes would eat you." I promised. My father climbed on a burro and they started off. I kept my eyes upon them until finally they disappeared in the direction of Oraibi. I moaned and began to cry, fearing that I should never see them again. A Hopi boy named Nash, whom I did not know, spoke to me and told me to stop crying. My parents would come back again, he reassured me, and they might bring me some good Hopi food. He took me through the Canyon to the other end, where the school building stood. There we gathered some wild roseberries and began eating them until I discovered that they were full of worms.

At noon we all lined up, with the smallest boys in the lead. I was the tallest and the last boy for our dining room. At the table somebody spoke a few words to God, but failed to offer him any of the food. It was very good.

After lunch we smaller boys were given a job cleaning up trash in the yard. When we had finished, Nash and I took a walk up the southeast mesa to the highest point. As we reached the top, Nash turned and said, "Look over to the west." I looked and saw the top of Mount Beautiful, just beyond Oraibi. It seemed far away and I cried a little, wondering whether I would ever get home again. Nash told me not to worry, because I was put there to learn the white people's way of life. He said that when he first came he was homesick, too, but that now he was in the third grade and satisfied. He promised me that when his relatives brought some good Hopi food he would share it with me. His talk encouraged me. As we climbed down the mesa, we heard the supper bell ringing and ran but arrived late. The disciplinarian stepped up to us and struck Nash twice on the buttocks saying, "You are late." Since I was a new boy, he did not put his hands on me—I was lucky.

We went to the dining room and ate bread and a thing called hash, which I did not like. It contained different kinds of food mixed together; some were good and some were bad, but the bad outdid the good. We also had prunes, rice, and tea. I had never tasted tea. The smell of it made me feel so sick that I thought I would vomit. We ate our supper but it did not satisfy me. I thought I would never like hash.

I had trouble defecating, too. A person had to be very careful where he sat. Little houses called privies were provided—one for boys and another for girls. I went into one of them but was afraid to sit down. I thought something might seize me or push me from below and was uneasy about this for several days.

After supper we played a little. Some of the older boys, who had been in school before, wrestled with me. I had been a big, brave lad at home, but now I was timid and afraid. It seemed that I was a little nobody and that any boy could beat me. When it came time for bed the matron took us to the small boys' dormitory, where she made us undress except for our underwear, kneel, and put our elbows on the bed. She taught us to ask Jesus to watch over us while we slept. I had tried praying to Jesus for oranges and candy without success, but I tried it again anyway.

The next day we had to go to school. The little boys went both morning and afternoon. I had to commence at the very bottom in the kindergarten class. When we had entered the classroom and taken our seats, the teacher asked me my name. I did not like my name, Max, so I kept quiet. "Well," said the teacher, "your name shall be Don," and wrote it down in a little book.

The teacher used to pick up a stick, turn the leaves of a chart, and tell us to read. Some of the little boys from First Mesa, who had been there before, could read right along. Although I was the biggest boy in the class, I could not read at all. I felt uncomfortable, especially since they had dressed me in little brown knee pants which I did not like. The first things to learn were "A hat," "A cat," "A horse," "A cow," "An eagle," etc. Then came such things as "A cow has four feet," and "The man had two feet." Another step was, "Put a ball on the box," "Count up to ten." After several days I finally began to understand the words. Soon we were reading long sentences like " 'A rat, a rat,' cried Mae."

I grew tired of school and thought of running away. But one of my father's nephews, Harry Kopi, was watching me and noticed that my face was growing sorrowful. One afternoon, as I was sitting still and sad in the building, he came to me and said, "Come out with me to the place where the pigs live." As we walked along he asked me if I were lonesome, and I almost cried. "I have brought you out here to see the pigs," he said. "When I used to get homesick I would come here and look at them; they made me laugh and feel better." There were about twenty pigs in the pen, all of different sizes. They were funny animals—like dogs with hooves. They looked horrible with their little eyes, sharp mouths, and dirty faces. "Let's go into the pen and ride a pig," said Harry. He caught one by the tail and I clambered on its back and rode it about the pen. It was great fun. I felt better when I got off, and thought to myself that if my homesickness returned I would ride a pig again. . . .

On June the fourteenth my father came for me and we returned home, riding burros and bringing presents of calico, lamps, shovels, axes, and other tools. It was a joy to get home again, to see all my folks, and to tell about my experiences at school. I had learned many English words and could recite part of the Ten Command-

ments. I knew how to sleep on a bed, pray to Jesus, comb my
hair, eat with a knife and fork, and use a toilet. I had learned that
the world is round instead of flat, that it is indecent to go naked
in the presence of girls, and to eat the testes of sheep or goats. I
had also learned that a person thinks with his head instead of his
heart. . . .

By the end of summer I had had enough of hoeing weeds and
tending sheep. Helping my father was hard work and I thought
it was better to be educated. My grandfather agreed that it was
useful to know something of the white man's ways, but said that
he feared I might neglect the Hopi rules which were more important. He cautioned me that if I had bad dreams while at school,
I should spit four times in order to drive them from my mind
and counteract their evil influences.

Before sunrise on the tenth of September the police came to
Oraibi and surrounded the village, with the intention of capturing
the children of the Hostile families and taking them to school by
force. They herded us all together at the east edge of the mesa.
Although I had planned to go later, they put me with the others.
The people were excited, the children and the mothers were crying,
and the men wanted to fight. I was not much afraid because I had
learned a little about education and knew that the police had not
come without orders. One of the captured boys was Dick, the son
of "Uncle Joe" who had stirred up most of the trouble among the
Hostiles. I was glad. Clara, the granddaughter of Chief Lolulomai,
was also taken. The Chief went up to Mr. Burton, who was writing
our names on a piece of paper, and said, "This girl must be left
until she is older." She was allowed to return to her mother. They
also captured my clan brother Archie, the son of my mother's
sister, Nuvahunka.

When Mr. Burton saw me in the group, he said, "Well, well,
what are you doing here? I thought you were back in school at
the Agency." I told him that I was glad to go with him. This
seemed to please him, and he let me go to my house to get my things.
When I returned with a bag of fresh peaches, I discovered that
they had marched the children to New Oraibi to be placed in the
wagons. I followed and found my grandfather in a group near the
wagons. When I noticed how crowded the wagons were, I asked
Mr. Burton if I might ride a horse. He sent me with Archie, Dick,
and my grandfather to ask the police. Two of them were my clan
uncles, Adam from First Mesa and Secavaima from Shipaulovi.
I walked up to Adam, smiling, shook hands with him, and introduced my clan brother Archie. "You don't need to fear us," said my
uncle, "we are policemen." I asked him whether Archie and I might
ride double on horseback to the Agency. They laughed and said
that I had a brave heart. They warned me that the Hostiles might
follow us on the road and give battle, but they were only teasing.

When we were ready to leave the police took us three boys
behind their saddles. Near the foothill of First Mesa we made
a short cut through the gap to the mission house, where we
stopped and waited for the wagons to bring our lunch. After

eating, Adam told me that his week's term as policeman was up and that this was as far as he was going. He took me to Mr. Burton, who told me that I might ride with him in his buckboard. When we were ready to start, I climbed on the buckboard back of the seat. Rex Moona, an educated Hopi who worked in the office at Keams Canyon, was riding in the seat with the superintendent. We drove on ahead of the procession and reached Keams Canyon about sunset.

The children already at the school were eating their supper when we arrived. Rex and I went to the kitchen and asked for food. We each got a loaf of bread and ate it with some syrup. The cook asked me if I would like some hash. I said, "No." We ate our food at the door and told the people in the kitchen that the children were coming in wagons. Then we went to the dormitory and rested. The next morning we took a bath, had our hair clipped, put on new clothes, and were schoolboys again.

HOW ALLOTMENT IMPOVERISHES THE INDIANS: TESTIMONY BEFORE A SENATE COMMITTEE INVESTIGATING CONDITIONS IN THE INDIAN TERRITORY, NOVEMBER, 1906

D. W. C. Duncan (Cherokee)

I am a Cherokee, as I informed you at the outset of my remarks, not without a purpose, and I am going to base a part of my arguments upon my own experiences. Under the old régime, when we were enjoying our vast estate in common here, we all had enough and more than enough to fill up the cup of our enjoyment, for every Cherokee that wanted a home or wanted a farm could go and open it up and enjoy it under the guarantees given us by that incomparable old President, Jackson, years ago. While that was the case I had developed a farm of 300 acres up north of town, not more than 3 miles from where you gentlemen are sitting. I had expended all the labor of a lifetime and worked hard, looking forward to the future, when these gray hairs should come upon my head; looking forward to the time when I should become disqualified by the weight of years to labor and wanted to rest, and I had accumulated a competency sufficient to maintain me in my old age; but when the Dawes Commission sent its survey party around and cut me off up there all but 60 acres, I went to work on that, and to-day the allot-

From Senate Report No. 5013, 59th Congress, 2d Session, Part I, pp. 180–90.

ment process that has been brought upon us by the Federal Government has written destruction of property and capital more terrible than that which was visited upon the isle of Galveston years ago by the anger of the ocean.

Senators, just let me present to you a picture; I know this is a little digression, but let me present it. Suppose the Federal Government should send a survey company into the midst of some of your central counties of Kansas or Colorado or Connecticut and run off the surface of the earth into sections and quarter sections and quarter quarter sections and set apart to each one of the inhabitants of that county 60 acres, rescinding and annulling all title to every inch of the earth's surface which was not included in that 60 acres, would the State of Connecticut submit to it? Would Colorado submit to it? Would Kansas brook such an outrage? No! It would be ruin, immeasurable ruin—devastation. There is not an American citizen in any one of those States would submit to it, if it cost him every drop of his heart's blood. That, my Senators, permit me—I am honest, candid, and fraternal in my feelings—but let me ask a question: Who is that hastened on this terrible destruction upon these Cherokee people? Pardon me, it was the Federal Government. It is a fact; and, old as I am, I am not capable of indulging in euphuisms.

Before this allotment scheme was put in effect in the Cherokee Nation we were a prosperous people. We had farms. Every Indian in this nation that needed one and felt that he needed one had it. Orchards and gardens—everything that promoted the comforts of private life was ours, even as you—probably not so extensively—so far as we went, even as you in the States. The result has been— which I now want to illustrate, as I set out, by my own personal experience.

Under our old Cherokee régime I spent the early days of my life on the farm up here of 300 acres, and arranged to be comfortable in my old age; but the allotment scheme came along and struck me during the crop season, while my corn was ripening in full ear. I was looking forward to the crop of corn hopefully for some comforts to be derived from it during the months of the winter. When I was assigned to that 60 acres, and I could take no more under the inexorable law of allotment enforced upon us Cherokees, I had to relinquish every inch of my premises outside of that little 60 acres. What is the result? There is a great scramble of persons to find land—the office was located here in our town—to file upon. Some of the friends in here, especially a white intermarried citizen, goes up and files upon a part of my farm—on a part of my growing crop, upon the crop upon which I had spent my labor and my money, and upon which I had based my hopes. I remonstrated with him. I said to him, "Sir, you don't want to treat me that way. We are neighbors and friends. You can't afford to take my property that way. Of course the Dawes Commission and the Curtis law will give you the land, although I have subdued it, and I have fenced it, and cultivated it. But for God's sake, my friend, don't take my crop." "Well," says he, "I had to surrender my crop to a fellow down here. He allotted on me, and I don't know why I should be any more lenient on you than others are on me. If you don't let that corn alone, I will go to the court and get an order." That was new to me, but when I came to examine the Curtis law, and investigated the orders and rules established by the Dawes Commission, I just folded my hands and said, "I give it up." Away went my crop, and if the same rule had been established in your counties in your State you would have lost your dwelling house; you would have lost your improvements. Now, that is what has been done to these Cherokees. . . .

What a condition! I have 60 acres of land left me; the balance is all gone. I am an old man, not able to follow the plow as I used to when a boy. What am I going to do with it? For the last few years, since I have had my allotment, I have gone out there on that farm day after day. I have used the ax, the hoe, the spade, the plow, hour for hour, until fatigue would throw me exhausted upon the ground. Next day I repeated the operation, and let me tell you, Senators, I have exerted all my ability, all industry, all my intelligence, if I have any, my will, my ambition, the love of my wife— all these agencies I have employed to make my living out of that 60 acres, and, God be my judge, I have not been able to do it. I am not able to do it. I can't do it. I have not been able to clear expenses. It will take every ear of the bounteous crop on that 60 acres—for this year is a pretty good crop year—it will take every bushel of it to satisfy the debts that I have incurred to eke out a living during the meager years just passed. And I am here to-day, a poor man upon the verge of starvation—my muscular energy gone, hope gone. I have nothing to charge my calamity to but the unwise legislation of Congress in reference to my Cherokee people. . . .

I am in that fix, Senators; you will not forget now that when I use the word "I" I mean the whole Cherokee people. I am in that fix. What am I to do? I have a piece of property that doesn't support me, and is not worth a cent to me, under the same inexorable, cruel provisions of the Curtis law that swept away our treaties, our system of nationality, our every existence, and wrested out of our possession our vast territory. The same provisions of that Curtis law that ought to have been satisfied with these achievements didn't stop there. The law goes on, and that 60 acres of land, it says, shall not be worth one cent to me; although the Curtis law has given me 60 acres as the only inheritance I have in God's world, even that shall not be worth anything. Let me explain.

If you had a horse that you couldn't use, and some competent power ordained that that horse should have no value in any market on the face of the earth, and at the same time you should be compelled to keep that horse as long as he should live, or at least twenty-five years, at your expense; now, in the name of common

An Indian speaking in front of the statue of Massosoit, "protector of the Pilgrims" in 1621, during a Thanksgiving Day demonstration at Plymouth Rock, Massachusetts. The demonstrators, members of about twenty-five tribes, declared that Thanksgiving Day should be a day of national mourning for the American Indian.

A drummer in the costume of the Eagle Dance of the Tesuque Pueblo in northern New Mexico. Many Indians and non-Indians are now taking a new look at the heritage of the original Americans.

Buffalo dance in New Mexico.

New York Public Library Picture Collection

In the twelfth and thirteenth
centuries, ancestors of the
present-day Pueblo Indians
built communal dwellings
on ledges in canyon walls
and on the flat tops of mesas.
Here an archaeologist
lectures to a group near
"Cliff Palace" in Mesa
Verde National Park,
Colorado.

A Hopi snake priest,
photographed by
A. C. Vroman in 1901.

*Religious News
Service Photo*

Navajo country, a land
of high buttes and
dry, eroded soil
on the Arizona–
New Mexico border.

Woman and child on a Navajo Indian reservation.

Yakima Indian woman
grinding grain for
making bread on a
Yakima reservation in a
national park
in Washington.

*Religious News
Service Photos*

Self-contained community of Tinglit Indians
in the heart of downtown Juneau, Alaska.

Members of the Taos Pueblo
tribe who appeared before
a Senate subcommittee on
Indian affairs to request
the return of lands known
as the Blue Lake area in
northern New Mexico.
The lands were seized
in 1906 and made part
of the National Forest
Preserve.

Dennis Banks of the
American Indian Movement
asking a church group
for funds to aid the
nation's Indians.

*Religious News
Service Photos*

Indians occupying Alcatraz Island in San Francisco Bay. They claimed the island under an 1868 treaty.

Wide World Photos

John Trudell, a leader of the Indians who claimed Alcatraz, standing beside a symbolic tepee erected on the island. In the background is the Golden Gate Bridge.

Wide World Photos

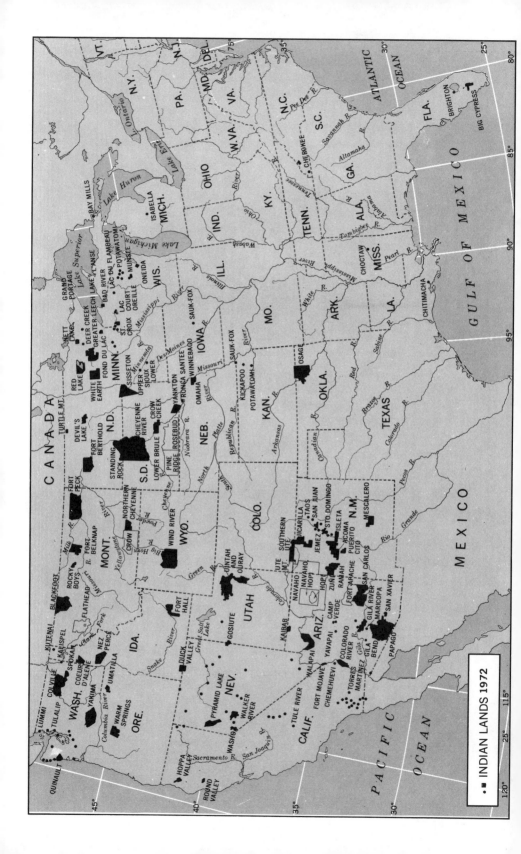

■ INDIAN LANDS 1972

sense, what would you do with that horse? He is not worth anything; his services are not worth anything to me; I can't ride him; I can't use him. There is no man in the world that will give me a cent for him; the law won't allow me to sell him. I would get rid of that horse somehow sure.

The point I am making here is applicable to every species of property, whether real or personal. Prevent the property from being purchasable in open market and you destroy it. Upon the same principle, my allotment up here is absolutely destroyed. What am I going to do with it? What can any Indian do with his allotment under similar circumstances?

Let me allude to myself again. It is not egotism. I will tell you what I am going to do with my allotment. I sat down one day and wrote out my application for the removal of my restrictions. I went to work and pushed it through all the Federal machinery up to the Secretary of the Interior and back again, and a few days ago I was notified my restrictions were raised. Now for the next step. What am I going to do with that worthless piece of property? I am going to hold it—how long I don't know—but I am going to wait until the white population becomes a little more multitudinous, when the price of real estate will rise. When I can get anything like an adequate value for my farm I am going to sell it. It is worthless to me.

The Government of the United States knows that these allotments of the Indians are not sufficient. Congress recognizes the fact forcibly, by implication, that these allotments are not sufficient. Why, one American citizen goes out on the western plain in North Dakota to make a home. What is the amount of land allotted to him? Isn't it 160 acres? Why, it is the general consensus all over the country that nothing less would be sufficient to support any family; and there are many years when you think, too, that 160 acres is not sufficient. Since this country has been split up, the Cherokee government abolished, and the allotments attained, immigration has come in from the surrounding States, consisting of persons of different kinds. I have tested them, and know what I am talking about, personally. Persons in pursuit of a sufficient quantity of land upon which to rear their families and take care of themselves. I have interrogated them time and again. I have said to them. "Look here, my friend, where are you going?" "To Indian Territory." "What for?" "To get a piece of land." "Did you have any land in Missouri or Kansas?" "Yes, sir; I had some up there, but it was too small and wasn't sufficient." "How much was it?" "Eighty or one hundred acres," as the case may be; "I have leased out my land up there to parties, and thought I would come down here and get a larger piece of ground." Well, now, that is the state of the case. I think, gentlemen, when you investigate the case fully you will find that these people have been put off with a piece of land that is absolutely inadequate for their needs.

THE RESERVATION SYSTEM
Thomas L. Sloan (Omaha)

Early in the administration of Indian affairs it became evident that the Indian could not rely upon the statements of the Indian Service officials, the laws made by Congress for their protection, nor the treaties made between them and the United States of America. The rights to hunt, to fish, to make homes and to occupy the lands of their fathers were never held sacred to the Indian, although declared to be so by law or treaty. Public policy and political policy joined in the administration to deprive him of his rights.

In Arizona, New Mexico and Colorado an official first named to protect his water interests, without which the lands were of no value, recommended that he hold his rights under the State and territorial laws. This was in States where the Indian's rights are least considered, and where it is the practice to steal water and take advantage by the use of it. This protecting Indian official wanted those rights turned over to the State. He even admits under oath that where the courts have decreed that a certain quantity of water on specifically described lands, he, as an official of the Indian Office, ignored the decrees of the court, the previously acquired water rights and the established rule of law as announced by the court for the protection of Indian lands and water. When asked what he had done to recover the stolen water rights for the Indians, he said he did not think it right to take it away from the whites who had used it so long. He was paid to protect and look after the interests of the Indian, but he had no desire to recover

From *Proceedings of the First Annual Conference of the Society of American Indians* (Washington, D.C., 1912), pp. 112–21.

that which belonged to him. The long years of use by the Indian had no effect upon him as to their established water rights. But when it had been stolen from them by the whites and used for a shorter time, it was wrong to take it from them and give it back to the Indians to whom it belonged. That is an example of administration protection, and a disgrace to the nation, against which complaint should be made.

In the administration of the lands of deceased allottees by the Indian Office, the decision of the Secretary of the Interior is attempted to be made final and conclusive. In one case, after the heirs had established their rights in a hearing after due notice, and the Secretary of the Interior had approved and promulgated the order and given notice to the heirs of their respective rights, the Secretary of the Interior, upon the request of a senator, without notice, hearing, evidence, or any legal papers being filed, has taken up the case and reversed his previous decision. The heirs were afterwards informed that they had no rights in these lands. This is a confiscation of property rights. It is the most extreme disregard of property rights and interests that can be found in modern times. A "star-chamber" proceeding, without notice of hearing, depriving the individual Indian of property rights and interests without due process of law. This is some of the recent administration protection. The most solemn safeguards of vested property rights are overridden by the very power that was designed to protect the Indian's rights.

It has gone on to such an extent that in one case the Supreme Court of the United States has said that the action of the Interior Department was so arbitrary that it had no place in American jurisdiction; and in that particular case they restored the rights of which the Indian had been deprived by decree of court, and made the statement that there was no place even in the Executive Department of the Government for such arbitrary action and disregard of law. Still the very thing which the Supreme Court of the United States found to be arbitrary and unreasonable is the very thing that has been done and will continue to be done until it is limited by wholesome and just laws.

Think of a politician who had never had any court experience acting as a judge in controversies involving land titles by descent, worth millions of dollars, and who, without experience, attempted to adjudicate thirty or forty cases in a single day. He not only acted as judge, but also as attorney for both sides. The record shows that this acting judge in some cases heard all of the evidence upon one side and then gave notice to the other side. One of the fundamental rights in the courts of law concerning controversies over property is to be faced with witnesses, and to examine and cross-examine them upon the testimony which they offer. But in these cases the acting judge saw fit to hear all the testimony upon one side before giving notice of hearing to the other side.

Appeals from the acting judge go to the superior who appointed him. The idea of the Indian Office seems to be that they are better fitted to handle all the affairs of the Indian than the Indian himself, or the other departments of a republican form of government. The Indian Office says, "The Indian does not know what is best for him in the administration of these inheritances." So a politician is selected to act as judge for them, and this politician acting as judge violates every rule of law for the protection of property, and the Indian subjected to rules and regulations and arbitrary action that violates constitutional limitations. The evil seems to be that the Indian Bureau administers as if the Indian was selected for their benefit, to exploit them, and not they that were created for the benefit of the Indian. This spirit prevails generally in the Indian service.

It seems that there is no step forward in the Indian service. With less lands now to administer, with fewer ignorant Indians, they still have more employees, greater expenditures, and a greater per capita cost to maintain their work than before. More rules and regulations, and when an Indian learns to comply with one set of rules and regulations they are changed so that he is compelled to begin again.

Although the President of the United States appointed a so-called competency commission to determine the competency of the Omaha Indians, and they made their report, which was approved, and the Indians declared competent, still the superintendent in charge may, without hearing or notice of any kind, declare a citizen Indian of the tribe to be incompetent. Should the superintendent in charge report favorably upon any such man, a clerk or some one else in the Indian Office may overrule it, and the communications which are submitted to the Indian Office are treated as confidential and therefore not open to an investigation by the party affected. It is in effect a star chamber proceeding that determines that a citizen of the United States is an incompetent person. Their status as men and women determined in such a manner is not by law, but by autocratic and arbitrary power. The practice of subjecting a man or woman to investigation without notice, hearing or trial, and declaring him or her incompetent upon a secret order, is one that cannot be defended under any circumstances. Such men and women, being citizens of the United States and of the States wherein they live, are entitled to all the rights, privileges and immunities of citizens of the several States, but they are treated as arbitrarily as the subjects of the Czar of Russia. Men, through political accident, and most likely through business failure preceding it, are placed in positions of arbitrary power. They evolve new theories, discover latent powers, old and new wrongs, and remedies for all. They are followed by a horde of their appointees who know nothing more than themselves about the people and their conditions. About the time they have discovered their success or failure some new politician is found or some "land duck" requires a berth. Then begins some new idea.

The local communities about the reservation always desire something to be done with it. The representatives of the business people of the town adjoining a reservation desire that the land be obtained in fee, sold or otherwise disposed of, not for the welfare of the Indian, but to enable them to develop business or trade. Business men, politicians, farmers, railroad men, grafters and sharks in the vicinity of a reservation wish it open, not for the benefit of the Indian, but for a larger opportunity for each in his own line. Such influences reach the executive branches of the government as well as Congress more readily than the Indian, and when something is to be done with the Indian land or property under the general guise of some good for him, he is the last person to know about it, through some action taken that affects his property or his income. Among the Omaha Indians, admittedly among the most advanced, there was a new scheme about leasing their allotments. It was discussed at Washington by the commissioner and the delegates from the towns around the reservation, and with the superintendent in charge and the leading citizens about the reservation, but not with the Indian. The last to know anything about it were the Indians. Yet it was their property; they were affected most by any change as to their income or manner which they should get it, but they were the last to learn anything about it and were not consulted as to what might be best in reference to their land. Those people who were consulted were those who had interests adverse to the Indian. They, because of their position or political influence or the two combined, were the first who were given consideration, and those who were most affected, whose rights were being considered, were the last to be notified, *not consulted*, simply notified.

Sales of Indian land have been made under the directions of agency officials. Usually the Indians, before the sale, obtained more money in a year from rentals than they can get from the proceeds of the sale of the land in the same length of time while held in the agency office. In some cases after the sale of such lands and its dissipations in a few years, the Indian is without any income at all, and he would have had an income through rents during that same period, an amount equal to the sum which was paid to him from the principal. The money is held at the agency for the sale of land, which furnishes some means of living, and the only means of living for many Indians.

On the Rosebud Reservation it costs the Indian as much in time and money and effort to collect the small sums of money at the agency as it would to have gone out and earned it. Others with sums of money at the agency have suffered in want. One old man past seventy years of age, living near Bonesteel, on what was formerly a part of the Rosebud Sioux Reservation, was told in a letter from the Office at Washington, in answer to his application to be paid some money, that if he would go to the agency he would receive from his four thousand dollars there on deposit such amount of money as would be necessary to provide for his needs. It was one hundred and fifty miles across the country to the agency. To go around by railroad was more than three hundred miles, and the stage route twenty-five miles more. He had neither the means nor the physical ability to make the trip, and this particular old man died in absolute want, except such means as were provided him by the neighbors. An inspector of the Indian service says there are many such cases.

An old Indian woman past eighty years of age, in order to get from the agency a check of ten dollars, money due her derived from the sale of her land, had to travel seven or eight miles each month to get the check. During the severest kind of cold weather, about the 1st of January, it was necessary for her grandson to carry her to the wagon and cover her carefully and drive a distance of seven or eight miles and return, and the hardship upon that old lady was more than it was worth to get it. Had she paid her grandson a reasonable compensation for taking care of her there, she should have had five or six dollars left out of the ten dollars that was paid her.

The ration system is no worse than the present money system, which holds the Indian a bondsman and makes him eke out the same kind of living or existence that he had when he received the rations. It takes from him every incentive for development, and holds him in such subjection that his independence and manliness are destroyed. He gets no experience, and he is subservient at all times through the control of this money to the agency official and to the reservation system. It is only a continuation of the old system, which was admitted by the Indian Office, by the Indians, and those who have any general knowledge of those affairs as detrimental to the Indian.

In some instances where Indians have lived from the reservation, and because of the law which provided that when an Indian separates himself from his tribe and adopts habits of civilized life, he is a citizen of the community in which he lives. Such an Indian may hold an allotment upon the reservation. The Indian Office seems desirous of bringing such Indians into bondage through the control and supervision of his lands. Such men have made application for fee patents and they have been refused. Some of them, where they have a section of land, have been offered a fee patent for one hundred and sixty; and Pine Ridge Reservation at this time, would just about yield the expenses of going up there and selling it and coming back. I think that about five dollars an acre is all that could be demanded for the ordinary lands upon the Pine Ridge Reservation at this time.

One young man who was doing business in the city of Chicago made several trips to Washington to obtain a fee patent for his land. Although he had been in the general grocery business in that city and had deposited in the bank the sum of a thousand dollars and a little more, still he is not considered competent by the

Indian Office, through their star-chamber proceedings, so that he might handle the proceeds of three hundred and twenty acres of land that might bring at most ten dollars an acre in the Sioux country. It seems that in order for such a man to be free it would be absolutely necessary for him to abandon his rights upon the reservation and live separate and apart and independent of the Indian nations and everything that he might have.

To those who only know reservation life among their own people and nothing of what can be done away from it, a breaking away cannot well be expected. The long years of reservation life and the dominant official control has been exercised to such length that the reservation Indian does not know the limit when it is reached. An allotment has no property value to the Indian citizen living in Chicago or other places away from the Indian country unless he can use it to some advantage, and that is denied him absolutely by the present policy of the Indian Office. He may have been unfitted for life in the open, no means of making use of land because of want of teams and agricultural implements and a house in which to live, and the necessities of life to live upon until he could break up his land and raise a crop.

The country in the immediate vicinity of Pine Ridge was a number of years ago broken up by hordes of homesteaders, who, when the dry season came on, abandoned the country, left their land, their houses, their barns, their fences, and were glad to be able to get back to some of the more prosperous parts of the country with their teams and families, and the country was absolutely abandoned, and still it is expected of an Indian that he shall make a living and thrive under the same conditions and upon the same kind of land where the educated and prepared white man failed.

No man in Washington, neither the head nor the subordinate, can know the conditions of the man or his opportunities or his capabilities. The Indians are individuals and are not bound directly or controlled by any set of rules and regulations which may be promulgated by the Secretary of the Interior or the Commissioner of Indian Affairs. The man on the ground, the agency official is overwhelmed by official duties and does not know, perhaps does not care, about the individual; he has more than he can do, and he is expected to do that which only the individual can do for himself. He is not given a chance to get away from supervision long enough to assert his individuality, and it may be that he will only develop manliness after he has been defrauded out of his lands or has frittered it away. At any rate the present system is not making men and women. There is a lack of development of the man in dealing with the Indians.

A missionary on the Rosebud Reservation said that the Sioux Indian was simply eking out an existence upon the inherited lands which had come to him and which he had sold, and that he was not as manly, as independent, or as strong as he was some fifteen years ago when he made efforts on his own behalf.

How many inspectors of the Indian service have sustained the Indian in an investigation against an Indian Office official? Most of them have sought to sustain the official against any Indian who complained. Complaint was made about a certain Indian official and an inspector was sent to the agency. Witnesses were examined and the acts complained [of] were practically admitted. It appeared that he had held an open honest meeting, and here for once was an opportunity where the truth could be reached and something decisively done where a wrong had been committed. The officials were transferred. It was thought that everything had been done honestly and fairly. The report disclosed "that the thing complained of had been done, but the inspector said the officials employed at that agency were faithful to the government, and it was wrong to condemn or punish them. That to do so would be detrimental to the service and would encourage complaints."

These are some of the things of which the Indian should complain, and in which the administration should be improved. When you think of inspectors, you expect them to investigate for the benefit of the Indian, but it has happened in many instances their inspection has been to the detriment of the Indian.

This covers sufficiently the matter of administration, and the law applying to it, so that the subject is open for discussion. In the administration of Indian affairs there should be such reforms as will give the Indian in hearings and investigations those rights which belong to him under the Constitution of the United States. That his property may be protected by regular court proceedings, and that when the court decrees certain rights, no Indian official be permitted to disregard the decree of the court and the law protecting the Indian, and not to violate his own oath of office to the detriment of the Indian. We should ask for reforms, and the repeal of this Act of Congress, which provides that the investigation of the Secretary of the Interior as to the heirs of deceased allottees shall be final and binding, as in violation of the express limitation of the Constitution of the United States, which provides that the government of the United States shall be vested in the three departments: legislative, executive and judicial. The Supreme Court of the United States has said that the action of an executive officer can never be a judicial power. Even the layman can see that when a controversy arises between two parties in reference to the vesting of property rights by descent, that controversy is one for judicial determination as to the claims of the parties under the law. We are having these lands administered in a manner that is a shame and a disgrace to any civilized nation, let alone these United States, and we ought to ask for such reform as will guarantee to us the protection of the laws and the privileges with reference to our property rights, which are given to every citizen, and for that matter, to non-citizens who hold property within the United States.

TESTIMONY DURING A 1915 TRIAL FOR VIOLATING A WASHINGTON STATE CODE ON SALMON FISHING

Chiefs Meninock and Wallahee (Yakima)

The defendant chief, Meninock, gave the following forceful and convincing testimony:

"God created this Indian country and it was like He spread out a big blanket. He put the Indians on it. They were created here in this country, truly and honestly, and that was the time this river started to run. Then God created fish in this river and put deer in these mountains and made laws through which has come the increase of fish and game. Then the Creator gave us Indians life; we awakened and as soon as we saw the game and fish we knew that they were made for us. For the women God made roots and berries to gather, and the Indians grew and multiplied as a people. When we were created we were given our ground to live on, and from that time these were our rights. This is all true. We had the fish before the missionaries came, before the white man came. We were put here by the Creator and these were our rights as far as my memory to my great-grandfather. This was the food on which we lived. My mother gathered berries; my father fished and killed the game. These words are mine and they are true. It matters not how long I live, I cannot change these thoughts. My strength is from the fish; my blood is from the fish, from the roots and the berries. The fish and the game are the essence of my life. I was not brought from a foreign country and did not come here. I was put

From *The Washington Historical Quarterly*, July, 1928, pp. 170–74.

here by the Creator. We had no cattle, no hogs, no grain, only berries and roots and game and fish. We never thought we would be troubled about these things, and I tell my people, and I believe it, it is not wrong for us to get this food. Whenever the seasons open I raise my heart in thanks to the Creator for his bounty that this food has come.

"I want this treaty to show the officers what our fishing rights were. I was at the council at Walla Walla with my father, who was one of the chiefs who signed that treaty. His name was Meninock, too. Jim Wallahee, who was arrested when I was and who is a defendant too, had an uncle whose name was Owhi, who was at that council and who also signed the treaty. I well remember hearing the talk about the treaty. There were more Indians there at Walla Walla than ever came together any place in this country. Besides the women and the children, there were two thousand Indian warriors, and they were there for about one moon, during the same part of the year as now, in May and June.

"The Indians and the Commissioners were many days talking about making this treaty. One day Governor Stevens read what he had written down, and had one of his interpreters explain it to the Indians. After everybody had talked and Pu-pu-mox-mox had talked, General Stevens wanted to hear from the head chief of the Yakimas. He said, 'Kamiaken, the great chief of the Yakimas, has not spoken at all. His people have had no voice here today. He is not afraid to speak—let him speak out.'

"Something had been said about more and more whites coming into the Indian's country and that then the Indians would be driven away from their hunting grounds and fishing places; then Governor Stevens told the Indians that the Government would see that when the white men came here the rights of the Indians would be protected; then Chief Kamiaken said: 'I am afraid that the white men are not speaking straight; that their children will not do what is right by our children; that they will not do what you have promised for them.' To this Governor Stevens said: 'My brothers and myself have talked straight to the council. You and your children will not be troubled in the use of your streams. The Indians will be allowed to take fish from them at the usual fishing places, and this promise will be kept by the Americans as long as the sun shines, as long as the mountains stand, and as long as the rivers run.' "

Chief Wallahee, another defendant, testified:

"What Chief Meninock and Chief Alex McCoy have said is true, as all our people know. I want to speak some words to tell the judge why I feel I do no wrong when I catch salmon at the old Top-tut fishing place at the Prosser Falls.

"When the treaty was made at Walla Walla the Indians were told to give up all the Indian country except the Reservation. They did not like to do this, and there was much talk. The Indians were told that the whites would come in large numbers and that they would want to raise crops and stock and unless there was an understanding about what lands and places were to be used by each, there would be trouble and bad feeling between the Indians and the whites all the time. But after a while the Indians were persuaded to sign the treaty and they gave up all the country except the Reservation and a few fishing places and the right to catch fish at these places like Top-tut where our people have always fished.

"There is a reason why the Indians reserve the right to fish at these ancient fishing places, which I will try to tell.

"At Top-tut there always was a kind of a fall. The river at this place was so made and the rocks so formed by God that when the salmon came from the sea they would go up to this place where the water was shallow and in ripples so that the fish could be caught with our hooks, spears and nets, so when an Indian got hold of a big fish there, he could land it without danger of being pulled in and being drowned in the deep, swift high water. That is why these accustomed fishing places which were created for the Indians were set aside in the treaty for the use of the Indians.

"That is why I do not think I do any wrong when I fish at this place my father saved for me and which the Great Spirit made for the Indians. Is it right for the white man to build a dam at the falls and then say that his act destroys the bounty of the Creator?

"I am telling the truth. Indians do not bother white people. Anything they raise we do not bother. I do not go into a white man's field or destroy his things. I keep out, but the salmon does not belong to him. It is sent free from the ocean by God for my use.

"I do not think it would be right for the white man to say, 'Indians, I do not want you to have even a few fish for your own use.' I do not think all white people are like the Fish Commissioner. He wants us to act like little children and go some place else and fish at places where we know and he knows we cannot catch any."

The case was submitted to the jury and under the instructions of the Court a verdict of guilty was returned. Before sentence was imposed the head chief, Meninock, made the following impassioned plea to the Court, as copied from a report in the Spokesman-Review:

"I am about to open my heart to speak to you of my griefs and troubles. Open yours to receive my words.

"I first salute the Great Spirit, the Master of Life, and the author of the natural law upon which all justice rests. Then I turn to you my earthly judge. Let me say a word for our fathers, who are dead. My father, Meninock, was one of the chiefs who signed the Yakima Treaty. Had he lived he would speak today and you would have heard a good man; and truth would flow from his lips. But our fathers are gone and they can not speak and they pray you to listen to the living.

"I was at Walla Walla in June, 1855, with my father when the treaty was signed. Our chiefs did not want to sign the treaty proposed by General Stevens. Our father said, 'You will take away our rights and we cannot fish and hunt,' and they would not sign the treaty. There was much trouble then.

"General Stevens said: 'You listen to me. I am going to protect you in your rights to fish. I will put in the record never to be wiped out that the Indians shall have the right to fish at their fishing places. I will see that your children get their rights. If, when I am gone, any of my white children violate this agreement the government will punish them—the Government will take up and protect you always as long as the sun shines, as long as the mountains stand and as long as the rivers run.'

"Then our chiefs were persuaded and they believed what General Stevens said and they signed the treaty and the clouds cleared away and the day was bright. My father when he was about to die charged us to abide in peace and live up to the treaty and we have done so all our lives. Now I am told that the high court of the state of Washington says: 'This treaty is no good.' They close their ears to the truth. They make out that General Stevens did not speak to our people truthfully after all—that he deceived the Indians with sweet words.

"Judge, is this so? I loved the land on which I was born, the trees which covered it and the grass growing on it. I am thankful to the Creator for the food fish which he sends to us in his streams and I am not here to beg, but I came to ask for the right which was guaranteed us to take this food for our selves.

"No people can fight against the Americans. Only the great God himself can punish them when they do wrong. I am now old; you are powerful; you can wipe away our tears, order your officers to be just; forbid them to arrest the Indians when they fish at places reserved in the treaty; have pity on us. You have many red children here; grant them their rights.

"We have followed the treaty. We think it is the highest law. We think it was made before the state law and you should decide our rights. We do not kill the fish for the market; we make no money. Look at me! How much money did I make on this fishing? I have nothing. We have heard how the white man kills the fish and sells them for money. That is why the fish are getting scarce.

"I follow my father—I stand by what the treaty says. Let me take back the tidings to my people that the whites also stand by the treaty. Then all will be well."

"LET MY PEOPLE GO": AN ADDRESS DELIVERED AT THE CONFERENCE OF THE SOCIETY OF AMERICAN INDIANS IN LAWRENCE, KANSAS, SEPTEMBER 30, 1915

Carlos Montezuma (Apache)

Somehow or other the idea prevails that the Indian's sphere of action in this life and in America should be limited within the wigwam, and when an Indian boy or girl goes away to school you hear the hounding voices saying, "Go back, go back to your home and people." These good people and many others seem to convey the idea that Indians are strangers in America; and strange to say, these people have the whole world for their action, and they are far away from their place of birth, and when they came the Indian was here; and, of course, the Indians, too, must have the whole world for their sphere of action.

There are hundreds of Indian employees in the Indian Service. To a casual observer this may appear as though the United States Government is magnanimous, considerate of its wards by giving employment to the schooled Indian boys and girls and to others who can fill positions and pass civil-service examinations. Man is the outcome of his environment. If employed in the Indian Service of the Government, that person will carry with him the atmosphere of that service, be he from any race. Anyone who conscientiously

From Congressional Record, 64th Congress, 1st Session, pp. 7843–45.

and unselfishly starts in the Indian Service to sacrifice his ambition in behalf of the Indian in time will fall into the rut, get tired, disgusted, and lose interest, and finally see no use, and he will fall into the level of his surroundings and stick to his job. He has lost sight of the grand object that he had at first, but he sticks to his job.

Just so with the Indian employees in the Indian Service; their personality is destroyed. To keep their positions, to be in the swim, they must not express themselves: they have nothing to say. They stick to the Indian Service and hate to lose their jobs.

Indian employees in the Indian Service are working against the freedom of their race.

Truth hurts, but it is never wrong, and in the long run it conquers. The Indian Bureau is the only obstacle that stands in the way, that hinders our people's freedom. It seems so strange, so incredible, and so unheard of that we Indians must fight and kill the very organ that was organized to free us in order to free ourselves.

What is the Society of American Indians good for? Dare we shy? Dare we run? Dare we cower? And dare we hide when our duty is so plainly written before us? As a society with the greatest object for our people, it should be no longer possible to evade the issue; the responsibility rests with us to be message runners to every camp and to let every Indian know that it remains with every individual Indian to be free.

It is appalling and inexplicable that the palefaces have taken all of the Indian's property—the continent of America—which was all he had in the world. The Indian asks for public school, college, and university education for his children. To refuse such a noble request would be as cruel as to give a stone when he asks for bread. Will the department defray the expenses of any college or university Indian students? The Indian Bureau's motto seems to be, "Eighth grade and no more." And therefore we may assume that the Indian Department does not want the Indian educated. It may be wise, and is afraid that they will make too many lawyers who will fight to a finish. It may be that the Indian Bureau fears something may happen from the Indian's knowledge of doing something.

To dominate a race you do not want to educate them. All one needs to do is to make them believe black is white and get them to believe everything you do is all right. Let them live Indian life. Let them fear you. Let them quibble among themselves. Give them plenty of sweets and tell them things will come out all right, for them not to worry, but leave it all to their "Washington father"; for he is "good medicine," and all will be well. Blessed is the superintendent who has this executive ability.

The life of the Indian Bureau is supported by plausibilities and by civil service. No discredit to the principles of civil service, but when it comes to clinch and hold the lid down and keep the Indians from their liberty by its good name, then it is time that a loud protest should come from the Society of American Indians. The merit system has a limit when it stands in the way of human rights.

The Indian Bureau is willing and anxious to do everything for the Indians, but! It says: "If there is anything wrong, we can remedy it ourselves, because we are in a position to know the needs of the Indians, and do not believe, but!"

"Thou good and faithful servant" cannot be applied to the Indian Bureau; from a lamb it has grown to be a strong monster. It looks with furious glare at every movement we make, lest we take away the Indians from its blood-stained paws, because it pays to continue the same old policy, to keep us within due bonds.

The Indian Bureau could dissolve itself and go out of business, but what is the use? Just think, 8,000 employees would be jobless and there would be no $11,000,000 appropriation. By dissolving it would be killing its hen that lays the golden egg. Having nursed the Indians for so long, they might be lonesome living without Indians. There is no other race to draw upon to keep the wolf from the door. The last thing it thinks of is to let go of the Indians. It will fight to the last ditch, because they are its bread and butter; they are its money and have sacrificed their services to the cause.

Therefore it is useless to look within the Indian Department for relief. It must come from the outside—from Congress and the people.

Some may ask, Can we not adjust or reform the Indian Bureau so that it will accomplish something for the Indians? The Indian Bureau system is wrong. The only way to adjust wrong is to abolish it, and the only reform is to let my people go. After freeing the Indian from the shackles of Government supervision, what is the Indian going to do? Leave that with the Indian, and it is none of your business. Leave an Indian and a Yankee on a desert to live or die. I will vouch on an Indian every time—that he will make a living. This idea that the Indian will starve to death when the Indian Bureau is abolished is all talk, and there is nothing to it. He has to settle everything for himself. He has to do the same as you and I—and that is freedom.

The Indian Bureau has not left the Indians but is awfully busy with a third party. The third party wants this and wants that, backed by Congressmen and by Senators and by a long list of petitioners. The Indian Bureau jibes in with the third party, and they both agree that the Indian has too much land. "He has no use for so much. Let us open up a part of it to the public, sell the land, and deposit the money to his credit in the Treasury, and have the interest money paid to him quarterly." If the Indian wants 50 cents and the tribe has $200 in the Treasury, the department takes the 50 cents from the $200, and the Indian believes it comes from Washington by taxing the public. That honest, if you can call it honest, method is called the reimbursement mind.

Reimbursement charity is the most damnable charity conceivable, and it takes away as much burden from the Indians as that good and kind-hearted old lady did when she held her heavy market basket out of the wagon on scaling the steep hill so that the poor horses would not have such a heavy load to pull up the hill. The Indians have to pull the heavy load up the hill of the Indian Bureau system, while the Indian Bureau rides and thinks it is helping us by holding its heavy basket out of the wagon.

What did the Indians get for their land that is flooded? How much did the Indians get for the land that irrigation ditches pass through? How much did the Indians get from the forest reserve and the natural park reserve? These are the questions yet to be settled, if the Government has not protected us as its wards.

Is the Indian's reimbursement fund Government appropriation, or is it the Indian paying himself?

Has the Indian no right to express himself or to be consulted and give his approval and disapproval of the construction of a dam on his domain?

Has he no right to say what part of his reservation may be sold?

Coming down to the fine point, has the Indian any right to open his mouth, to think for himself, or to do for himself, or even to live and breathe for himself?

Not at all; not at all! The Indian Bureau—the Indian Bureau does it all. If there is such a place as hell, O, it's like hell! O, it's like hell to me.

Fairly speaking, the *Century of Dishonor*, by Helen Hunt Jackson, bears a tale that is mild in comparison to the present Indian administration.

The iron hand of the Indian Bureau has us in charge. The slimy clutches of horrid greed and selfish interests are gripping the Indian's property. Little by little the Indian's land and everything else is fading into a dim and unknown realm.

The Indian's prognosis is bad—unfavorable, no hope. The foreboding prodromic signs are visible here and there now; and when all the Indian's money in the United States Treasury is disposed of; when the Indian's property is all taken from him; when the Indians have nothing in this wide, wide world; when the Indians will have no rights, no place to lay their heads; and when the Indians will be permitted to exist only on the outskirts of the towns; when they must go to the garbage boxes in alleys to keep them from starving; when the Indians will be driven into the streets, and finally the streets will be no place for them, then, what will the Indian Bureau do for them? Nothing, but drop them. The Indian Department will go out of business.

In other words, when the Indians will need the most help in this world, that philanthropic department of the Government that we call the Indian Bureau will cease to exist; bankrupt with liabilities —billions and billions—no assets. O Lord, my God, what a fate has the Indian Bureau for my people.

If we depend upon the employees of the Indian Bureau for our life, liberty, and pursuit of happiness, we wait a long while. They are too busy looking after the machinery of Indian Affairs; they have no time to look ahead; they have no time to feel the pulse of the Indian; they have no time to think of outside matters; they have no time to adjust matters. "Well, what time have they?" you may ask. All of their time is devoted to the pleasure and will of their master at Washington that we call the Indian Bureau.

Blindly they think they are helping and uplifting, when in reality they are a hindrance, a drawback, and a blockade on the road that would lead the Indian to freedom, that he may find his true place in the realms of mortal beings.

The reservation Indians are prisoners; they cannot do anything for themselves. We are on the outside, and it is the outsiders that must work to free the Indians from bureauism. There is no fear of the general public; they are our friends. When they find out that we are not free they will free us. We have a running chance with the public, but no chance with the Indian Bureau.

The abolishment of the Indian Bureau will not only benefit the Indians, but the country will derive more money annually from the Indians than the Government has appropriated to them. Why? Because by doing away with the Indian Bureau you stop making paupers and useless beings and start the making of producers and workers.

WHAT THE INDIAN MEANS TO AMERICA (1933)

Luther Standing Bear (Sioux)

The feathered and blanketed figure of the American Indian has come to symbolize the American continent. He is the man who through centuries has been moulded and sculpted by the same hand that shaped its mountains, forests, and plains, and marked the course of its rivers.

The American Indian is of the soil, whether it be the region of forests, plains, pueblos, or mesas. He fits into the landscape, for the hand that fashioned the continent also fashioned the man for his surroundings. He once grew as naturally as the wild sunflowers; he belongs just as the buffalo belonged.

With a physique that fitted, the man developed fitting skills—crafts which today are called American. And the body had a soul, also formed and moulded by the same master hand of harmony. Out of the Indian approach to existence there came a great freedom—an intense and absorbing love for nature; a respect for life; enriching faith in a Supreme Power; and principles of truth, honesty, generosity, equity, and brotherhood as a guide to mundane relations.

Becoming possessed of a fitting philosophy and art, it was by them that native man perpetuated his identity; stamped it into the history and soul of this country—made land and man one.

By living—struggling, losing, meditating, imbibing, aspiring, achieving—he wrote himself into ineraceable evidence—an evidence that can be and often has been ignored, but never totally

From Chief Standing Bear, *Land of the Spotted Eagle* (Boston, 1933), Chapter 9.

destroyed. Living—and all the intangible forces that constitute that phenomenon—are brought into being by Spirit, that which no man can alter. Only the hand of the Supreme Power can transform man; only Wakan Tanka can transform the Indian. But of such deep and infinite graces finite man has little comprehension. He has, therefore, no weapons with which to slay the unassailable. He can only foolishly trample.

The white man does not understand the Indian for the reason that he does not understand America. He is too far removed from its formative processes. The roots of the tree of his life have not yet grasped the rock and soil. The white man is still troubled with primitive fears; he still has in his consciousness the perils of this frontier continent, some of its fastnesses not yet having yielded to his questing footsteps and inquiring eyes. He shudders still with the memory of the loss of his forefathers upon its scorching deserts and forbidding mountain-tops. The man from Europe is still a foreigner and an alien. And he still hates the man who questioned his path across the continent.

But in the Indian the spirit of the land is still vested; it will be until other men are able to divine and meet its rhythm. Men must be born and reborn to belong. Their bodies must be formed of the dust of their forefathers' bones.

The attempted transformation of the Indian by the white man and the chaos that has resulted are but the fruits of the white man's disobedience of a fundamental and spiritual law. The pressure that has been brought to bear upon the native people, since the cessation of armed conflict, in the attempt to force conformity of custom and habit has caused a reaction more destructive than war, and the injury has not only affected the Indian, but has extended to the white population as well. Tyranny, stupidity, and lack of vision have brought about the situation now alluded to as the "Indian Problem."

There is, I insist, no Indian problem as created by the Indian himself. Every problem that exists today in regard to the native population is due to the white man's cast of mind, which is unable, at least reluctant, to seek understanding and achieve adjustment in a new and a significant environment into which it has so recently come.

The white man excused his presence here by saying that he had been guided by the will of his God; and in so saying absolved himself of all responsibility for his appearance in a land occupied by other men.

Then, too, his law was a written law; his divine decalogue reposed in a book. And what better proof that his advent into this country and his subsequent acts were the result of divine will! He brought the Word! There ensued a blind worship of written history, of books, of the written word, that has denuded the spoken word of its power and sacredness. The written word became established as a criterion of the superior man—a symbol of emotional fineness.

The man who could write his name on a piece of paper, whether or not he possessed the spiritual fineness to honor those words in speech, was by some miraculous formula a more highly developed and sensitized person than the one who had never had a pen in hand, but whose spoken word was inviolable and whose sense of honor and truth was paramount. With false reasoning was the quality of human character measured by man's ability to make with an implement a mark upon paper. But granting this mode of reasoning be correct and just, then where are to be placed the thousands of illiterate whites who are unable to read and write? Are they, too, "savages"? Is not humanness a matter of heart and mind, and is it not evident in the form of relationship with men? Is not kindness more powerful than arrogance; and truth more powerful than the sword?

True, the white man brought great change. But the varied fruits of his civilization, though highly colored and inviting, are sickening and deadening. And if it be the part of civilization to maim, rob, and thwart, then what is progress?

I am going to venture that the man who sat on the ground in his tipi meditating on life and its meaning, accepting the kinship of all creatures, and acknowledging unity with the universe of things was infusing into his being the true essence of civilization. And when native man left off this form of development, his humanization was retarded in growth.

Another most powerful agent that gave native man promise of developing into a true human was the responsibility accepted by parenthood. Mating among Lakotas was motivated, of course, by the same laws of attraction that motivate all beings; however, considerable thought was given by parents of both boy and girl to the choosing of mates. And a still greater advantage accrued to the race by the law of self-mastery which the young couple voluntarily placed upon themselves as soon as they discovered they were to become parents. Immediately, and for some time after, the sole thought of the parents was in preparing the child for life. And true civilization lies in the dominance of self and not in the dominance of other men.

How far this idea would have gone in carrying my people upward and toward a better plane of existence, or how much of an influence it was in the development of their spiritual being, it is not possible to say. But it had its promises. And it cannot be gainsaid that the man who is rising to a higher estate is the man who is putting into his being the essence of humanism. It is self-effort that develops, and by this token the greatest factor today in dehumanizing races is the manner in which the machine is used—the product of one man's brain doing the work for another. The hand is the tool that has built man's mind; it, too, can refine it.

INDIAN SELF-DETERMINATION (1934)

Ralph Fredenberg (Menominee)

Mr. FREDENBERG:
The Menominee Reservation is located in north-central Wisconsin. It comprises 233,000 acres and has a timber stand of about 800,-000,000 feet. The Menominees are located on land where the white man first found them, a portion of the original habitat. We have never been allotted. Our property is all in communal ownership. There are about 2,000 Menominees.

Senator THOMAS of Oklahoma: Do you live on the reservation?

Mr. FREDENBERG: Yes, sir; in 1908 the senior Senator La Follette introduced a bill in Congress that set up on our reservation a modern sawmill. The Indians, from 1870 to 1908, had been logging and selling the timber to outside operators, floating it down the river and in other manners getting it to the outside mills; but in 1908 the Senator came to Wisconsin and visited with the Menominees for a period of about a week, and he suggested the possibilities of creating a commercial industry there and making it possible for these people to become competent mill operators as well as competent loggers, which they were at that time.

The La Follette Act was the result of this conference, and it was probably the first scientific forestry act that ever came through this Congress. It provided for the selective cutting of timber, meaning that only the grown, ripe, fully matured timber would be taken.

In the report made by Senator La Follette at that time he especially stressed this point—that he hoped that under that law we

From Hearings before the Committee on Indian Affairs, United States Senate. 73d Congress, 2d Session. On S. 2755 and S. 3645, Part 2, pp. 110-13.

could preserve that which the white people surrounding us had completely destroyed. The Indians, in the conference with the Senator, asked that some method be applied under this law so that they would be permitted to log as long as there was any reservation there; that is, over a long period of years, by this selective-cutting method.

The plant in connection with that law was also to be an educational institution and one from which the Menominees would benefit financially. From 1909 until within the last year the Indians have had nothing to say about the operation of this plant.

Senator THOMAS of Oklahoma: Who operated it?

Mr. FREDENBERG: The Government operated it, but under various managers and various appointees.

Senator THOMAS of Oklahoma: Under the Indian Bureau?

Mr. FREDENBERG: Under the Indian Bureau. There is nothing in the Civil Service regulations that provides for an examination for a manager. In other words, a man that had a good political pull might go in there and get the job. It was a desirable position. It paid a good salary and the requirements were not very high as to qualifications. Anyway, the Menominees were exploited over this period of years and were not given a chance to do anything on their own. A year ago, however, an Indian foreman has been on the reservation. Within the last year, under this administration, we have had Indian foremen placed in each department.

It was not necessary to send these fellows to school or give them any more practical experience than they already had; but the policy of this administration was to go out and pick fellows that had the ability within the tribe and they were put in the responsible position of foreman. We hope that within a very reasonably short time we will have a hundred percent of our industry operated by Indians. We employ about 300 men in our logging and in our milling operations.

Senator THOMAS of Oklahoma: There is no legislation required to enable you to have a hundred percent Indian supervision and help in this particular industry, is there?

Mr. FREDENBERG: Yes; there is. The provision of the 1908 act says that Menominees shall be employed insofar as practicable. Under the operation of that phase in the past our experience has been that Indians were not employed because the manager did not think it was practicable.

Senator THOMAS of Oklahoma: If the Indian Office should say it was practicable, that would end the difficulty, would it not?

Mr. FREDENBERG: That did not seem to make any difference. We have had the Indian Office post up notices around the reservation to that effect.

Senator THOMAS of Oklahoma: But suppose the Indian Office should select an Indian manager or someone who had the viewpoint of the Indians; then the Indian manager could employ Indians for the positions?

Mr. FREDENBERG: There is no law required for that. However, there is a loophole in the present law where it would be possible—

Senator THOMAS of Oklahoma: That is only under the construction of the Indian Office that a white man is more satisfactory to them than an Indian, which I do not agree with. I have your viewpoint of the matter entirely.

If the Indians are competent, which they are in your case, they ought to manage their affairs as fully as they are capable of doing, and if they are sufficiently capable they should manage them entirely.

Mr. FREDENBERG: I am only giving you this information because I think I will be able to enlighten you as to the reason why we are especially interested in one phase of the Wheeler-Howard bill.

Under the act of 1908, for a period of 16 or 18 years, the Government went in there with white employees and they destroyed about 26,000 acres, denuded it of timber completely, and then burned the brush and refuse that was left. We protested here over a period of several years, asking that they follow the provisions of the law, but we got no satisfaction nor recognition.

Senator THOMAS of Oklahoma: You have an Indian agency there, have you not?

Mr. FREDENBERG: Yes.

Senator THOMAS of Oklahoma: Did your tribesmen protest to the agent against the destruction on this tract of ground?

Mr. FREDENBERG: We did.

Senator THOMAS of Oklahoma: But no attention was paid to it?

Mr. FREDENBERG: Nothing. In 1927 they finally recognized the provision of the law, and they have started now what they consider to be selective cutting, and in this selective cutting we employ Menominees entirely. The Indians cut out the lumber and timber themselves.

If we were to get the benefit of the Wheeler-Howard bill that provides that the Indians might set up their own form of organization, might form their own self-government, that would secure for us in the future the thing that we now enjoy. When we first set up and operated our own mill we had Indians in every responsible position.

Senator THOMAS of Oklahoma: Supposing that the Indian Office should pick out a competent Indian to be supervisor of that agency and filled every position in the agency with Indians. Then the superintendent would appoint a foreman of the sawmill and the foreman would appoint Indians to run it; do you not believe that under the law the Indian Bureau could give you full control over your properties so that you can run them as you see fit?

Mr. FREDENBERG: I think they could; but are we secure in the belief that they would? Are we secure in the belief that we would have a similarly sympathetic administration in the future? That is the thing we fear.

Senator THOMAS of Oklahoma: Then it reverts back to the viewpoint of the Indian Office?

Mr. FREDENBERG: Entirely.

Senator THOMAS of Oklahoma: Do you think that would be changed if you had some legislation on the matter?

Mr. FREDENBERG: I think under the provisions of this bill, which allows us to set up our own system of self-government and our own system of incorporation, or whatever we might make, which would be a cooperative organization prescribed by legislation, we would be secure and we would be able to hold and protect this property.

Senator THOMAS of Oklahoma: Supposing that the next administration comes along and does not have the viewpoint of the present administration, which is entirely sympathetic with the Indian—and I agree to that and approve of it—but assuming that they did not; then they would come in and presume to tell you what to do and perhaps do it for you, if you did not have as sympathetic an administration as you have now. Is not that possible?

Mr. FREDENBERG: That is possible.

Senator THOMAS of Oklahoma: Then we cannot control the matter by legislation unless we entirely divest your tribe of Indians from the control by the Bureau in Washington. So long as they have this control, you are likely to be at any time interfered with as you have been in the past, as I see it.

Senator FRAZIER: That is why you are for this bill. It will give the Indians something to say about their own situation instead of leaving it up to the attitude of the Bureau?

Mr. FREDENBERG: That is the thing we want. That is what we would like to accomplish.

Senator THOMPSON: What portion of the bill gives you that authority?

Mr. FREDENBERG: The self-government title, I understand, will give us the authority to organize and to submit a charter.

I recollect very distinctly that when the last administration came in there were a number of letters written to the chairman of the committee here setting forth the need of allowing Indians to organize, and we felt that something would be done under that administration, some proposal would be offered that would answer this thing that everybody recognizes is a need of the Indians—the right to govern their own lives and work out their own destiny. But while we got some very encouraging letters, and the attitude of everybody seemed to be to give the Indian that thing, nothing has been done. This is the first move I know of of any significance and that at least is working toward some method by which the Indian could get the thing he desired.

Senator THOMPSON: Can you give me an idea of how you operate, as to your schools, and so forth, and how you live; whether you live in tribal relations or whether you live in separate families?

Mr. FREDENBERG: We live very much as any other community does.

We have our own schools. We operate everything on our reservation out of our own funds, and we have about $1,600,000 in the treasury. We have never cost this Government any money. We maintain our entire life out of our own tribal funds. We have our own milling industry, and we hope to be able to do that continuously. Some of our people are in the lumbering industry and some of them log; others work in the mill, and a large portion of them follow agriculture. They have farms, dairy herds, and modern machinery; not all of them, but a great number of them.

THE INDIAN IN WARTIME (1944)

Ella Deloria (Sioux)

In spite of laudable efforts put forth to help the Indians along and rehabilitate them, only a small minority have been reached so far. There are countless families in the remote pockets of reservations still in great poverty. Anyone who drives through their country can see it. The clergy who minister to their spiritual wants see it constantly. Visitors, students of sociology, evaluators and surveyors of the reservation situation come away depressed by the shabbiness and drabness of existence surrounding many families and the general apathy and passivity that pervade the whole picture.

I do not minimize, by failing to dwell on it, all that our churches and our government have done in offering higher education for the young people. Many of them have made a success that is outstanding and are now out working and receiving incomes commensurate with those earned by young people of other races for similar work. But I am talking only of the reservation—of the homes from which these individuals have gone forth and of the state of mind and the outward appearance of the majority of their people. Life on the reservation has always been seemingly inactive. The people have rarely had very much, sometimes nothing, and many homes are dismal and the life in them is listless by contrast with the homes of the white settlers. It is no wonder that these homes have provoked harsh comments from superficial observers. "Look at their homes! Those people certainly have no initiative," critics said of them, and stopped there, not curious enough to find out *why*. "They are beggars," some said with more harshness than

From Ella Deloria, *Speaking of Indians* (New York, 1944), Chapter 14.

judgment. "They wait only on the government and accept charity without shame."

But they were wrong who said that. To the older people, especially, it was not charity. Don't you see, it was part of that same old ideal of interdependence expressed in giving. It was right that Uncle Sam should help the Indians. They were poor, made poor through circumstances they could not control. It was Uncle Sam's duty to show himself a man in that way. They could not return the compliment now, maybe never. But if ever a time came when they could, they would not be found wanting. Nor were they, for a time *did* come.

As soon as our country became involved in war, the Indians of all tribes got into action. They did it in 1917 and they did it again and in fuller measure in 1941 and the years following. Who can say they are apathetic and listless now? They have something to bestir themselves about at last—what a pity it had to be a war! And it has called forth all those dormant qualities that had been thought killed long ago—initiative, industry, alertness. And they had generally retained their infinite patience, sympathy, gentleness, religious devotion, tolerance, showing an amazing lack of bitterness—amazing, because they have had plenty to be bitter about. They are not bitter, not because they are childish and don't know enough to be, but because they are wise. They know that bitterness endangers dignity—another inalienable trait—and solves nothing. . . .

Indian boys are in every branch of service. From General Tinker, who lost his life at the very start of the war, down to the last private, they qualify for any post and are serving everywhere, courageously.

Indian girls are Red Cross nurses, WACs, and WAVEs. They, too, are everywhere. When a missionary's wife asked where his sister was now, a little full-blood boy answered quite casually, "In Iceland." Iceland was now part of his world.

These new experiences of Indian youth raise some vital questions about their training, and this may be a good place to stop and consider them.

Before the war some of the educational planning was directed to a very special kind of life. It was predicated on the common statement, "Ninety per cent of the Indians return to the reservation anyway," the assumption always being that there is little need of training them for the outside world since they will not be in it. The course of study and training was thus devised for the limited, expectable needs of reservation life. And now, see where the young people are! How well prepared were they for the world at large? It seemed a good idea at the time, no doubt. But in future a course of study that corresponds in all essentials to the requirements of the various state boards of education might be safer—and fairer to the Indians in the long run.

We might well ask ourselves, "Why do they return to the reservation, anyway?" Well, partly it is that pull toward home and family, a universal human need but peculiarly accentuated in the Indian nature from centuries of close family and clan and *tiyospaye* life. But that is not all. It is also because Indian young people had not been prepared to get into American general society and feel at home in it. If they had known the ordinary, commonplace things that other American youth take for granted, they would not have felt ill at ease and lonely there. If one is not familiar with the allusions and casual references that pepper the conversation of a particular group, one is bound to feel left out. Indian people are by nature reticent and retiring; when they feel a lack of social ease and self-confidence, they want to run away from the crowd, knowing they are ill-prepared to hold their own. It is not enough to be a good mechanic or a well trained stenographer at such times.

I sometimes listen to quiz programs on the radio to see if I can answer the questions. It challenges me to find out the things I miss. I don't like *not* to know the answers. Some Americans know them; why not I? That is the way I think other Indians feel. That is how some parents have been feeling of late. They have been saying they want their children to learn what the other children in their state are required to learn. They can teach them all the Indian lore and language they themselves choose, they say, and do a better job of it. They want the schools to concentrate on things the children cannot learn at home. I think they have something there.

The war has indeed wrought an overnight change in the outlook, horizon, and even the habits of the Indian people—a change that might not have come about for many years yet. For weal or woe, the former reservation life has been altered radically. As it looks now, that idea of a special course of study set up for Indians alone shows up a bit negatively as a kind of race discrimination. What is right and necessary for the majority of American school children and is made available to them ought not to be denied to other American children. It is a challenge, moreover, to be expected to measure up, the same as anyone else, rather than to have allowances continually made on the basis of race. . . .

Whole families have moved into the cities and are meeting problems they have never faced before. As workers they are valuable. Skillful with their hands at tasks requiring meticulous care, they are extremely accurate, patient, dependable. If they are a split second more deliberate than some others, they make correspondingly fewer mistakes that might prove fatal. They will not stop to bargain for themselves; it is not in their tradition to think of self first; and they will not grumble. They will never do anything to hinder the war effort. They are too peculiarly American for that.

One of their problems is that of paying rent. They find it an irksome concomitant to living away from their own homes. They have never paid rent before. Naturally they try to find the least expensive places—with the result that they sometimes find themselves among undesirable neighbors. And of course there are numerous other problems. What to do with their children and adolescent girls in these surroundings is one of the hardest problems. How to get wholesome entertainment is another, and where to go to church, a third.

These Indians are earning "big money" now, and for many of them it is their first experience. They like it and will want to keep on earning and being able to buy, out of their own efforts entirely, what they desire, instead of waiting endlessly for their money from leases handled by the agency.

But do they all know how to take care of their money? What knowledge have they of practical business? Can they budget wisely? Many of them have till now had little chance to handle money, since the agency office has always managed even personal accounts for the majority of them.

And then what of the great problem they share with peoples on every continent—the new ordering of their life when their sons and daughters return from the armed services and the war industries are closed?

What will the workers in war plants do then? Many will doubtless want to stay in the cities, having become urbanized and liking it. Some will doubtless get on there; but others may quite possibly be forced out of work. Reticent and uncompetitive, as some of their tribal societies have made their people, perhaps they will have their jobs snatched by the aggressive and blatant type of workers who are used to competition.

The vast majority will probably want to go home. It is natural to want to be near one's own people. Many Indians cannot yet feel complete with just their little family, their spouse and children. They have been used to thinking in terms of the larger family groups for many generations. Even while they work their hearts turn homeward. "This is transitory," they think. "We will soon be home again." For many, that means the reservation, and it seems very good to them, however drab and bare it may look to outsiders. It will be good to get into their own homes, be they ever so humble. At least they won't have to feel beholden to landlords and will be able once again to reckon without rent. Owning one's own home will take on a new meaning. . . .

The Indians' progress has been slow and discouraging at times; but *there are reasons why.* I never hear a speaker who tells about the depressing aspects of the problem in detail and then stops there, but that I want to ask, "Why?" For the American people need to understand *why,* so that they will not blame the people unduly, as if there were something congenitally wrong with them, but will understand the causes. . . .

Part of the apathy and hopelessness apparent among Indians may sometimes be due to the absence of a clear plan. Without being really impressed with the urgency of their achieving full readiness to participate in American life, they have been carried along throughout the many decades of their history. They have never been aroused and deeply stirred to get ready by any special time, for any special thing, in any special way. Their life has been separated by a wide gulf from that of all other Americans.

To quote John Stuart Mill, "a state which dwarfs its men in order that they may be more docile instruments in its hands *even for beneficial purposes* will find that with small men no great thing can really be accomplished." (The italics are mine.) In a way, I believe that this is what has happened to the Indian people. They have always been so supervised and so taken care of that it has been hard to "try their wings" without self-consciousness. And they have been so remote from general American life that they don't always know what to try.

"Very well," you say, "if that's all, it can be taken care of." But not so fast. That isn't all. Unfortunately these many decades of paternalism and protection and gratuity have left their mark. That is not so strange, nor is such a result peculiar to Indians. Have we not in our own time seen how spoiled and weakened people may become with a little of that sort of thing? So, along with all the other problems is that of re-education, this time for eventual qualification for full citizenship with all its duties and responsibilities as well as all its privileges.

It will take time, but with a definite end in plain view and with consistent hammering at the job of getting ready, tribe by tribe, I believe it can be accomplished. In the old days the Indians had dignity and pride. They still do. An appeal to their pride, their manhood, their tribehood, would bring a response. But they must be approached with dignity and sincerity, and told earnestly by their friends that here is a profoundly critical, essential task for them all to unite on *for the good of their children.* I am optimistic enough to think they would respond, especially if they are told to go ahead *in their own way*—that too is important—and if a chance is given them to do this without a kind of stifling oversight.

"SHALL WE REPEAT INDIAN HISTORY IN ALASKA?": SPEECH TO THE ANNUAL MEETING OF THE INDIAN RIGHTS ASSOCIATION, JANUARY 23, 1947

Ruth Muskrat Bronson (Cherokee)

If I were forced to choose one word to portray the spirit of the Indians of southeast Alaska, as I interpreted it, that word would have to be "despair." The Indians know they are standing with their backs to a wall, fighting a situation which they see clearly has a single, inevitable ending if help does not come to them soon. That ending is poverty —a property-less, marginal existence on the fringes of dependency so long as they survive as a race.

The natives of Alaska are today in much the same predicament the Indians of the United States faced a century and a half ago. They are despised and unwanted by those Alaskans, and there are many of them, who are dominated by the "get rich and get out" psychology that is a relic of the gold-rush days. They are despised and unwanted because they own property which this element in Alaska wants and intends to get at any cost. They are being stripped of their property by every means possible, sometimes even by agencies of our Government which has sworn to protect them. Their old avenues of livelihood are constantly being whittled down as more and more white people come into their country. They are

From *Indian Truth*, January–April, 1947.

being pushed ruthlessly and inexorably lower and lower in the economic scale, not because they are less able but because they are defenseless under discriminatory laws and practices. Even the same things are said of them by white settlers of the territory of Alaska as were said of Indians in the continental United States in the days of Helen Hunt Jackson—that they are a menace to the advance of civilization; that they are obstructing commercial development of the territory; that they should not be allowed to hold onto valuable property which business interests could develop so much better and faster; that they are a vanishing people whose future security need not be taken seriously into account; that they are a helpless and childlike people who will always have to be looked after anyhow, and the looking after will have to be the Federal Government's responsibility. The parallels are all there, a repetition of history so faithful that one question hammers itself out with desperate clarity—"Will the decent people of the United States stand idle while another century of dishonor is written in Alaska?"

The Tlingits and Haidas number roughly 5,000 people. They have always claimed southeast Alaska as their home. They are a fiercely proud and highly competent people. They were skillful and fearless sailors even before they ever met a white man, and were probably the most advanced and wealthiest native people north of Mexico. They are even today good traders and very skillful fishermen. Today the general consensus in Alaska is that these Indians can beat any other fishermen in Alaskan waters given an even break with boats and good fishing gear. Many of them are excellent boat builders and skilled craftsmen.

There is a comparatively large number of educated men in the group and a few educated women. The mayors of at least three of the native towns I visited were college graduates. While every town except Hydaburg and Klawock chose to use an interpreter at meetings I attended I had the feeling that in most instances this was not actually necessary, even for the very old who were present. English is in common usage. There is at least a grade school in each town, and the Women's School Committee of the Alaska Native Sisterhood make it their responsibility to see that the children come to school clean and on time. Some of the native towns of southeast Alaska have Government day schools, always poorly equipped, and sometimes poorly staffed. A few have Territorial schools, no better by comparison. All but two or three of the towns would prefer the Territorial schools, however, because of the greater chance for some community control.

The native Indians of southeast Alaska seemed to me to be, on the average, more at home in the white way of life than many of our Indian groups here in the States, probably because the southeastern Alaskan native culture more nearly approximated white culture concepts even before the two came in contact. The Tlingits and Haidas accumulated personal wealth; their culture was aggressive and competitive; they understood and practiced trading. They have not needed to be "civilized" in order to use and understand the techniques of white civilization. They understand and have used to to their own advantage the white man's organizational methods. Both men and women belong to labor unions, and for thirty-three years the Alaska Native Brotherhood, and the women's auxiliary, the Alaska Native Sisterhood, have been indigenous organizations that have held the people steady through terrific pressures. These two bodies have frequently wielded genuine political power, for when the Indians stand solidly together they can often determine a political issue or unseat a political candidate. This year they elected three Indians to the Territorial legislature. Today the Alaska Native Brotherhood is the strongest force operating in the lives of the people, and the greatest source of hope and courage to meet the heavy odds crowding down upon them.

These are a strong and able people who, given even half a chance, can make their own way and become a solid asset to any country.

But today they do not have that half chance. They are having to fight every inch of the way for the precarious foothold they have been able to keep in Alaska. They are enormously proud of their citizenship status, and they have resisted almost to the point of frenzy anything they think might even endanger that citizenship or might set them apart as a special group. Their enemies know this and have used even this sentiment for their destruction, by convincing some of them that if they try to keep land for themselves they will lose their citizenship rights in the territory. In spite of this almost worshipful attitude toward citizenship, however, the Indians occupy a position of inferiority in the Territory. One thing I found difficult at first to understand, because it was so different from what I have known here at home, was the almost frantic desire of so many of the younger group to repudiate entirely their native heritage. Most of the Indians I know here in the States would rather be Indians than to have gold or rubies. This is not always true in Alaska. As I got deeper into the Alaska situation, however, I came to understand this attempted repudiation was in reality a blind effort to escape from an intolerable position. I believe this is a partial explanation, too, of the terrific liquor problem among the natives of Alaska. These passionately proud people who were once top men in this region cannot endure the constant and grueling slights put upon them. Alcohol to the point of oblivion offers one sure means of respite. One educated Tlingit told me that the "natives in Alaska" occupy a position in many respects no better than that of the Negro in the States. This is true. They often have to endure the same kind of exclusions and discriminations. Just a year ago, after a bitter fight, they were able to get through the Territorial legislature a law making it illegal for business places serving the public to exclude individuals because of color or creed. Many Indians feel this was an empty victory, while others are convinced that the situation has been somewhat bettered.

The schools, both Government and Territorial, are doing little to build in Indians a respect for the culture that produced them, or to point out to white children the many splendid qualities Indians possess, or the magnificent episodes of Indian history. On the contrary, the schools too have their part in the destruction of Indian self-respect, though this is apt to be by indirect methods, such as tolerating, too often, teachers who "look down" on the native children. I saw enough of this in Alaska schools to be shocked. In the library of one of the large Federal high schools, filled to bulging walls with mixed-blood youngsters, or relatives of mixed bloods, I found a book entitled "The Half-Breed—the Abomination of Civilization." There can be no hope of a secure future for a people whose self-respect has been destroyed.

There are signs that the Territory has no intention of accepting the natives of Alaska as an integral part of the commonwealth if this can be avoided. The strongest evidence of this is the recent effort of the Director of Education and the Governor of the Territory to secure a special appropriation for the education of Indians in Territorial schools on the ground that education of Indians is a Federal responsibility, although the Indians of Alaska pay every kind of tax any other Territorial citizen pays. This and other signals lead one to suspect that after Indians of Alaska have been entirely dispossessed (if this can be accomplished) the Territory will follow the pattern of the continental United States and declare these pauperized victims to be the full responsibility of Federal largesse.

The downhill road to poverty has already been laid out for the Alaska native. One by one each of their various means of livelihood has been wiped out. The enormous trading enterprise they had built up under the Russians and even before this period was destroyed with our purchase of Alaska and the establishment of new national boundaries that cut them off from trade with the Canadian Indians. The game laws and white competition have reduced trapping to a barely profitable venture. In fact, even here, the Indians feel big business is crowding them out, in that the owners of mink farms are having far too much influence on the game regulations governing the trapping of mink. The increased numbers of trappers, and renegade trappers who will not observe game laws, are destroying the supply of fur-bearing animals. When the United States bought Alaska, Indian rights were ignored in that valuable timberlands then in Indian possession were summarily seized by the Federal Government and swallowed up by the Tongass National Forest. Now these public lands are being given out, piecemeal and with disregard of Indian rights, to white homesteaders, to mining interests, lumber companies, and the fishing canneries. The original land holdings of the Indians of southeast Alaska have shrunk from tremendous acreage that insured a living on a regal basis to bare stretches of sandy beach surrounding their towns and not through any fault of the Indians themselves, but because our Government usurped their property. Not enough land resources are now in actual possession of these Indians to guarantee a decent standard of living on a civilized basis. The best fishing sites, once belonging exclusively to these people, have been seized by the fishing corporations with the connivance of the Federal Government. And the fish traps established at these sites, Indians claim, are rapidly destroying the source of salmon supply. Salmon is the last great natural resource left to these people to ensure them a decent living. The present terror confronting them is that these too will be destroyed and a future too miserable to contemplate left open to them. They feel grievously wronged, and deprived of that which by law should belong to them. And they are right. They feel too that the Federal Government through the Fish and Wildlife Service constantly, by its fishing regulations, its granting of trapsites, favors the great fishing corporations at the expense of the Indians. And many of their decisions must bear out the Indians' suspicion in this. The most glaring evidence in support of the Indians' contention is the fact that for about 30 years now no native group has been or is now able to get a really productive trapsite, while the fishing corporations have more than four hundred of these scattered all over southeast Alaska, and many of them on Indian land.

In 1944–45 the Department of the Interior initiated a policy of holding hearings to determine what lands rightfully belonged to the Indians of southeast Alaska by right of aboriginal possession. These hearings were held in the towns of Hydaburg, Kake, and Klawock, and then apparently, with the change of Secretaries, the policy was abandoned or is now at a standstill. The plan was that after the ownership of the land was established, if the Indians wanted it, reservations would be set up to prevent further aggression upon Indian property, and to assure Indians control over their actual holdings. The Indians all feel that the three towns did not fare very well in their hearings. They say the lands awarded were the poorest lands under consideration, and the poorest fishing sites. They did not get the 3,000 feet of water rights they feel is so essential to them as fishermen. But their worst grievance is the fact that the decisions of the Secretary have never been enforced. They say they have only a paper ownership which everyone goes merrily on ignoring. The Forestry Service is still awarding logging permits for timber on land the Secretary of the Interior says belongs exclusively to Indians, without allowing the Indians any share in the timber sales. The fishing corporations are still operating fish traps on Indian land, and so far Indians have found no means of enforcing "no trespass" warnings, and the Department of the Interior has taken no effective steps to protect Indian property. The powerful fishing industry has fought Indian rights bitterly through the press, through their attorneys, and through a campaign of misrepresentation to the Indians themselves. They have put on a tremendous propaganda campaign against reservations for Indians in Alaska. They have told the Indians, and are still telling them, that reservations are degrading; and that reservations will cost them their citizenship, and their right to vote in the Territory. They have told the

white settlers of the Territory that Indian rights, if they are established, will wipe out all white homesteads and other property
holdings. All this false propaganda has been solely for the purpose
of creating a hysteria that would defeat any move to accord justice
to the Indians.

Four things need desperately to be done at once to help the
Alaska Indians before all their holdings are lost. . . . The Indian
people must have immediately competent legal assistance to help
them fight for their land rights in the courts. Their cases will have
to be appealed beyond the courts of the Territory of Alaska if they
are to secure justice, for the majority of the judges in the Territorial courts are violently anti-Indian. Prolonged legal fights cost
a great deal of money, and the Indians are no longer well-off financially. If they are to have the quality of legal help they need to win
we are going to have to help them provide the money to pay for it.
The fishing corporations which will be their chief antagonists are,
according to the Congressional Record, paying a Washington attorney $250.00 per day *to assist the Department of the Interior* [to]
protect the interests of the corporations. The Indian people cannot
meet that kind of competition without outside help and they ought
not to have to depend entirely on help from lawyers from the
Indian Office or the Department of the Interior, for these attorneys,
however able and honest they may be, are compelled to give divided allegiance. This fight is desperate enough to demand that the
Indians have legal counsel fighting on their side only. If, as has
happened in the memory of all of us, men in high authority in
Government service should be more sympathetic to the desires and
enticements of big business interests than they are to the cause
of the Indians, attorneys in the Government service responsible to
them can fight only as hard as their superior officers will allow.
The Indian people ought to be protected against such a possibility
by having attorneys who have only their orders to carry out. Nor
can the Alaska Indian people hope for legal aid from the Attorney
General of Alaska territory who should defend them as part of his
electorate. He has declared himself as entirely against them. The
first and immediate task of those Americans who believe in justice
and fair play is to see that the best available legal ability is at the
service of the Indians of Alaska if they are to secure justice. The
National Congress of American Indians has offered the service of
its legal counsel, but this organization's budget is limited and it
cannot carry the burden alone. Other organizations will have to
help. The Robert Marshall Civil Liberties Trust gave the National
Congress of American Indians funds to make the initial investigation of the Alaska situation. Other funds from many sources will
have to be forthcoming if justice and fair play is to prevail.

A second thing we need to be doing is to keep constant and
diligent watch on the activities of those Government agencies concerned with determining policies in Alaskan Indian Affairs—the
Department of the Interior; the Fish and Wildlife Service; the

National Park Service; the Forestry Service under the Department of Agriculture; the Office of Indian Affairs, to insure that no predatory official within the ranks of any one of these agencies can formulate policies or make important decisions prejudicial to Indian interests. The danger of another Teapot Dome did not pass away with the apprehension of Albert Fall. Nor does all the cupidity in dealing with Indians and Indian property belong to the generation of our forefathers. Alaska is full of possibilities of Federal chicanery yet to be perpetrated on Indians, and it is our responsibility as conscientious citizens to prevent it. That is what organizations such as this exist to do.

Organizations such as the Indian Rights Association, the Association on American Indian Affairs, and other groups interested in full opportunity for all people can and should insist that the aboriginal rights hearings, promised to the Indians of Alaska and already undertaken, be carried out for all of the native towns that want them. The towns of Kasaan, Saxman, and Klukwan have been asking for these hearings for two and a half years, but the Department of the Interior delays action. Many think this is because the powerful fishing industry is objecting to a further clarification of Indian land rights.

Our fourth task right now is to watch legislation on Alaskan matters to insure that Indians do not suffer therefrom. If, as the Congressional Record suggests, legislation is to be presented which has been prepared by the Federal Government with the help of an attorney employed by the fishing corporations, you may be sure it will be prejudicial to Indian interests. We need to defeat any further attempts to take property or other rights away from the Alaska Indians. We need, I think, to go even further than this and take a more positive approach by seeing that legislation friendly to Indians and other residents of Alaska who are the common people, is introduced and passed so that these people can be assured a just and fair opportunity under the flag of the United States.

Here is a fight before us that is immediate and urgent. To help in the winning of it will justify all the years of our existence as an organization to protect the rights of a defenseless minority, and it will help to keep our national honor clean. We cannot ignore our responsibility.

PROBLEMS OF OFF-RESERVATION EMPLOYMENT (1948)

Jim Becenti (Navajo)

It is hard for us to go outside the reservation where we meet strangers. I have been off the reservation ever since I was sixteen. Today I am sorry I quit the Santa Fe R.R. I worked for them in 1912–13. You are enjoying life, liberty, and happiness on the soil the American Indian had, so it is your responsibility to give us a hand, brother. Take us out of distress. I have never been to vocational school. I have very little education. I look at the white man who is a skilled laborer. When I was a young man I worked for a man in Gallup as a carpenter's helper. He treated me as his own brother. I used his tools. Then he took his tools and gave me a list of tools I should buy and I started carpentering just from what I had seen.

We have no alphabetical language. We see things with our eyes and can always remember it. I urge that we help my people to progress in skilled labor as well as common labor. The hope of my people is to change our ways and means in certain directions, so they can help you someday as taxpayers. If not, as you are going now, you will be burdened the rest of your life. The hope of my people is that you will continue to help so that we will be all over the United States and have a hand with you, and give us a brotherly hand so we will be happy as you are. Our reservation is awful small. We did not know the capacity of the range until the white man come and say "you raise too much sheep, got to go somewhere else," resulting in reduction to a skeleton where the Indians

From *The American Indian*, Vol. 4, No. 3 (1948).

can't make a living on it. For 80 years we have been confused by the general public, and what is the condition of the Navajo today? Starvation! We are starving for education. Education is the main thing and the only thing that is going to make us able to compete with you great men here talking to us.

AN APPEAL FOR JUSTICE (1948)

Indians of the St. Regis Reservation, Hogansburg, New York

Many winters ago your forefathers came to our country. They were poor, weak and feeble. They asked for a little land to plant corn on for their women and children, a place to spread their blankets. We took pity on them. We gave them a great tract of land. Our forefathers taught them how to live in America. They showed them many things: how to plant corn, beans, squashes, potatoes, tomatoes and many more vegetables; showed them how to make sugar from the sap of the maple; told them that the clam and oyster were good to eat; showed them how to make the canoe, the moccasin, the sleeping bag, the snowshoe; they taught them how to smoke the pipe of friendship and peace; taught them healing roots and herbs; showed them the workings, the operations of a great democracy, the Iroquois Government, a system unknown in Europe or Asia. During times of hardship when their little ones cried for bread, it was the Indian who brought them meat, corn and fish.

Now the white man has become strong. Our little countries (Reservations you call them) are all that we have left of this beautiful country, the gift of the Great Spirit to us, his Red Children. We have the right to call this our country. It is ours. We have the written pledge of George Washington that we should have it forever as against him or his successors, and he and his ministers promised to protect us in it. We didn't think we would ever live long enough to find that an American promise was not good. An

From *The American Indian*, Vol. 4, No. 3 (1948).

enemy's foot (New York State) is on our country, and the United States knows it, for our chiefs have told him.

There are many reasons why we wish the United States to live up to its treaties. First, as a people, we love the land of our birth, our little reservations, the place of our fathers' graves and could we be permitted to remain unmolested on our lands, the gift of the Great Spirit to his Red Children, we would be content. We are satisfied with our country! We neither ask nor seek a better one!

A few years ago you won a great war. We fought by the side of your generals. We were told that we were fighting for democracy, for the rights of little peoples! Your generals still live to bear testimony of our fidelity. Yes, the blood of our warriors was shed on the battlefields of France, Germany and Japan for what you then told us was our common cause, *Democracy!* Why then, should you wish to break the sacred agreements between your country and the Six Nations? Our sacred treaties have been broken like saplings and your land speculators come forth to cheat and rob us, your former protector, once a great and powerful nation, the Iroquois. What harm can our retaining our reservations and treaties do to you? What are a few thousand acres of land to a nation like the United States? Neither have you any lack of wealth that your people need become rich at our expense. Neither have we given you any grounds of complaint against us.

We want justice from now on. After all that has happened to us, that is not much for us to ask. When your Thirteen Colonies won their freedom from Great Britain you took a brand from our Council Fire (our government) and kindled your own fire. Now the same fire is trying to consume the very people who taught you the worth of such a fire!

Your government has just decided to take away the political liberties of all the Red Men you promised to protect forever, by passing such laws through your Congress in defiance of the treaties made by George Washington. Those laws, of course, would mean the breaking up of the tribes, if enforced. Our people would rather be deprived of their money than their political liberties. So would you!

We believe that if the people of the United States knew our story, that they would not allow their government to pass these bills, in violation of our sacred treaties and without our consent. If you think the Indian is being wronged, *write letters to your Congress and tell them so.* They will listen to you, for you elect them. If they are against us, ask them to tell you when and how they got the right to govern people who have no part in your government and wish to retain their own way of life,—guaranteed by your fathers. They can't tell you that!

The hand that guided and protected your ancestors is now open to you for justice!

"WHITHER THE AMERICAN INDIAN?": A SYMPOSIUM, 1954

Daisy Albert (Hopi), Clarence Wesley (Apache), and N. B. Johnson (Cherokee)

DAISY ALBERT: In the old days our ancestors fought for land which was their own, and for their way of living. But the white man took our morale away from us by trying to "civilize" us. He has trampled on the Indians since he set foot in America and has destroyed everything which is good in the Indian culture, or tried to. He worked his way into the Indians' confidence with bribes, lies, and promises.

Some Indians are now so confused by sweet promises of the white man that many of them have denounced their way of life (religion and tradition) to become "white men." Many have called their own Indian people "pagans" and "heathens." This because they must bow to the majority, the white man.

Some white men have even taken our religion, the snake dance, and made a mockery of it. To the Hopi Indians it is a very sacred religious dance. For the Hopi people the snake dance brings rivers full of rain. For the whites, who imitate it, it brings buckets full of money.

I speak from the experience of my people, the Hopi, who have faced many serious problems brought on them by a white man's tool, the so-called Hopi Tribal Council. Through this the Hopi peo-

From *The Rotarian*, August, 1954.

ple found out that the white man's ways and his laws are not the life they want to live. But Hopi people have retained their identity despite all efforts to destroy them with hostile laws and ways.

Some misinformed whites call the real Hopis, those who are sincerely religious and determined to keep the good things given them by the Supreme Being, "hostiles." The real "hostiles" are the whites who are trying to destroy us.

The reason for the survival of the Hopis has been our dedication to and faithfulness to our one God of the universe, and our adherence to our tradition and learnings. As long as we do this same thing, we will survive as a people and be of service to the rest of humanity.

By learning about our Hopi ways, and the good things about our faith and beliefs, we will build up in ourselves the strength to withstand the lies and libels aimed at us. We have learned that. We can learn a lot from our struggle for existence and self-respect, and respect of all other people, and for all other people.

The white man has forced himself upon the Indian nation of America to be their "guardian." He has tried to take everything the Indians had, talking his way with sweet language and promises. These promises have not yet been fulfilled.

New laws are being promoted in Congress, laws which would sever our tribal relations. They would bring in hordes of people alien to our ways. These are laws aimed at obliterating us.

CLARENCE WESLEY: In 1934 the Wheeler-Howard or so-called Indian Reorganization Act reversed policies operative since 1887. The Dawes Act of that year provided for the allotment land system which had led to loss of some 86,000,000 acres of Indian holdings and created many landless and destitute Indians.

Taking advantage of the 1934 legislation, we San Carlos Apaches have organized as a tribal unit but along modernized lines. It is difficult to tell in a few words how it works. But think of it as a corporation with all members of our tribal community as stockholders. Our operating revenue is derived from the sale of cattle, royalties from mining leases, and miscellaneous sources. . . .

Several other tribes, like my own, are now federal corporations. The plan is not perfect, but it seems to be working out quite well. I hope soon to see the government monies given direct to these tribal organizations for them to plan and use. It is by doing things for ourselves that we best learn self-government and self-reliance.

The tribal self-government system is, however, not the only solution to the Indian problem. It doesn't apply at all to Indians who have left their reservation and are assimilated elsewhere. But experience of the San Carlos Apaches indicates it is a workable plan for Indians who remain with their people on tribal lands, who cling to many old ways and beliefs, and who do not want to hurry about following the white man's road in the white man's way.

N. B. JOHNSON: I advocate the assimilation of Indians into the general citizenship wherever and whenever such course is feasible. The time is here for the establishment of a planned program for the progressive liquidation of the United States Indian Service.

The Congress, the Indian Bureau, the states with Indian population, and the Indians working together should evolve a plan which will lead the American Indians down the road to independence and complete absorption into general citizenship. This is being accomplished through intermarriage; by migration of Indians away from reservations into the non-Indian communities; and by association with non-Indians in the armed forces, war plants, and other industries. The educational contracts being made between the Indian Bureau and the various state departments of education, authorized by the Johnson-O'Malley Act, whereby Indian children attend the public schools with non-Indian children, are doing much to achieve this end.

Today many tribes are possessed of material resources in reservation status which require only additional development and utilization by Indians in order to provide an adequate standard of living for the tribe. Assistance should come from the federal government for this development in the form of either loans or grants, or both, so that Indians may have an opportunity to improve their standards of living and at the same time hasten the day when they will be self-supporting citizens and integrated into the life of the community.

However, a number of unwise bills have been introduced in Congress to terminate federal supervision of tribes for some of our more depressed or illiterate Indians. One of the tribes included is the Seminole tribe of Florida. Ninety percent of these Indians are unable to read or write and nearly half of their children receive no schooling. Another tribe for whom abandonment of federal supervision and responsibility is proposed is the Turtle Mountain Chippewas of North Dakota. Their average family income was $500 in 1950 and they are generally submarginal socially and economically.

It would be tragic indeed for these Indian tribes if the federal government should abruptly withdraw its responsibility and obligations to them. The states in which they live would be unprepared to meet the requirements of education, welfare, health, conservation, and road construction. Immediate relinquishment of federal responsibility and supervision in such states as New Mexico and particularly Arizona, with more than 60,000 Indians, would place a burden on those states which could not be assumed because of lack of schools, hospitals, and other facilities now administered and maintained by the federal government for Indians.

Steps are now being taken by the Congress and the Bureau of Indian Affairs for the gradual liquidation of the Indian Service. This cannot be done overnight, but should be realized tribe by tribe, area by area, and state by state, and in carrying out this program the federal government should not disregard or forget its obligations to the Indians under its treaties and agreements with them.

Indians in such states as Oklahoma, Minnesota, California, and Washington, before too long, should be ready for complete relinquishment of federal control and supervision.

Such a program can be accomplished or fulfilled only through the cooperation by the Indians and the government in all phases of program operations from the planning stage to the final execution.

THE IMPORTANCE OF KEEPING THE LAND (1955)

Don Monongye (Hopi)

We who are following this life pattern of the Hopi and protested against many of the policies coming to us from Washington have been criticized by many of our own people who want to get ahead. It seems that we are denying them many things by doing this way, but we are not. You all know that many of our people own cars and many of the things that these white men have in their houses and in their fields. These young boys have worked hard and earned these things for themselves. It is in keeping with our traditional instructions that we must never be indebted by obtaining things free by not working for them. We were told not to be lazy, to work at anything that we are able to do and make our own livelihood as best we can and get all the things we desire and want to use, but we must work for all of them. That is the good instructions that we must never forget. We must work and not beg for things. We all know this, but many people criticize us with the words that just because I want to live the Hopi way I should not have these things. Let us not criticize in this manner any more, but work and earn our own livelihood so we will not lose this life and land. These are the most sacred instructions passed down to us that we must not forget.

Many of our teachings point out the things that will take place at this time. One of the things that we were warned never to take part in is the present Tribal Council. We were warned that once

From *Hopi Hearings*, July 15-30, 1955. Bureau of Indian Affairs, Phoenix Area Office.

that happened it would lead us to breaking up our own life pattern. We were told never to take part or support that organization. Knowing these instructions, we have never taken part in the Tribal Council organization which was formed under the Indian Reorganization Act and have never supported them or approved those leaders, because we know that it will create more trouble among us. And we are realizing those troubles today because of it. Many troubles have come upon us. I have noticed that same thing is happening in other parts of the country in other Indian tribes. . . .

I have mentioned before that when we went to Washington one of the men told me that this Indian Reorganization from which the Tribal Council has been formed is the key to the whole problem and he suggested that we look into this more thoroughly and find out more about it. We have made several attempts in the past to invite the Council members to meet with us so that we can ask them questions—not to argue—not to fight among ourselves—but to find out whether we fully understand the contents of these by-laws of the Indian Reorganization Act, to find out where it will lead us eventually. But we all know that whenever we do get together and begin to ask questions the Council members walk out of the meeting and go home and never give us a chance to ask questions, and because we do not want to come to these troubles in this manner we tried several times to do this. Today we are faced with many problems because of this.

This is not only for this Village, or for the Hopi people, but for all the Indian people who are following that Council organization and have lost many of their lands because of it. It is happening everywhere under this new plan. Now we must not allow this to happen in this land of ours. This is our own, our very own, and I speak this not for the Hopis but for all Indian people who were here first, and for those Hopi people who are working away from home so that whenever they get into trouble or cannot make a go of it outside they will have a home to come back to, and we will welcome them back because they are our people and have a right to this land and we want them to feel that they are a part of us and help us in our Village life and on their farms and help us to uphold this life pattern of the Hopi. Let us not be lazy and work our fields so that we will not go hungry. These are the instructions we know. We will not make a mistake if we follow these teachings. This is what we are striving for; a good peaceful way of life where we will be able to support ourselves with our own determination and with our own hard work and have a good life. I want to say again I am not arguing or creating trouble, but I am speaking frankly and hoping that we will work together for this goal. These are the many things that were told to me by my father. He told me several times that some time there will be a time someone will come and attempt to cut up your land. He did not know when that would take place, but he told me to watch and if we ever come to that time I must support the one who is standing for the Hopi traditional life pattern because with that we are holding this life and land for the Hopi people. He said "I am from the Sand clan whose duty it is to keep this earth and life going. This earth is our mother from which we obtain our livelihood which keeps all life going and which we must never cut up at any time." So as I go along year by year watching and waiting for the time when this will come before us, then later a Mormon man from Salt Lake City, Utah, John S. Boyden, came along and started work on the land problem of the Hopis and I recognized this as the time when they would be cutting up our land so I began to work and help those leaders who are holding this life plan for us. Our religious leaders are the ones who are upholding this life pattern for all of us in this land and are keeping this life going. So I began to work and help in protesting against any plans which appear to cut up our land in any manner. And this is our instructions because this is our land and this earth is our mother that we must never cut it up, so let us not do that. We are not going to ever cut it up or give this life and land to anyone but will continue this life that our forefathers have followed so that we will not make a mistake. This is why we have many protests and have opposed many plans that come to us from Washington.

I know that many of us do not understand many of these teachings or the reason why some of us are opposing these new policies that are coming to us. It is because of these instructions, because of these religious beliefs and warnings that were taught us by our forefathers. When we oppose any of these new policies we simply make ourselves a laughing stock. Many people are laughing at us, but this life is a very serious matter to us and the teachings that were handed down to us are instilled in us that we must never make this mistake of losing this land and life because there is someone above watching us and is hearing us speak these words and if we ever make a mistake He will know and will punish us. That is His mission, and we must never allow ourselves to come to this end. This is the instructions that the Hopi knows will protect our life and our land. We are not to hurt or to hate anyone, but only to humble ourselves and go on with our stand and work toward that life that the Great Spirit gave us.

THE VOICE OF THE AMERICAN INDIAN

[In June, 1961, more than four hundred Indians from sixty-seven tribes met at the University of Chicago to discuss all aspects of Indian affairs. The purpose of the conference was to present the concerns of the tribes with a united voice to the new Kennedy administration in Washington. In spite of the apparent unanimity of the conference document, reprinted here in part, the year 1961 saw a series of schisms in Indian leadership. In the fall, the National Indian Youth Council was organized, further emphasizing an already evident split between the older leaders and the young, urbanized, educated Indians. A significant amount of intertribal rivalry also emerged, which was to hamper Indian progress during the 1960's.]

CREED

WE BELIEVE in the inherent right of all people to retain spiritual and cultural values, and that the free exercise of these values is necessary to the normal development of any people. Indians exercised this inherent right to live their own lives for thousands of years before the white man came and took their lands. It is a more complex world in which Indians live today, but the Indian people who first settled the New World and built the great civilizations which only now are being dug out of the past, long ago demonstrated that they could master complexity.

From *Declaration of Indian Purpose*. American Indian Chicago Conference, June 13-20, 1961.

WE BELIEVE that the history and development of America show that the Indian has been subjected to duress, stifling influence, unwarranted pressures, and self-destroying policies which have produced uncertainty, frustration, and despair. Only when the public understands these conditions and is moved to take action toward the formulation and adoption of sound and consistent policies and programs will these destroying factors be removed and the Indian resume his normal growth and make his maximum contribution to modern society.

WE BELIEVE in the future of a greater America, an America which we were the first to love, where life, liberty, and the pursuit of happiness will be a reality. In such a future, with Indians and all other Americans cooperating, a cultural climate will be created in which the Indian people will grow and develop as members of a free society.

THE AMERICAN INDIAN PLEDGE

1. We are steadfast, as all other true Americans, in our absolute faith in the wisdom and justice of our American system of Government.
2. We join with all other loyal citizens of our beloved country in offering our lives, our property and our sacred honor in the defense of this country and of its institutions.
3. We denounce in emphatic terms the efforts of the promoters of any alien form.

RESOURCE AND ECONOMIC DEVELOPMENT

Due to the wide variation of economic status and geographical location of tribes, the needs of Indians vary. Consequently, it is necessary that careful consideration be given to the needs of each Indian community. Programs that may be good for one tribe of Indians may not necessarily achieve desirable results for another. Proper evaluation of Indian needs requires qualified field personnel who understand Indians, and, equally important, who are understood by Indians. It is the consensus of the delegates to the American Indian Chicago Conference that the following are the needs of the Indian people.

Economic Assistance. There is need for providing economic assistance to Indian tribes and their members by the establishment upon Indian reservations of industries and other activities which will provide employment and otherwise improve the economic status of Indians. Adequate staffing of this industrial development division of the Bureau of Indian Affairs is highly essential.

Legislative assistance including tax inducements, is necessary to accomplish this end. Also, states and other local agencies should

be requested to lend encouragement and offer inducements to industries to locate plants and establishments on or near Indian
reservations.

Indian participation in development programs. We believe that
where programs have failed in the past, the reasons were lack of
Indian understanding, planning, participation, and approval.

A plan of development should be prepared by each Indian group,
whose lands or other assets are held in trust, whether such lands
or assets are fully defined or not; such plans to be designed to
bring about maximum utilization of physical resources by the dependent population and the development of that population to its
full potential; such plans to be prepared by the Indians of the
respective groups, with authority to call upon the agencies of the
federal government for technical assistance, and the ultimate purpose of such planning to be the growth and development of the
resources and the people.

That requests for annual appropriations of funds be based on
the requirements for carrying into effect these individual development plans, including credit needs and capital investment, and the
annual operating budget for the Bureau of Indian Affairs to include sufficient funds to cover the costs of preparing plans and
estimates similar in operation to a Point IV plan.

That any transfer of services now provided by the United States
for the benefit of Indians be jointly planned with the Indians.

Land Purchase Funds. The land purchase funds authorized by
the Indian Reorganization Act should again be appropriated on an
annual basis, to permit tribes to add to their inadequate land
base, to purchase heirship lands and allotments on which restrictions are removed, and otherwise improve their economy.

That a concentrated effort be made to retain, rather than dispose
of, Indian lands in order to allow the Indians sufficient economic
units upon which to improve their economic conditions; and that
administrative regulations and practices be reviewed, modified, and
amended to bring about such results.

Economic Development and Credit. There is need for adequate
revolving loan funds so that the Indian will have full opportunity
to take advantage of the potentials of his property.

Conclusion of Projects. Too often both the government and private
agencies fail to provide sufficient continuity in funds or personnel
to carry a program through to conclusion. Therefore all groups
that wish to help Indians should plan to make their help sufficient
and available over a long enough period of time to permit the
successful conclusion of a project.

Indian Preference in BIA Employment. Preference to Indians in
BIA employment should be reinstated and given encouragement.
As recently as early 1961 Indian graduates of business schools have
been counselled and urged by BIA to go to distant cities to use
their newly acquired training while at the same time BIA clerical

positions were open in their home community agencies and were
filled by non-Indian BIA employees' wives or other relatives. Propaganda pressure on Indian graduates to go to distant cities should
be stopped.

*Force Account Method of Getting Construction Work Done by
BIA.* As one way of bringing additional employment opportunities
to Indian reservations, the BIA should return to the force account
method of doing construction work. The present policy of contracting construction jobs has withdrawn from Indians many valuable opportunities for on-the-job training and needed employment.
Many persons who lost employment because of this change in
policy over the last ten years have often been forced on federal
or tribal relief assistance which has resulted in a greater total
public burden than in the savings on construction jobs. When contracts for construction projects are made on reservations they
should include stipulations that the resident Indians be given
preferential job opportunities and that they be exempt from union
requirements to obtain and hold such jobs.

Where certain Indian-owned private businesses exist they too
should be permitted on a negotiated contract basis such as dirt
moving, construction, surveying, etc., when force account is not
attempted.

Service Contracts. The policy of contracting with private business
to take over such functions as school lunch feeding, laundry and
bakery services, and dairying should be discouraged and BIA
should conduct these services where feasible as adult training programs.

Relocation Programs. The volume of relocatees should not be
an objective and large numbers exceed the ability of the relocation
staff. The number should be determined not only by the job
market, but by the ability of the office to provide continuing services
to relocatees. Relocation personnel should be trained to give each
client their utmost attention, and should not be under the pressure
of large numbers.

Statements to Indians being relocated of what they will need,
what services are available, how long they may have to wait for a
job, that there may be periods of unemployment, etc., should be
more clearly stated to the relocatee. A written statement should
be given to each relocatee of his rights and privileges. Qualification
of the proposed relocatee should indicate possible success of relocation effort.

The temporary housing for new families should be improved. At
the time of arrival, there is the greatest sense of strangeness. And,
the temporary housing should be as cheerful and as good as
possible.

Welfare provisions for relocatees should be greatly increased.
They are still inadequate to the needs of many families due to
periodic unemployment. It is a waste of money to pay the way out

for an Indian family only to have them return because of inadequate finances, or inadequate preparation. The Program should provide for adequate financial assistance to relocatees until such time as they are eligible for assistance from local agencies.

Self-relocated Indians should be provided employment aid by the Relocation Office.

Federal assistance in purchasing homes in the area should be made by a group which is independent of the Bureau. Indians elected from the area should be represented on this body. General publication should be made of financial transactions of relocation services.

BIA should re-case the Relocation Program to include an adult education program. Counting success or failure in terms of those who stay relocated should be discontinued. The BIA should immediately review its program of financial assistance to take into full account the varying eligibility requirements for welfare assistance and other services by the several states and counties. Within reasonable limits relocatees should get their transportation paid to return home when adjustments to urban life prove too difficult; this would also serve to force better screening before relocatees are sent away from home, and sinking into the slum areas to live.

Job Opportunities. It is recommended that a special conference be held of federal and state governments to act upon the recommendations of such conference, enacting protective laws or measures as needed.

LAW AND JURISDICTION

In view of the termination policy and particulary Public Law 280, many Indian people have been vitally concerned and fearful that their law and order systems will be supplanted, without their consent, by state law enforcement agencies which, perhaps, might be hostile toward them. In *US.* vs. *Kagama* (1885) 118 U.S. 375, 383, the court speaking of Indians said:

They are communities dependent on the United States; dependent for their political rights. They owe no allegiance to the States, and receive from them no protection, because of the local ill feeling of the people, states where they are found are often their deadliest enemies. From their very weakness and helplessness, so largely due to the course of dealing of the Federal Government with them and treaties in which it has been promised, there arises the duty of protection, and with it the power.

That statement by the Supreme Court is considered to be as true today as when written. The repeated breaking of solemn treaties by the United States has also been a concern which is disheartening to the tribes and it is felt that there is no apparent concern by the Government about breaking treaties.

Recommendations

1. Return of Indian Lands: We urge the Congress to direct by appropriate legislation the return of that part of the Public Domain formerly owned by an Indian tribe or nation which the Secretary of Interior shall determine to be excess and non-essential to the purpose for which such land was originally taken or which was covered by a reversionary clause in the treaty or cession or other lands declared to be surplus to the government's needs.

2. Indian Claims Commission: We urge that Congress ascertain the reasons for the inordinate delay of the Indian Claims Commission in finishing its important assignment. The Congress should request the views of the attorneys for the tribes on this subject in order to balance the views already expressed to Congress by the attorneys for the United States.

The woeful lack of sufficient personnel to handle the case load in the Justice Department, we believe, is the sole cause for the delay, so damaging to the tribes, in expediting the Commission's work.

The law clearly directs that each tribe be represented by counsel and there would seem to exist no possible reason why the Justice Department should not be required to increase its personnel in the Indian Claims Section of the Lands Division to remove this just criticism. Simple justice suggests that this be speedily done or else irreparable damage to the tribes will result. We believe the Congress will want to correct this situation as promptly as possible.

3. Title to Reservations: The Secretary, if he has the authority, or the Congress should act to determine the legal beneficiaries of reservations created under the Indian Reorganization Act or other authority for "Landless and Homeless Indians," also reservations established by executive order or prior act of Congress, where the naming of the beneficial users has been left indefinite or ambiguous. As Indians improve such lands, or as mineral wealth or other assets of value are discovered, ownership is in jeopardy unless clearly defined.

4. Submarginal Lands: Submarginal lands adjoining or within the exterior boundaries of Indian reservations and purchased for the benefit of the Indians, should be transferred to the tribes under trust.

5. Land Purchase Funds: The land purchase funds authorized by the Indian Reorganization Act should again be appropriated on an annual basis, to permit tribes to add to their inadequate land base, to purchase heirship lands and allotments on which restrictions are removed, and otherwise improve their economy.

6. Voting on the Indian Reorganization Act: Amend the Indian Reorganization Act to permit tribes to vote on its acceptance at any time.

7. Protect Indian Water Rights: Adopt legislation to protect all

Indian water rights of Indian Reservations against appropriators who, because the government may be negligent in providing for Indian development, are able to establish a record of prior use.

8. Heirship Lands: Adopt a manageable and equitable heirship lands bill.

9. Amend P. L. 280 (83rd Congress) to require Indian consent to past and future transactions of jurisdiction over civil and criminal cases to the state in which a reservation is located, and to permit such transfers to take place with Indian consent, on a progressive or item-by-item basis.

10. Reservation Boundaries: In order that Indian tribes may be properly protected in their reservation and may proceed with the orderly development of their resources. It is recommended that authority, if required, and funds be appropriated for the immediate survey and establishment of reservation boundaries.

Taxation

Grave concern has arisen as a result of the recent rulings of the Bureau of Internal Revenue which in substance directly violate the solemn treaty obligations made with the American Indian.

In fact, within the past few years, there has been a steady trend by both the federal and state taxing department to encroach upon the rights of the Indian in the taxing of Indian property.

Recently, the Bureau of Internal Revenue has claimed that it has the right to levy upon and collect income taxes upon income received by Indians which is derived from the sale of livestock grazed upon restricted Indian lands. Already the Internal Revenue Service has levied upon, assessed and collected income taxes upon income received from restricted Indian production.

The taxing department of the federal government has arbitrarily made these rulings which are wholly contrary to the solemn provisions of the treaties made with the American Indian. These rulings have been made and are being enforced notwithstanding the fact that it was never intended that the Indian was to be taxed in any manner upon his restricted Indian lands, or upon the income derived from the same.

In fact the greater amount of Indian lands located in the western part of the nation are dry and arid lands and suitable for grazing purposes only. In other words, the Indian is by nature restricted as to the use of his lands since the same can only be used for grazing purposes.

Therefore, in order to further prevent the establishment of such arbitrary rules of the Bureau of Internal Revenue, and to correct the rules already existing, we deem it necessary that legislation be enacted which will clearly spell out the clear intent and purposes of the existing tragedies and agreements made with Indian tribes. Specifically, a clear statement must be made by law that income received by an enrolled member of an Indian tribe, which is derived from tribal, allotted and restricted Indian lands, whether by original allotment, by inheritance, by exchange or purchase, or as a leasee thereof, while such lands are held in trust by the United States in trust is exempt from Federal and State income taxes.

Treaty Rights

It is a universal desire among all Indians that their treaties and trust-protected lands remain intact and beyond the reach of predatory men.

This is not special pleading, though Indians have been told often enough by members of Congress and the courts that the United States has the plenary power to wipe out treaties at will. Governments, when powerful enough, can act in this arbitrary and immoral manner.

Still we insist that we are not pleading for special treatment at the hands of the American people. When we ask that our treaties be respected, we are mindful of the opinion of Chief Justice John Marshall on the nature of the treaty obligations between the United States and the Indian tribes.

Marshall said that a treaty ". . . is a compact between two nations or committees, having the right of self-government. Is it essential that each party shall possess the same attributes of sovereignty to give force to the treaty? This will not be pretended, for on this ground, very few valid treaties could be formed. The only requisite is, that each of the contracting parties shall possess the right of self government, and the power to perform the stipulation of the treaty."

And he said; "We have made treaties with (the Indians); and are those treaties to be disregarded on our part, because they were entered into with an uncivilized people? Does this lessen the obligation of such treaties? By entering into them have we not admitted the power of this people to bind themselves, and to impose obligations on us?"

The right of self-government, a right which the Indians possessed before the coming of the white man, has never been extinguished; indeed, it has been repeatedly sustained by the courts of the United States. Our leaders made binding agreements—ceding lands as requested by the United States: keeping the peace; harboring no enemies of the nation. And the people stood with the leaders in accepting these obligations.

A treaty, in the minds of our people, is an eternal word. Events often make it seem expedient to depart from the pledged word, but we are conscious that the first departure creates a logic for the second departure, until there is nothing left of the word.

We recognize that our view of these matters differs at times from the prevailing legal view regarding due process.

When our lands are taken for a declared public purpose, scattering our people and threatening our continued existence, it grieves us to be told that a money payment is the equivalent of all the things we surrender. Our forefathers could be generous when all the continent was theirs. They could cast away whole empires for a handful of trinkets for their children. But in our day, each remaining acre is a promise that we will still be here tomorrow. Were we paid a thousand times the market value of our lost holdings, still the payment would not suffice. Money never mothered the Indian people, as the land has mothered them, nor have any people become more closely attached to the land, religiously and traditionally.

We insist again that this is not special pleading. We ask only that the United States be true to its own traditions and set an example to the world in fair dealing.

CONCLUDING STATEMENT

To complete our Declaration, we point out that in the beginning the people of the New World, called Indians by accident of geography, were possessed of a continent and a way of life. In the course of many lifetimes, our people had adjusted to every climate and condition from the Arctic to the torrid zones. In their livelihood and family relationships, their ceremonial observances, they reflected the diversity of the physical world they occupied.

The conditions in which Indians live today reflect a world in which every basic aspect of life has been transformed. Even the physical world is no longer the controlling factor in determining where and under what conditions men may live. In region after region, Indian groups found their means of existence either totally destroyed or materially modified. Newly introduced diseases swept away or reduced regional populations. These changes were followed by major shifts in the internal life of tribe and family.

The time came when the Indian people were no longer the masters of their situation. Their life ways survived subject to the will of a dominant sovereign power. This is said, not in a spirit of complaint; we understand that in the lives of all nations of people, there are times of plenty and times of famine. But we do speak out in a plea for understanding.

When we go before the American people, as we do in this Declaration, and ask for material assistance in developing our resources and developing our opportunities, we pose a moral problem which cannot be left unanswered. For the problem we raise affects the standing which our nation sustains before world opinion.

Our situation cannot be relieved by appropriated funds alone, though it is equally obvious that without capital investment and funded services, solutions will be delayed. Nor will the passage of time lessen the complexities which beset a people moving toward new meaning and purpose.

The answers we seek are not commodities to be purchased, neither are they evolved automatically through the passing of time.

The effort to place social adjustment on a money-time interval scale which has characterized Indian administration, has resulted in unwanted pressure and frustration.

When Indians speak of the continent they yielded, they are not referring only to the loss of some millions of acres in real estate. They have in mind that the land supported a universe of things they knew, valued, and loved.

With that continent gone, except for the few poor parcels they still retain, the basis of life is precariously held, but they mean to hold the scraps and parcels as earnestly as any small nation or ethnic group was ever determined to hold to identity and survival.

What we ask of America is not charity, not paternalism, even when benevolent. We ask only that the nature of our situation be recognized and made the basis of policy and action.

In short, the Indians ask for assistance, technical and financial, for the time needed, however long that may be, to regain in the America of the space age some measure of the adjustment they enjoyed as the original possessors of their native land.

THE INDIAN TESTS THE MAINSTREAM
D'Arcy McNickle (Flathead)

Clearly, the Indians
have changed. In their meetings of thirty years ago, they talked
mostly about "the big claims"—the folk term applied to land claims
against the government, but which conveyed an overburden of dis-
trust and hostility vis-à-vis the white man. When John Collier convened regional meetings throughout the Indian country to elicit
tribal views about the then pending Wheeler-Howard bill (subsequently adopted as the Indian Reorganization Act of 1934), he received mostly complaints directed at local bureau personnel and
local hardship conditions. The complaints were real, but they conveyed no sense of an "Indian" dialectic of involvement in their own
fate.

It is still said that Indians cannot agree on what they want, and
the allegation is used to justify action in Congress or the Executive
branch without waiting for or even seeking Indian consent. This
was especially noticeable in the Eisenhower administration, when
various dismembering laws were adopted because, as the herd-rid-
ing Senator Watkins charged, the Indians would never "make up
their minds" (to accept tribal disintegration) if left to themselves.

The fact is that Indians do know their needs, as they always have.
The problem has always been to get such outsiders as administrators and Congressmen to listen when they fail to hear what they
want to hear. What has been happening in these later years is that
Indians more and more are talking in the language of politics. "Give
us home rule," they are saying, in effect, "and we will vote for you or

From *The Nation*, September 26, 1966.

your party." It may not be a renaissance, but the Indians have mounted an appeal to democratic conscience.

Thus far they have come, and there they hang—the least involved in and the least served by the social upheaval of our times.

The same Senate committee report referred to in the second paragraph found that "Indians remain at the bottom of the economic ladder, have the highest rate of unemployment, live in the poorest housing, and suffer chronic poverty." It quoted the Secretary of Health, Education and Welfare, who found that "in 1965, 16,000 Indian children between the ages of 8 and 16 were not enrolled in school; half of these were forced to forgo education because of lack of facilities . . . [and] the dropout rate among Indians is 50 per cent compared to a national average of 29 per cent."

The committee expressed itself as "shocked."

Two motivating factors need to be mentioned at this point, the first of minor importance but effective in its way. It was discussed by a young Montana tribesman, speaking at the annual convention of the National Congress of American Indians last year. He remarked: "We find it difficult to move some of our older people because they think if they show progress of any kind, the federal government will start termination proceedings against the tribe. . . . The fear of termination is impeding progress of Indians in this area rather than helping develop self-sufficiency."

Related to this state of mind is the hesitancy to accept grants for programs offered by the Office of Economic Opportunity. The Indians want to know whether the funds received from this source will later be charged against them if their tribe should be awarded a money judgment in a claims case against the government.

A more constant and pervasive factor in the Indian situation is the concern with identity. For a very long time, since in fact the first arrival of Europeans in the New World, the Indian people were told that they were an inferior human stock. Nothing that has happened in recent years—notwithstanding civil rights legislation—has indicated a radical re-evaluation by the white man of his racist ideas. Discrimination on grounds of race or creed has been found to be a drag on the economy and the cause of social unrest—and it makes America look bad in the eyes of the world—but the drive to eliminate racism can hardly be ascribed to a fundamental moral revulsion. And indications to the contrary are not lacking in Indian experience.

One of the supremacist objections to Indian landholding is that Indians make inferior use of the land. A kindred argument is used in the drive to abrogate treaty-guaranteed fishing rights in Indian waters in the Northwest—the allegation being that Indians are wasteful in the taking of fish, an allegation that ignores two sets of facts: (1) that Indians fish for subsistence primarily, not for sport; and (2) Indians followed conservation practices long before there were conservation laws.

The land-utilization argument has been especially effective in blocking the efforts of the Alaska natives to establish rightful ownership to areas on which they have subsisted since long before Russian occupation. Many such areas are now found to be mineral rich. If such lands should be vested in the Indians, as the treaty with Russia and subsequent acts of Congress promised, some natives might become wealthy, and some white men be denied. Senator Gruening is willing to let the taxpayer relieve Uncle Sam of embarrassment by paying for these inchoate rights, but he is vigorously opposed to passing title to the lands on which Indians and Eskimos depend for a living.

The Navajo Indians learned some years ago that they could not prevail against white men when they attempted, with the support of Secretary Ickes' Department of the Interior, to regain possession of the lands lying east of the present reservation which had been part of their original home territory. Some 8,000 to 9,000 Navajos were actually living in the area as squatters, renters or holders of individual trust allotments, as against fewer than 100 white families. But the white owners included some very large cattle and sheep men, heavily financed by local bankers, whereas the Navajos were subsistence farmers, who planted their little fields in the hollows of the land where spring moisture accumulated, and at other times followed their small bands of sheep and goats from dawn to dusk. Not an efficient use of the land, but it supported the people and their independence. Legislation designed to transfer the land to the tribe in 1936 was defeated single-handedly by New Mexico's Senator Chavez, who owed no political obligations to the Navajo people. . . .

The recital of these details takes on significance when we turn finally to the reasons for the dismissal of Philleo Nash as Commissioner of Indian Affairs. The imminence of Nash's removal was rumored in the Indian country for several months, but never with any clearly stated reasons as to why this was to come about. When it did not happen at once, Indians became hopeful that the rumor would fade away. . . .

President Johnson, in accepting Nash's resignation, noted:

During your incumbency, the Indian people have renewed their confidence in government. . . . You led an early attack in the war on poverty before that war was formally declared. Your sensitive guidance of programs on Indian reservations furnished a valuable blueprint for the larger effort which followed.

Whatever the accomplishment, it was "not enough," in Udall's phrasing. Soon after the resignation, he called a meeting of top bureau officials in Santa Fe, at which he expressed what probably was his major concern:

Our country has moved into an unprecedented period of peacetime prosperity. The increase in our Gross National Product in the past five years has been larger than the total GNP of most nations in the world. . . . Yet in that period of rising economy the poverty question, of which the Indians are only a part, becomes more and more embarrassing. . . . This is an inconsistency that is intolerable in a country as rich and wealthy as ours. . . . The Indian people should be tied to the great things that have been happening.

Part of the answer Udall brought to the Santa Fe conference was more involvement by other areas of government, federal and state, by the universities and by private business. He asked, "What would IBM or A.T.&T. or Standard Oil of New Jersey do with the resources owned by the Indian people?"

And answered himself: "We may need some new laws and some some new help. I think the Indian trusteeship way that we have operated in the past has been like having hobbles and handcuffs on at the same time. . . . I hope to get Congressional support for new ideas." He drew the thought out further by saying: "We could single out ten or twelve reservations with good resources, some of the best in the country, for development—and not a major corporation in this country that would not take resources these Indians have and increase the value ten or twenty times in the next twenty years."

While these ideas were being aired behind closed doors (in an Episcopal church building), Indians cooled their heels on the outside. An emergency meeting of the National Congress of American Indians had been called for the same time, in the hope that a dialogue might develop between the government men and the Indians whose affairs were being discussed. . . .

The outcome of these events cannot be casually estimated. The notion that what is needed to solve Indian problems is the determined use of power—the big push—is not new. It has been employed at various times—in forcing the division of tribal lands, in kidnaping Indian children for distant boarding schools, in insisting that tribes such as the Klamath and Menominee divide up their assets and release the government of further responsibility. Whenever force has been used, it has been necessary to go back later and try to repair the damage inflicted—and the problem which called out the show of power remained unsolved. . . .

The difficulties which burden the Indian will not yield to mere pressure, and the proposal to involve men talented in market operations, who wouldn't know a powwow from a pogo stick, is less than reassuring.

The odds are strictly against solution by government, whatever pressures or gimmicks or legislative attacks are invoked. The Indian Bureau is usually pictured as a monolithic structure moving mindlessly through time when, in fact, it is not self-contained and is not a continuity. Its commissioner, the nominal head, cannot move independently of the Secretary of the Interior. The latter cannot move independently of the Bureau of the Budget. And all are subject to the policies of Congress, whatever they may be.

TESTIMONY AGAINST PROPOSED CONGRESSIONAL LEGISLATION, 1966

Earl Old Person (Blackfoot)

It cannot be denied that every time the Bureau of Indian Affairs goes to Congress for money, they justify their request for appropriations on the grounds that they are trying "to get themselves out of the Indian business." This means termination to members of Congress and to Indians.

It is important to note that in our Indian language the only translation for termination is to "wipe out" or "kill off." We have no Indian words for termination. And there should be no English word for termination as it is applied to modern day terms regarding the relationship of the U.S. Government and the American Indian. Why scare us to death every year by going to Congress for money and justifying the request on the grounds that the money is necessary to "terminate the trust relationship of the U.S. to the American Indian"?

You have caused us to jump every time we hear this word. We made treaties with the U.S. Government which guaranteed our right to develop our reservations and to develop as a people free from interference. In order to bring about this development, careful planning must be done on the part of not only the agencies of Government, but by the tribes themselves. But how can we plan our future when the Indian Bureau constantly threatens to wipe us out as a race? It is like trying to cook a meal in your tipi when someone is standing outside trying to burn the tipi down.

From Vine Deloria, Jr., ed., *Of Utmost Good Faith* (San Francisco, 1971), pp. 219-21.

So let's agree to forget the termination talk and instead talk of development of Indian people, their land, and their culture.

Land and the animals it fed are the backbone of Indian existence. We worshipped the Great Spirit who created the land; we worshipped the Sun who gave life to the grasses and plants that provided food and clothing for us; and we worshipped the water and the rain by praying to the Great Spirit that he give us water and rain to make the plants and animals plentiful. That was the way of our ancestors. Now we realize that the ways are disappearing, and we must find new ones to take their place. The old ways of the Indian Bureau have disappeared also. And we hope you find new ones to take their place.

In the past 190 years, the U.S. Government has tried every possible way to get rid of the troublesome Indian problem he feels he has on his hands. First the Government tried extinction through destruction—where money was paid for the scalps of every dead Indian. Then the Government tried mass relocation and containment through concentration—the moving of entire tribes or parts of tribes to isolated parts of the country where they were herded like animals and fed like animals for the most part. Then the Government tried assimilation—where reservations were broken up into allotments (an ownership system the Indians did not understand) and Indians were forced to try to live like "white men." Indian dances and Indian hand work was forbidden. A family's ration of food was cut off if anyone in the family was caught singing Indian songs or doing Indian hand craft. Children were physically beaten if they were caught speaking Indian languages. Then termination was tried by issuing forced patents in fee to Indian land owners— land was taken out of the trust relationship with the U.S. Government and an unrestricted patent in fee was issued to the Indian whether he wanted it or not or whether he understood what was going on or not.

None of these policies worked. They only seemed to make the Indians more determined than ever to keep their Indian ways and their Indian identity.

The first breakthrough came with the Indian Reorganization Act of 1934. This permitted a Government policy of organization by allowing tribes to adopt constitutions which provided terms for managing their own affairs. But the Indian Bureau became impatient with the progress of Indians under this system. So in 1953 they again turned to the policy of termination. Several tribes were terminated as a result of this old policy revived and sold to Congress. I do not need to tell you of the poverty and hopelessness these terminated tribes now suffer.

Again I say, "Let's forget termination and try a policy that has never been tried before—development of the Indian reservations for Indians and development of Indians as human beings with a personality and a soul and dreams for a bright future." Why is it so important that Indians be brought into the "mainstream of American life"? What is the "mainstream of American life"? I would not know how to interpret the phrase to my people in our language. The closest I would be able to come to "mainstream" would be to say, in Indian, "a big wide river." Am I then going to tell my people that they will be "thrown into the Big, Wide River of the United States"?

As first Americans, we had a truly American way of life. And we mixed this with the way of life of the white man who came to live among us. The result is the most democratic form of government in the world.

On this point, will the mainstream of American life as we know it now be the same fifty, or even twenty-five years from now? Is it the same now as it was twenty-five years ago?

The white man has borrowed much from the Indian way of life. For example, the Indians probably saved the United States when they taught the white man to grow corn and plant potatoes. We feel that we can contribute still further to a better way of life for all Americans by an example of co-operation which we can hold up to the world as a model.

Let's do what the President asked at your swearing in ceremony, Commissioner Bennet. Let's also say to Indian people, "We are not going to force anything upon you which you do not want. We will give you time to develop your land and your people in your own way. The policy of each Indian tribe will be the policy of the Bureau of Indian Affairs."

Our people are eager to learn. They are proud of being American. They are proud of being Indians. They are proud to welcome non-Indians onto the reservations. We feel that we have dealt with honor with the Government through the many treaties we have made. We respect these treaties and expect the Government to do the same. We do not demonstrate in the streets to get our rights. We feel we have rights guaranteed to us by these treaties and we trust the Government to respect these rights.

We accept your word that Indians will be furnished copies of any legislation affecting their rights before such legislation is proposed to Congress. We hope that after reviewing such legislation, we will have another series of meetings to keep what is good for the Indians and take out what Indian people feel is not in their best interests at this stage in their development.

We have learned to live with what we have while we hope for a better future for our children, more dignity for our old people, and better opportunity for ourselves. All we need is time and coopera-tion. We do not need termination or all the other programs that have not worked in the past. And what will it cost for the Indian Bureau and the Congress to say, "Go home and develop your plans. You do not have to be afraid to take the time you need. We are not going to sell your land out from under you or force your people off the reservation."

If this is done, the time will surely come when Indian people everywhere can say in both word and deed that a special agency to handle their affairs is no longer needed. In closing, I would like permission to submit a statement at a later date proposing specific approaches to our problem.

THE WAR ON POVERTY (1967)
Clyde Warrior (Ponca)

Most members of the National Indian Youth Council can remember when we were children and spent many hours at the feet of our grandfathers listening to stories of the time when the Indians were a great people, when we were free, when we were rich, when we lived the good life. At the same time we hear stories of droughts, famines, and pestilence among Indian people. But it is only recently that we realized that there was surely great material deprivation in those days, and that our old people felt rich because they were free. They were rich in the things of spirit. But if there is one thing that characterizes Indian life today it is poverty of the spirit. We still have human passion and depth of feeling, which is something rare today, but we are poor in spirit because we are not free, free in the most basic sense of the word. We as American Indians are not allowed to make those basic human choices and decisions about our personal life and about the best need of our communities, which is the mark of free, mature people.

We sit on our front porches or in our yards, and the world and our lives in it pass us by without our desires or aspirations having any effect. We are not free. We do not make choices. Our choices are made for us; we are the poor. For those of us who live on reservations these choices and decisions are made by Federal administrators, bureaucrats, and their "yes men," euphemistically called tribal governments. Those of us who live in nonreservation areas have our lives controlled by local white power elites. We have many rulers. They are called social workers, "cops," school teach-

From *Rural Poverty*, Hearings before the National Advisory Committee on Rural Poverty, Memphis, Tennessee (Washington, D.C., 1967), pp. 143–47.

ers, churches, et cetera, and recently OEO employees, because in
the meeting they tell us what is good for us and how they pro-
gramed us, for they come into our homes and instruct us, and their
manners are not what one would always call polite by Indian standards, or perhaps by any standards. We are rarely accorded respect
as fellow human beings. Our children come home from school to us
with shame in their hearts and a sneer on their lips for their home
and parents. We are the "poverty problem," and that is true; and
perhaps it is also true that our lack of reasonable choices, our lack
of freedom, our poverty of spirit is not unconnected with our material poverty.

The National Indian Youth Council realizes there is a great struggle going on in America now between those who want more "local"
control of programs and those who would keep the power and the
purse strings in the hands of the Federal Government. We are un-
concerned with that struggle because we know that no one is arguing that the dispossessed, the poor, be given any control over their
own destiny. The local white power elites who protest the loudest
against Federal control are the very ones who would keep us poor
in spirit and worldly goods in order to enhance their own personal
and economic station in the world. Nor have those of us on reservations fared any better under the paternalistic control of Federal administrators. In fact, we shudder at the specter of what seems to be
the forming alliances in Indian areas between Federal administrators and local elites.

Some of us fear that this is the shape of things to come in the
War on Poverty effort. Certainly it is in those areas where such an
alliance is taking place, that the poverty program seems to be
"working well." That is to say, it is in those areas of the country
where the Federal Government is getting the least "static," and
where Federal money is being used to bolster the local power structure and local institutions. By "everybody being satisfied," I mean
the people who count, and the Indian or poor does not count.

Let us take the Headstart program as an instance. We are told in
the not-so-subtle racist vocabulary of the modern middle class that
our children are "deprived." Exactly what they are deprived of
seems to be unstated. We give our children love, warmth, and respect in our homes and the qualities necessary to be a warm
human being. Perhaps many of them get into trouble in their teens
because we have given them too much warmth, love, passion, and
respect. Perhaps they have a hard time reconciling themselves to
being a number on an IBM card. Nevertheless, many educators and
politicians seem to assume that we, the poor, the Indians, are not
capable of handling our own affairs and even raising our own children and that State institutions must do that job for us and take
them away from us as soon as they can. My grandmother said last
week, "Train your child well now for soon she will belong to her
teacher and the schools."

Many of our fears about the Headstart program which we had

from listening to the vocabulary of educators and their intentions were not justified, however. In our rural areas the program seems to have turned out to be just a federally subsidized kindergarten which no one takes too seriously. It has not turned out to be, as we feared, an attempt to "rethread the twisted head" of the child from a poor home. Headstart, as a program, may not have fulfilled the expectations of "elitist" educators in our educational colleges, and the poor may not be ecstatic over the results, but local powers are overjoyed. This is the one program which has not upset anyone's applecart and which has strengthened local institutions in an acceptable manner, acceptable at least to our local "patrons."

Fifty years ago the Federal Government came into our communities and by force carried most of our children away to distant boarding schools for 10 or 12 years. My father's and many of my generation lived their childhoods in an almost prisonlike atmosphere. Many returned unable even to speak their own language. Some returned to become drunks. Most of them had become white haters or that most pathetic of all modern Indians, Indian haters. Very few ever became more than very confused, ambivalent, and immobilized individuals, never able to reconcile the tensions and contradictions built inside themselves by outside institutions. As you can imagine, we have little faith in such kinds of Federal programs devised for our betterment, nor do we see education as a panacea for all ills.

In recent days, however, some of us have been thinking that perhaps the damage done to our community by forced assimilation and directed acculturative programs was minor compared to the situation in which our children find themselves. There is a whole generation of Indian children who are growing up in the American school system. They still look to their relatives, my generation and my fathers, to see if they are worthy people. Their judgment and definition of what is worthy is now the judgment which most Americans make. They judge worthiness as competence and competence as worthiness. And I am afraid my fathers and I do not fare well in the light of this situation and judgment. Our children are learning that their people are not worthy and thus that they individually are not worthy. But even if by some stroke of good fortune prosperity was handed to us on a platter, that still would not soften the negative judgment our youngsters have of their people and themselves. As you know, people who feel themselves to be unworthy and feel they cannot escape this unworthiness turn to drink and crime and self-destructive acts. Unless there is some way that we as Indian individuals and communities can prove ourselves competent and worthy in the eyes of our youngsters there will be a generation of Indians grown to adulthood whose reactions to their situation will make previous social ills seem like a Sunday school picnic.

For the sake of our children, for the sake of the spiritual and material well-being of our total community, we must be able to demonstrate competence to ourselves. For the sake of our psychic stability as well as our physical well-being, we must be free men and exercise free choices. We must make decisions about our own destinies. We must be able to learn and profit by our own mistakes. Only then can we become competent and prosperous communities. We must be free in the most literal sense of the word, not sold or coerced into accepting programs for our own good, not of our own making or choice. Too much of what passes for grassroots democracy on the American scene is really a slick job of salesmanship. It is not hard for sophisticated administrators to sell tinsel and glitter programs to simple people, programs which are not theirs, which they do not understand, and which cannot but ultimately fail to contribute to already strong feelings of inadequacy.

Community development must be just what the word implies, community development. It cannot be packaged programs wheeled into Indian communities by outsiders which Indians can "buy" or once again brand themselves as unprogressive if they do not "cooperate." Even the best of outside programs suffer from one very large defect: If the program falters, helpful outsiders too often step in to smooth over the rough spots. At that point any program ceases to belong to the people involved and ceases to be a learning experience for them. Programs must be Indian creations, Indian choices, Indian experiences. Even the failures must be Indian experiences because only then will Indians understand why a program failed and not blame themselves for personal inadequacy. A better program built upon the failure of an old program is the path of progress. But to achieve this experience, competence, worthiness, sense of achievement, and the resultant material prosperity, Indians must have the responsibility in the ultimate sense of the word. Indians must be free in the sense that other, more prosperous Americans are free. Freedom and prosperity are different sides of the same coin and there can be no freedom without complete responsibility. And I do not mean the fictional responsibility and democracy of passive consumers of programs—programs which emanate from and whose responsibility for success rests in the hands of outsiders, be they Federal administrators or local white elitist groups.

Many of our young people are captivated by the lure of the American city with its excitement and promise of unlimited opportunity. But even if educated they come from powerless and inexperienced communities and many times carry with them a strong sense of unworthiness. For many of them the promise of opportunity ends in the gutter on the skid rows of Los Angeles and Chicago. They should and must be given a better chance to take advantage of the opportunities they have. They must grow up in a decent community with a strong sense of personal adequacy and competence.

America cannot afford to have whole areas and communities of people in such dire social and economic circumstances. Not only for her economic well-being, but for her moral well-being as well. America has given a great social and moral message to the world and demonstrated, perhaps not forcefully enough, that freedom and responsibility as an ethic is inseparable from and, in fact, the cause of the fabulous American standard of living. America has not, however, been diligent enough in promulgating this philosophy within her own borders. American Indians need to be given this freedom and responsibility which most Americans assume as their birthright. Only then will poverty and powerlessness cease to hang like the sword of Damocles over our heads, stifling us. Only then can we enjoy the fruits of the American system and become participating citizens—Indian Americans rather than American Indians.

A SYMPOSIUM ON INDIAN EDUCATION, JUNE, 1968

Allen Quetone (Kiowa), Alex Saluskin (Yakima), Joshua Wetsit (Assiniboine), and Ben Black Elk (Oglala Sioux)

ALLEN QUETONE: This is the second part of today's subject and the question is, "How is it possible to teach today's children the old Indian way, or the intuitive way? In other words, how to modernize or modify this old way or translate it into language that younger people can understand today and use in solving their problems, man's problems?"

ALEX SALUSKIN: In our tribal custom, which was handed down to my grandfather, Chief Saluskin Wee-al-wick, each of his children were assigned to a tutor, like he had been by his grandparents, so that each child, each of his descendants, should be trained by an expert. These experts were proficient in hunting and everything for survival, as well as teaching the blessing of the Great Creator. I was assigned to my uncle and his name was Twi-nant in Indian name, in English they call him Billy Saluskin. So he and his wife had undertaken to bring me under their wing for a season. (This was after I had one year of schooling.)

My grandfather came and asked my father if I would make a trip with them to the mountains where they hunt for deer, as well as mountain sheep, and gather huckleberries. They caught salmon

From Sylvester M. Morey, ed., *Can the Red Man Help the White Man?*, A Denver Conference with the Indian Elders (New York, 1970), Chapter 3.

from the spawning beds there and dried them for their provisions while they were staying in the mountains. Naturally, they depended for their livelihood on what they could catch and kill, as well as catch small fish from the streams.

When we began, first I was to learn how to control my horse, which was given to me with a complete outfit, as well as a gun. Then we came to the first camp. Early in the morning my uncle started to assume his responsibilities, got me out of bed, and he says, "Nephew, let's hurry down to the creek. It's my duty now to train you, to equip you with the wisdom and knowledge that I had acquired. First of all, we're going to go down to this swift stream and we're going to plunge in that stream and we will disturb the old lady." (We referred to the stream as an old lady.) "We'll disturb her and the old lady will rub you down and soothe up your sore muscles and give you an endurance for the rest of the day." I knew I had to do the things that I was told. We went down and we stripped off and jumped into this swift water, very cold. We stayed in the water until my body was numb. We came up and pranced around, jumped up and down to get our circulation gcing. We put on our clothes and by the time we got back to the camp, the breakfast was ready.

Again we were taught how to care for the horses and how to handle them. As we traveled, the same processes were conducted until we reached our destination.

As soon as we reached our destination, I was told that the sweat house and the hot rocks which were prepared for the sweat house were blessings taught and handed down from the Great Spirit. This hot water caused by cold water on the hot rocks would cleanse you and purify your scent, so the wild animals wouldn't detect you. You would have the scent the same as the fir bough and reeds that grow in the mountains. So naturally I had to believe that this was the case. I followed through this system and we had to do this every morning about three o'clock while we were in the mountains.

At the end of our trip, I was wiry; I could walk probably for days and weeks if I had to. I had gone through my course of training for survival. I learned every herb, root, berries and how to take care of them. This kind uncle of mine and his wife took time to explain these things step by step. They didn't leave one thing untold and it was shown physically to me, then asked me if I could do it.

After we reached the mountain, my uncle killed a bear. The old man, my grandfather, had told the other man, "You boys better go back down there and take care of him (the bear). We'll just have to let somebody stay down there and watch it all night." You know who got the assignment! I got the assignment to watch that bear all night.

Like I said yesterday, the marriage is through Indian custom. They never abandon their family under that religious marriage. But these young people now, like the gentleman says here, since World War II they don't want that any more. Yet we have, I would say, about ten percent, maybe fifteen percent, of our Indians still on the Yakima Reservation, still onto their Indian religion and teaching.

ALLEN QUETONE: How do they get this to their young people, to this ten percent?

ALEX SALUSKIN: Through their families. Each of these old people had a family: daughter or son, they still hang onto their beliefs. These little fellows are taught under that religion by their participating, right from the little fellow on up.

ALLEN QUETONE: Supposing you were chosen as a teacher to translate some of these things you have said, to conceptualize this so you could make the young people understand what you are saying or what you would like for them to know, would you have to form a system, or would you follow the old pattern that you experienced?

ALEX SALUSKIN: I believe you would have to set up a system. May I add just one more point there which I went through when my parents were living.

When we were children, one time about five or six of us took our horse swimming. We used him as a sort of ferry boat. A few of us would get on him and let him take us across the water, and finally we got that horse so tired swimming, he almost drowned. We thought we had done something bad, so we turned him loose, but the horse got sick. He didn't pull out of it for a couple of weeks and we couldn't use him any more. The grandfolks wondered what was wrong with the horse but nobody would say anything. We weren't volunteering any information, but it was the responsibility of the young boys and girls in those days, if they were asked, they would have to tell the truth. One girl was asked, "What were you doing with the horse down there?"

"We were using him to swim across the river and when we all got across, we'd come back again. We got him tired and almost lost him in the river." The mother of that girl went to report. Nothing was said then, but we were festering our little mischiefs. One group did something else and another group did something, and things were piled up.

After construction of the long houses of a new village, there was a ceremony to whip these little fellows that had been mischievous for a certain period of time. Each family came and had a report. How many children were involved in this mischief? And we have to say we were. How about this other mischief that was committed? A lot of them were in that too. No one denied it, because they were asked. They were taught honesty. The result was that a hired whipper delivered the punishment. He lined you up, tied the willow rods together, about seven. He let you kneel down in front of all the families, relatives and old folks. That fellow brings his whip up and right across your back just as hard as he could. By about the third blow, you don't feel anything. That was what they give you—three. Some of those smart ones think, "If I turn over and start to whimper, they'll take pity on me and won't whip me." That was worse on them, as that whip man was going to let that punishment come down. All received the same, even the one that was good enough to report us.

The philosophy of that was that if you're playing and someone commences to suggest some mischief, you know somebody is bound to have to tell, somebody of our group is bound to tell, and we'll get a licking. Let's not do it.

JOSHUA WETSIT: We cannot teach our children. They have white teachers, and the children get so that they don't care to learn anything from home. Although I know most of our Indian people among the Assiniboine and Sioux, where I am there, insist on pushing and urging their children to go and try and compete with the whites. Even though they don't have much schooling themselves, they tried hard so that those children could make their grades every year.

When we're speaking about getting back to our days of Indian life, it's pretty hard to make them understand. We have to put it in their language, that would be understandable by common people. In order to get them to practice that, we have to teach them so it could be something that would be interesting. Lot of times they don't understand it, and they lose interest. It's something you've got to offer, the goal that we're working for.

I picked up a paper not long ago and read an article regarding education: a professor teaching among white people in public schools, teaching religion to American people. I suppose we all know about how they've been struggling about the religion in the public schools. In our constitution it is open for freedom of religion, but we don't permit them to use even one short prayer before they start the day of schooling. On the other hand, when any public officer takes the oath of office, they raise their right hand to the Great Spirit or the God. Congress, they have prayers. They have certain one come in to say prayers.

But our Indian religion is all one religion, the Great Spirit. We're thankful that we're on this Mother Earth. That's the first thing when we wake up in the morning, is to be thankful to the Great Spirit for the Mother Earth: how we live, what it produces, what keeps everything alive.

I know my old father—died about twenty years ago, almost a hundred years old—he never neglected his thanks early in the morning when he'd be out and the sun came up, shining—that's the eye of the Great Spirit. No matter what he's doing, certain times, he looked up, just before it got into the middle of here in the sky— that's the throne of the Great Spirit. When the sun got about there, noon, he stopped, just for a few seconds, gave thanks to the Great Spirit and asked to be blessed. Then again when the sun was going down, he watched that until it got out of sight. Those are the things I always think is wonderful when we're talking about our Indian life.

My father was a medicine man. He did lot of doctoring and he cured lot of sickness. I don't know how he did it. I asked him to show me how to do it. You got to make an offering. You got to make a suffering to show your faith that you're sincere. You got to know what the power is you're going to use, what kind of bird or animal. Even from flowers or something that's pretty, you can never tell what you can use.

Every man is born under a certain thing. He may not know how to do many things, but there's something a man is going to be expert at. If he practices it, he can use it. He has a power to use it.

So to speak, this is quite a subject we're on and I hope something can be worked out to interpret that, so we could use it for the good of our country. The way the young people are going, it's not so good. That's what we have to protect. The jet age makes a lot of things different now from what it used to be. Time for a change. Like that travel I was telling you about—I saw them travel and then today in the jet age, that's entirely different. It is the same in the way of life, too. We have to make these new ways, new methods, all that is coming about. Somebody said, "We get education, things are going to get so that it won't be much problem." But it's different, and the more education we have, our problems are getting worse and bigger all the time.

ALLEN QUETONE: You have commented well on some of the problems that would be faced by Indian people who forget or do not use this intuitive power, intuitive or Indian way. As Dr. Winkler explained earlier, the intuitive way is from the inside, which explains the natural knowledge that Indian people have. There was no formal schooling; instead, a personal training had to relate you to the world about you. I think this is part of the quest that we have here.

Today Indian people who are still holding on to the remnants of their Indian way, at least try to find a manner of expressing this Indian way of life in today's world. They have done it in their own native way.

This is a method or idea that has to be worked out if a new way is found to strengthen and perpetuate our Indian life. It's difficult for young people. For instance, Kiowa people—and I'm sure all Indian people—teach their young people to be patient, especially among their elders. It's a quality that has high importance in Indian life. You're taught this from the very beginning. But then today, the young Indian has to go out into the world and compete. The outside world is a competitive, aggressive world which will leave behind the man that has patience, that stands back and lets the next man have the way. So in the modern world there has to be a balancing, a reconciling of ways.

These are the things that need to be deliberated on by Indian people. Some of these are realities that have caused our Indian way of life to suffer, because it's hard, especially for the younger Indians, to practice some of these things in a different setting.

BEN BLACK ELK: That's the point we have to teach our children. They have to be proud they're Indians. We raise our children that way; but these kids raise their kids, it is modern. In the modern time, it's different. We have to go accordingly, and we have to teach our children to be proud because they're Indians.

We were created by a Great Spirit. We have a primitive way of living and we survive. We didn't know what the dollar was, whiskey was, and coffee was. That's the point we have to go back to for our answer. We have a culture of our own so great, it's greater than any culture in the world. This honesty, that's the way we have to teach our children to go forth.

ALEX SALUSKIN: As one of the Indians who had direct communications with the past, especially from the old people, I'm hopeful my contribution could be of some help in bringing the light to the Christian world. We have heard a great deal about how, when the Europeans came to this continent, they claimed that we were totally savage. We didn't know right from wrong. To my own belief, from what I could learn and from what I have learned from my old people, the Indians were worshipping all the time. There was direct contact with the spirits from the heaven, and they knew what was right and what was wrong.

FISHING RIGHTS FOR THE INDIANS OF WASHINGTON STATE (1968)

Sidney Mills (Yakima-Cherokee)

[What the buffalo were for the Plains Indians, fishing has been for the tribes of the Puget Sound area. Thus the nineteenth-century treaties with these Indians guaranteed their fishing rights in perpetuity. Unfortunately, with the depletion of fish owing to commercial fisheries, dams, pollution, and avid white sportsmen in this century, state conservation laws have been enacted that conflict with the old treaties. The states prefer to enforce their own laws and ignore the treaties; and so far the federal government has been very lax in living up to its treaty obligations with the Indians. There have resulted, in the past few years, numerous arrests of Indians and occasional violent clashes between them and state officials or sportsmen.]

I am a Yakima and Cherokee Indian, and a man. For two years and four months, I've been a soldier in the United States Army. I served in combat in Vietnam—until critically wounded. I recently made a decision and publicly declare it today—a decision of conscience, of commitment and allegiance.

I owe and swear first allegiance to Indian People in the sovereign rights of our many Tribes. Owing to this allegiance and the commitment it now draws me to, I hereby renounce further obligation in service or duty to the United States Army.

My first obligation now lies with the Indian People fighting for the lawful Treaty Rights to fish in usual and accustomed waters of the Nisqually, Columbia and other rivers of the Pacific Northwest, and in serving them in this fight in any way possible.

Anyone fully aware of the facts and issues involved in this fight can understand that my decision is not difficult. What is difficult to understand is why these United States, and the State of Washington in particular, make it necessary for such decisions to be made. Why do the United States and the State of Washington command me to such a decision by their actions in seeking to effectively destroy the Indian people of this State and our way of life by denying rights that are essential to our existence?

This fight is real—as is the threat to Indian existence under the enforced policy objectives of the State of Washington, as permitted by the compromised position and abdication of responsibilities by the U.S. Government.

The defense of Indian People and a chosen way of life in this fight for unrelinquished fishing rights is more compelling and more demanding of my time and commitment than any duty to the U.S. military. I renounce, and no longer consider myself under, the authorities and jurisdiction of the U.S. Army.

I have served the United States in a less compelling struggle in Vietnam and will not be restricted from doing less for my People within the United States.

The U.S. would have accepted sacrifice of my life in Vietnam in a less legitimate cause—in fact, nearly secured such sacrifice and would have honored such death. Yet I have my life and am now prepared to stand in another battle, a cause to which the United States owes its protection—a fight for People who the United States has instead abandoned. My action is taken with the knowledge that the nation that would have accepted and "honored death" by its requirement may now offer only severe consequence and punishment because I now choose to commit myself to Indian People.

I have given enough to the U.S. Army—I choose now to serve my People.

My decision is influenced by the fact that we have already buried Indian fishermen returned dead from Vietnam, while Indian fishermen live here without protection and under steady attack from the power processes of this Nation and the States of Washington and Oregon. I note that less than a month ago, we counted the death of another Indian fisherman, Jimmy Alexander, because of conditions imposed upon our People to secure a livelihood while avoiding arrest. These conditions continued off Cook's Landing on the Columbia River, where Jimmy drowned, largely because the President of the United States ignored a direct appeal to intervene in the arrest case of Army Sergeant Richard Sohappy, a friend and fellow fisherman of Jimmy Alexander.

Sergeant Sohappy is back in Vietnam on this third tour of duty there [as of May, 1969 Sgt. Sohappy had been returned to San Francisco, California; to the hospital to be exact. Ed.] He was arrested three times in June for illegal net fishing, while home on recuperative furlough, recovering from his fourth series of combat wounds, and while attempting to secure income for his large family.

For his stand in Vietnam, this Nation awarded him Silver and Bronze Stars, among other awards. For fighting for his family and People, this Nation permitted a professional barber acting as Justice of the Peace to interpret his Treaty, to ignore his rights, and to impose punishment and record under criminal conviction. His Commander-in-Chief, Lyndon Johnson, routinely referred the appeal for intervention to the Department of Interior, which routinely refused to act on basis of false information and facts—and on basis of a presumption of guilt on the part of Sergeant Sohappy.

He now continues to fight for this Nation in Vietnam. His fellow Yakima tribesman Jimmy Alexander is dead, and the United States stands indifferent while his People and their rights are destroyed.

Equally, I have been influenced by the fact that many Indian women and children have become obligated by conditions and necessity to sustain a major burden in this fight. These women and children have sustained some of the most brutal and mercenary attacks upon their lives and persons that have been suffered by any Indian People since prior Indian wars.

Just three years ago today, on October 13, 1965, 19 women and children were brutalized by more than 45 armed agents of the State of Washington at Frank's Landing on the Nisqually River in a vicious, unwarranted attack.

It is not that this is the anniversary of that occasion that brings us here or which prompts my declaration on this day—but rather the fact such actions have gained in frequency and have come to be an everyday expectation in their lives. As recently as last night we witnessed the beating or injury of women simply because they are among the limited numbers who will not surrender our limited rights.

This consideration, as much as any, gives immediacy to my decision and prompts me to act upon it now. I will not be among those who draw pride from a past in which I had no part nor from a proud heritage I will not uphold.

We must give of ourselves today—and I will not be content to have women and children fighting in my stead. At the least, I will be among them—at the least they will not be alone.

The disturbing question is, "Why must our People fight?"

Why can't an Al Bridges or Lewis Squally fish on the Nisqually without placing their lives and property in jeopardy, when 45,000 non-Indian citizens of this State draw their income from the commercial salmon industry? Why can't a Bob Satiacum or Frankie Mounts continue their ancestral way of life in fishing, when 500,000 sports fishermen pleasure themselves upon this resource? Why must the life patterns of a Richard Sohappy be altered and the subsistence of a family be denied, when two or three times the total annual salmon catch by Indians of this State are alone escaping past Bonneville Dam and as many being caught by non-Indians below it? Why must a Jimmy Alexander lose his life under unnatural conditions, when non-Indians were able to catch 11,000,000 salmon to the Indians' half million in the last year before restrictions were enforceably imposed upon my people?

Is it because the U.S. Constitution, which declares all Treaties made to be the Supreme Law of the Land and contradictory state laws void, is almost 200 years old? But treaties are still being made under force of that document. Or, is it because the Indian Treaties involved here are slightly more than one hundred? Or is it because the non-Indian population in this area has increased in that century from 3,900 to more than 3,000,000?

We do not believe that either antiquity in years or numerical superiority in population act to diminish legitimate rights not granted by this Nation, but rights retained in valid agreement and guaranteed the protection of the United States in their continued existence and exercise.

The Treaties define the extent of these fishing rights, as well as their limitation. The Indian "right of taking fish" exists only in the traditional waters of each respective Tribe and do not extend beyond these geographical boundaries.

State laws act to permit commercial fishing of salmon almost exclusively in areas where the Indian rights to fish do not exist. There are no State laws or regulations which would specifically permit Indian commercial fishing on the Nisqually River where several Tribes or bands of Indians hold co-existing rights. In no way do state laws and regulations account for the existence of Indian fishing rights in the waters where these rights exist.

The greatest impact upon the salmon resource, or 80% of the total catch, is made by non-Indians permitted to fish commercially by all types of gear and equipment in areas where Indian fishing rights do not exist. Roughly 15% of the salmon catch is annually taken by sport fishermen.

Indian fishermen have shown the utmost regard for conservation, but have maintained that the question of conservation must involve all elements which or who have impact upon the salmon resources. All adult salmon caught are returning to spawning grounds to engage in reproduction processes—whether they be among an 11,000,000 salmon caught by non-Indians or among the few hundred thousand caught by Indians.

The State must deal with conservation issues at the point where adult salmon return to its territorial waters. Conservation must draw its validity in force from consideration of the total resource, irrespective of its being salt water or freshwater fisheries, and of being on or off reservations.

The State claims it seeks only to give equal application of law to all persons. Yet their equal application of law would permit non-Indians to catch up to 11 million salmon in all waters—yet can and does prohibit Indians from catching any in areas where the Supreme Law and their rights exist. The State claims that any other situation would give superior status to Indian "citizens", not recognizing under law that a separate and distinct status or legal dimension of the Indian exists.

Citizenship of the Indian has too frequently been used as a convenience of government for deprivation of rights or property held owing to our being Indians.

We did not generally become citizens of this nation nor lawful residents of its states until June 2, 1924—and not when all other people gained nationality and citizenship under the Fourteenth Amendment since it was immediately held in the U.S. Supreme Court that Indians were born unto the allegiance of their Tribes and not unto the allegiance of the United States. The granting of citizenship was not to act negatively upon Indian allegiance nor rights.

It is such first allegiance that I now declare and embrace in making total commitment to the Indian Cause and the immediate fight for undiminished Fishing Rights.

There is no legitimate reason why this nation and the State of Washington can not respect the equitable interests and rights of Indian People and be responsive to our needs.

Interestingly, the oldest human skeletal remains ever found in the Western Hemisphere were recently uncovered on the banks of the Columbia River—the remains of Indian fishermen. What kind of government or society would spend millions of dollars to pick upon our bones, restore our ancestral life patterns, and protect our ancient remains from damage—while at the same time eating upon the flesh of our living People with power processes that hate our existence as Indians, and which would now destroy us and the way of life we now choose—and by all rights are entitled to live?

We will fight for our rights.

THE NATIVE ALASKANS' LAND RIGHTS (1969)

John Borbridge (Tlingit)

The natives of Alaska (Eskimos, Indians, and Aleuts), who are estimated to number approximately 54,000, today use and occupy extensive areas in Alaska for hunting, trapping, fishing, and other purposes. These are the same lands which they used and occupied for many centuries prior to the coming of the first Europeans.

Today, the descendants of these native groups still continue to hold, by "rights of aboriginal occupancy," the great bulk of the same territory.

Today, Alaska, the last great frontier and wilderness region of our nation, is the sole remaining part of the United States which includes extensive areas still used and claimed by the indigenous inhabitants, based on *rights of aboriginal occupancy*. Except for these large areas in Alaska, the Indian or native title to lands of our nation has, over the years, been acquired by the federal government.

As repeatedly held by the Supreme Court of the United States, aboriginal Indian title to lands embraces the *complete beneficial ownership based on the right of perpetual and exclusive use and occupancy*. Such title also carries with it the *right* of the tribe or native group *to be protected fully by the United States in such exclusive occupancy against any interference or conflicting use or taking by all others, including protection against the state governments*. In short, as declared by the Supreme Court, aboriginal Indian ownership is as sacred as the white man's ownership.

From some lips fall the familiar complaints that the native occu-

From *Congressional Record*, 91st Congress, 1st Session.

pancy of lands is impeding the economic development and progress of the state of Alaska.

Our answer is that though we have the right of complete beneficial use of our aboriginally occupied lands and all the resources of such lands, we have been prevented and restrained from exercising our rights to deal with and develop such lands and resources. We say that only after we have been permitted the reasonable opportunity to exercise such rights a judgment may fairly be made as to whether our occupancy is hampering the economic development and progress of Alaska.

We believe that we have sufficient leadership ability to direct the development of our lands and resources.

We believe that we have the capacity—at least equal to the federal and state bureaucracies—to make wise selection of experts and technicians to assist us, including engineers, geologists, foresters, managers, investment advisors, accountants, economists, and lawyers.

Some argue that since the discoveries of valuable oil and gas resources on the native lands have been recent and since the natives in their aboriginal way of life did not exploit their lands for oil and gas, the natives have no basis for complaint if the federal government permits the natives to continue to use the land solely for hunting, trapping, and fishing purposes, or if the federal government appropriates the lands and compensates the natives only for the value of the lands for such aboriginal uses without regard to the oil and gas values.

This is an argument which has been repeatedly rejected by the Supreme Court and the court of claims in cases involving Indian tribal lands.

By a parity of poor reasoning, it may be suggested that if Senator Jackson or Congressman Aspinall owned a 5,000 acre tract of mountain lands in his home state, which he used exclusively for hunting and for enjoying its beauty, and then valuable mineral deposits were discovered on the land, the federal government could, lawfully and in good conscience, appropriate the tract and pay Congressman Aspinall only for its value for hunting purposes and for its beauty.

Many have suggested that since the Alaska Statehood Act gave to the state of Alaska the right of selection of some 103,000,000 acres of land, a serious dilemma has been created in that the exercise of such right by the state would necessarily require the selection of much land presently held by the Alaska natives.

Our answer is that Congress was fully aware of this problem when the statehood act was passed. In accordance with the uniform federal policy to honor and protect lands held by aboriginal occupancy rights, Congress explicitly required the state of Alaska in the statehood act to "forever disclaim" all right or title to any lands held by Indian, Eskimo, and Aleut groups.

We say that any state selection of lands which are held by native aboriginal title is violative of the terms, intent, and spirit of the statehood act and contrary to other acts of Congress as well as federal policy.

Alaska natives have assumed a statesmanlike posture, reflective of a conscientious awareness of the welfare of all citizens by their expressed willingness to negotiate on a political or legislative solution through the United States Congress. We, who are the first Alaskans, desire the development of our home state. We only ask that justice and equity be done and that, in the future, Alaska's native people may become active participants in Alaska's development.

Although Alaska natives have agreed to negotiate politically and are, therefore, not making recourse to the courts, we must emphasize that we are negotiating from a position of right and strength. We stress the fact that while we eschew the litigatory route, we still choose to retain the right to define our substantive legal rights, for therein lies the strength of our bargaining position and the basis of our negotiating effectiveness. Nevertheless, *litigation is a viable alternative, which we have, thus far, chosen to avoid.*

We Alaska natives envision that provisions of an equitable settlement of the land claims will enable us to uplift the qualities of life for our people. Recognizing that frustrations may be derived from a minority status due to ethnic origin and economic powerlessness, we anticipate our ability to exercise the *prerogative of choice* within the context of our needs, our goals, and our desires. We will recognize that many of our people will choose life in the villages, because it is, for them, a fulfillment and a satisfaction, while others, desirous of projecting themselves into a competitive society, will have the means to do so.

PLANNING GRANT PROPOSAL TO DEVELOP AN ALL-INDIAN UNIVERSITY AND CULTURAL COMPLEX ON INDIAN LAND, ALCATRAZ

Indians of All Tribes

[One of the more spectacular instances of Indian activism in the late 1960's was the seizing of Alcatraz island in San Francisco Bay in late November, 1969. San Francisco's Indian Center had burned down during the month, and there seemed little prospect of getting any help from the federal government for a new one, since the Bureau of Indian Affairs expends very little of its resources on urban Indians. A group of Bay Area Indians, mostly university students, took over the island and proclaimed their intention to turn it into a cultural-educational center. The following statement was issued by the group, calling itself "Indians of All Tribes," in February, 1970. Later that year, the federal government ousted the Indians from the island after several months of a precarious existence during which all supplies—even water—had to be brought over from the mainland.]

Indians of All Tribes greet our brothers and sisters of all races and tongues upon our Earth Mother. We here on Indian land, Alcatraz, represent many tribes of Indians.

We are still holding the island of Alcatraz in the true names of

From *Congressional Record*, 91st Congress, 2d Session.

freedom, justice, and equality, because our brothers and sisters of this earth have lent support to our just cause. We reach out our hands and hearts and send spirit messages to all Indians.

Our anger at the many injustices forced upon us since the first white men landed on these sacred shores has been transformed into a hope that we be allowed the long suppressed right of all men to plan and to live their own lives in harmony and cooperation with all fellow creatures and with nature. We have learned that violence breeds only more violence and we therefore have carried on our occupation of Alcatraz in a peaceful manner, hoping that the government will act accordingly.

Be it known, however, that we are quite serious in our demand to be given ownership of this island in the name of Indians of All Tribes. We are here to stay, men, women, and children. We feel that this request is but little to ask from a government which has systematically stolen our lands, destroyed a once beautiful landscape, killed off the creatures of nature, polluted air and water, ripped open the very bowels of our earth in senseless greed, and instituted a program to annihilate the many Indian tribes of this land by theft, suppression, prejudice, termination, and so-called relocation and assimilation.

We are a proud people! We are Indians! We have observed and rejected much of what so-called civilization offers. We are Indians! We will preserve our traditions and ways of life by educating our own children. We are Indians! We will join hands in a unity never before put into practice. Our Earth Mother awaits our voices. We are Indians of All Tribes!!!

We came to Alcatraz because we were sick and tired of being pushed around, exploited, and degraded everywhere we turned in our own country. We selected Alcatraz for many reasons but most importantly, we came to Alcatraz because it is a place of our own. Somewhere that is geographically unfeasible for everybody to come and interfere with what we would like to do with our lives. We can beat our drums all night long if we want to and not be bothered or harassed by non-Indians and police. We can worship, we can sing, and we can make plans for our lives and the future of our Indian people and Alcatraz.

After we landed on Alcatraz, we got a lot of attention and publicity. Support came in from the local areas and the nation, and even worldwide. People wanted to give us benefits, have us speak at schools, be in programs on television and radio, and even have movie premiers on the island. We were flooded with everything and everybody, from opportunists and vultures to sincere and dedicated people. Somehow, we survived all the glory and confusion even though we have never been the victims of attention before and the symbol of the American Indian shined out before the nation and the whole world.

Indians of All Tribes united on the Alcatraz issue and for the first time in the Bay area, Indian organizations representing over 40,000

Indian people, united and formed the Bay Area Native American Council, in order to push the government to deal with Alcatraz as the priority issue.

The Bay Area Native American Council is a support group for Alcatraz. They do not speak for Indians on Alcatraz, although we consult with them, and support them in their work to help Indians in the Bay area.

Our work on Alcatraz is different from BANAC. We are maintaining the island during the occupation, as a way of promoting the general welfare of all Indian people, which means that our occupation is not strictly Alcatraz but rather for all Indian people. We hope to concern and involve ourselves with national Indian problems as well as planning and building our own Indian university and cultural center.

We on Alcatraz formed a nonprofit corporation called Indians of All Tribes, Inc. We represent who we are, and we are Indians of All Tribes.

We don't speak for Indians all over the country. The Indians all over the country speak for themselves.

When Indian people come to see what Alcatraz is all about and to see what they can do for the Alcatraz movement, then they speak for themselves. We have a radio station that broadcasts live from the island where they speak about their reservations and it draws attention to their particular problems. We have a newsletter as well. Anyone is welcome to write what they have to say.

Before we took Alcatraz, people in San Francisco didn't even know that Indians were alive, and if that's a sample of what the local people knew, considering that this is the main relocation point for Indians through the Bureau of Indian Affairs, then there are people across the nation who never even knew that Indians were alive or ever even knew our problems. They never knew anything about our suicide rate that is ten times the national average, or our education level that is to the fifth grade. Alcatraz focused on the Indian people. Now the Indian people have a chance for the first time to say what they have to say and to make decisions about themselves, which has never happened before.

The decision we want to make is in governing ourselves and our own people, without interference from non-Indians. Naturally we don't have all the tools that we need in order to make decisions on the engineering or structural engineering on Alcatraz or the planning of the island, so we would need non-Indian advice as well. We need everyone's advice who has something to contribute.

Our main concern is with Indian people everywhere. One of the reasons we took Alcatraz was because the students were having problems in the universities and colleges they were attending. This was the first time that Indian people had ever had the chance to get into a university or college because relocation was all vocation-oriented and it was not until 1968 and 1969 that Indians started getting into the universities and colleges. So, when this happened, we all realized that we didn't want to go through the university machinery coming out white-orientated like the few Indian people before us, or like the non-Indian people who were running our government, our Indian government, or our Indian Affairs. We didn't want to alienate ourselves from the non-Indian people because we were learning from everyone else as well, but we also wished to retain our own identity, with the whole conglomeration of everybody. We didn't want to melt with the melting pot, which was the object of federal relocation programs. We wanted to remain Indians. That's why native American studies became a prime issue, and when we had a big confrontation with the administration, we could see that we weren't going to fool ourselves about the university; we could see that we could never get everything through it. They would make small concessions, but still didn't give us what we needed. It was just a token of what we actually wanted and we didn't want to be used like that.

This was one of the reasons why we wanted our own Indian university, so that they would stop whitewashing Indians, which was happening, not only on the university level, but in the Indian boarding schools and summer home programs for Indians and just everything that the government had to do with Indians.

We were also concerned about our own lives and our children and what was happening on the reservations as well, because while we were physically away, we still had our families and people in our hearts and on our minds, the problems that they were facing, and the frustration of not being able to help them because we were trying to get the necessary tools so we could return to our reservations some day. In the meantime, there were all types of roadblocks. We needed attention brought to our people, and we needed a place to get together in the city so that we didn't become victims of assimilation. It finally all came to a point and we decided we would just go liberate our own land since all of our other lands had been taken away and the cities were so crowded and we had no where to go together for Indian dances or powwows or anything, or even to have our own religious ceremonies. We'd get arrested if we practised our own religion and had peyote in our home. In 1964 a Sioux landing party had taken Alcatraz which was federal surplus land that, according to the Sioux treaty, should revert back to the Indians after use. The Sioux wanted the government to live up to their treaty and they landed on Alcatraz and staked their claim. They were rejected and turned away, so we followed it through, when all of the proposals came out from Hunt, Treshman, and other millionaires.

What we want to do in the long range view is to get some type of help for our people all across the nation. We must look at the problem back on the reservation, where it all begins, with the Bureau of Indian Affairs. There's going to have to be some changes made within our own government structure. We often thought of ourselves as a sovereign nation within a nation, but through the years, this has fallen apart, because the state has beaten us on jurisdiction rights on different reservations, and the termination of the Indian people is close in sight. We all can see those things that are coming on and we want to avoid having our life taken away from us. What few lands we do have left on the reservations, we want to keep. We have no government for our own people and we live under what is really a colonial system because we do not select the people who govern us, like the commissioner of Indian Affairs, who is appointed by the secretary of the interior, who is appointed by the President, and the superintendent on every reservation, who is appointed by the commissioner. We must somehow make up our own plan of government for ourselves and for our people, rather than have someone else decide or plan what is ahead for us. We must make up those plans and decisions for ourselves.

Alcatraz is a beginning, because we are doing that on Alcatraz now. We are making up our own plans. . . .

We'd like to change laws, which are not made for us. Even the Constitution of the United States, which says that all men are created equal, was made for white men at the time it was written, and didn't include any Third World people. The Constitution has not included us, as history will bear out. It's hard for us to look around and see all the destruction that has happened to our country and feel good about it. Every day that we go over on the boat, we can see all that garbage and junk that's in the water, and it makes us sad. The air that is being polluted around us covers the sun and the sun is our giver of life and without the sun there will be no life on this earth. Part of us is being taken away by this destruction of nature. If you destroy everything around us, then you are destroying us. Maybe other people who are living in this country will have more respect and pride for the home that they are living in if we bring this to their attention.

We want to establish a center on ecology, as part of our cultural complex. The cultural complex also involves the tradition of our religion. The base of anything we do is our religion. We must have a place for our spiritual leaders and our medicine men to come. We also plan to have our own library and archives to help us document the wrongs which have been done in this country and the wisdom that has been lost. Also, we plan to have a place where we can practise our dances and songs and music and drums, where we can teach our children and not let this die, as it's dying on the reservation today.

Our parents were forbidden to speak their own language, or dance their own dances, and they were pushed into government boarding schools that were trying to teach them how to be "civilized," which meant losing their own identity. We have been forced to fit into a pattern which had been thought out a long time ago, not by us, but by the government that was over us. When there's no employment on the reservation, the only jobs that you would get were with the Bureau of Indian Affairs or the government and in this way, they can continue to indoctrinate the Indian people on the reservation by holding money in front of their faces. Because the non-Indians live in another world where they have cars and clothes and food to eat, they can always use that as a lure to get our people to want the same things, and by doing this, then they can brainwash our people the way they want them to be so that they would eventually work against their own Indian people. This is what has been happening when the Bureau of Indian Affairs set up the mock tribal governments on reservations. Since the Civil Rights law has passed, it hasn't affected the Indian that much because they've only taken down the signs that say "No Dogs and Indians Allowed." The feeling is still there.

We feel that the island is the only bargaining power that we have with the federal government. It is the only way we have to get them to notice us or even want to deal with us. We are going to maintain our occupation, until the island which is rightfully ours is formally granted to us. Otherwise, they will forget us, the way they always have, but we will not be forgotten.

CONSOLIDATING INDIAN EFFORTS (1970)
Vine Deloria, Jr. (Standing Rock Sioux)

In 1964, while attending the annual convention of the National Congress of American Indians, I was elected its executive director. I learned more about life in the N.C.A.I. in three years than I had in the previous thirty. Every conceivable problem that could occur in an Indian society was suddenly thrust at me from 315 different directions. I discovered that I was one of the people who were supposed to solve the problems. The only trouble was that Indian people locally and on the national level were being played off one against the other by clever whites who had either ego or income at stake. While there were many feasible solutions, few could be tried without whites with vested interests working night and day to destroy the unity we were seeking on a national basis.

In the mid-1960's the whole generation that had grown up after World War II and had left the reservations during the fifties to get an education was returning to Indian life as "educated Indians." But we soon knew better. Tribal societies had existed for centuries without going outside themselves for education and information. Yet many of us thought that we would be able to improve the traditional tribal methods. We were wrong.

For three years we ran around the conference circuit attending numerous meetings called to "solve" the Indian problems. We lis-

From "This Country Was a Lot Better Off When the Indians Were Running It," *New York Times Magazine*, March 3, 1970.

tened to and spoke with anthropologists, historians, sociologists, psychologists, economists, educators and missionaries. We worked with many Government agencies and with every conceivable doctrine, idea and program ever created. At the end of this happy round of consultations the reservation people were still plodding along on their own time schedule, doing the things they considered important. They continued to solve their problems their way in spite of the advice given them by "Indian experts."

By 1967 there was a radical change in thinking on the part of many of us. Conferences were proving unproductive. Where non-Indians had been pushed out to make room for Indian people, they had wormed their way back into power and again controlled the major programs serving Indians. The poverty programs, reservation and university technical assistance groups were dominated by whites who had pushed Indian administrators aside.

Reservation people, meanwhile, were making steady progress in spite of the numerous setbacks suffered by the national Indian community. So, in large part, younger Indian leaders who had been playing the national conference field began working at the local level to build community movements from the ground up. By consolidating local organizations into power groups they felt that they would be in a better position to influence national thinking.

Robert Hunter, director of the Nevada Intertribal Council, had already begun to build a strong state organization of tribes and communities. In South Dakota, Gerald One Feather, Frank LaPointe and Ray Briggs formed the American Indian Leadership Conference, which quickly welded the educated young Sioux in that state into a strong regional organization active in nearly every phase of Sioux life. Gerald is now running for the prestigious post of chairman of the Oglala Sioux, the largest Sioux tribe, numbering some 15,000 members. Ernie Stevens, an Oneida from Wisconsin, and Lee Cook, a Chippewa from Minnesota, developed a strong program for economic and community development in Arizona. Just recently Ernie has moved into the post of director of the California Intertribal Council, a statewide organization representing some 130,000 California Indians in cities and on the scattered reservations of that state.

By the fall of 1967, it was apparent that the national Indian scene was collapsing in favor of strong regional organizations, although the major national organizations such as the National Congress of American Indians and the National Indian Youth Council continued to grow. There was yet another factor emerging on the Indian scene: the oldtimers of the Depression days had educated a group of younger Indians in the old ways and these people were now becoming a major force in Indian life. Led by Thomas Banyaca of the Hopi, Mad Bear Anderson of the Tuscaroras, Clifton Hill of the Creeks, and Rolling Thunder of the Shoshones, the traditional Indians were forcing the whole Indian community to rethink its understanding of Indian life.

The message of the traditionalists is simple. They demand a return to basic Indian philosophy, establishment of ancient methods of government by open council instead of elected officials, a revival of Indian religions and replacement of white laws with Indian customs; in short, a complete return to the ways of the old people. In an age dominated by tribalizing communications media, their message makes a great deal of sense.

But in some areas their thinking is opposed to that of the National Congress of American Indians, which represents officially elected tribal governments organized under the Indian Reorganization Act as Federal corporations. The contemporary problem is therefore one of defining the meaning of "tribe." Is it a traditionally organized band of Indians following customs with medicine men and chiefs dominating the policies of the tribe, or is it a modern corporate structure attempting to compromise at least in part with modern white culture?

The problem has been complicated by private foundations' and Government agencies' funding of Indian programs. In general this process, although it has brought a great amount of money into Indian country, has been one of cooptation. Government agencies must justify their appropriation requests every year and can only take chances on spectacular programs that will serve as showcases of progress. They are not willing to invest the capital funds necessary to build viable self-supporting communities on the reservations because these programs do not have an immediate publicity potential. Thus, the Government agencies are forever committed to conducting conferences to discover that one "key" to Indian life that will give them the edge over their rival agencies in the annual appropriations derby.

Churches and foundations have merely purchased an Indian leader or program that conforms with their ideas of what Indian people should be doing. The large foundations have bought up the well-dressed, handsome "new image" Indian who is comfortable in the big cities but virtually helpless at an Indian meeting. Churches have given money to Indians who have been willing to copy black militant activist tactics, and the more violent and insulting the Indian can be, the more the churches seem to love it. They are wallowing in self-guilt and piety over the lot of the poor, yet funding demagogues of their own choosing to speak for the poor.

I did not run for re-election as executive director of the N.C.A.I in the fall of 1967, but entered law school at the University of Colorado instead. It was apparent to me that the Indian revolution was well under way and that someone had better get a legal education so that we could have our own legal program for defense of Indian treaty rights. Thanks to a Ford Foundation program, nearly fifty Indians are now in law school, assuring the Indian community of legal talent in the years ahead. Within four years I foresee another radical shift in Indian leadership patterns as the growing local movements are affected by the new Indian lawyers.

There is an increasing scent of victory in the air in Indian country these days. The mood is comparable to the old days of the Depression when the men began to dance once again. As the Indian movement gathers momentum and individual Indians cast their lot with the tribe, it will become apparent that not only will Indians survive the electronic world of Marshall McLuhan, they will thrive in it. At the present time everyone is watching how mainstream America will handle the issues of pollution, poverty, crime and racism when it does not fundamentally understand the issues. Knowing the importance of tribal survival, Indian people are speaking more and more of sovereignty, of the great political technique of the open council, and of the need for gaining the community's consensus on all programs before putting them into effect.

One can watch this same issue emerge in white society as the "Woodstock Nation," the "Blackstone Nation" and the block organizations are developed. This is a full tribalizing process involving a nontribal people, and it is apparent that some people are frightened by it. But it is the kind of social phenomenon upon which Indians feast.

In 1965 I had a long conversation with an old Papago. I was trying to get the tribe to pay its dues to the National Congress of American Indians and I had asked him to speak to the tribal council for me. He said that he would but that the Papagos didn't really need the N.C.A.I. They were like, he told me, the old mountain in the distance. The Spanish had come and dominated them for 300 years and then left. The Mexicans had come and ruled them for a century, but they also left. "The Americans," he said, "have been here only about eighty years. They, too, will vanish, but the Papagos and the mountain will always be here."

This attitude and understanding of life is what American society is searching for.

I wish the Government would give Alcatraz to the Indians now occupying it. They want to create five centers on the island. One center would be for a North American studies program; another would be a spiritual and medical center where Indian religions and medicines would be used and studied. A third center would concentrate on ecological studies based on an Indian view of nature—that man should live *with* the land and not simply *on* it. A job-training center and a museum would also be founded on the island. Certain of these programs would obviously require Federal assistance.

Some people may object to this approach, yet Health, Education and Welfare gave out $10 million last year to non-Indians to study Indians. Not one single dollar went to an Indian scholar or researcher to present the point of view of Indian people. And the studies done by non-Indians added nothing to what was already known about Indians.

Indian people have managed to maintain a viable and cohesive social order in spite of everything the non-Indian society has thrown at them in an effort to break the tribal structure. At the same time, non-Indian society has created a monstrosity of a culture where people starve while the granaries are filled and the sun can never break through the smog.

By making Alcatraz an experimental Indian center operated and planned by Indian people, we would be given a chance to see what we could do toward developing answers to modern social problems. Ancient tribalism can be incorporated with modern technology in an urban setting. Perhaps we would not succeed in the effort, but the Government is spending billions every year and still the situation is rapidly growing worse. It just seems to a lot of Indians that this continent was a lot better off when we were running it.

APPEAL TO CONGRESS FOR THE RETURN OF BLUE LAKE, 1970

Taos, New Mexico, Pueblo Delegation

[Early in 1971, subsequent to the appeal, presented here, Congress passed legislation, signed by President Nixon, authorizing the return of the Blue Lake region in Colfax County, New Mexico, to the Taos Pueblo.]

Mr. Chairman, it has been many years and several congresses since we first came before this subcommittee to appeal for the return of our sacred Blue Lake lands. Our spirits were lifted yesterday as we heard the President of the United States endorse H.R. 471. Like Job in the Biblical story, our people have patiently endured great hardship and deprivation fighting to save the religious heritage embodied in this holy land. In this fight we are also struggling to preserve the identity of our people as a tribe, to preserve our Indian way of life, and to obtain restitution of land wrongfully taken from us.

We are poor village people, and it has been hard for us to bear the costs of this long struggle for justice over the years since 1906 when the federal government first took the land and put it in the national forest. Even the young children of our village have contributed their pennies to bring our representatives to Washington time and again.

Apart from the financial hardship, we have had to contend with the irreverent curiosity and even mockery that this distasteful, prolonged public conflict has engendered among some white men—

From *Congressional Record*, 91st Congress, 2d Session.

such as the threat reported by one of our tribal members in 1968 of a stranger who had declared that he would force his way with a gun into our ceremonies at Blue Lake. That man did not carry out his threat; perhaps because we responded by posting guards to protect our people and the sanctity of their worship. But the incident typifies how difficult it is for everyone—non-Indians as well as Indians —to tolerate the present permit system under which the sacred land is treated on the one hand as an Indian special-use area, on the other as a public multiple-use area.

We ask you to resolve this inherent conflict once and for all by returning the sacred area to our stewardship for religious and traditional use, and by doing so to extend to our people the Constitutional right of all Americans to religious freedom and self-determination.

Of the two bills now pending before this committee, H.R. 471 and S. 750, the Senate bill, S. 750, makes a mockery in every important respect of the religious and cultural needs of our Indian people. What does it do? We testify in good faith that our religious needs require the entire watershed to be maintained intact as an ecological unit, as is provided by H.R. 471; in direct repudiation of our simple request, S. 750 breaks this natural unit into four separate and distinct pieces for the benefit of others; one piece, a tiny island of 1,640 acres around Blue Lake, would be earmarked for our exclusive use; a second piece, about 3,000 acres surrounding that island, is added to the Wheeler Peak Wilderness and opened to the public without restriction; the third piece, 34,500 acres mainly in the existing Permit Area, is made available for logging and other Forest Service uses with minor Indian use; and the fourth piece of approximately 8,000 acres is opened for logging and multiple use by the Forest Service and the public, with no provision whatever for our Indian needs.

Then we plead for protection of our religious privacy—as it is guaranteed by H.R. 471—so that our religion and strength will not be destroyed as those of other tribes have been; the response to this plea under S. 750 is to take away 4,600 acres from the Special Permit Area and convert 3,000 of those acres into a corridor around Blue Lake for free and unimpeded public access through the Wheeler Peak Wilderness Area into the remaining areas of the watershed. Under those conditions it would be impossible to preserve our sacred area from public intrusions under S. 750.

Again, we assert the profound belief of our people that the trees and all life and the earth itself within the watershed are comparable to human life and must not be cut or injured, but must be protected by wilderness status as is provided by H.R. 471. What does S. 750 do about this? S. 750 gives the Secretary of Agriculture discretion to harvest timber in 34,500 acres (including most of the watershed), to "manipulate vegetation" and fence off pastures in the interest of "water yield," and entirely excludes the 8,000 acres of critical drainage only one-half mile from the Rio Pueblo de Taos from any protection whatever against such desecration.

We ask this committee to reject S. 750 as the very opposite of the principles of religious freedom and self-determination upon which this nation was founded.

H.R. 471, on the other hand, would uphold those principles by placing the sacred area under the jurisdiction of the Interior Department in trust for Taos Pueblo—the normal arrangement for Indian lands—and by requiring that it be maintained forever in wilderness status in accordance with the most fundamental tenets of our religion. The wasteful conflicts and confusion as between the purposes of the Forest Service and the real needs of Taos Pueblo would be ended without harming any other interests. . . .

Religious Use and Interferences. The entire watershed is permeated with holy places and shrines used regularly by our Indian people; there is no place the does not have religious significance to us. Each of the peaks or valleys or lakes, springs, and streams has a time in our religious calendar when homage in one form or another must be given, or plants that we have studied and used for centuries gathered, or rituals performed. Our religious leaders and societies go regularly to perform these duties in accordance with this yearly calendar throughout the area. They also supervise, for a period of 18 months, the preparation of our sons for manhood at various places throughout the sacred area.

In addition to the actual and threatened interference with our religious practices by disruptions of the natural condition of the watershed cited above, there have been continued and repeated interferences with those practices by non-Indian Forest Service employees and sportsmen. These include Forest Service trail-builders or construction workers from adjacent areas, and pleasure-seekers who treat the land as a public part of the national forest. They have been found camping and fishing at Blue Lake and at other places in the sacred area; they have been encountered at places where rituals were to be performed, and on the route to such places. . . .

Conservation and Water Rights. Taos Pueblo has used and occupied the watersheds of the Rio Pueblo and Rio Lucero for 700 years or more. We have always practiced conservation of those watersheds; they yield clear water today because of our long-standing care. Today it is more important than ever that the natural condition of those watersheds be preserved as the source of pure water in those streams. Our life depends upon that water even more than does the welfare of the non-Indians downstream because we obtain our drinking water directly from the Rio Pueblo. For these reasons we want the protections of H.R. 471, which require the Secretary of the Interior to "be responsible for the establishment and maintenance of conservation measures for these lands, including without limitation, protection of forests from fire, disease, insects or trespass, prevention or elimination of erosion, damaging land use, or stream pollution, and maintenance of stream flow and sanitary conditions."

We also want the protection of wilderness status for the watershed, which will prevent destruction of the natural values of that area more effectively than the present system. The Wilderness Society has inspected the area and has reported that it is suitable for wilderness status. Indeed, the Forest Service itself has repeatedly testified that the watershed is presently a "wild" area. . . .

Precedent Issue. It has been asserted that justice cannot be done for Taos pueblo because other tribes might then seek similar legislation. The Interior Department has pointed out, however, that this is the only instance in which land claimed by a tribe has been continuously used and occupied by the claimant, and that no other tribe has a claim pending solely for religious and traditional use. . . .

All Indians yearn for Congress' recognition of the right to preserve their cultures, their religion, their tribal governments, and pride in their heritage. We want to take our rightful place in American society as Indians. Enactment of H.R. 471 would signal a new policy that will henceforth support Indian efforts to sustain their culture, their religions, and their tribal governments. Thus, H.R. 471 poses issues that are national in scope and touch Indians everywhere. We urge you to proclaim such a policy by recommending enactment of H.R. 471.

The past and the future of our Indian heritage is in your hands.

AFTERWORD

"... AND INDIAN ALWAYS"

by **ROBERT POWLESS**, Director
American Indian Studies
University of Minnesota—Duluth

"Indians are in."

This slogan might characterize American Indian affairs in the 1970's. (How long this particular phenomenon will remain, however, is still to be seen.) This does not necessarily mean that many of the social and economic problems facing American Indians will be solved within this decade. Nevertheless, I suspect it may be somewhat comforting for Indian people to understand that there is considerable concern about them at local, state, and national political levels. There is more interest than ever before concerning the directions in which Indians see themselves heading, as well as in the roles that non-Indian people can play in helping them to attain their goals.

I would like to state immediately that I do not presume, in any way, to speak for all American Indians. There are many people, both Indian and non-Indian, who claim, rather extravagantly to know what Indians are thinking and what Indians want. I make no such claims. My information and observations are to a certain extent gleaned from the literature available, but they mostly come from my own observations and from conversations with Indians across the country. My thoughts, hopes, and dreams regarding American Indians, are, I'm sure, shared by many. I am not quite presumptuous enough to assume that they are shared by all. I hope to give as fair a picture as I can of what I believe to be the goals that the American Indians would like to achieve, and describe as well some of the problems that the Indian people must overcome at this point in their history.

By way of introduction, I would like to make two points. First, diversity has always been a factor in all areas of American Indian life. ("Pan-Indianism" is a relatively new concept.) In the early history of Indian-white relations in America, there were many attempts to unite different tribes, but the Indians were, and still are, a tribal people. Their language, their religion, their customs, and

their life-styles differed to some degree at every stage of their development in North America. Today it is probably in only three
areas that Indians have certain characteristics, certain basic philosophies, that tend to cut across tribal lines. These three are:

1. *The relationship of the Indian to the land.* The Indian feels
that land is sacred. He reveres the land and includes this feeling for
land in some form or another in the particular religion espoused
by his tribe or band.
2. *The way that Indian people relate to the idea of freedom.* The
concept of "pure democracy," which is often attributed solely to
the Greeks, has been a function of Indian political life throughout
the known history of Indian society. "Pure freedom" is an idea that
can be seen in the deliberations of the great, and once-powerful,
Great Tree of Peace of the Iroquois. It also extends into child-
rearing practices, and can be seen today in the reaction of Indian
children when they come into contact with the bureaucratic and
sometimes rather harsh structures (and strictures) of public or
federal school systems.
3. *The feeling of Indians about "dancing Indian."* This is often
something that many people overlook as being either a display of
local color or a physical exercise to blow off steam. It is, however,
a very important part of Indian life today and cuts across tribal
lines throughout the United States. I know very few Indians, no
matter how traditional or how assimilated, who do not have certain
positive feelings about attending powwows or ceremonial dances of
some kind. This applies to both men and women, young and old.
One Menominee woman of my acquaintance expressed this feeling
very simply. She said, just before leaving for a powwow in another
state, "I must go down and recharge my batteries." I suspect that
this is the way many Indian people feel about "dancing Indian."
Any Indian person can go almost anywhere in the country and feel
comfortable taking part in the dancing of another region.

The second important point, particularly for non-Indians, is that
the Indian present cannot be understood without a knowledge of
the Indian past. I am especially concerned about people's understanding of the period in Indian history from c. 1887 to the present.
Non-Indians generally continue to relate to the pre-1887 "historical
Indian," who has always been depicted wearing a large (usually
plains-type) headdress and riding a swift pony off into the gathering twilight—powerful, handsome, and free. (There are some non-
Indians who, I suspect, living amid the pressures and concerns of
our highly technological society, long for that kind of image for
themselves.)
It is also easier to "love" the "historical Indian" of that period,
because he is so far removed from the present. A young Tuscarora
associate of mine, who is somewhat of a philosopher, said on one
occasion that he felt the non-Indian's love for the Indian had a
great deal to do with proximity—the farther away the Indians
were, the greater the love. I would say there is considerable jus-
tification for his statement, and would merely emphasize that not
only is geographical distance involved but distance in time as well.

Non-Indian people seem to feel, erroneously, that Indians suddenly disappeared at the time of the Dawes Allotment Act and then
suddenly reappeared in the 1960's as a highly militant people. This
nationwide lack of knowledge about Indian history since 1887 has, I
think, created many current misconceptions about what Indians
are like today and what they are trying to do for themselves. Therefore, even this piece on contemporary Indian life should not be
read without a consideration of the Indian past.

Contemporary Problems: Where Do We Begin?

A discussion of the major problems facing Indian people today
could, of course, be endless. As one Menominee friend of mine is
often fond of saying, "You name it, we don't have it." Some of the
contemporary studies on Indian problems would seem to indicate
that this statement is very largely true in all of the major social
areas—health, education, etc. I would like to briefly discuss five
areas that I consider to be of high priority for solution in the 1970's.

1. *"Destruction of self-esteem."* There is a current fad among
Indian youth for a T-shirt with the words "Indian and Proud"
emblazoned on back. While Indians have much to be proud of in
their contribution to America's heritage, I'm not so sure that pride
isn't often used as a substitute for self-esteem. It seems to me that
the feelings of Indian people about themselves are crucial to any
kind of solution to both their individual and collective problems.
That the Indian self-image has been basically negative in the past
one hundred years seems to be fairly well proved. In our time,
Senate report 91–501, *Indian Education: A National Tragedy—A
National Challenge*, documents this fact very clearly in the critical
area of education. In the heart of this report, we find:

> Condemned for his language and his culture, berated because his
> values aren't those of his teacher, treated demeaningly simply
> because he is Indian, the Indian student begins asking himself if
> he really isn't inferior. He becomes the object of a self-fulfilling
> prophecy which says "Indians are no good."

Further on, we find these words:

> Substantial evidence indicates that the question of identity is
> uppermost in the minds of Indians and that feelings of alienation,
> anxiety, and inadequacy are problems with which they are trying
> to cope.

If pride in one's heritage can indeed have a positive effect on one's
self-esteem then I am very much in favor of any kind of program,
any kind of writing, any kind of teaching effort that moves in this
area. I would hope, however, that in our attempts to revive the
concept of heritage among our young people we do not forget to
deal with the specific, and often very contemporary, kinds of self-
esteem problems that these young people must contend with in our
particular era of Indian history.

2. *Perpetuation of stereotypes.* This area, relating to the enhancing or perpetuating of certain stereotypes regarding American Indian people, cannot be separated from "self-esteem." Stereotypes have been very debilitating to Indians, not only in the present, but also for many decades in the past. The stereotypes relating to Indian feelings about work, Indian abilities to relate to time, and Indian relationship to alcohol are among the most common. These negative stereotypes have developed, like most stereotypes, because of misunderstanding and because of some people wanting to find a negative rap to pin on people "different" from them. They result mainly from a basic lack of knowledge of the life-style and philosophies of Indian people.

Stereotypes do not die easily, and non-Indians seem to take a peculiar delight in perpetuating them through the media. One does not have to view the television very long to observe the proliferation of advertising that places Indians either in a somewhat less than intelligent role in our current society, or in a sort of "savage" role in the society of the past. Neither of these descriptions is very accurate. A non-Indian public, however, brainwashed for decades with this type of misinformation, continues to clutch the stereotypes to its intellectual bosom.

Unfortunately, we as Indian people do not always help by our behavior to eradicate these stereotypes. If one goes from Indian community to Indian community, Indian people can be seen still acting out the negative roles which white people have placed on them. So in this second area, I believe we need a more aggressive approach by Indian people not only to rid books, TV, and other media of these kinds of images, but also to re-evaluate our own actions and our own behavior to see if we are not many times guilty of carrying on these ancient stereotypes.

3. *Lack of understanding and knowledge on the part of non-Indians regarding Indian people.* I am particularly concerned about non-Indian people not understanding how crucial it is that Indian people be called upon to help solve the many problems facing American society today. Former Commissioner of the Bureau of Indian Affairs John Collier (a non-Indian), who was a prophet in this area, stated in his book, *Indians of the Americas* (1947):

> They had what the world has lost, they have it now, what the world has lost, the world must have again lest it die. Not many years are left to have or have not, to recapture the lost ingredient.
> This is not merely a passing reference to World War III or the atom bomb—although the reference includes these ways of death, too. These deaths will mean the end if they come—racial death, self-inflicted because we have lost the way, and the power to live is dead.
> What, in our human world, is this power to live? It is the ancient, lost reverence and passion for human personality, joined with the ancient, lost reverence and passion for the earth and its web of life.
> This indivisible reverence and passion is what the American

Indians almost universally had; and representative groups of them have it still.

They had and have this power for living which our modern world has lost—as world view and self view, as tradition and institution, as practical philosophy dominating their societies and as an art supreme among all the arts.

Today, almost everywhere one goes in this country, Indians are seeking out ways of learning more about their heritage. Multitudes of non-Indian people, especially the young, are also trying to find, as Collier put it, "the lost ingredient" that lies within the traditional philosophies and life-styles of Indian people.

It should be of concern, then, that in the 1970's we establish some mechanism for overcoming the dearth of accurate and descriptive information regarding the Indian people's way of life, in both the past and the present.

4. *"Alcohol-related": a term of despair and frustration.* That Indians may have alcohol problems should not imply that Indians are any more susceptible to alcohol than any other people. Despite what some Indians and non-Indians seem to feel in this area, there are no scientific data to support such a contention. It is fairly obvious, however, if you go from one Indian community to another, that alcohol-related crime is of great significance. In a study entitled "American Indian Criminality," by Omer C. Stewart, we find the following statement:

An examination of the causes for arrests indicates that Indians are particularly vulnerable to arrest for drunkeness and other crimes involving alcohol. In fact, drunkeness alone accounted for 71% of all Indian arrests reported in 1960. The Indian arrests for all alcohol-related crimes is 12 times greater than the national average, and over five times that of Negroes.

With this in mind, then, it would be foolish to say that there is no problem. I think it is important, however, that Indian people define the problem, and find the solutions as well. Perhaps the best definition of why alcohol abuse seems to be a problem among Indians was given by Dr. Ed Dozier, Professor of Anthropology at the University of Arizona, in a 1964 address entitled "Alcohol Abuse and the American Indian":

We have, I think, indicated sufficient deprivational factors to account for the deep sense of inferiority and inadequacy which the American Indian suffers—factors which in bulk and intensity would seem to be greater than that to which other ethnic groups have been subjected. . . . To all this we must add that American Indians share with other racially visible ethnic minority groups of low economic status the following circumstances: discrimination, poverty, poor housing, lack of education, and other conditions which we recognize can contribute to delinquent behavior and high rates of crime everywhere. Under the weight of these deprivational factors it is not surprising that American Indians have sought relief in alcohol. Alcoholic beverages have been the easiest and quickest way to deaden the senses and forget the feeling of inadequacy. Under the influence of liquor the real world becomes substituted by an unreal one where the Indian sees himself as an equal to others, and with physical and psychological support provided by drinking companions, the world appears less hostile and even tolerable.

I must emphasize again at this point that if there is an alcohol problem on an Indian reservation or in an Indian community the solution is one that must be undertaken by Indian people. The efficacy of this approach can be supported by historical fact. It is interesting to note, for instance, that the first temperance society in the United States was Indian. The Iroquois Temperance League was formed in New York State by Indian people fifteen years before the beginning of the Women's Christian Temperance Union. Also, it is well known among Indians that the religion of Handsome Lake among the Iroquois and many of the other Messianic Indian religions that followed were based largely on doing away with the evils and the problems of the white man's alcohol. With this kind of background, and with this kind of knowledge, it is very plausible to assume that Indian people will, in their own time and way, find solutions to this difficult problem.

5. *Factionalism: the "green monster."* Factionalism manifests itself in a variety of ways both within reservation governments and in Indian organizations in the urban centers. Unfortunately, it doesn't only evolve out of differences in philosophy. Philosophical differences are something that all people have had to contend with and Indians, like everyone else, seem generally able to work with others even given such differences. But personality conflicts so often arise—and these are the "green monsters" that, in my opinion, are tearing the Indian world asunder even today. The first Indian organization of the modern period, the Society of American Indians, founded in 1911, was ultimately destroyed by personality differences, which had individuals and small groups within the organization at each other's throats.

Too often, reservation government and urban organizations have been used by a few people as a means of self-aggrandizement. This has caused splinter groups to break off so that, in one of our large urban centers, there are now as many as fifty separate Indian organizations ostensibly serving the Indian people. Despite some protestations to the contrary, factionalism is a very real thing among Indian people today. And careful attention must be given to find ways of alleviating this problem. Fortunately, there are people across the Indian world who, by using Indian religious concepts and establishing certain viable purposes with which all people can agree, are attempting to bring Indians of all tribes, all bands, and all philosophies together in order to set out on some united course of action. I do not believe that a complete bringing together of all Indians into one large body will ever be achieved. Neither do I believe that it would be particularly desirable to do so. I believe, however, that on certain issues Indian people today cannot hope to have political power, cannot hope to have the kind of impact on the society that we need to make, if we cannot settle some of our differences and curb some of our personality quirks. We must submerge them for the good of the Cause. This problem needs immediate attention and immediate care by all Indian people, not by just a few.

Seven: "The Magic Number"

In many Indian tribes, "seven" was a magic or mystical number. While it is not very likely that all Indian people will find too much magic in my seven "solutions" to Indian problems in our times, I believe that my approaches could at least lead us in some positive direction in this decade. I certainly have no pat answers to the problems that exist. I believe that these ideas are practical and have evolved from what many Indian people throughout the country have been saying about what should be done as Indian people attempt to move forward toward new horizons.

1. *Tough decisions = tough people?* Perhaps again the problem that is most obvious to many white people is the problem of alcohol abuse. How do we deal with this? Many solutions have been offered. One of the best approaches, it seems to me, was suggested to me in a letter from a young Indian man from Montana, who will remain anonymous. These are his feelings:

> We need to research, find, and examine our Indian principles and values. Once we have indentified the ones that will be good for us in this day and age then we should apply them to our lives as Indian people; in other words, take the best of our culture and the best of the dominant culture and use it.
>
> I believe that the white man's religion will never really meet the needs of all the Indian people. We should search and find our own ways. They will meet our needs as Indian people.
>
> The Indian today is searching for who he really is, however many of our people are misguided in the fact that they are turning and searching and believing in what the white man has made him out to be, and believe me, that is not the real Indian. The Indian should turn back to his Maker, the way he understands him; then, and only then, will he find himself.

We can see in this writing the strong feelings that Indian people do have regarding the need for finding oneself in our time by reawakening the spirit of the Indian in each of our lives. It would appear that only by doing this can the many social problems afflicting us be solved. Dozier talks again about this approach, but takes a somewhat more pragmatic view when he says:

> Perhaps the most promising for postive long-enduring results are group oriented programs where Indian participation is engaged in planning and implementing the programs. Community

or "Indian centers" are potential focal points for the establishment of organizations which will bring about successful rehabilitation to Indian drinkers. Before group or gang type drinking can be eliminated, there is need for a satisfying substitute activity and organization. Community centers can work actively toward the creation of such organizations. The establishment of successful community centers requires initial outside help by church and civic groups, for Indians are typically inexperienced in organization and leadership. Such a coordinated approach in setting up Indian centers in Indian communities and in urban areas where Indians reside would appear to be the best method in combating pathological Indian drinking.

While the many Indian AA organizations, which exist primarily in urban centers across the country, as well as the development of Indian half-way houses, would seem to belie Dozier's statement that Indians are "typically inexperienced in organization and leadership," nevertheless his points are well taken, and we can see the results (if only in a very subjective way) of these kinds of efforts in Indian communities everywhere. I would suggest that we also need examples for Indian young people to follow in regard to the use of alcohol. I think we need a sort of cadre or coterie of what I call "tough" Indian individuals, tough physically and tough mentally—people who can withstand the peer pressure, and who have been able to cope with the dominant society's pressures to follow the old patterns of Indian drinking. Because they have been able to cope, because they have been able to stand up strongly for a more positive image of Indian people, these kinds of individuals will so stand out that young Indians in particular will, hopefully, use them as models for their lives, instead of using some of the other more negative models that are available.

2. *New models: to whom can I turn?* If different models have some chance of success in the area of alcohol problems, perhaps we should be developing new models in all areas. It is difficult for an Indian student coming into a public school in which there are no Indian teachers to look around and find someone with whom he can relate; someone about whom he can say, "This is the kind of Indian person I would like to be like." Much of pre-white Indian education was of the role-model type, that is, the young people learned, by observing their elders, how to handle certain situations, how to successfully complete certain tasks, how to function within the societal structure. As our young people now are expected to learn from books in a more theoretical way, it is much more difficult for them to perceive exactly how to function in the new society. It is my contention that in the schools, for instance, we must make more use than ever done before of Indian para-professionals. It is not so important, it seems to me, that everybody working with young people have a college degree. It does matter what kind of people they are. We must adjust our hiring practices, if necessary at this time, so that Indian people both young and old (but particularly young) can have new models to follow, new models to look up to, new models after whom to pattern their lives.

3. *Indian inmates: potential powerhouses?* We must set about recovering one of our lost sources of human resources. These are the Indian inmates in our federal, state and local correctional institutions. Omer Stewart points out the following for our benefit in his article, "American Indian Criminality":

When a table is prepared showing the rate of 100,000 population, however, the amount of Indian criminality relative to population size seems to be exceptionally large. For the nation as a whole, the rate of Indian criminality is nearly seven times that of the national average. Nationally, the Indian rate for all types of arrests is nearly three times that of Negroes and about eight times that of Whites.

If this is so, and we have no reason to doubt Stewart's figures, there would appear to be a significant number of Indian people in correctional institutions at any given time. From experience gained working in two projects in Minnesota, in both a state and a federal institution, I feel certain that some of our high potential people are in these institutions. They are high potential from the standpoint of intelligence quotient, from the standpoint of training, and from the standpoint of motivation to serve Indian people. It behooves us, as Indians, to make some kind of consistent effort to encourage these often forgotten Indians and to show them in some way that we are concerned about their welfare and that we need them back in our Indian communities. At a federal correctional institution I recently obtained a newsletter put out by the Indian inmates. A young Sioux, who had been elected the chief, or president, of the American Indian group in the institution, wrote a small piece in this newsletter, part of which goes as follows:

Brothers, you have chosen me as your chief, and I will perform my duties to the utmost of my abilities. If this is not enough, I can still look within myself and know that I did my best. As you know I too stand beside you in this prison afflicted with the monotonous time which discourages us all. Conflicting personalities and grievous monotones about it doesn't do anyone any good, and I appeal to you as brothers—let us unite in brotherhood, and stand together and work as such.

"The monotonous time which discourages us all." Can those of us on the outside relate to such a feeling? We often think that our jobs are drudgery, but at least we are, in a very real sense, free. This is not true of the men in our institutions. Should we not, if we truly believe in the Indian values which we so often expound on, be out at these institutions showing these men that we care, and setting up the kind of communication with them that will bring them back to us, so they can point out from experience that the road they took is a hard road at best and one that should be avoided by young Indian men and women? Could they not be better counselors, more human and understanding perhaps, than you or I?

4. *Tourism: to sell or not to sell?* The creation of new economic

opportunities always has high priority in most Indian discussions. How does one do this? Is a certain kind of industry feasible on a reservation? These kinds of questions have to be asked. They particularly have to be asked from an Indian standpoint, that is, will a certain kind of industry destroy the land or pollute the streams, air, and water? Also, are the kinds of jobs really such that people can be happy at them over a long period of time with a feeling of satisfaction? These questions are being asked more and more by reservation business committees and by Indians in federal agencies that support these kinds of programs. There are two areas of economic development in which we sometimes fail to see the tremendous potential for reservations. These are the areas of tourism and cooperative crafts. Without a doubt the two go together, but I think that in some places full scale tourism is not feasible; a cooperaive craft outlet, however, is. This outlet would be a place where Indian people could bring their items for sale and distribution and could feel that they were getting a fair price without having to go through a non-Indian middleman. On the other hand, because of their location and because of the kind of talent available among the Indian people, some areas could have a full scale tourist program with perhaps weekly Indian powwows to which tourists would be invited for a nominal fee. Indian run campgrounds, grocery stores, etc., would be a part of the whole. All of the proceeds would go into a communal pot and be divided up on a per capita basis among all those contributing to the operation. Too often Indian people turn thumbs down on this kind of operation and then see non-Indian people develop the same kind of programs on the edge of reservations and make their living off of the Indian "theme."

5. *Urban-reservation split: myth or reality?* Can Indians in the urban centers and Indians on the reservation agree? Is there a real urban-reservation split? These are also questions that Indians must ask themselves today. Through talking with Indian people in both of these areas it has become fairly apparent to me that the urban-reservation split exists primarily in the minds of the leadership. It seems that many of the leaders of urban organizations and of reservation business committees use the idea of the split to maintain a certain amount of control over the people in their particular area. A leader in an urban center can say that the reservation people don't want "urban Indians" to have money for programs, and that they want to retain the money for themselves. By so doing he can enhance his position as a "fighter for the rights of urban Indians," and so solidify his leadership position. A reservation Business Committee member can do essentially the same thing. In talking with the so-called grass roots people in these two areas, I found that they take a quite different view. I suspect it may have something to do with the fact that so many of us are related to each other. It is a little bit more difficult to damn your first cousin (at least on certain occasions) than it is to put down a total stranger. It also seems that there is so much mobility today between the urban centers and the reservation that it is pretty difficult to label people as urban or reservation types. With these things in

mind, I would suggest that perhaps we take a slightly different view and try to establish programs that will encompass both areas. One example of this might be setting up a kind of half-way house in an urban center to which visitors, transient workers, or people seriously considering settling in the urban center might come for a couple of days to get a room, a little money, counseling, etc. Such a place could also provide a person with the opportunity to find and talk with other Indian people—something very important to most Indians. This type of half-way house, planned and run by Indians, would help alleviate the tremendous hardship and trauma many Indians have undergone when coming to the urban center as part of white instigated programs such as the old "Relocation Program," as well as similar operations. These places would be manned on a rotating basis by Indians both from the urban center and the reservation. Hopefully, all involved would be "educated" to better understand why people come to the city, why they return to the reservation periodically (or sometimes permanently), and how this emigration can be accomplished without the failures of the past. It would enable reservation people to see the city in a new light, and would help urban people to recall some of the problems and some of the feelings that they had when they first came to the city.

6. *Indian input: catch phrase of the 1970's?* Can we set up better procedures for "Indian Input" in our Indian organizations both on the reservation and in the urban centers? Both regionally and nationally it is my observation that many reservation business committees and many Indian organizations become "closed corporations," wherein certain types of people take over the operation and the programs and pretty much control the kinds of input that they are going to receive. Even more critically, they control the kinds of people who find their way into the leadership positions of the organizations. I think this is very unfortunate, especially for our young people. They often feel left out and discriminated against when they try to make themselves heard by the so-called Indian leaders in today's society.

I would propose that we set up special advisory groups to all Indian organizations at the federal, regional, and local levels. These advisory committees would be made up entirely of young people, selected by themselves. These committees would hopefully provide input regarding how they feel the organization is functioning and what changes they feel should be made. This would be only one small step, but it would seem to be eminently better than the kind of situation that exists today. Many so-called Indian leaders talk about involving people from the "grass roots" level, but, practically speaking, this seldom occurs. Our young people, as well as our adults, are being alienated from Indian organizations. We cannot afford this kind of alienation of our potential leadership. If young people are to really lead in the future, they must have an opportunity to feel that their needs are being met today, and that their ideas and their opinions are being given at least some consideration. One of the reasons why there is somewhat of a dearth of real Indian leadership today is that our organizations have functioned in an "exclusive" fashion so often in the past.

7. *Red power* = *voter power?* Indians are living at a time when our numbers are increasing. People are turning to us more and more for the kinds of ideas they feel have been lost over the centuries. We must realize that Indians are getting into a better and better political situation. It would seem then that we must take stronger measures to make ourselves into a political force, with political organization, candidates, and officeholders. In many areas of the country it would be possible to elect local officials (county sheriffs, mayors, or assemblymen) if we would only get organized. Rather than think about electing an Indian state senator, it would perhaps be more realistic to think of an alderman in a community. We must start at a realistic level, at a level where we can enjoy some immediate success. From these kinds of beginnings, however, it is a natural movement into the upper echelons of politics—state offices and Congress. I would propose that we start now to build the kind of political organization in the Indian world that would enable us by 1976 or 1980 to be able to have an Indian Vice-Presidential candidate in one of the two major parties. I realize that right now this looks like the "impossible dream," but it need not be if we start to organize, to plan, and to work—today.

If we are going to fragment ourselves and, like the man in the old story, "get on his horse and ride off in all directions," we are not going to succeed in such an endeavor. I believe, however, that I see Indian people beginning to think more strongly along these lines. Certainly we had more delegates at the recent Democratic convention than we have ever had. Three or four decades ago, no one would have ever deemed this small triumph possible. The time is very ripe politically for bold moves. If we don't undertake them for Indians, other groups will seize the opportunity for themselves. While some Indians may scoff at political power, it is a fact of life in our time. To ignore it is to be unrealistic. We must begin to deal with voting and with political organizations in a very pragmatic way. We must begin to overcome the factionalism that has existed among Indian people and support candidates who are well qualified and who will do the job for us when they are elected.

We must not be afraid of Indian people who have achieved a formal education. Peter McDonald, the current Chairman of the Navajo Nation, is a good example of the kind of young, educated leadership that is available, and also of the kind of leadership that will consider all groups, young and old, conservative and progressive, militant and non-militant. These men (and women) are now coming to the fore, and it is important for us to set up the kind of political organization that will put them in a position to take over offices at local, state, and national levels. From these offices they can not only serve us better, but also serve all the people of the country in the "Indian way."

Final Thoughts

What should all of us (both Indians and non-Indians) have learned from all this? First of all, I would say that non-Indians must recognize that Indians are not all the same, and that there is also a certain strength in diversity. Indian people, on the other hand, must learn to overcome negative diversity (factionalism) so that on certain major issues a united front can be presented to the Bureau of Indian Affairs, to the Congress, and to other agencies affecting our lives.

Secondly, we should have learned that this is a time of Indian input and control. An old friend and former colleague of mine, Ms. Ada Deer, has said on many occasions that Indians must "stand up and speak out." It is much easier to do this in the present era than at any other time in the history of Indian Affairs. It is particularly important for organizations that have been staffed primarily by non-Indians but have dealt almost exclusively with Indian people to understand that this kind of arrangement is on the way out. Indian people are seeking and obtaining positions that will help them to control their own destinies. Some of these non-Indian people have previously provided reasonably adequate service. Hopefully, if these same non-Indians are truly dedicated to the progress of Indians in this country, they will be willing to step aside so that Indian people can assume the responsibilities of helping themselves. This may not be an easy task on either side, but it is quite apparent that it is going to happen.

So then, in keeping with directions that Indians are taking in the 1970's, non-Indians must be willing to accept their "negative legacy of the past" and be willing to ask: "How do you as Indians see your needs?" and "Can (or may) we be of some help in meeting those needs?"

As Indians, we should realize that, though many negative things have happened to us, we must try, if we are to continue to survive as a people, to think positively most of the time—and Indian always.

GLOSSARY OF TRIBES

ALGONQUIAN. The name denoting the largest of the Indian language families, comprising tribes in all parts of the present United States, from New England to California. Among the many Algonquian tribes were the Penobscot, Narragansett, Pequot, Delaware, Shawnee, Kickapoo, Miami, Sauk, Fox, Ottawa, Blackfoot, Cheyenne, Nootka, Nisquali, and Squamish.

APACHE. A name applied to six tribes of the Athapascan language group: the Mescalero, Jicarilla, Lipan, Chiricahua, Kiowa, and Navajo. Centuries ago, they were native to western Canada and southern Alaska, but in modern times they lived in the western Plains region. At the time of America's discovery, they ranged over Arizona, New Mexico, Colorado, western Texas, and northern Mexico. Among the fiercest resisters of European encroachment, they live today in Oklahoma, Arizona, and New Mexico.

ARAPAHOE. A Plains tribe of Algonquian Indians, native to western Kansas and Nebraska and eastern Colorado and Wyoming. Currently, most of them live on reservations in Oklahoma or Wyoming.

ARIKARA. A tribe of the Caddoan language group, native to the upper Missouri River region of South Dakota. Most of them now live in North Dakota on the Fort Berthold reservation.

ASSINIBOINE. A tribe of the Siouan-Hokan language group, native to the upper Missouri River area of the northern Great Plains, often at war with the Sioux and Blackfoot tribes.

BLACKFOOT. A name applied to three tribes of the Algonquian language group, native to Montana and neighboring Alberta, Canada. They ranged widely over the Plains as buffalo hunters and resisted white settlement until the 1880's. Most of them live today on a reservation in Montana, though there is a sizable group in Alberta.

CAYUGA. A tribe of the Iroquois federation, they lived near Lake Cayuga in upper New York. Today, most of them live at Grand River, Canada, with some survivors in western New York.

CHEROKEE. A tribe of the Iroquois language family, they were native to eastern Tennessee and the western part of the Carolinas. They progressed rapidly in "civilization" after the arrival of whites, but in the first half of the nineteenth century they were uprooted by legal decree, deprived of their lands and property, and forcibly removed to Indian Territory beyond the Mississippi.

CHEYENNE. A tribe of the Algonquian language group, native to Minnesota, they were driven by pressure of the Sioux to the western Plains area. Extremely hostile to white inroads in the West, they became Plains warriors, once they obtained horses. Early in the nineteenth century, the tribe divided into Northern and Southern Cheyenne.

CHIPPEWA. Another name for the Ojibway tribes of the Algonquian language group, native to Ontario, Manitoba, and the northern sections of Minnesota, Wisconsin, and Michigan. Originally, they were probably the largest tribe in North America outside Mexico.

CHOCTAW. A tribe of the Muskhogean family, closely related to the Chickasaw and native to the present state of Mississippi. They now live in Oklahoma as one of the "five civilized tribes," having gone there in the 1830's as part of the Indian removal policy.

COMANCHE. A tribe of the Uto-Aztecan language stock, related to the Wind River and Northern Shoshones. Probably native to Wyoming, they were among the first Indians to get horses and became the best horsemen in the West, the terror of the Plains, and the most warlike of all the tribes. They raided far and wide, even into Mexico. After the late-nineteenth-century Indian wars, most of the Comanches were confined to Indian Territory (Oklahoma).

CROW. A tribe of the Hokan-Siouan language stock, native to the upper Missouri area of the northern Plains. They now live mostly in Montana and northern Wyoming.

DELAWARE. A name applied to tribes of the Algonquian language stock, native to the Middle Atlantic region from Maryland to Long Island. Currently, they live in Oklahoma, Ontario, and Wisconsin.

FIVE CIVILIZED TRIBES. A loose federation of independent tribes in Indian Territory (Oklahoma), comprising the Cherokee, Choctaw, Creek, Chickasaw, and Seminole. They were called "civilized" by whites because they seemed more amenable to Anglo-Saxon ways. The federation was formed in 1859, but it ceased functioning as an independent unit when Oklahoma became a state in 1907.

FLATHEAD. A Salishan tribe of the Algonquian language family, native to western Montana and eastern Idaho. They were a Plains tribe of buffalo hunters, and today they live primarily on a reservation at Flathead Lake, Montana.

FOX. A tribe of the Algonquian family, native to southern Wisconsin and long allied with the Sauk tribes. White incursions drove them into Illinois, then into Iowa, where they now live, near Tama.

GROS VENTRE. A term applied variously to two separate Indian groups: the Hidatsa and the Atsina. The Hidatsa, closely related to the Crow, lived along the upper Missouri, largely in North Dakota. The Atsina, or Gros Ventres of the Plains, were an Arapahoe tribe living in Montana and Alberta.

HOPI. A tribe of the Shoshones, they adopted a pueblo culture centuries ago and were native to the northeast section of Arizona. They live in six pueblos on three large mesas dating back to pre-Columbian times, and remain generally uninfluenced by white society.

IROQUOIS FEDERATION. A league of tribes called originally the Five Nations, then, with the addition of the Tuscarora, the Six Nations.

The original member tribes were: the Mohawk, Oneida, Cayuga, Onondaga, and Seneca. Calling themselves the "people of the long house," they lived in upper New York and adjacent areas of Canada. More unified and better organized than any other Indians north of Mexico, they were the most powerful political force east of the Mississippi before the arrival of the white man. The League was formed, according to tradition, sometime in the sixteenth century, instigated by Deganawida, a Huron, and Hiawatha, an Onondaga. During the American Revolution, the League began to disintegrate, and by 1800 it was no longer an effective political force.

KICKAPOO. A tribe of the Algonquian family, native to lower Michigan and central Wisconsin, they were closely related to the Sauk and Fox. Pressure from white settlers drove them into southern Illinois, then into Missouri and Kansas. Some of them went as far as Mexico.

KIOWA. A tribe of the Tanoan language family, divided into seven bands, they were Plains Indians who lived the nomadic existence of buffalo hunters. The Apache band that became associated with them were called Kiowa Apaches. Since 1868, they have lived in Oklahoma, on a reservation shared with the Comanche.

MAHICAN. A tribe of the Algonquian family, associated with the Mohegan. Native to the Hudson River Valley and Connecticut, they survive at Norwich, Connecticut; Stockbridge, Massachusetts; and Oneida, Wisconsin.

MENOMINEE. A tribe of the Algonquian family, native to northeast Wisconsin. As white settlement increased, they were concentrated on reservations but remained in Wisconsin to engage in farming and the lumber industry.

MINGO. A name applied to a band of Iroquois-speaking Indians in western Pennsylvania. Eventually, they drifted into Ohio country, joined with the Wyandots, and ended up in Oklahoma.

MODOC. A tribe of the Penutian language family, native to southern Oregon and northern California. They resisted reservation life with the Klamath tribe and, in rebellion, initiated the "Modoc War" of 1872–73, led by Kintpuash (Captain Jack). The Modoc were removed to Oklahoma, but some remained with the Klamaths in Oregon.

MOHAWK. The easternmost tribe of the Iroquois federation, originally natives of New York State, they now live mostly in Ontario, with a few hundred of them near Hogansburg, New York.

NAVAJO. Currently the largest of the tribes, they are a branch of the Apaches. Coming to the United States from Canada centuries ago, they settled in the Southwest, where they lived by agriculture, hunting, and raiding other tribes. During the Civil War, the U.S. Army rounded them up and confined them at Bosque Redondo in eastern New Mexico, near Fort Sumner, from 1864 to 1868. In the latter year, they were permitted to return to their traditional home in the "four corners" area of Arizona, New Mexico, Utah, and Colorado.

NEZ PERCÉS. The largest tribe of the Shahoptin language group, they were native to Idaho and eastern Oregon. Under their most noted leader, Chief Joseph, they fought the United States in 1877, hoping

to be allowed to remain on their lands. Today, most of the Nez
Percés are on reservations in Washington, Oregon, and Idaho.

OJIBWAY. See Chippewa.

OMAHA. A tribe of the Siouan language group, related to the Poncas,
Quapaws, and Osages. Native to the Ohio Valley, they had settled
in Nebraska by the early 1700's.

ONONDAGA. The central tribe of the original Iroquois federation,
they lived in the central portion of upper New York, from the
Thousands Islands in the St. Lawrence River south to the Pennsylvania border. Currently, they live on a reservation near Syracuse.

OTTAWA. A tribe of the Algonquian family, native to the Great Lakes
region from Ontario south to the Ohio country. Eventually, they
settled in Michigan and eastern Wisconsin.

PAIUTE. A term designating two subgroups of the Shoshone-language
Indians. The Northern Paiutes were native to western Nevada,
eastern Oregon, and east-central California. The Southern Paiutes
lived in southern Utah, Arizona, southern Nevada, and southeastern California. Wovoka, the "Paiute Messiah," belonged to the
northern branch.

PAWNEE. A tribe of the Caddoan language family, native to the
Platte River area of Nebraska. The tribe was divided into four
bands: Skidi, Kitkehahki, Chaui, and Pitahauerat. By the twentieth century, this once populous tribe had been nearly decimated
by the white man.

PONCA. A tribe of the Siouan language group, closely related to the
Omahas. Native to southwest Minnesota, they were pressured by
the Dakota tribes into settling in the Black Hills. Later, they
moved south into Nebraska and Iowa and eventually were located
on reservations in Oklahoma.

POTAWATOMI. A tribe of the Algonquian family, native to the Atlantic
seaboard, they migrated to Wisconsin. White settlements caught
up with them, and, although some remained in Wisconsin, others
went to Kansas and Oklahoma.

PUEBLO INDIANS. The term "pueblo" is from Spanish usage, meaning
town or village. The pueblos of New Mexico and Arizona represent a settled form of Indian life, with relatively permanent
homesites, in contrast to the nomadic or forest existence of so
many American tribes. There are basically six language groups of
pueblo Indians: Tewa, Tiwa, Jamez, Zuni, Hopi, and Keresan. The
Hopi live in northeast Arizona, while the other five groups dwell
in New Mexico, primarily in the northern Rio Grande Valley.
There are eighteen pueblos in New Mexico and only one in Arizona.

PUGET SOUND TRIBES. A collective reference to a number of small
tribes native to western Washington, including the Squamish,
Twana, Nisquali, Tenino, and Nootka.

SAC, OR SAUK. A tribe of the Algonquian family, allied to the Fox
and related to the Kickapoos. Native to the Ohio Valley, they had
been pushed by the Iroquois into central Wisconsin. White settlement drove them into the area of western Illinois, along the
Mississippi, between Rock Island and St. Louis, Missouri. After

the Black Hawk War of the early 1830's, they settled in the Indian Territory.

SEMINOLE. A tribe of the Muskhogean family, native to Florida and Georgia. After the United States purchased Florida from Spain, the Seminole War broke out. Although the United States did not win the war decisively, many of the Seminoles were forced to go to Indian Territory, while others remained in the more inaccessible parts of southern Florida.

SENECA. The largest tribe of the Iroquois federation. Native to upper New York State west of Seneca Lake, they were largely responsible for disrupting the Huron federation in 1649.

SHAWNEE. Most southern of the Algonquian language family. Probably native to the Cumberland Basin of Tennessee, with a colony in South Carolina, they had migrated into Ohio country by the eighteenth century and lived along the upper Miami River. Most of the survivors now reside in Oklahoma, incorporated with the Cherokee.

SHOSHONE. A large family of tribes: the Bannock, Comanche, Hopi, Paiutes, Snake, Penamint, Chemehuevi, Pima, Papago, and several California tribes. They lived throughout the Far West.

SIOUX. A misnomer applied to the Lakota, or Dakota, Indians of the northern Great Plains. They were among the largest of the Indian groups and called themselves the "seven council fires." Of the seven branches, the Teton Sioux was the largest, comprising the Brulé, Hunkpapa, Mineconjou, Oglala, Oohenonpa, San Arcs, and Blackfoot Sioux. The other groups were the Sisseton, Wahpeton, Yankton, Wahpekute, Mdewkanton, and Yanktonai. Of all the hundreds of tribes in the United States, the Sioux have become, for the white man, the archetypal Indians in the country because of their customs, colorful dress, and overwhelming presence in the Plains. Among famous Indian names, Crazy Horse, Sitting Bull, Red Cloud, Spotted Tail, Rain-in-the-Face, and Black Elk were all Sioux.

TAOS. A Tiwa pueblo of the Tanoan language group, located in the northern Rio Grande Valley of New Mexico. It was at Taos that the great rebellion of 1680 against Spanish rule was plotted by Popé, the medicine man, and his confederates.

TLINGIT. A tribe of the Nadene language group, native to the southeast coast of Alaska. They are the makers of totem poles and other fine wood carvings. Tribal divisions of the Tlingit are Auk, Chilkat, and Sitka.

WANAPUM. One of the Shahaptin tribes, native to the far Northwest, in the area along the Oregon-Washington border near Idaho.

WINNEBAGO. A tribe of the Siouan language group, native to eastern Wisconsin. Some of them were relocated in Nebraska after 1865, but others remained in Wisconsin, despite wide pressure to leave.

WYANDOT. Another name for the Huron tribes native to the St. Lawrence River Valley. They are of the Iroquois language family but were enemies of the Iroquois federation. In colonial times, they allied themselves with the French against the British. In 1648–50, an Iroquois invasion drove many of the Hurons west to Michigan, Wisconsin, and Ontario.

YAKIMA. A tribe of the Shahaptin family, related to the Nez Percés. They were native to the west-central region of Washington and Oregon, where they still live, on reservations.

YAZOO. Indians of the Tunica tribe, of the Siouan language group, native to Louisiana and Mississippi. What few survivors there are live in Oklahoma or continue in Louisiana.

ZUÑI. A tribe of the Aztec-Tanoan language family, native to New Mexico, where they live in a pueblo south of Gallup. Their ancient habitations, as discovered by the Spanish, were the famed Seven Cities of Cibola.

Note: The tribes listed in this glossary are but a fraction of the hundreds of bands and tribes that lived within the continental United States prior to European colonization. For a comprehensive survey, the reader should turn to a volume such as Wissler's *Indians of the United States* or Terrell's *American Indian Almanac.*

RECOMMENDED READING

The literature on the American Indian is vast almost beyond measure. The following short list of titles serves as a general guide for American Indian history to supplement the material in this volume.

THE INDIAN IN HISTORY

BROWN, DEE. *Bury My Heart at Wounded Knee: An Indian History of the American West.* New York, 1970.

CERAM, C. W. *The First American: A Story of North American Anthropology.* New York, 1971.

COLLIER, JOHN. *Indians of the Americas.* New York, 1947.

DEBO, ANGIE. *A History of the Indians of the United States.* Norman, Oklahoma, 1970.

DELORIA, VINE, JR. *Of Utmost Good Faith: The Case of the American Indian Against the Federal Government.* San Francisco, 1971.

DRIVER, HAROLD E. *Indians of North America.* 2d ed., rev. Chicago, 1969.

JOSEPHY, ALVIN M., JR. *The Indian Heritage of America.* New York, 1968.

NIEHARDT, JOHN G. *Black Elk Speaks* (1932). Lincoln, Nebraska, 1961.

TERRELL, JOHN UPTON. *American Indian Almanac.* New York, 1971.

WISE, JENNINGS C. *The Red Man in the New World Drama.* Revised and edited by Vine Deloria, Jr. New York, 1971.

WISSLER, CLARK. *Indians of the United States.* Rev. ed. New York, 1966.

THE INDIAN IN THE TWENTIETH CENTURY

BURNETTE, ROBERT. *The Tortured Americans.* Englewood Cliffs, N.J., 1971.

DELORIA, VINE, JR. *Custer Died for Your Sins.* New York, 1969.
———. *We Talk, You Listen: New Tribes, New Turf.* New York,
1970.
HERTZBERG, HAZEL W. *The Search for an American Indian Identity:
Modern Pan-Indian Movements.* Syracuse, N.Y., 1971.
LEVINE, STUART, and NANCY O. LURIE, eds. *The American Indian
Today.* Baltimore, 1970.
SHORRIS, EARL. *The Death of the Great Spirit.* New York, 1971.
STEINER, STAN. *The New Indians.* New York, 1968.

INDEX

Abenaquis, 16, 17
Acoma pueblo, 70
Acton (Minnesota), 176
Adodarho, 25
Alaska, 319–25, 371–73
Alaska Native Brotherhood, 321
Alaska Native Sisterhood, 320, 321
Alaska Statehood Act, 372
Albany (New York), 159
Albert, Daisy, 330
Alcatraz Island, 374–79, 383–84
Aleuts, 371
Alexander, Jim, 367, 368, 369
Allotment, 286–89, 331
American-British relations, 132
American Horse, 267–71
American Indian Leadership Conference, 381
American Indian Movement, 274
Americans for Indian Opportunity, 274
Amherst, Jeffrey, 105
Anthony, Scott J., 191
Apaches, 214–15, 259–61, 301, 330, 331
Applegate, Ivon, 216, 217
Arapahoes, 66–69, 191–94, 210, 223, 230–31
Arikaras, 10–15
Arizona, 256
Arkansas River, 209
Ashurst, William, 106
Aspinall, Wayne, 372
Assiniboines, 38–40, 62–65, 360

Bad Lands, 265
Bald Eagle, 59
Bannock Indians, 84, 85
Banyaca, Thomas, 381
Barbour, James, 107
Baxter Springs (Kansas), 250
Bay Area Native American Council, 376

Bear Paw Mountain, 249
Becenti, Jim, 326–27
Bent, George, 191
Between-the-Logs, 139
Big Eagle, 172
Big Foot, 267
Big Snake, 254–55
Big Tree, 129
Birch Coulee Agency, 179
Bitter Root Valley, 246, 251
Black Coal, 230
Black Elk, 101
Black Elk, Ben, 360
Black Hawk, 154
Black Hawk War, 154
Black Hills, 66, 226, 230–31
Black Kettle, 191–94
Black Thunder, 141
Blackfoot Indians, 94, 222, 351
Blackfoot Sioux, 232–34
Blue Earth, 179, 181
Blue Jacket, 131
Blue Lake (New Mexico), 385–88
Bogus Charley, 217
Bourier, Louis, 182
Boyden, John S., 336
Brackenridge, Hugh H., 108–9
Bradford, William, 104–5
Bramhall, John T., 110
Bridges, Al, 368
Briggs, 381
British-American relations, 139–40
British-French relations, 122–25, 131–32
Bronson, Ruth Muskrat, 319
Brown, Dee, 277
Brulé Sioux, 230
buffalo hunting, 62–65
Buffalo (New York), 159
Buffalo Bill (William Cody), 252
Buffalo Creek (New York), 135
Bureau of Indian Affairs (also Indian Bureau, Indian Department,

Indian Office), 102, 103, 186, 266, 273, 291–96, 301–5, 311–12, 332, 339–40, 341, 350, 351–54, 374

Caddoes, 210
Cahnawaas, 117, 118
Caldwell v. *State of Alabama*, 109
California, 216–21
California Intertribal Council, 381
Campbell, David, 106
Campbell, Joe, 183
Canada, 122, 124
Canassatego, 119
Canby, Edward R. S., 216, 219, 221
Canzas (Kansas) Indians, 18
Captain Jack, 216–21
Captain Sword, 267–71
Carlisle Indian School, 110
Catiti, Alonso, 114
Catlin, George, 4–5, 106
Cayugas, 20–26, 116, 159
Century of Dishonor (Jackson), 304
Chaouanous, 16
Charles I of England, 117
Charleston (South Carolina), 132
Chaska, 178
Chautaughque (New York), 130
Cherokee Nation v. *State of Georgia*, 107
Cherokees, 105, 149–50, 286–89, 319, 330, 366
Cheyennes, 60–61, 67, 84, 191–94, 210, 223, 226–29, 230–31, 248
Chicago Tribune, 90
Chicasaws, 16
Chinook, 37
Chippewas, 122–23, 131, 175, 332, 381
Chiracahua Apaches, 259–61
Chivington, John, 191–94
Choctaws, 151–53
Chutepalu (Nez Percés), 237; *see also* Nez Percés
Clark, William, 146
Coacooche, 156
Cochise, 214
Cody, William (Buffalo Bill), 252
Colfax County (New Mexico), 385
Collier, John, 6, 274, 276
Columbia River, 366
Columbus, Christopher, 3
Comanches, 208–10, 257
Conestogas, 104
Connewaugus (New York), 143
Cook, Lee, 381
Cooper Union, 211
Cornplanter, 129, 143
Crawley, Dennis, 217
Crazy Horse, 226–29
Cresap, Colonel, 126
Crook, George, 226, 259, 265
Crow Beast, 95
Crow Indians, 66–69, 95, 222–25
Cunningham, William, 4
Curtis law, 287, 288
Custer, George A.

Dakota (Sioux) Indians, 174, 230–31
Dakota Territory, 205
Davenport (Iowa), 185
Dawes Act (1887), 331
Dawes Commission, 286, 287
Degandawida, 20
Delawares, 27–30, 120, 124–25, 127, 167
Deloria, Ella, 314
Deloria, Vine, Jr., 380–84
Department of the Interior, *see* Interior, Department of
Detroit, 127
Donehogawa (Ely S. Parker), 186
Du Pratz, Le Page, 16
Duncan, D. W. C., 286
Dunmore's War, Lord, 126

Eagle Chief, 77
Eastman, Charles, 54
Eastman, John, 173
education, 46–53, 278–85, 360–65, 374–79
Emerson, Ralph Waldo, 105
employment, 326–27
environmental problems, 306–8
Eskimos, 371
Eustis, William, 137

family life and customs, 38–45
Faribault, Alex, 182
Farmers-Brother, 137
Fish and Wildlife Service, 323, 349
fishing rights, 297–300, 366–70
Five Nations (Iroquois) Indian Confederacy, 20–26
Flaming Arrow, 70
Flandreau (South Dakota), 173
Flathead Indians, 397
Florida, 156
Forest City (Iowa), 180
Forestry Service, 323
Fort Berthold, 94
Fort Brooke, 156
Fort Hall, 84
Fort Lapwai, 242
Fort Laramie, 212, 222, 224
Fort Lyon, 191
Fort McKenney, 226
Fort Randall, 201, 202, 205
Fort Ridgely, 179, 180
Fort Snelling, 178
Fort Stanwix, 130, 144, 145
Fort Washakie, 84
Forum, 108
Fox Indians, 125, 141–42
Franklin, Benjamin, 104
Frazer, Jack, 182
Fredenberg, Ralph, 309–13
French-British relations, 122–25, 131–32
funeral ritual, 96

Gall, Chief, 228
Ganada-Mucho, Chief, 256
Garland, Hamlin, 275

Garreau, Pierre, 95
Genesee River, 137, 143
George III of England, 132
Geronimo, 259–61
Ghost Dance religion, 84–91, 102, 263–71
Gibbon, John, 247
Granger, Gordon, 214
Grant, Ulysses S., 186, 211, 226
Grass, John, 232–34, 269
Gray Bird, 181
Great Lakes region, 131
Greenville (Ohio), 131
Grinnel, George B., 6
Gros Ventres, 92–95

Haidas, 320
Hairy Bear, 254
Half-Town, 129
Harkins, George W., 151
Harrison, William Henry, 133
Headstart Program, 356–57
Hill, Clifton, 381
History of Louisiana (Du Pratz), 16
Hogansburg (New York), 328
Holcombe (Rhode Island), 173
Hooker, Jim, 218, 220, 221
Hopi (Moqui), 70–73, 113, 278–85, 330–31, 334–36; see also Moqui
Horse Creek treaty, 212
Hot Creek Indians, 217, 218
Housatonics, 168
Howard, Oliver Otis, 242–49
Hoyt, John W., 235
Hubbard, A. W., 195
Hudson's Bay Company, 37
Huggan, Nancy, 173
Hunkpapa Sioux, 252–53, 262
hunting, 54–59, 62–65, 70–73
Hutchinson (Minnesota), 180
Hydaburg (Alaska), 320

Illinois, 146
Indian Atrocities (Brackenridge), 109
Indian removal, 149–53
Indian Reorganization Act of 1934 (Wheeler-Howard Act), 274, 311, 331, 347, 352, 382
Indian Rights Association, 319, 325
Indian Territory (Oklahoma), 151, 216, 250
Indians of All Tribes, 374–79
Interior, Department of, 186, 291
Iroquois federation, 14, 16, 20–26, 130, 144, 159, 329; see also Six Nations

Jackson, Andrew, 109, 148
Jackson, Helen Hunt, 304, 320
Jackson, Henry M., 372
Jefferson, Thomas, 4, 106, 107, 126, 131, 133
Johnson, Andrew, 105
Johnson, Lyndon B., 349
Johnson, N. B., 330

Johnson-O'Malley Act, 332
Jones, Robinson, 177
Jones, W. A., 275
Joseph, Chief, 237–51
Juniata (Pennsylvania), 120

Känakûk, 146
Kansas (Canzas) Indians, 18
Kaomdeiyeydan, 177
Kariwhiyo, 24
Katcina, 280
Keams Canyon agency, 279
Kickapoos, 146–48
Kiowas, 210, 360
Kittochtinning Hills, 120
Klamaths, 216
Klawock, Alaska, 320
Knife River, 92

La Farge, Oliver, 276
La Follette, Robert, 309
La Isleta pueblo, 112
La Pointe, Frank, 381
Lakota (Sioux) Indians, 41–45, 308
land tenure problems, 135–36, 146–48, 160–62, 230–31, 334–36, 371–73, 385–88
Lapwai reservation, 240
Las Casas, Bartolome de, 4, 104
Le Blanc, George, 179
Left Hand, 191
Leupp, Francis, 275
Lewis and Clarke expedition, 238
Literary Digest, 275–76
Little Big Horn, Battle of, 226–29
Little Crow, 171, 174, 176–80, 184, 185; see also Taoyaleduta
Little Hill, 204
Little Swan, 201
Little Wound, 269
Logan, 126
Lone Chief, 52
Lone Wolf v. Hitchcock, 108
Long, James Larpenteur, 38, 62
Long House, 159
Longman's Magazine, 110
Lost River, 56
Luther Standing Bear, 41, 306–8

McCoy, Alex, 298
McLean, William, 107
McNickle, D'Arcy, 347
Madison, James, 133
Mahicans, 166–70
Malockese, 131
Malominese, 131
Manhattans, 116, 168
Manitoba, 175
Manitou (Menetto), 29
Mankato, Chief, 179, 181, 182, 185
Mankato (Minnesota), 179
Manuelito, 256
Marshall, John, 107
Maryland, 116–18
Masse Hadjo, 90
Medicine Lodge Indian Council, 208

Meeker County (Minnesota), 176
Mékinak, 125
Menetto (Manitou), 3, 29
Meninock, Chief, 297
Menominees, 309–13
Mexican War, 257
Michaelius, Jonas, 3
Michilimakinak, 125
Miles, Nelson, 248–50
Mills, Sidney, 366
Minavavana, 122
Mingo, 126
Minneapolis, 179
Minnesota, 163, 171–85, 204, 205, 207
Mississippi, 151, 152
Mississippi River, 17
Missouri River, 17
Modoc War, 216–21
Mohawks, 20–26, 118
Mohegans, 167, 168
Moncachtape, 16–19
Monongye, Dan, 334
Monroe, James, 109, 188
Montezuma, Carlos, 301
Moqui (Hopi), 113; see also Hopi
Morris, Robert, 137
Mounts, Frankie, 368
Muhheconnew Indians, 167–69
Munsees, 167
Muscogees, 149
Myrick, Andrew, 178
mythology, 7–15, 96–99

Nagiwicakte, 177
Naragansetts, 167
Naranjo, Pedro, 112
Narrative of the Late Massacres in Lancaster County (Franklin), 104
Nash, Philleo, 349
National Congress of American Indians, 274, 324, 348, 380–83
National Council of American Indians, 274
National Indian Youth Council, 274, 337, 355, 356, 381
Navajos, 256–58, 326–27, 349
Nebraska, 204–7
Nevada, 84, 85, 86
Nevada Intertribal Council, 381
New Mexico, 256
New York, 116–18, 144, 145
New York Historical Society, 159
New York Times, 106
New Ulm (Minnesota), 179, 180
Newhouse, Seth, 20
Nez Percés (Chutepalu), 237–51; see also Chutepalu
Niagara, 17
Nisqually River, 366, 367
Nixon, Richard, M., 276, 385
North American Indians, The (Catlin), 106
North American Review, 110, 275
Northwest Ordinance, 108

Office of Economic Opportunity, 348
Oglala Sioux, 101, 211–13, 230, 263, 360, 381
Ohio River, 17
Ohiyesa (Charles Eastman), 54
Ojibways, 58, 160–62, 171, 172
Old-Knife, 95
Old Person, Earl, 351
Omahas, 206, 290
One Feather, Gerald, 381
Oneidas, 20–26, 381
Onondagas, 20–26, 116
Oraibi pueblo, 278–85
Oregon, 216
Oshkosh (Wisconsin) Democrat, 5
Ottawas, 27, 125
Otters, 18
Overland Monthly, 110

Pages, Pierre Marie François de, 4
Paiutes, 84, 263
Palaneapope, 195
Parker, Ely S., 186
Parkman, Francis, 5
Parsons, William, 256
Pawnees, 52–53, 77–79, 97–99
Paytaino, James, 70
Pazoiyopa, 177
Peanuts comic strip, 103
Peau de Chat, 160
Penn, William, 117, 119
Pennsylvania, 119–21, 143–45
Penobscotts, 167
Pequots, 104–5, 167
Philadelphia, 144
Pickering, Timothy, 107
Piegans, 224
Pine Ridge reservation, 267, 268, 269, 294, 295
Pipe, Captain, 127
Pitahaunat Pawnee, 97–99
Plenty-Coups, 66
Plymouth Plantation, Of (Bradford), 104–5
Pockmark, Jim, 210
Poncas, 254–55, 355
Pontiac, 27, 124
Poor Wolf, 92
Popé, El, 113, 114, 115
Porcupine, 84
Porter, Bradford L., 205
Potawatamies, 131
Poverty, War on, 355–59
Powder River, 224, 225, 226
Powell, John Wesley, 108
Powhatan, 111
Powhatan confederacy, 111
Prairie du Chien (Wisconsin), 141, 154
Pratt, Richard H., 110
Proclamation of 1763, 106–7
Prophet, the 131
Pueblo revolt of 1680, 112–15
Puget Sound tribes, 80–83, 366–70
Putnam, Israel, 144
Pyramid Lake (Nevada), 86

Queres Indians, 112
Quetone, Allen, 360
Quinney, John, 166

Ramsey, Alexander, 163–65
Red Cloud, Chief, 211, 232, 233, 263
Red Cloud, Jack, 269
Red Feather, 38
Red Iron, 163–65
Red Jacket, 31, 135
"Red Power," 274
Redwood agency, 180
Reidsville (New York), 166
religion, 7-9, 27–37, 74–79, 84–91, 97–99
removal policy, 149–53
Renville County (Minnesota), 175
Renville Rangers, 175
reservation policy, 259–61, 290–96, 326–29
revolts, Indian, 112–15, 171–85, 216–21, 237–51
Ridgeway, James, 276
Rio Grande, 209
ritual, 74–79, 91
Robert Marshall Civil Liberties Trust, 324
Robinson, Tom, 183
Rolling Thunder, 381
Roosevelt, Theodore, 108
Rosebud reservation, 268, 293

Sacs, 125
Sacs-Potowatomis, 154–55
Saghalee Tyee, 36
St. Lawrence River, 17
St. Louis (Missouri), 146
St. Paul (Minnesota), 179
St. Paul Pioneer Press, 173
St. Regis reservation, 328–29
Salmon River, 246
Saluskin, Alex, 360
San Carlos Apaches, 331
Sanborn, John B., 107–8
San Felipe pueblo, 112
San Francisco Indian Center, 374
Sand Creek massacre, 106, 191–94
Santa Fe (New Mexico), 256
Santa Fe Railroad, 326
Santee Sioux, 171–85
Santeux, 125
Sargent, John, 167
Sault Ste. Marie, 160
Schulz, Charles, 103
Schurz, Carl, 110
Seattle, Chief, 80
Secawgoes, 131
self-government, 20–26, 331–33
Seminoles, 156–58, 332
Senecas, 20–26, 31–33, 116, 119, 129–30, 135–38, 143–45, 186
Sesquehanna, 120
Sesquehanna River, 117
Seven Years' War, 122, 124
Seventh Cavalry (Custer's), 226–29
Sewall, Samuel, 106

Seward, William, 109–10
Shakopee, Chief, 175, 177
Shawnees, 131–34
Sheridan, Philip, 106
Sherman, William T., 257
Shonkaska, 175
Shoshone, 74–76, 85, 235–36
Sibley, Henry H., 183–85
Sioux tribes, 41–45, 54–59, 67, 68, 90, 93, 94, 101, 102, 163–65, 195–203, 211–13, 223–29, 232–34, 252–53, 262–71, 306, 380
Sioux uprising of 1862, 163, 171–85
Sisseton Sioux, 163–65, 180
Sitting Bull, Chief, 226–29, 249, 252, 262, 266, 267
Six Nations (Iroquois federation), 130, 144; see also Iroquois federation
Six Point Cloud People (Hopi), 276–79; see also Hopi; Moqui
Skidi Pawnee, 77–79
Sloan, Thomas L., 290
Smith, John, 111
Smoky Day, 58
Smohalla, 36
Snake Indians, 84
Snake River, 244
Society of American Indians, 274, 301, 302
Sohappy, Richard, 367
South Dakota, 195, 381
Spaulding, Henry H., 237, 238, 239
Speckled Snake, 149
Spencer, George H., 178
Spirit They Live In, The, 276
Spotted Horse, 267–71
Spotted Tail, 232, 233, 253
Squally, Lewis, 368
Standing Rock agency, 94, 252
Standing Rock Sioux, 380
Statiacum, Bob, 368
Stevens, Ernie, 381
Stevens, Isaac, 80, 239, 298, 299, 300
Stevenson, Robert Louis, 110
Stockbridge (Massachusetts), 167
Sully, Alfred, 200, 201
sun dance, 74–76
Swimming Mound (Kansas), 97

Talayesva, Don C., 278
Tamaroas, 17
Tampa (Florida), 156
Taopi, 175, 179
Taos pueblo, 113, 114, 385–88
Taoyaleduta, 171–72; see also Little Crow
Tawas, 131
Taylor, Nathaniel G., 208
Tecumseh, 131, 133
Ten Bears, 208
Terry, Alfred G., 226
Teton Sioux, 198
Thomas, J. W. Elmer, 309–13
Thompson, Clark, 175, 205
Tillich, Paul, 1

Tirawa (Pawnee god), 52, 77-79, 97, 98
Tlingits, 320
Tongass National Forest (Alaska), 322
Tongue River, 66, 224, 225, 227, 249
Traverse des Sioux treaty, 173
Tule Lake (California), 216, 218
Turning Hawk, 267–71
Turtle Mountain Chippewas, 332
Turtle Mountain's Heart, 57
Two-Kettle band, 200
Two Moons, 226

Udall, Stewart, 349
Ugarte y la Concha, Hernando, 113
Umatilla agency, 242
U.S. government policy, and failures
    of, 163–65, 186–90, 195–207, 211–13, 222–
    25, 232–36, 252–53, 262–66, 286–96, 301–5,
    309–13, 319–25, 328–33, 337–59
U.S. v. Kagama, 341
U.S. v. Lucerno, 107
University of Chicago Indian Confer-
    ence (1961), 337

Van Buren, Martin, 105
Vietnam War, 367–68
Vincennes (Indiana), 133
Virginia, 116–18

Wabasha, 174, 177
Wacouta, 177
Wakpaton Sioux, 180
Walker, Francis A., 110
Walker Lake (Nevada), 86
Walla Walla (Washington), 242, 243,
    298, 299
Wallahee, Chief, 297
Wallamatkin (Nez-Percés band), 237
Wallowa Valley (Washington), 243, 244
Wanapums, 36–37
Wapetonhonska, 180
War of 1812, 139–40
War on Poverty, 355–59
Warrent (Pennsylvania), 145
Warrior, Clyde, 355
wars between tribes, 60–61
Washakie, Dick, 74, 235

Washington, 80, 297 300, 366–70
Washington, George, 105, 128
Wayne, Anthony, 107
Wesley, Clarence, 330
Wetsit, Joshua, 360
Wheeler-Howard Act, see Indian Re-
    organization Act of 1934
White Crane, 58
White Hand, 191
White River, 224
Whitman, Walt, 5–6
Wichita Indians, 14
Wilson, Jack (Wovoka), 84, 263; see
    also Wovoka
Wilson, Peter, 159
Wind River, 224, 225
Winnebagos, 46–51, 175, 204–7
Winnepaus, 131
Winning of the West, The (Theodore
    Roosevelt), 108
Wolf (Delaware) Indians, 27–30
Wood Lake, 183
Wooden Leg, 60–61
World War II, Indians in, 314–18
Worth, William, 156
Wounded Knee (South Dakota), 102,
    267–71
Wovoka (Jack Wilson), 84–89, 90, 263;
    see also Wilson, Jack
Wyandots, 131, 132, 139
Wyncoop, Edward W., 105–6, 191
Wyoming Territory, 235

Xavier, Francisco, 113

Yakimas, 297–300, 360, 366
Yankton (South Dakota), 206
Yankton Sioux, 195–203
Yazoo tribe, 16–19
Yellow Bull, 248, 249
Yellow Medicine agency, 184
Yellowstone River, 92, 223, 247
York, Duke of, 116, 117
Young Bull, 97
Young-Man-Afraid-of-His-Horses, 269

Zuñi tribe and pueblo, 7–9

Other titles of interest

**PERSONAL MEMOIRS OF
P. H. SHERIDAN**
New introd. by Jeffry D. Wert
560 pp., 16 illus., 16 maps
80487-5 $15.95

**MEMOIRS OF GENERAL
WILLIAM T. SHERMAN**
New introd. by William S. McFeely
820 pp.   80213-9 $17.95

**COMANCHES
The Destruction of a People**
T. R. Fehrenbach
596 pp., 43 illus., 2 maps
80586-3 $16.95

**CRIMSONED PRAIRIE
The Indian Wars**
S.L.A. Marshall
270 pp., 20 photos
80226-0 $12.95

**ENCYCLOPEDIA OF WESTERN
LAWMEN & OUTLAWS**
Jay Robert Nash
581 pp., 530 illus.
80591-X $24.95

**FIRE AND BLOOD
A History of Mexico
Updated Edition**
T. R Fehrenbach
687 pp., 1 map
80628-2 $18.95

GERONIMO
Alexander B. Adams
381 pp., 18 illus.
80394-1 $14.95

**MONTCALM AND WOLFE
The French and Indian War**
Francis Parkman
Foreword by C. Vann Woodward
674 pp., 116 illus., 9 maps
80621-5 $18.95

**AMATEURS, TO ARMS!
A Military History of the
War of 1812**
John R. Elting
318 pp., 19 photos, 16 maps
80653-3 $14.95

THE WAR OF 1812
John K. Mahon
476 pp., 35 illus.
80429-8 $15.95

**THE STORY OF THE
MEXICAN WAR**
Robert Selph Henry
424 pp., 25 maps and illus.
80349-6 $14.95

**WIND ON THE BUFFALO GRASS
Native American Artist-Historians**
Edited by Leslie Tillett
176 pp., 111 illus.
80357-7 $18.95

Available at your bookstore

OR ORDER DIRECTLY FROM

DA CAPO PRESS, INC.

1-800-321-0050